# Pragmatics & Language Learning

# Pragmatics & Language Learning

*Gabriele Kasper, Series Editor*
*Marta González-Lloret, Series Editor*

Pragmatics & Language Learning ("PLL"), a refereed series sponsored by the National Foreign Language Resource Center at the University of Hawai'i, publishes selected papers from the biennial International Conference on Pragmatics & Language Learning under the editorship of the conference hosts and the series editor. Check the NFLRC website (nflrc.hawaii.edu) for upcoming PLL conferences and PLL volumes.

**Pragmatics and language learning (Vol. 13)**
Tim Greer, Donna Tatsuki, & Carsten Roever (Eds.), 2013
ISBN 978-0-9835816-4-2

**Pragmatics and language learning (Vol. 12)**
Gabriele Kasper, Hanh thi Nguyen, Dina Rudolph Yoshimi,
Jim K. Yoshioka (Eds.), 2010
ISBN 978-09800459-6-3

**Pragmatics and language learning (Vol. 11)**
Kathleen Bardovi-Harlig, César Félix-Brasdefer, & Alwiya S. Omar (Eds.), 2006
ISBN 978-0-8248313-7-0

# Pragmatics & Language Learning

volume 14, 2016

*editors*   Kathleen Bardovi-Harlig
J. César Félix-Brasdefer

©2016 Kathleen Bardovi Harlig, J. César Félix-Brasdefer
Some rights reserved. See: http://creativecommons.org/licenses/by/4.0/
Manufactured in the United States of America.

The contents of this publication were developed in part under grants from the U.S. Department of Education (CFDA 84.229, P229A100001 and P229A140012). However, the contents do not necessarily represent the policy of the Department of Education, and one should not assume endorsement by the Federal Government.

ISBN: 978–0–9835816–8–0
ISSN: 1943–6947
Library of Congress Control Number:

distributed by
**National Foreign Language Resource Center**
University of Hawai'i
1859 East-West Road #106
Honolulu HI 96822–2322
**nflrc.hawaii.edu**

# contents

vii    Acknowledgments

1    Introduction
*Kathleen Bardovi-Harlig*
*J. César Félix-Brasdefer*

## Acquisition of Second-Language Pragmatics

13    Offering Advice: Length of Residence or Intensity of Interaction?
*Elizabeth Flores-Salgado*

37    Semantic and Pragmatic Causal Relations in Native Speaker and L2 Learner Oral Discourse: The Use of the Spanish Connective *Porque*
*Sarah E. Blackwell*
*Margaret Lubbers Quesada*

65    Perceptions of Spanish L2 Writing Quality: The Role of Discourse Markers and Sentence-level Phenomena
*Mai Kuha*
*Lisa M. Kurisack*
*Elizabeth M. Riddle*

93    The Interactional Establishment of the Membership Category 'Nonnative Speaker' in Gatekeeping Encounters'
*Louise Tranekjær*
*Katherine Kappa*

## Research in Pedagogical Contexts

125 Effects of Metapragmatic Instruction on the Production of Compliments and Compliment Responses: Learner–Learner Role-plays in the Foreign Language Classroom
*Maria Hasler-Barker*

153 Challenges Facing Mexican EFL learners: Disagreement and local pragmatic practices
*Gerrard Mugford*

179 Playful Performances of Russianness and L2 Symbolic Competence
*Maria Shardakova*

207 Do EFL Teachers in Serbia Have What They Need to Teach L2 Pragmatics? Novice Teachers' Views of Politeness
*Milica Savić*

233 Noticing of Pragmatic Features During Spoken Interaction
*Tetyana Sydorenko*
*Gwen Heller Tuason*

265 "Always remember to say please and thank you": Teaching Politeness with German EFL Textbooks
*Holger Limberg*

293 A Research-based Teaching Unit for ESL/EFL Students: Responses to Gratitude
*Sara Gesuato*

## Brief Summaries and Reports

325 How Formulaic is Pragmatics?
*Kathleen Bardovi-Harlig*

341 The Design and Construction of Websites to Promote L2 Pragmatics
*Andrew D. Cohen*

357 A Corpus Linguistic Analysis of On-line Peer Commentary
*Naoko Taguchi*
*David Kaufer*
*María Pía Gómez-Laich*
*Helen Zhao*

371 About the Contributors

# acknowledgments

This volume has greatly benefited from helpful commentaries at different stages of the editorial process. The editors gratefully acknowledge the following reviewers:

Eva Alcón, *Universitat Jaume I, Spain*
William Allendorfer, *Indiana University*
Patricia Amaral, *Indiana University*
Robert Baxter, *Indiana University*
Spyridoula Bella, *University of Athens, Greece*
Sarah Blackwell, *The University of Georgia*
Diana Boxer, *University of Florida*
Adam Brandt, *Newcastle University, UK*
Andrew Cohen, *University of Minnesota*
Vanessa Elias, *Indiana University*
Catherine Evans Davies, *The University of Alabama*
Nydia Flores-Ferrán, *Rutgers University*
Debra Friedman, *Indiana University*
Carmen García, *Arizona State University*
Maria Hasler-Barker, *Sam Houston State University*
Noriko Ishihara, *Hosei University, Japan*
Dale Koike, *University of Texas at Austin*
Celeste Kinginger, *The Pennsylvania State University*
Erin Lavin, *University of Michigan*
Scott Ledbetter, *Indiana University*
Ji Hye Lee, *Cornell University*
Virginia LoCastro, *University of Florida*
Sean McKinnon, *Indiana University*

Patrick Moore, *Indiana University*
Sabrina Mossman, *Indiana University*
Gerrard Mugford, *Universidad de Guadalajara, Mexico*
Lynn Pearson, *Bowling Green State University*
Maria Elena Placencia, *Birkbeck, University of London*
Tom Salsbury, *Washington State University*
Gila Schauer, *Universität Erfurt, Germany*
Maria Shardakova, *Indiana University*
Klaus Schneider, *Universität Bonn, Germany*
Rachel Shively, *Illinois State University*
Yunwen Su, *Indiana University*
Satomi Takahashi, *Rikkyo University, Japan*
Rémi A. van Compernolle, *Carnegie Mellon University*
Lynda Yates, *Macquarie University, Australia*

# Introduction

Kathleen Bardovi-Harlig
J. César Félix-Brasdefer
*Indiana University, USA*

The international conference of Pragmatics and Language Learning has been around the world since its revitalization in Bloomington at Indiana University in 2005. The conference was hosted by the University of Hawai'i in 2007 and by Kobe University in Kobe, Japan in 2010; it returned to Indiana University in 2014. The previous three conferences produced excellent volumes of *Pragmatics and Language Learning* (Volumes, 11, 12, and 13) including new and innovative research in the field covering a variety of languages examined in a range of analytic frameworks. We offer this volume in the same spirit. When we published our first *Pragmatics and Language Learning* volume in 2006, we were fortunate that the *Pragmatics and Language Learning* publication was taken on by the National Foreign Language Resource Center at the University of Hawai'i at Mānoa. Publication of the *Pragmatics and Language Learning* volumes by the NFLRC transformed the series and its distribution. In the expert hands of Deborah Masterson, NFRLC publications and graphic design specialist, the volumes became not only innovative in content, but beautiful and professional publications. We would like to dedicate this volume to Deborah on the occasion of her retirement and express our thanks for her work on this series and her contribution to the field.

## Overview

This volume contains a selection of papers presented at the 2014 International Conference of Pragmatics and Language Learning at Indiana University. It includes 14 papers on a variety of topics, with a diversity of first and second languages. Reflecting the topics represented by the papers, this volume is divided into three main sections: Acquisition of Second-Language Pragmatics, Research in Pedagogical Contexts, and Brief Reports and Summaries.

In the first section, *Acquisition of Second-Language Pragmatics*, four papers explore a range of topics from speech acts which include offering advice and contentious disagreement in English, to the use of *porque* in oral Spanish discourse, the use of discourse markers in the assessment of L2 Spanish writing, and identity in gatekeeping interviews in L2 Danish.

In her paper "Offering Advice: Length of Residence or Intensity of Interaction?" Elizabeth Flores-Salgado looks at the effects of length of residence and intensity of interaction among Mexican students after returning from a summer camp experience in the US. Sarah Blackwell and Margaret Lubbers Quesada examine causal relations of the Spanish connector *porque* among L2 learners in "Semantic and Pragmatic Causal Relations in Native Speaker and L2 Learner Oral Discourse: The Use of the Spanish Connective *Porque*." In their paper "Perceptions of Spanish L2 Writing Quality: The Role of Discourse Markers and Sentence-level Phenomena," Mai Kuha, Lisa Kurisack, and Elizabeth Riddle investigate the presence versus absence of discourse markers in L2 writing. Finally, Louise Tranekjær and Katherine Kappa explore how the membership category *nonnative speaker* is interactionally established and initiated by the native speaker in "The Interactional Establishment of the Membership Category *Nonnative Speaker* in Gatekeeping Encounters."

In the section *Research in Pedagogical Contexts*, seven papers explore several issues in pragmatics and language learning related to the classroom. Maria Hasler-Barker, "Effects of Metapragmatic Instruction on the Production of Compliments and Compliment responses: Learner–Learner Role-plays in the Foreign Language Classroom," undertakes a classic instructional effect study. Gerrard Mugford, in "Challenges Facing Mexican EFL Learners: Disagreement and Local Pragmatic Practices," focuses on how users of English as a Foreign Language (EFL) in Mexico express disagreement in uncomfortable situations. Maria Shardakova, in "Playful Performances of Russianness and L2 Symbolic Competence," documents classroom interactions between students and their Russian-speaking instructors that chart the development of what being Russian (and being a speaker of Russian) means to a classroom learner. Milica Savić, "Do EFL Teachers in Serbia Have What They Need to Teach L2 Pragmatics?", investigates the preparedness of Serbian EFL teachers to teach L2 pragmatics, echoing a concern raised by Sykes (2013) that lack of teacher knowledge about pragmatics is one of the obstacles to a fuller embracing of pragmatics in a general language teaching curriculum. Tetyana Sydorenko and Gwen Heller Tuason, "Noticing of Pragmatic Features during Spoken Interaction," probe what advanced learners of English notice in the input in a classroom request activity through an analysis of production and interview data. Holger Limberg's "Always Remember to Say 'Please' and 'Thank You': Teaching Politeness with German EFL Textbooks" undertakes a review of the presentation of pragmatics in commercially available texts, one of the further points raised by Sykes (2013). The last paper in this section proposes a remedy to the state of commercially available instructional materials. Sara Gesuato reports on a study of responses to gratitude in North America and demonstrates how naturalistic data can be used as a basis for instruction in "A Research-based Teaching Unit for ESL/EFL Students: Responding to Gratitude."

We introduce the section Brief Summaries and Reports to present essays and reports which include essays based on empirical work, a retrospective on website development, and an early-stage empirical report. In "How Formulaic is Pragmatics," Kathleen Bardovi-Harlig positions formulaic language as one pragmalinguistic resource among many. Andrew Cohen presents an insider's account of the construction of the invaluable University of Minnesota websites devoted to pragmatics in "The Design and Construction of Websites to Promote L2 Pragmatics." Naoko Taguchi, David Kaufer, Maria Pia Gómez-Laich, and Helen Zhao report on the preliminary use of Docu-Scope for pragmatics analysis in "A Corpus Linguistics Analysis of On-Line Peer Commentary."

## Acquisition of second-language pragmatics

In "Offering Advice: Length of Residence or Intensity of Interaction?", Elizabeth Flores-Salgado investigates the influence of length of stay and intensity of interaction at a summer camp in the Unites States. The opportunity to use the target language outside the classroom may encourage pragmatic development. Flores-Salgado investigates length of residence in the target community and the intensity of the interaction undertaken with native speakers and their influence on Mexican students' sociocultural perceptions of social status when offering advice in English. The participants include 16 learners who had recently returned from a 3–5 month long summer camp program in the United States, 20 of their Mexican peers who had never travelled to an English speaking country, and 20 native speakers of American English. Results show that both groups of non-native speakers differed from native speakers in terms of frequency and strategy choice. The fact that non-native speakers who travel to work at a summer camp often experience social seclusion shows that they cannot rely on length of residence alone to acquire pragmatic competence.

Sarah E. Blackwell and Margaret Lubbers Quesada examine causal relations expressed by the Spanish connective *porque* ('because') in oral texts in "Semantic and Pragmatic Causal Relations in Native Speaker and L2 Learner Oral Discourse: The Use of the Spanish Connective *Porque*." Working with Sweetser's (1990) three categories of causal conjunction—content (semantic), epistemic, and speech act—they analyze causal relations with *porque* in two narrative and two nonnarrative texts (a description, and an account of future plans) by second language (L2) learners of Spanish at three levels of proficiency and native speakers. They use heuristic tests to determine whether *porque* is used semantically to encode relations of CONSEQUENCE-CAUSE, or pragmatically to express epistemic (CONCLUSION/CLAIM-ARGUMENT) or speech-act (UTTERANCE-MOTIVATION) relations (Sanders & Sweetser, 2009) and compare the effect of task type and group on the production, distribution, and relations expressed by *porque*.

Mai Kuha, Lisa Kuriscak, and Elizabeth Riddle explore the role that discourse markers, and sentence-level grammar, and vocabulary play in the evaluation of L2 writing quality in "Perceptions of Spanish L2 Writing Quality: The Role of Discourse Markers and Sentence-Level Phenomena." L2 Pragmatics research often focuses on spoken discourse and spoken interaction, and English has been the dominant target language. Recent research on the L2 acquisition and comprehension of Spanish discourse markers (e.g., Gánem-Gutiérrez & Roehr, 2011; Hernández, 2011; Lahuerta Martínez, 2009) lays the ground work for Kuha, Kuriscak, and Riddle's investigation of the use of Spanish discourse markers versus grammatical correctness and sentence-level vocabulary choices on native speaker evaluation of writing quality. They report on an experimental study that investigated (a) whether presence versus absence of appropriate DMs in L2 writing affected participants' evaluation of the quality of the texts, (b) whether DMs or grammatical/lexical errors weigh more heavily in such evaluations, and (c) whether evaluations by native and near-native speaker Spanish instructors differ from non-instructor native speakers.

In "The Interactional Establishment of the Membership Category 'Nonnative Speaker' in Gatekeeping Encounters," Louise Tranekjær and Katherine Kappa examine how the membership category *nonnative speaker* is established interactionally and initiated by the native speaker interviewers during confirmation internship interviews between Danish employers and born-abroad candidates. Tranekjær and Kappa offer close analyses of three excerpts from a set of 16 recorded interviews for nursing-home internships. At the time of the interviews, the interns had already been placed in the internships. Analysis of the interviews demonstrates how membership categories are fundamentally indexical of the context of interaction. Employing membership categorization analysis and utilizing conversation analytic tools, Tranekjær and Kappa identify three different ways in which the interviewers orient to and establish the candidates as members of the category *nonnative speaker* without performing other-repair, by (a) an interviewer inquiring about a candidate's ability to understand, followed by interlanguage forms used by the interviewee,(b) an interviewer inquiring about a candidate's ability to understand with no nontargetlike production by the interviewee, and (c) reference to nationality of the candidate and her husband.

## Research in pedagogical contexts

In "Effects of Metapragmatic Instruction on the Production of Compliments and Compliment Responses: Learner–Learner Role-plays in the Foreign Language Classroom," Maria Hasler-Barker reports on the effects of metapragmatic instruction of the compliment-response sequence on intermediate learners of Spanish as a foreign language. Though there is research on both compliments and compliment responses, this study analyzes both acts in the compliment-compliment response sequence together. Twenty-six intermediate-level learners of Spanish received instruction across three conditions (explicit instruction, implicit instruction, and a control group). Instructed learners participated in awareness activities and cross-cultural analysis using authentic language samples, and had an opportunity for controlled and guided practice. Learner role-play data was compared at the pretest, posttest, and delayed posttest to native speaker groups, across testing times, and between learner groups. The results show advantages for learners in both instructional conditions over the control group, indicating that intermediate-level learners can benefit from instruction, and that both types of instruction are advantageous and may be combined for pedagogical success.

"Challenges Facing Mexican EFL Learners: Disagreement and Local Pragmatic Practices" by Gerrard Mugford focuses on how users of English as a Foreign Language (EFL) in Mexico express disagreement in 10 potentially uncomfortable and unfriendly situations (discourse completion tasks). While much current research examines disagreement in terms of appropriate and acceptable strategies, this paper concerns politeness and disagreement strategies that give learners choices when negotiating difficult situations. Participants completed 10 potentially difficult and antagonistic situations that reflected negative or misguided comments about the participants or and their country. Working with politeness strategies based on Scollon and Wong Scollon's (1995) notions of solidarity, deference, and hierarchical politeness, and following Walkinshaw (2009), Mugford describes disagreement strategies in terms of high involvement disagreement, conciliative involvement, and suppression. The paper brings to light both situations and analyses that have not been widely investigated in pragmatics and language learning.

Maria Shardakova provides an intimate view of humorous classroom interactions among students and teachers as the students try out various Russian identities in "Playful Performances of Russianness and L2 Symbolic Competence." This paper reports on a classroom study that focuses on spontaneous humorous performances of Russianness by university-level students with varying proficiency levels in Russian who are enrolled in an intensive summer program at a university. Approaching the students' performances from the language socialization standpoint (Ochs, 1993; Ochs & Schieffelin, 2012), the study investigates whether the playful double-voicing can provide opportunities for the development of symbolic competence, the ability to access contextually relevant social memories and symbols, including social roles and identities. Shardakova's excerpts show the increased sophistication of the portrayals of Russianness as proficiency increases, accompanied by students' increased ability to sustain the identity across multiple turns. The study also highlights the key role of the instructor in response to these performances and in the students' acquisition of symbolic competence. The beneficial role of spontaneous performances of Russianness in the students' acquisition of new voices and semiotic resources is contrasted with the students' ability to access target culture social memories, discourses, and scripts.

Milica Savić addresses the issue of teacher knowledge—which is arguably the most important in Sykes's (2013) list of reasons that pragmatics is not more widely taught in language classes—in "Do EFL Teachers in Serbia Have What They Need to Teach L2 Pragmatics?" The lack of attention to pragmatics in foreign language programs, from which future foreign language teachers often graduate, compounded by infrequent focus on pragmatics in teacher preparation programs, often results in L2 teachers having limited pragmatic competence and/or metapragmatic awareness. However, teachers need a high degree of metapragmatic awareness to be able to support their students' pragmatic learning (Kasper & Rose, 2002). To determine the degree of pragmatic awareness in her local setting, Savić investigated novice English teachers' metapragmatic awareness as reflected in their views of general politeness and L2 politeness employing semi-structured interviews of 13 novice Serbian teachers of English as a foreign language (EFL). A content analysis of the interviews revealed the novice teachers' perceptions of the nature of politeness, especially its universal and culture-specific aspects, sometimes heavily colored by their own cultural perspective as well as considerable individual differences. The findings suggest a need for including both theoretical and pedagogically-oriented pragmatics courses in EFL teacher education in Serbia. Readers may find a resonance for local second and foreign language teacher-preparation programs.

In "Noticing of Pragmatic Features during Spoken Interaction," Tetyana Sydorenko and Gwen Heller Tuason employ a multiple-case study design to explore what learners are able to notice during a repeated request activity. Five graduate students participated in a request role-play with native speakers of English three times. The authors measured noticing as the difference between the learners' performance in first and third role plays (their uptake) and their verbal reports via interviews, stimulated recalls, note-taking, and reflections. Learners predominantly noticed and incorporated pragmatic strategies rather than forms. Sydorenko and Tuason also reported individual variation, including knowledge of linguistic expressions, ability to memorize, awareness of differences between L1 and L2 cultures, learners' goals, proficiency level, and degree of access to native speakers. The authors observe that these findings suggest that learners may be able to autonomously notice and make use of some native-speaker input outside of classrooms.

"Always Remember to Say 'Please' and 'Thank You': Teaching Politeness with German EFL Textbooks" by Holger Limberg investigates the presentation of politeness in commercially available textbooks. Language textbooks are an important pedagogical resource in all educational settings, and their significance increases in foreign-language settings in which they are often the only resource. In this paper, Limberg documents how EFL textbooks for secondary schools from three major publishers in Germany provide input for learners on politeness. The review identifies the aspects of politeness that are explicitly addressed in textbooks and what in-class activities are suggested for learners to develop their politeness competence. The analysis emphasizes the importance of politeness as a learning objective and illustrates how textbooks conceptualize politeness as a pragmatic discourse phenomenon.

In "A Research-Based Teaching Unit for ESL/EFL Students: Responses to Gratitude," Sara Gesuato explores responses to gratitude as expressed in elicited oral interaction (open role-plays) by native speakers of American English, giving an overview of the conventions of means and conventions of forms of the head acts and supporting moves of these reacting speech acts. She discusses their frequency of occurrence and combinatorial options across situations differing in terms of the social distance and power relationships between the interactants. She then presents a proposal for familiarizing ESL/EFL students with the speech act of responding to gratitude in two complete 90-minute lessons that include conversations from the role plays as input and models, noticing activities, worksheets, production opportunities, and answer keys for teachers. In addition to being a ready-to-use lesson plan (which can be divided to fit any class length), the lesson provides a model for developing additional instructional units on pragmatics.

## Brief summaries and reports

In the first essay, Kathleen Bardovi-Harlig addresses the title question, "How Formulaic is Pragmatics?" With the growing interest in formulaic language in pragmatics, it is important to understand how formulaic language fits into the larger set of pragmalinguistic resources. This essay reviews ways in which the frequency or recurrence of formulaic language has been assessed, particularly in pragmatics, and discusses the challenges to learners that the formulaic (or not so formulaic) nature of pragmatics presents to learners, including linguistic characteristics such as nativelike selection, distribution, transfer, and the changing nature of formulas, and learner variables such as proficiency, attitude, and exposure to the target. It also briefly considers instruction, materials development, and assessment.

Andrew Cohen gives an account of the development of the well-known University of Minnesota pragmatics websites in "The Design and Construction of Websites to Promote L2 Pragmatics." These websites were the first of their kind and continue to support research as well as the teaching and learning of second- and foreign-language pragmatics. The websites included information on a wide range of languages, with a specially developed website for Japanese pragmatics and one for Spanish pragmatics. On the basis of the continued success of these websites, Cohen discusses future plans for the creation of a wiki that will serve as a repository of knowledge about pragmatics within and across languages.

Naoko Taguchi, David Kaufer, María Pía Gómez-Laich, and Helen Zhao, "A Corpus Linguistics Analysis of On-line Peer Commentary," describe a preliminary attempt to apply *DocuScope* (Ishizaki & Kaufer, 2011), a computer platform for classifying text into rhetorical categories, to the analysis of an interactive educational task. The authors compiled and analyzed two corpora of peers critiquing each other's essays in classes teaching academic and professional writing were. One corpus was constructed from a graduate-level, narrative and argumentation class in a U.S. university where 12 participants shared critiques of each other's essays in a collaborative online environment (21,485 words). The other corpus was compiled in an undergraduate-level composition class in Hong Kong where 13 learners of L2 English commented on one another's essays online (29,900-words). The two corpora were automatically tagged in the DocuScope environment and statistically analyzed; a manual analysis followed. The DocuScope analysis identified a range of linguistic dimensions that were significantly different between the two corpora indicating that the common pragmatic act of critiquing others' essays was practiced differently in these two writing classes. The combined quantitative and manual analyses combined suggest great potential for the use of the DocuScope as a tool for pragmatic analysis.

Taken together, the articles included in this volume advance our understanding of second language pragmatics with regard to learning and the use of pragmalinguistic resources necessary to produce and comprehend speech acts (advice, disagreements, compliments and compliment responses, expressions of gratitude), conventional expressions, discourse markers, relational talk to develop L2 symbolic competence in the classroom, and polite expressions in language textbooks. Other chapters underscore the importance of instruction in L2 and FL settings, in particular, the need to raise sociopragmatic awareness about cultural expectations among second language learners and teachers. This volume also highlights the diversity of methods used to collect pragmatic data in L2 and FL learning contexts. Finally, three brief reports provide theoretical and methodological contributions to development of pragmatic competence in formula use as well as through online formats and pedagogical websites.

## References

Gánem-Gutiérrez, G. A., & Roehr, K. (2011). Use of L1, metalanguage, and discourse markers: L2 learners' regulation during individual task performance. *International Journal of Applied Linguistics, 21*(3), 297–318.

Hernández, T. A. (2011). Re-examining the role of explicit instruction and input flood on the acquisition of Spanish discourse markers. *Language Teaching Research, 15,* 159–182.

Ishizaki, S., & Kaufer, D. (2011). Computer-aided rhetorical analysis. In P. McCarthy & C. Boonthum-Denecke (Eds.), *Applied natural language processing and content analysis* (pp. 276–296). Hershey, PA: Information Science Reference.

Kasper, G., & Rose, K. R. (2002). *Pragmatic development in a second language.* Oxford, England: Blackwell Publishing Limited.

Lahuerta Martínez, A. C. (2009). Empirical study of the effects of discourse markers on the reading comprehension of Spanish students of English as a foreign language. *International Journal of English Studies, 9*(2), 19–43.

Ochs, E. (1993). Constructing social identity: A language socialization perspective. *Research on Language and Social Interaction, 26,* 287–306.

Ochs, E., & Schieffelin, B. B. (2012). The theory of language socialization. In A. Duranti, E. Ochs, & B. B. Schieffelin (Eds.), *The handbook of language socialization* (pp. 1–21). Malden, MA: Wiley-Blackwell.

Sanders, T., & Sweetser, E. (2009). Introduction: Causality in language and cognition—what causal connectives and causal verbs reveal about the way we think. In T. Sanders & E. Sweetser (Eds.), *Causal categories in discourse and cognition* (pp. 1–18). Berlin,Germany: Mouton de Gruyter.

Scollon, R., & Wong Scollon, S. (1995). *Intercultural communication: A discourse approach.* Oxford, England: Blackwell.

Sweetser, E. (1990). *From etymology to pragmatics: Metaphorical and cultural aspects of semantic structure.* Cambridge, England: Cambridge University Press.

Sykes, J. M. (2013). Multiuser virtual environments: Learner apologies in Spanish. In N.Taguchi & J. M. Sykes (Eds.), *Technology in interlanguage pragmatics research and teaching* (pp. 71–100). Philadelphia, PA: John Benjamins.

Walkinshaw, I. (2009). *Learning politeness: Disagreement in a second language.* Oxford, England: Lang.

# Acquisition of
# Second-Language Pragmatics

# Offering Advice: Length of Residence or Intensity of Interaction?

Elizabeth Flores-Salgado
*Benemérita Universidad Autónoma de Puebla, México*

Language acquisition requires that learners have access to the target language to use its linguistic and pragmatic rules appropriately and effectively in a particular situation. Research has shown that study abroad affords learners the opportunity to use the target language outside the classroom. This opportunity allows them to acquire different pragmatic abilities such as conventional expressions and speech acts (Bardovi-Harlig & Bastos, 2011; Félix-Brasdefer, 2004; Félix-Brasdefer & Hasler Barker 2015). This paper investigates whether either the length of residence in the target community or the intensity of the interaction undertaken with native speakers influences the Mexican students' sociocultural perceptions of social status when offering advice. The instrument used in this study was a multiple-choice questionnaire with 12 scenarios designed to elicit perceptions of social status. Three groups participated in the present study: 16 Mexican students recently returned from a foreign exchange (+abroad experience), 20 of their Mexican peers who had never travelled to an English speaking country (−abroad experience), and 20 native speakers of American English. Results show that both groups of non-native speakers differed from native speakers in terms of frequency and strategy choice. The fact that non-native speakers who travel to work at a summer camp often experience social seclusion shows that they cannot rely on length of residence alone to acquire pragmatic competence. It is argued that, at least in relation to the specific speech act of offering advice, length of residence does not guarantee pragmatic appropriateness, and that intensity of interaction can actually guarantee better results.

## Introduction

In order to interact effectively and appropriately in a situation, each speaker needs to know the linguistic forms, the functions of these forms, and the social rules that allow him/her to interpret and perform a message in a specific language. This knowledge is known as pragmatic competence (Kasper, 1992). Kasper and Rose (2002) consider that this competence may increase if learners receive a vast amount of input in the target language (TL). Therefore, the knowledge that is determined by experiences in a particular culture plays an important role in the development of pragmatic competence. This knowledge cannot be fully acquired in the language classroom, due to fact that there are limited opportunities to practice the TL in this setting. Language acquisition requires that learners have access to the TL in order to learn how to use its linguistic and pragmatic rules appropriately and effectively in a particular situation. More specifically, research has shown that studying abroad allows learners to acquire different pragmatic abilities, and that the opportunity to use the TL outside the classroom could contribute to that acquisition (Alcón-Soler, 2015; Bardovi-Harlig & Bastos, 2011; Félix-Brasdefer, 2004; Félix-Brasdefer & Hasler Barker, 2015; Shardakova, 2005).

The most important aspect to acquire a language is the ability to use and interpret it appropriately in context, as well as knowledge of how the relationship between participants influences the structure of the message (Matsumura, 2001). Some of the aspects that must be recognized in a situation are the setting, the age of the participants, the degree of intimacy, and social status. Several researchers (Blum-Kulka, 1983; Félix-Brasdefer, 2007; Matsumoto, 1988, 1989) have pointed out that the selection of strategies in a speech act is governed by social status variables. These variables are conveyed during the conversation through the form and content of the participants' actions and it is important to recognize such status at the moment the speech act of offering advice is performed. Using a multiple-choice questionnaire, this paper investigates the influence of sociocultural perceptions on the selection of linguistic strategies by intermediate learners of English for offering advice and compares these strategies with those selected by native speakers (NSs). A second objective is to analyze the roles of length of residence (LoR) and intensity of interaction on the recognition of sociocultural perceptions of social status when offering advice among learners of English.

## Theoretical framework

Offering advice is considered a directive speech act (Searle, 1979). Like all directives, offering advice attempts to get the H (hearer) to do something. It implies a future act embodying what could or should be done in a situation or regarding a certain problem, with the action suggested being for the benefit of the H. Pinto (2010) observes that even though advice benefits the H, it can be considered a face-threatening act, especially when the H has not asked for advice. It can be interpreted as negative criticism and the H can be offended. DeCapua and Huber (1995) consider that it can impinge upon the H's personal space. At the moment the S (speaker) offers unsolicited advice, s/he puts himself/

herself in a superior position where s/he is the expert (Pinto, 2010). According to Wardhaugh (1985), the advice given is a strong suggestion to carry out a certain course of action. While it is the S who is stating his/her point of view and lending his/her authority to what is proposed, it is the H who will be at risk when s/he does what was suggested. On the other hand, when advice is solicited, it is generally appreciated, especially when coming from acquaintances or intimates (such as friends, relatives, and status equals). Pinto (2010) adds that in close relationships, people look for advice in order to obtain a second opinion, rather than because they consider the speaker an authority. Offering advice is of interest to pragmatics because its performance involves recognizing the social status of the participants in order to select the appropriate strategy and form.

LoR and intensity of interaction have long been two variables of interest in second language acquisition research. Bella (2011) considers that these variables are affected by two different types of input quantity and quality, and that there are quantitative and qualitative aspects to both LoR and intensity of interaction that influence learners' pragmatic development and performance. LoR is also referred to as "length of stay", and specifically refers to a temporary residence undertaken by non-immigrant language learners (Bardovi-Harlig & Bastos, 2011) in which they are exposed to the TL and its full social context over a limited period of time. Studies undertaken in this area have investigated the effects of time spent in the host environment on language development. The latter variable, length of intensity or intensity of interaction, refers to the extent of social contact experienced by learners in the host community; in other words, the learners' social exposure to and the social contacts they have cultivated in the TL during their residence in the host environment.

The literature on the effect of the LoR on learners' pragmatic development has examined various aspects (comprehension and production; second and foreign language learners with different levels of proficiency and different LoR) in several languages when performing different speech acts. However, the literature is not very extensive and has covered the following research lines: requests (Hassall, 2003; House & Kasper, 1987), apologies (Bataineh & Bataineh, 2006; Cohen & Olshtain, 1993; Shardakova, 2005), requests and apologies (Márquez-Reiter, 2000), offering advice (Matsumura, 2001), refusals (Beebe, Takahashi & Uliss-Welts, 1990; Bella, 2011; Félix-Brasdefer, 2003, 2004), suggestions (Koike, 1996), complaints (Trosborg, 1995), and conventional expressions (Bardovi-Harlig & Bastos, 2011). Overall, these studies have shown that LoR may be one of the variables responsible for the development and performance of pragmatics.

Some studies support this possibility and have demonstrated that LoR in the target community is one of the factors that can reduce negative transfer and increase pragmatic competence in the L2 (Olshtain & Blum-Kulka, 1985; Blum-Kulka & Olshtain, 1986). Bouton (1994) found that with longer lengths of stay in the United States, English as a second language learners enrolled at an American university were able to become increasingly target-like in their interpretation of implicatures, without special training in pragmatics. In the same vein, Alcón-Soler (2015) examined request mitigators performed by 60 Spanish-speaking learners of English enrolled for a year at an English University. She explored the extent to which pragmatic instruction and length of study abroad influence learners' ability to mitigate requests in e-mail communication. In contrast with Bouton's (1994) results, Alcón-Soler (2015) found that pragmatic instruction is more effective and significant when language learners are exposed to the TL because they have to use and reconstruct acquired knowledge; thus, it may be suggested that LoR interacts with instruction.

Similarly, Shardakova (2005) carried out a study on apologies performed by 90 American learners of Russian at two different proficiency levels. She analyzed the combined effects of L2 proficiency and exposure to the target culture on learners' pragmatic development. Learners were divided according to their proficiency level and their exposure to the TL. The author found that the low proficiency group with direct exposure to Russian culture approximated more to the Russian norm than the high proficiency group without exposure to the TL. The low proficiency learners expanded their apologetic vocabularies and adjusted their apologies to contextual factors, bringing them closer to the NS norms than the high proficiency learners. Although the high proficiency learners exhibited changes in their repertoire of apologies, these proved insufficient for them to approximate the NS patterns, meaning that they did not change their contextual perception. Only exposure to the target culture enabled learners to see things from the point of view of a Russian.

Félix-Brasdefer (2004) analyzed the effect of LoR on learners' pragmatic development across refusal interactions. Using role plays and retrospective verbal reports, 24 advanced learners of Spanish who had been studying in Latin America participated in the study. The participants had different periods of residence in the target community. Félix-Brasdefer (2004) found that there was no correlation between proficiency level and LoR in the L2 culture and that these aspects should be considered independently, as exposure to input in the L2 culture did not seem to influence the learners' pragmatic development. However, his results show that learners with more extended lengths of residence made more frequent attempts to negotiate and mitigate their refusals and also approximated NS norms.

With respect to offering advice, Matsumura (2001) compared the development of 97 Japanese foreign exchange students' pragmatic competence with that of 102 of their peers in Japan, and analyzed the changes in the exchange students' sociocultural perceptions with respect to the speech act of offering advice during the year they were studying in Canada. While his results indicated that pragmatic development was not necessarily associated with the LoR, he did consider that richness of input had more influence on the acquisition of pragmatics. Bardovi-Harlig and Bastos (2011) examined whether the ability of 122 learners of English to recognize and use conventional expressions in the TL was influenced by proficiency, LoR, or intensity of interaction. Their results indicated that both proficiency and intensity of interaction have a significant influence on the production of conventional expressions, whereas LoR did not have a significant effect on either recognition or production. Using role plays, Bella (2011) investigated the politeness strategies and mitigating devices used by NSs and non-native speakers (NNSs) of Greek when refusing an invitation from an intimate and their consequences for using norms of expressing politeness. She also examined whether the LoR or intensity of interaction with NSs affect NNS' performance. Bella (2011) found that the acquisition of sociocultural norms can only be affected by the LoR if participants have sufficient interaction opportunities. Overall, it does seem as though both variables, LoR and length of interaction, influence the acquisition of pragmatics in the TL.

Although these studies have contributed to our understanding of the relationship between pragmatic development and time in the host community, they should be viewed with caution, as Félix-Brasdefer (2004) suggests. Different methods have been used (perception of politeness strategy, written production, comprehension of implicature, and refusal interactions) to establish pragmatic acquisition, with different types of subjects with different periods of residence in the L2 (10 years, 5 years, 17 months, 2 years). Therefore, the diverse nature of the research makes it particularly challenging to draw comparisons across languages or discern conclusive patterns. Some findings seem to indicate that there are other variables that have more influence on pragmatic development; specifically, they highlight the need to analyze the quality of input received by learners during their residence in the target community (intensity of interaction).

The purpose of this paper is to compare the pragmatic development of 16 Mexican students recently returned from a foreign exchange with 20 of their Mexican peers who have never travelled to an English-speaking country. The aim was to analyze whether either the LoR in the target community or the intensity of the interaction undertaken with NSs has more influence on the Mexican students' sociocultural perceptions of social status when offering advice. Unlike previous studies of LoR (Barron, 2002; Bouton, 1994; Félix-Bradesfer, 2004, Matsumura, 2001), which analyzed the development of L2 pragmatics in long-term residents (either immigrants or long-term university students), recent interest in this area has focused on what learners can acquire over a shorter timeframe. Hence, this study will examine the acquisition of L2 pragmatics in an under-researched group of learners, who, instead of going abroad to study, go to work at a 10 to 15 week summer camp program. The specific questions to be addressed in this investigation are:

- What are the similarities and differences between Mexican college students who have travelled to the US and Mexican college students

who have not, in terms of the sociocultural perceptions of social status when offering advice?
- Which is the most influential factor for the development of pragmatic competence, LoR or intensity of interaction?

## Method

### Participants

The participants in this study were divided into three groups: 20 NSs of American English who were exchange students (age range 20–28) at the *Universidad de las Américas Puebla* (UDLAP) in Puebla, Mexico and 36 NSs of Mexican Spanish learners of English (age range 20–26) who were divided into two groups. The first group consisted of 16 intermediate learners (NNSs1 [+abroad experience]) who had participated in a summer camp program in the United States for 3 to 5 months. The second group included 20 intermediate learners who had never been to an English-speaking country (NNSs2 [–abroad experience]).

All of the Mexican participants completed a background questionnaire in order to ensure that the groups were as homogeneous as possible and to achieve optimum comparability among the non-native groups so that the differences could not be attributed to variables other than those being studied. The background questionnaire included the following information: (a) the number of English courses that they had taken; (b) the course level at which they were currently studying; (c) their last grade in an English course; (d) where they started learning English; (e) whether they had taken a proficiency exam; (f) the name of the proficiency exam and the score that they obtained; (g) whether they had visited an English speaking country; and, (h) if they had, how long they were there. The Mexican Spanish groups did not differ significantly in terms of average age and contained individuals from both urban and suburban areas, with males and females fully represented in each group. However, gender was not considered in this study. The characteristics of the groups are described below.

*American English NSs.* In order to analyze whether (and to what degree) the responses of EFL learners approach American English norms, it was necessary to establish those norms. Twenty American English NSs and exchange students who had recently arrived in Mexico as part of a study-abroad program at the UDLAP, agreed to participate. The data were collected during the first month after the subjects' arrival. They were recruited individually to participate outside the classroom. The average length of time to complete the task was approximately 15 minutes.

*Mexican Spanish NSs.* The 36 learners were NSs of Mexican Spanish and natives of the state of Puebla, Mexico. They were undergraduate students studying Teaching English as a Foreign Language at *Benemérita Universidad*

Autónoma de Puebla (BUAP)[1] in Puebla, Mexico. With respect to social class, the population in this study may best be described as representing a continuum from middle to low social class. This particular aspect is important because most students have few opportunities to enroll in an exchange program outside Mexico due to their economic situation. The only opportunity that they have to travel to an English-speaking country is to apply for a Summer Camp Program (SCP) where they can work in the United States for 10 to 15 weeks.

These programs hire college students who are between 18 and 25 years of age and are able to work up to 40 hours per week over the summer. If they are accepted in the program, they live in a camp with other members of the staff who are from the United States and all over the world. Even though Mexican college students have the opportunity to choose the type of work they want to do in the summer camps (e.g., lifeguard, swimming instructor, counselor, housekeeping staff, kitchen staff, driver), they mainly prefer to be part of the kitchen or housekeeping staff so as to improve their chances of being recruited into the program. The Mexican learners applying to this program travel to the United States during the second or third week of May and return the first week of September.

In order to determine the proficiency level of both groups of learners, they were asked if they had passed the B1 level test, administered by the BUAP, which is based on the Common European Framework for the Teaching and Assessment of Languages (Council of Europe, 2001), and certifies them as being of an intermediate level in the four skills (reading, writing, speaking, and listening). All of them passed this exam. Data were collected once when the group of learners who participated in the SCP had just returned to Mexico. Before agreeing to participate in the study, all participants read and signed a consent form expressing their willingness to participate in the study.

### Instrument

Participants completed a background questionnaire and a multiple-choice questionnaire. The background questionnaire consisted of 19 questions in Spanish. The questions concerned their educational background; the position they had in the camp (Question 4); their LoR in the USA (Question 5); their opportunities for social contact with American English NSs, more specifically, the frequency with which they used English with NSs of English (Question 6); the frequency with which they employed English with the international staff (Question7); and the frequency that they used Spanish with NSs of Spanish (Question 8).

Some of the items of the questionnaire analyzed in the study are as follows: Indicate what percentage of time you interacted in English with NSs of English during the day.
    a. 0% b. 25% c. 50% d. 75% e. 100%

Indicate what percentage of time you interacted in English with international staff during the day.

a. 0% b. 25% c. 50% d. 75% e. 100%

Indicate what percentage of time you interacted in Spanish with NSs of Spanish during the day.

a. 0% b. 25% c. 50% d. 75% e. 100%

The second instrument used in this study was a multiple-choice questionnaire designed to elicit perceptions of social status. The data consisted of 12 scenarios and four response choices for each scenario that were modified and adapted from Matsumura (2001). A short description of the characters appears in the situations, explaining the setting, the social distance between the interlocutors, and their status relative to each other. This information allowed the respondents to understand the context and helped them to select the appropriate response. While the instructions and scenarios were written in learners' L1 (Spanish) to ensure full comprehension of the situation and avoid any misunderstanding, all the choices were offered in English (see Appendix). The social situations represented in each scenario took into account one of the three social status variables: higher status situations in which a university professor is addressed (situations 1, 4, 7, and 10); equal status situations in which a classmate is addressed (situations 2, 5, 8, and 11); and lower status situations in which a new classmate is addressed (situations 3, 6, 9, and 12). See Appendix.

As shown in Table 1, the four response choices represented the four speech act realizations in advice-giving situations: direct advice, hedge advice, indirect comment, and not giving advice.

**Table 1.** Strategies used in giving advice (Hinkel, 1997)

| type | strategy | structure |
|---|---|---|
| direct advice | declarative | You should... You shouldn't... |
| indirect comments | hints | |
| hedge advice | mitigators | Maybe... I think... I believe... |
| not giving advice | opting out | |

Based on Hinkel (1997) and Matsumura (2001), direct advice responses had the most literal pragmatic force and included the use of *should* without hedging. The second option – which featured hedged advice using lexical hedging *(I think, I believe, it seems that, it appeared)* – aimed to lessen the speaker's responsibility of what is said; these include expressions defined by Brown and Levinson (1987) as linguistic mitigating devices that protect the speaker from a commitment to the utterance. The third option used indirect comments with no advice. In this option, the speaker does not state his/her desires explicitly (Brown & Levinson, 1987); instead, it makes partial reference to the object or statement needed for the implementation of the act. The opting out option was always offered as the fourth choice in all scenarios. Participants could choose to opt out if they considered it unnecessary to offer advice. According to Rose and Ono (1995) and Rose (2000), opting out carries two potential meanings: (a) intentional non-performance due to the relevant contextual factors and (b) inability to carry out an act because of limited proficiency in the L2 or limited familiarity with the situation. Respondents were asked to select the appropriate answer – that which they considered would be appropriate in the given context, as can be observed in the following example:

1. Es muy tarde y ves a tu compañero de clase haciendo una tarea y se ve muy cansado. ¿Qué dirías en esta situación?
   You see your classmate working on the assignment late at night, and he is visibly tired. What would you say in this situation?
   a. Maybe it's better to go home. It's very late.
   b. I'm going home soon. It's very late.
   c. You shouldn't work so hard. It's very late.
   d. Nothing.

A group of 10 NSs (Mexican Spanish and American English) was asked to make comments on the scenarios and choices, check whether the descriptions and expressions were contextually appropriate in each situation, and make any cultural and stylistic modifications. Scenarios and choices that did not prove to be contextually appropriate were slightly changed, but the social context presented in each item remained intact. For example, instead of supervisor, *maestro de lengua meta* (target language professor) was used. The resulting version was pilot-tested with a group of 20 language learners at the BUAP. The final version was administered to all participants. This procedure produced a database of 648 answers.

## Data analysis

The data were analyzed according the levels of directness of the responses. The Mexican students' pragmatic development was examined by comparing the approximation of their preferences for advice type to NS preferences. LoR and intensity of interaction were self-reported variables. LoR in the host environment was reported in months, with the range reported for this factor being 3 to 5 months. Four learners who reported that they had previously lived for more than 5 years in the United States were excluded from the analysis; thus, 16 learners participated in the present study. In addition to the researcher, the data were coded by two coders. The coding produced by the coders coincided with the researcher's coding to a level of 97%. The discrepancies noted were discussed by the three coders, and a consensus was reached.

## Results

### Differences and similarities among the NSSs1 group (+abroad experience), the NNSs2 group (−abroad experience), and NSs of English.

This section presents the strategies, distributed into four coding types, selected by the three groups, and discusses their selection in terms of the sociocultural perceptions of social status when offering advice. The frequencies of these strategies are presented in Table 2 and show the differences and similarities among the groups. Table 2 shows that NNSs1 (+abroad experience) and NNSs2 (−abroad experience) did not exhibit major differences, while the native group showed differences compared to the two groups of NNSs.

**Table 2.** Strategies employed by the three groups.

| group | higher status | | | status equal | | | lower status | | |
|---|---|---|---|---|---|---|---|---|---|
| | NNSs1 +exp | NNSs2 −exp | NSs | NNSs1 +exp | NNSs2 −exp | NSs | NNSs1 +exp | NNSs2 −exp | NSs |
| direct | (20) 31% | (29) 36% | (10) 13% | (28) 44% | (28) 35% | (27) 34% | (23) 36% | (23) 29% | (19) 24% |
| hedged | (28) 44% | (34) 43% | (37) 46% | (26) 41% | (26) 32% | (22) 27% | (20) 31% | (24) 30% | (23) 29% |
| indirect | (7) 11% | (9) 11% | (27) 34% | (4) 6% | (10) 13% | (21) 26% | (18) 28% | (19) 24% | (33) 41% |
| opt out | (9) 14% | (8) 10% | (6) 7% | (6) 9% | (16) 20% | (10) 13% | (3) 5% | (14) 17% | (5) 6% |
| total | (64) 100% | (80) 100% | (80) 100% | (64) 100% | (80) 100% | (80) 100% | (64) 100% | (80) 100% | (80) 100% |

note: +exp = +abroad experience; −exp = −abroad experience

Findings revealed that the three groups preferred hedge advice solutions in higher status scenarios. However, the NNSs1 group (+abroad experience; 31%, 20/64) and the NNSs2 group (−abroad experience; 36%, 29/80) chose direct speech acts as the second most common strategy in offering advice to a higher status person when indirect speech was more appropriate and selected by NSs (34%, 27/80). It was expected that the preferences of the NNSs1 group (+abroad experience) would differ from the NNSs2 group (−abroad experience), and that L2 socialization in the target community would help language learners to understand both how native English speakers perceive higher social status and what advice strategy they employ in offering advice to a person of higher status. However, the NNSs1 group (+abroad experience) differed from the NSs group and not from the NNSs2 group. It can be observed that the third and fourth options most frequently chosen by NSs were direct advice and not giving advice (opting out).

On the other hand, both NNSs groups (+/−abroad experience) preferred indirect and not giving strategies in these scenarios.

Results show that with respect to preferences for giving advice to individuals of equal status, no considerable differences were observed between the most frequently selected strategies. All three groups showed a preference for direct advice (NNSs1=44%, 28/64; NNSs2=35%, 28/80; NSs=34%, 27/80) as the first choice and hedge for the second (NNSs1=41%, 26/64; NNSs2=32%, 26/80; NSs=27%, 22/80). In fact, both the NNSs1 group (+abroad experience) and the NNSs2 group (−abroad experience) exhibited the pragmatic competence required to choose appropriate strategies for giving advice in English to an equal status person. One possible explanation is that language learners and NSs may share the same perceptions of equal status. As DeCapua and Huber (1995) observe, offering advice is a common practice in everyday conversation. This type of speech act is not normally noticed, especially in situations with equals where the interlocutor adopts the role of expert and gives advice to a less experienced person. Casual and spontaneous advice is usually given in this type of relationship. However, in their third and fourth most frequent strategies, the language learners differed from the NSs. NSs chose indirect as the third choice (26%, 21/80) and not giving as the fourth (13%, 10/80), while the two groups of learners selected not giving (NNSs1 [+abroad experience]=9%, 6/64; NNSs2 [−abroad experience]=20%, 16/80) over indirect (NNSs1 [+abroad experience]=6%, 4/64; NNSs2 [−abroad experience]=13%, 10/80).

Regarding offering advice in lower status scenarios, the preferences of the NNSs1 group (+abroad experience) and NNSs2 group (−abroad experience) did not match the NS of English. Table 2 shows that indirect speech acts were preferred (41%, 33/80) by NSs, whereas the NNSs1 group (+abroad experience) selected direct strategies (36%, 23/64), with the NNSs2 group (−abroad experience) choosing hedge strategies (30%, 24/80) most frequently. With respect to the second most frequent option, the preferences of the NNSs1 group (+abroad experience) were similar to native English speakers, with both groups selecting hedge strategies, while the NNSs2 group (−abroad experience) chose direct strategies. In terms of the third preference, the two groups of learners and the native English speaker group differed again, with the NNSs1 (+abroad experience) and the NNSs2 (−abroad experience) groups selecting indirect strategies, while the native English speakers chose direct strategies. Table 3 presents the frequencies employed by the NS group for each situation.

**Table 3.** Native speaker group (Speakers of U.S. English)

|  | higher status | | | | | status equal | | | | | lower status | | | | | |
|---|---|---|---|---|---|---|---|---|---|---|---|---|---|---|---|---|
| scenario | 1 | 4 | 7 | 10 | % | 2 | 5 | 8 | 11 | % | 3 | 6 | 9 | 12 | % | total |
| direct | 1 | 3 | 3 | 3 | 13 | 4 | 13 | 9 | 1 | 34 | 3 | 3 | 3 | 10 | 24 | 56 (23) |
| hedged | 11 | 6 | 11 | 9 | 46 | 5 | 4 | 3 | 10 | 27 | 4 | 4 | 10 | 5 | 29 | 82 (34) |
| indirect | 6 | 10 | 5 | 6 | 34 | 10 | 2 | 6 | 3 | 26 | 11 | 12 | 6 | 4 | 41 | 81 (34) |
| not giving | 2 | 1 | 1 | 2 | 7 | 1 | 1 | 2 | 6 | 13 | 2 | 1 | 1 | 1 | 6 | 21 (9) |
| total | 20 | 20 | 20 | 20 | 100 | 20 | 20 | 20 | 20 | 100 | 20 | 20 | 20 | 20 | 100 | 240 (100) |

Table 3 shows that NSs of English preferred hedged and indirect speech acts in situations 1, 4, 7, 10, 2, 11, 3, 6, and 9, whereas more direct speech acts were only chosen in situations 5, 8, and 12. Table 4 and Table 5 indicate that the NNSs1 group (+abroad experience) selected hedged and indirect speech acts in situations 1, 4, 10, 11, 3, and 6. See Appendix for details. On the other hand, the NNSs2 group (–abroad experience) preferred this strategy in situations 1, 4, 8, 6, 12, and 3. The following is an example of the type of answers provided by NNS groups, with most participants selecting the indirect response choice indicated with the letter *c*:

2. You see your language professor working in the office late at night and looking very exhausted. What would you think be appropriate to say in this situation?
   c. Maybe it's better to go home. It's very late.

**Table 4.** Learners of English: NNSs1 group (+abroad experience)

|  | higher status | | | | | status equal | | | | | lower status | | | | | |
|---|---|---|---|---|---|---|---|---|---|---|---|---|---|---|---|---|
| scenario | 1 | 4 | 7 | 10 | % | 2 | 5 | 8 | 11 | % | 3 | 6 | 9 | 12 | % | total |
| direct | 3 | 4 | 7 | 7 | 30 | 9 | 8 | 7 | 4 | 44 | 0 | 6 | 11 | 6 | 36 | 71 (37) |
| hedged | 7 | 7 | 6 | 7 | 43 | 3 | 7 | 7 | 9 | 41 | 5 | 3 | 4 | 8 | 31 | 74 (39) |
| indirect | 3 | 1 | 1 | 2 | 11 | 3 | 0 | 1 | 0 | 6 | 9 | 7 | 1 | 1 | 28 | 29 (15) |
| not giving | 3 | 4 | 2 | 0 | 14 | 1 | 1 | 1 | 3 | 9 | 2 | 0 | 0 | 1 | 5 | 18 (9) |
| total | 16 | 16 | 16 | 16 | 100 | 16 | 16 | 16 | 16 | 100 | 16 | 16 | 16 | 16 | 100 | 192 (100) |

**Table 5.** Learners of English: NNSs2 group (–abroad experience)

| scenario | higher status | | | | | status equal | | | | | lower status | | | | | total |
|---|---|---|---|---|---|---|---|---|---|---|---|---|---|---|---|---|
| | 1 | 4 | 7 | 10 | % | 2 | 5 | 8 | 11 | % | 3 | 6 | 9 | 12 | % | |
| direct | 5 | 4 | 12 | 8 | 36 | 10 | 9 | 6 | 3 | 35 | 1 | 6 | 11 | 5 | 29 | 80 (33) |
| hedged | 12 | 12 | 4 | 6 | 43 | 5 | 9 | 9 | 3 | 32 | 2 | 7 | 5 | 10 | 30 | 84 (35) |
| indirect | 2 | 0 | 2 | 5 | 11 | 1 | 0 | 4 | 5 | 13 | 10 | 6 | 2 | 1 | 24 | 38 (16) |
| not giving | 1 | 4 | 2 | 1 | 10 | 4 | 2 | 1 | 9 | 20 | 7 | 1 | 2 | 4 | 17 | 38 (16) |
| total | 20 | 20 | 20 | 20 | 100 | 20 | 20 | 20 | 20 | 100 | 20 | 20 | 20 | 20 | 100 | 240 (100) |

As can be seen in Tables 4 and 5, direct speech acts were selected in situations of equal status and lower status (2, 5, 8, 9, and 12) by the NNSs1 group (+abroad experience) and in situations 2, 5, and 9 by the NNSs2 group (-a broad experience). An example for this strategy is as follows:

3. Your classmate considers skipping today's afternoon class. You happen to know that one absence loses one point from the final grade in the class. What do you think would be appropriate to say in this situation?
    b. *You should come to class. I've heard one absence loses one point from your final marks.*

In general, the results show that NSs preferred to use more hedged and indirect speech acts when they offer advice, especially when the interlocutor is in a higher position than him/her, and that they selected direct strategies only in specific situations with equals and in one situation with a person of lower status. On the other hand, both learner groups (+/–study abroad) showed some preference for direct strategies, choosing more direct speech acts with superiors, equals, and people of lower status.

### Length of residence or intensity of interaction

This section analyzes whether LoR or intensity of interaction is the most influential factor in the development of pragmatic competence. The responses to the background questionnaire by the learners who participated in a summer camp program in the US for the first time (NNSs1) are presented in Table 6 below. LoR was reported in months, with the range of reported LoR being 3 to 5 months. Among NNSs1, 56% reported a three-month stay (9 learners), 37% reported a four-month stay (6 learners), and 6% reported a five-month stay (1 learner). Intensity of interaction was measured by means of self-reporting on the respondents' opportunities for interaction in the TL during the day. This question provided eight categories and asked learners to circle all those that applied:

Native English-speaking friends; Native English-speaking superiors; service people (e.g., bus driver, salesperson, waiter, mechanic); maintenance people; international staff at the camp; campers; and NSs from the same church.

**Table 6.** Interaction in English at a U.S. summer camp program

| category | percentage |
|---|---|
| NS friends/peers | 3% |
| NS superiors | 15% |
| service people | 25% |
| maintenance people | 0% |
| international staff | 45% |
| campers | 15% |
| NS worship | 2% |
| other | 2% |

As can be seen in Table 6, a high percentage of learners reported interacting with members of the international staff (45%), service personnel (25%), campers (15%), and NS superiors (15%). These learners had very few opportunities to interact with NS peers in the camp or create intimate relationships with NSs in general. Although learners did report interaction with NS friends, it represented one of the lowest rates of contact with NSs of English or International speakers of English. Most of the learners mentioned that it was much easier for them to talk in English with NNSs than with NSs. Kasper and Rose (2002) have discussed the importance of creating opportunities to speak with NS peers or friends in order to improve pragmatic competence in the TL.

With respect to the type of work they carried out in the camp over the summer, 60% of the learners reported that they worked in the kitchen as part of the kitchen staff, 34% worked in the laundry, and 6% were housekeepers. The fact that they had these types of jobs reduced their opportunities to speak in English. Another aspect that was analyzed was the time learners spent talking to NSs of English, NSs of Spanish and NNSs of English speaking in English. The three groups represent input that can be measured in these terms.The three groups represent input that can be measured in terms of time. The learners reported spending 69% of their time in the camp using their mother tongue, 12% of their time speaking in English with NSs of English, and 19% of their time speaking with speakers of other languages in English.

In the participants' questionnaire responses, it is important to note their assertion that they used Spanish in the camp where they worked because there were other students from the same program and even their home university. Furthermore, there were other Spanish-speaking co-workers working in the same areas. Therefore, there were fewer opportunities to use English. They continued to use their mother tongue when interacting with their university classmates while carrying out their daily routines. These results suggest that the limited opportunities to interact with NSs of English may influence the lack of success in interlanguage pragmatic development.

## Discussion

With respect to the first question, the findings of the study demonstrate that the preferences of NNS1s (+abroad experience) and NNS2s groups (−abroad experience) presented important differences in comparison to NSs in relation to their preferences for particular strategies. The NSs preferred indirect speech acts in offering advice to a higher status person and a lower status person, and direct speech acts in equal status situations. NNS1s (+abroad experience), on the other hand, selected direct speech acts in high status situations and lower status situations, while NNS2s (−abroad experience) preferred direct strategies in high status situations, but favored hedging in low status situations. Regarding giving advice to individuals of equal status, the two groups of learners showed the same preference for advice type as NSs (direct advice and hedging).

It was expected that the perceptions of social status between the two groups of NNSs would be considerably different. However, the findings show that both learner groups, NNS1s (+abroad experience) and NNS2s (−abroad experience), had similar sociocultural perceptions. Both groups tended to select hedged advice strategies when they were asked to select an advice strategy for a higher status person and direct advice strategies for a person with equal status. The only difference was in the perception of lower status, with NNS1s (+abroad experience) preferring direct advice strategies, while NNS2s (−abroad experience) selected hedged advice strategies.

The results for research question two suggest that LoR did not play an important role in the acquisition of pragmatics in both this particular context and the population of L2 learners. The commonly shared belief among many Mexican learners that the longer they stay in the target community, the more their pragmatic knowledge will improve, did not hold true for the learners. In this study, NNS1s (with only 10 to 15 weeks of residence in the U.S. community) had few opportunities for social contact with NSs and were found to present several discrepancies when compared to NSs in this context. Some possible reasons behind these results were given in the questionnaire. One of them is that intensity of interaction had a considerable effect on the perception of social status in giving advice. The selection of direct strategies when indirect speech acts were more appropriate can be seen to confirm the idea that when the language learners give advice, they often prefer to be clear. Faerch and Kasper (1989) claim that learners tend to choose explicit and highly transparent forms when they realize a speech act. This finding suggests that grammatical knowledge does not imply that it will be used appropriately and effectively in a specific situation, and that learners need to acquire sociopragmatic and pragmalinguistic abilities in order to appropriately give advice. It appears that for these learners and for the specific situations examined here, LoR alone is not a sufficient condition for the development of sociocultural competence.

These findings appear to contradict the results of previous research that have emphasized the role played by LoR in the target community for the development of pragmatic competence. The cause of this contradiction can be explained based on the characteristics of the learners examined in this study as compared to those featured in previous research. As mentioned before, many studies discussing the positive effect of LoR have investigated the L2 pragmatics found in long-term university students (Alcón-Soler, 2015; Barron, 2002; Cheng, 2005; Félix-Brasdefer, 2003; Olshtain & Blum-Kulka, 1985). These learners have had more opportunities to be exposed to the TL through ordinary social life in the target speech community, having had many more opportunities for contact with NSs and, therefore, to receive more input. According to Bella (2011), this exposure gives the learners the opportunity to be aware of, and helps them to acquire, the pragmalinguistic and sociopragmatic rules of the TL.

The current study, on the other hand, has focused on the performance of a different population that consists of university learners who visit the US to work legally on a summer camp program for a short period of time (3 to 5 weeks). They go there because it is the only point of entry that they have to the TL community so they can practice and improve their language. Since they often experience social seclusion, they are unlikely to gain experience with a speech event such as giving advice, as NNSs are only likely to do so if exposed to real opportunities for socialization in the target community and for intimate relationships with NSs. Due to the type of work they carry out at the camp and the number of Spanish-speaking co-workers in the camp program, NNSs reported that they had more opportunities to interact in their L1 (Spanish) than in the TL (English). Bardovi-Harlig and Bastos (2011) consider that successful contact contributes to the acquisition of L2 pragmatics. Therefore, the lack of contact with NSs in the target community is reflected in the learners' low level of sociocultural knowledge of the target community rules.

## Conclusion

The aims of this study were to investigate the impact that the LoR and intensity of interaction had on the perception of giving advice. Specifically, it examined the strategies selected by Mexican learners who participated in a summer camp program in the US and Mexican learners who had never travelled to an English speaking country. By comparing three groups of participants, this study yields the following conclusions. Both groups of Mexican learners, NNS1s (+abroad experience) and NNS2s (−abroad experience) differed from the NSs of English in terms of frequency and choice of strategy. The two groups of learners exhibited almost exactly the same type of pragmatic competence. This may suggest that at least in relation to the speech act of offering advice, it is intensity of interaction rather than LoR that contributes to the acquisition of L2 pragmatics. It has been reported (Bouton, 1994; Olshtain & Blum-Kulka, 1985) that some aspects of pragmatic competence require more time to be acquired than others. However, even minimal LoR can have positive effects on the development of pragmatics if learners have opportunities to be exposed to NSs or other sources of input. More opportunities of contact with NSs during their stay in the target community will facilitate the development of pragmatic appropriateness in the L2. Bella (2011) notes that "length of residence does not guarantee pragmatic appropriateness and politeness when not combined with sufficient interaction opportunities" (p. 1737).

The results of this study cannot be generalized to hold for all NNSs of English because of the limited number of participants, their specific social characteristics, and the type of data obtained. The small number of participants provides only part of the picture with regard to non-native preferences for the speech under examination. However, the fact that they go to work, rather than study, during the summer camp program over a short period of time restricts the possibility of analyzing other types of input that they could have received if they had stayed under other conditions, such as social media and computer-mediated communication. The experience of the learner who goes to work is, in all likelihood, very different from that of a learner who goes to study. Furthermore, the use of a multiple-choice questionnaire to collect the data poses further limitations to the study. This limitation highlights the need to triangulate with other instruments, such as role plays. While recognition of the speech act was necessary, this was not a sufficient condition for its production, and, as such, it would be necessary to implement a productive task in order to fully analyze the performance of the participants. Thus, the examination of a larger corpus of data, another type of instrument and the use of statistical analysis would be necessary to obtain more valid conclusions and attain further insights into the acquisition of the strategies for offering advice.

Despite the limitations, the results of the present study show that LoR does not guarantee the acquisition of pragmatics in the TL when not combined with sufficient interaction opportunities. This highlights the need to encourage those learners who participate in the summer camp programs each year (the number of whom increases every year) to engage in more contact with NSs of English and to use the language in a variety of situations. In addition, the fact that both learner groups differed from NSs in terms of frequency and choice of strategy emphasizes the need for pedagogical intervention (see Hasler-Barker, this volume). Due to the fact that English is taught as a foreign language in Mexico and that it is thus difficult for learners to know what forms need to be used in a specific situation, explicit instruction in the classroom is recommended to raise EFL learners' awareness of the performance of speech acts in general, and L2 advice offering strategies in particular.

## Notes

1 Benemérita Universidad Autónoma de Puebla is a public university dependent on the state legislature for much of its basic funding, and on the federal government (through its many departments) for funding for research and training.

## References

Alcón-Soler, E. (2015). Pragmatic learning and study abroad: Effects of instruction and length of stay. *Pragmatic Learning across Contexts, 48*, 62–74.

Bardovi-Harlig, K., & Bastos, M. T. (2011). Proficiency, length of stay, and intensity of interaction, and the acquisition of conventional expressions in L2 pragmatics. *Intercultural Pragmatics, 8*(3), 347–384.

Barron, A. (2002). *Acquisition in interlanguage pragmatics: Learning how to do things with words in a study abroad context.* Amsterdam: John Benjamins.

Bataineh, R. F, & Bataineh, R. F. (2006). Apology strategies of Jordanian EFL university students. *Journal of Pragmatics, 38*(11), 1901–1927.

Beebe, L., Takahashi, T., & Uliss-Welts, R. (1990). Pragmatic transfer in ESL refusals. In R. Scarcella, E. Andersen, & S. Krashen (Eds.), *Developing communicative competence in a second language* (pp. 55–73). New York, NY: Newbury House.

Bella, S. (2011). Mitigation and politeness in Greek invitation refusals: Effects of length of residence in the target community and intensity of interaction on non-native speakers' performance. *Journal of Pragmatics, 43*, 1718–1740.

Blum-Kulka, S. (1983). Interpreting and performing speech acts in a second language: A cross-cultural study of Hebrew and English. In N. Wolfson & N. Judd (Eds.), *Sociolinguistics and language acquisition* (pp. 36–57). Roeley, MA: Newbury House.

Blum-Kulka, S., & Olshtain, E. (1986). Too many words: Length of utterances and pragmatic failure. *Journal of Pragmatics, 8*, 47–61.

Bouton, L. (1994). Conversational implicature in the second language: learned slowly when not deliberately taught. *Journal of Pragmatics, 22*, 157–167.

Brown, P., & Levinson, S. (1987). *Politeness: Some universals of language use.* Cambridge: Cambridge University Press.

Cheng, S. (2005). An exploratory cross-sectional study of interlanguage pragmatic development of expressions of gratitude by Chinese learners of English. (Doctoral dissertation). Retrieved from http://ir.uiowa.edu/etd/104.

Cohen, A., & Olshtain, E. (1993). The production of speech acts by EFL learners. *TESOL Quarterly, 27*, 33–56.

Council of Europe (2001). *Common European framework of reference for languages: Learning, teaching, assessment.* Cambridge, England: Cambridge University Press.

DeCapua, A., & Huber, L. (1995). If I were you…: Advice in American English. *Multilingual, 14*(2), 117–132.

Faerch, C., & Kasper, G. (1989). Internal and external modifications in interlanguage request realization. In S. Blum-Kulka, J. House, & G. Kasper (Eds.), *Cross-cultural pragmatics: Requests and apologies* (pp. 221–247). Norwood, NJ: Ablex.

Félix-Brasdefer, J. C. (2003). Validity in data collection methods in pragmatics research. In P. Kempchinsky & C. E. Piñeros (Eds.), *Theory practice, and acquisition. Papers from the 6th Hispanic Linguistics Symposium and the 5th Conference on the Acquisition of Spanish and Portuguese* (pp. 239–257). Somerville, MA: Cascadilla Press.

Félix-Brasdefer, J. C. (2004). Interlanguage refusals: Linguistic politeness and length of residence in the target community. *Language Learning, 54*(4), 587–653.

Félix-Brasdefer, J. C. (2007). Pragmatic development in the Spanish as a FL classroom: A cross-sectional study of learner requests. *Intercultural Pragmatics, 4*(2), 253–286.

Félix-Brasdefer, J. C., & Hasler Barker, M. (2015). Complimenting in Spanish in a short-term study abroad context. *System 48*, 75–85.

Hasler-Barker, M. (this volume). Effects of metapragmatic instruction on the production of compliments and compliment responses: Learner–learner role-plays in the foreign language classroom. In K. Bardovi-Harlig & J. C. Félix-Brasdefer (Eds.), *Pragmatics and language learning*, vol. 14. Honolulu: National Foreign Language Resource Center, University of Hawai'i at Mānoa.

Hassall. T. (2003). Requests by Australian learners of Indonesian. *Journal of Pragmatics, 35*, 1903–1928.

Hinkel, E. (1997). Appropriateness of advice: DCT and multiple choice data. *Applied Linguistics, 18*, 1–26.

House, J., & Kasper, G. (1987). Interlanguage pragmatics: requesting in a foreign language. In W. Loerscher & R. Schulze (Eds.). *Perspectives on language in performance* (pp. 1250–88). Tuebinge: Narr.

Kasper, G. (1992). Pragmatic transfer. *Second Language Research, 8*(3), 203–231.

Kasper, G., & Rose, K. (2002). *Pragmatic development in a second language*. Malden, MA: Blackwell.

Koike, D. A. (1996). Transfer of pragmatic competence and suggestions in Spanish foreign language learning. In S. Gass & J. Neu (Eds.), *Speech acts across cultures* (pp. 257–281). Berlin: Mouton de Gruyter.

Márquez-Reiter, R. (2000). *Linguistic politeness in Britain and Uruguay: Contrastive study of requests and apologies*. Amsterdam: John Benjamins.

Matsumoto, Y. (1988). Reexamination of the universality of face: Politeness phenomena in Japanese. *Journal of Pragmatics, 12*, 403–426.

Matsumoto, Y. (1989). Politeness and conversational universals: Observations from Japanese. *Multilingual, 82*, 207–221

Matsumura, S. (2001). Learning the rules of offering advice: A quantitative approach to second language socialization. *Language Learning, 51*(4), 635–679.

Olshtain, E., & Blum-Kulka, S. (1985). Degree of approximation: Nonnative reactions to native speech act behaviour. In S. M. Gass & C. Madden (Eds.), *Input in second language acquisition* (pp. 303–325). Rowley, MA: Newbury House.

Pinto, D. (2010). Lost in subtitle translations: The case of advice in the English subtitles of Spanish. *Intercultural Pragmatics, 7*(2), 257–277.
Rose, K. (2000). An exploratory cross-sectional study of interlanguage pragmatic development. *Studies in Second Language Acquisition, 22*, 27–67.
Rose, K., & Ono, R. (1995). Eliciting speech act data in Japanese: The effect of questionnaire type. *Language Learning, 45*, 191–223.
Searle, J. (1979). *Expression and meaning: Studies in the theory of speech acts.* Cambridge: Cambridge University Press.
Shardakova, M. (2005). Intercultural pragmatics in the speech of American L2 learners of Russian: Apologies offered by Americans in Russian. *Intercultural Pragmatics, 2*(4), 423–451.
Trosborg, A. (1995). *Interlanguage pragmatics: Requests, complaints and apologies.* Berlin, : Mouton de Gruyter.
Wardhaugh, R. (1985). *How conversation works.* Oxford,: Blackwell.

## Appendix

Instrucciones: Lee cuidadosamente cada situación: Al final de cada descripción encontrarás tres posibles opciones: A, B, y C. Selecciona la que consideres podría ser la más apropiada para cada situación. Si consideras que sería más apropiado no decir nada, escoge la opción D.

A continuación encontrarás una breve descripción de los personajes que aparecen en cada situación:

Instructions: Carefully read each situation. At the end of each description, you will find three possible options: A, B, and C. Choose the one that you think would be the most appropriate for each situation. If you think it would be more appropriate to say nothing, choose option D.

Below you will find a brief description of the characters that appear in each situation.

**Maestra de Lengua Meta:** Has tomado clases con él durante tres meses. El maestro y tú, junto con otros alumnos, han salido a comer varias veces después de clase. También, lo has visitado en su oficina varias veces para aclarar dudas sobre la clase.

**Target language instructor:** You have been taking classes with him for three months. The language instructor and you, together with other students, have gone out for dinner several times. You have visited his office several times to talk about questions related to the class.

**Compañero de clase:** Él y tú regularmente salen a desayunar juntos después de clase, varias veces le has pedido su libreta y lo consideras un buen amigo.

**Classmate:** He and you often go out for lunch together after class. You have borrowed his notes several times before. You regard him as a good friend.

**Compañero de nuevo ingreso:** Un amigo te lo presentó. Él y tú regularmente salen a comer juntos después de clase y te llevas bien con él.
**First-year university classmate:** A friend introduced him to you. He and you regularly go out for dinner after class and you have a good relationship with him.

## Situations
1. El maestro de lengua meta y tú están en un restaurante. El maestro comenta que va a pedir una hamburguesa. Tú ya la has comido en ese lugar y en tu opinión la hamburguesa tiene mucha grasa. ¿Qué le dirías?
   You and your language instructor are at a restaurant. The instructor says that he is going to order a hamburger. You have eaten in this restaurant before and, in your opinion, the hamburger was really greasy. What would you say?
   A. You shouldn't order the hamburger. I had it here before and it was really greasy.
   B. Maybe it's not a good idea to order a hamburger. I had one here before and it was really greasy.
   C. I had it here before and it was really greasy.
   D. Nothing
2. Tu compañero de clase esta pensando no entrar a la clase de la tarde. Tú sabes que con una falta se pierde un punto de la calificación final. ¿Qué le dirías?
   Your classmate is thinking about not going to class this afternoon. You know that one absence reduces one point from the final grade. What would you say?
   A. I've heard one absence loses one point from the final marks.
   B. You should come to class. I've heard one absence loses one point from the final marks.
   C. I think it's better to come to class. I've heard one absence loses one point from the final marks.
   D. Nothing.
3. Tu compañero de nuevo ingreso esta pensando tomar un curso de fonética. Has escuchado que el curso es muy difícil. ¿Qué le dirías?
   Your first-year classmate is considering taking a phonetics course. You have heard that the course is really difficult. What would you say?
   A. I don't think is a good idea to take this course. I've heard it's really difficult.
   B. I've heard it's really difficult.
   C. You shouldn't take this course. I've heard it's really difficult.
   D. Nothing.

4. Ves al maestro de lengua meta trabajando en su oficina. Ya es muy tarde y se nota cansado. ¿Qué dirías?
You see your language instructor working in his office. It's late and he looks tired. What would you say?
   A. I'm going home soon. It's very late.
   B. You shouldn't work so hard. It's very late.
   C. Maybe it's better to go home. It's very late.
   D. Nothing.
5. Tu compañero de clase metió una moneda de diez pesos en una máquina de dulces en la cafetería, pero está descompuesta. No recibe ni el dulce que quería ni la moneda. ¿Qué le dirías?
Your classmate put a ten peso coin in the vending machine in the cafeteria, but it's broken. Your classmate does not get any candy nor does he get the coin back. What would you say?
   A. Maybe it's better to complain about it. The cafeteria is downstairs.
   B. You should complain about it. The cafeteria is downstairs.
   C. The cafeteria is downstairs.
   D. Nothing.
6. Tu compañero de nuevo ingreso está pensando en llevar a reparar su carro a un taller mecánico. Tú sabes que el taller es conocido por su mala atención. ¿Qué le diriás?
Your first-year classmate is thinking about taking his car to a repair shop. You know that this place is known for bad customer service. What would you say?
   A. You shouldn't take your car to that shop. It has a really bad reputation.
   B. Maybe it's better to take your car to another shop. It has a really bad reputation.
   C. It has a really bad reputation.
   D. Nothing.
7. Te das cuenta de que el maestro de lengua meta está pensando en comprar un libro caro. Él no sabe que en otra librería venden el mismo libro más barato. ¿Qué le dirías?
You see that your language instructor is thinking about buying an expensive book. He doesn't know that another bookstore sells it cheaper. What would you say?
   A. You should buy the book at another store. This store is over-priced.
   B. This store is over-priced.
   C. Maybe, it's not a good idea to buy the book here. This store is over priced.
   D. Nothing.
8. Te das cuenta de que tu compañero de clase está haciendo su tarea y ya es muy tarde y se ve cansado. ¿Qué le dirías?

You see that your classmate is doing his homework. It's already late, and he looks tired. What would you say?
A. Maybe it's better to go home. It's very late.
B. I'm going home some. It's very late.
C. You shouldn't work so hard. It's very late.
D. Nothing.

9. Escuchaste que a tu compañero no le dieron su cambio completo en la cafetería. ¿Qué le dirías?
You heard that your classmate didn't get the exact amount of change at the cafeteria. What would you say?
A. Maybe it's better to complain about it. That person is still there.
B. You should complain about it. That person is still there.
C. That person is still there.
D. Nothing.

10. Acabas de escuchar que tu maestro de lengua meta que esta pensando ir a Veracruz en su coche que regularmente se descompone. ¿Qué le dirías?
You just heard that your language instructor is thinking about going to Veracruz (Mexico) in his car, which breaks down frequently. What would you say?
A. I think it may be risky for you to take such a long trip in this car.
B. Taking such a long trip in this car may be risky.
C. You shouldn't take this car for such a long trip. It may be risky.
D. Nothing.

11. Te has dado cuenta que tu compañero de clase olvidó dejar propina en el restaurante. ¿Qué le dirías?
You noticed that your classmate forgot to leave a tip at the restaurant. What would you say?
A. A tip is important. You shouldn't forget to leave one.
B. tip is important.
C. Maybe it's better to leave a tip. It's important.
D. Nothing.

12. Ves a tu compañero de nuevo ingreso estudiando en la biblioteca. Ya es muy tarde y se ve cansado. ¿Qué le dirías?
You see your first-year classmate studying at the library. It's very late and he looks tired. What would you say?
A. You shouldn't work so hard. It's very late.
B. Maybe it's better to go home. It's very late.
C. I'm going home soon. It's very late.
D. Nothing.

**Thank you!**

# Semantic and Pragmatic Causal Relations in Native Speaker and L2 Learner Oral Discourse: The Use of the Spanish Connective *Porque*

Sarah E. Blackwell
Margaret Lubbers Quesada
*The University of Georgia, USA*

This article examines causal relations with the Spanish connective porque ('because') in the oral texts of three groups of second language (L2) learners of Spanish and native speakers (NSs). We first distinguish causal relations with porque in terms of Sweetser's (1990) three categories of causal conjunction: content (semantic), epistemic, and speech act. We then explore the effects of task type on the speakers' use of porque-constructions. Specifically, we analyze 384 instances of porque in four different tasks, the participants' retelling of a silent film, a personal narrative, a description, and an account of future plans, using heuristic tests to determine whether porque is used semantically to encode relations of CONSEQUENCE-CAUSE, or pragmatically to express epistemic (CONCLUSION/CLAIM-ARGUMENT) or speech-act (UTTERANCE-MOTIVATION) relations (T. Sanders & Sweetser, 2009). We also examine the learner data to see how porque-constructions are used at different learner levels. Our findings reveal that text type and learning level condition the types of causal relations expressed by the participants. The NSs use semantic porque more frequently in past narratives, whereas the learners use more speech act porque, but in different narrative tasks according to level. Additionally, epistemic porque-relations are notably less frequent in the Spanish L2 learners' oral narratives, and most likely learned later than semantic and speech-act relations.

## Introduction

This article examines the acquisition and use of causal relations with the Spanish connective *porque* ('because') by second language (L2) learners of Spanish and compares their use of this connective with that of native speakers (NSs). We analyzed the oral production of 30 learners from three learner levels and 10 NSs who completed four different narrative tasks (the retelling of a silent film and three personal narratives). We first identified 384 instances of *porque* among the four groups and then applied heuristic tests to determine whether *porque* was used semantically to encode relations of CONSEQUENCE-CAUSE, or pragmatically to express epistemic (CONCLUSION/CLAIM-ARGUMENT) or speech-act (UTTERANCE-MOTIVATION) relations (T. Sanders & Sweetser, 2009). The general objective of this study was to determine whether L2 learners at different learning levels have acquired the pragmatic and semantic functions of causal *porque* in Spanish and are capable of producing them in narrative structure. More specifically, our aims are to (a) distinguish causal relations with *porque* in the narratives using Sweetser's (1990) three categories of causal conjunction: content (semantic), epistemic, and speech act; (b) explore the effects of narrative task type on the use of *porque*-constructions among L2 learners and NSs; and (c) determine whether L2 Spanish learners' and NSs use *porque*-constructions in narrative discourse in the same or different ways.

In section 2, we describe the semantics and pragmatics of causal connectives and review previous research on their use and interpretation. We present the framework of analysis applied in our study, known as the "domains" approach, and review earlier work on Spanish *porque*. Subsequently, we show how causal relations expressed with English *because* have been distinguished by causal domain through the use of heuristic tests and how these tests may also be applied to Spanish *porque*-constructions to determine their domain. Finally, we summarize previous work on the L2 acquisition of causal connectives. Section 3 describes the participants in the study and outlines the methods used to elicit, record, and transcribe their narratives, as well as the tests used to classify *porque*-relations. In section 4, we report the quantitative results of our analysis, and in section 5, we discuss these results and present representative examples of the participants' uses of *porque* in the four tasks. Conclusions and some limitations of the study, directions for future research, and pedagogical implications are presented in section 6.

## Theoretical background: Causal relations and connectives

According to T. Sanders and Sweetser (2009), speakers of all languages express causal relations with connectives (e.g., English *because*, *since*, *therefore*, and *so*), and "all humans in all cultures seem to interpret the world in terms of causal relations" (p. 1). Studies have been carried out on causal connectives in various languages, including Dutch (e.g., Degand, 2001; Pander Maat & Sanders, 2000, 2001; Pit, 2006; T. Sanders, 1997; J. Sanders, Sanders, & Sweetser, 2012; T. Sanders & Spooren, 2009, 2013); English (e.g., Dancygier & Sweetser, 2000; Sweetser, 1990); French (e.g., Degand & Fagard, 2012; Zufferey, 2012); and Greek (e.g., Bardzokas, 2012, 2014; Kitis, 2006). Cross-linguistically, causal connectives have been examined by Pander Maat and Degand (2001), who study French and Dutch; Zufferey and Cartoni (2012), who compare French and English; and Pit (2003) and Stukker and Sanders, T. (2012), who examine French, German, and Dutch (see also Couper-Kuhlen & Kortmann, 2000, and T. Sanders & Sweetser, 2009). However, despite the large volume of linguistic research on Spanish to date, relatively little work has been done on the Spanish causal connectives. Jordan (1989) analyzes the discourse-pragmatic functions of *porque*-clauses in Spanish conversational discourse. García (1992) examines the (non)-interchangeability of *porque* and *como* ('since') in literary texts. Goethals (2002) focuses on the description, classification, and distribution of the conjunctions *porque*, *pues* ('because', 'for'), *ya que* ('since'), and *como* ('as'), and later, he shows how *como*, *ya que*, and *pues* introduce causal clauses conveying justificational speech events (Goethals, 2010). Recently, Blackwell (2016) examines the *porque*-constructions in Peninsular Spanish film-retell narratives and shows that pragmatic constructions produce what could be considered Gricean implicatures involving metapragmatic commentary. However, to our knowledge, no previous studies have examined causal connectives in both NSs' and L2 Spanish learners' discourse.

## Distinguishing semantic and pragmatic causal relations

In her seminal work, Sweetser (1990) shows how causal conjunctions in English (e.g., *because* and *since*), as well as other conjunctions, are much like other areas of the lexicon in that they are pragmatically ambiguous. To account for these ambiguities, Sweetser proposes interpreting the syntactic conjunction of clauses in three distinct ways: "as conjunction of content, as conjunction of premises in the epistemic world, and as conjunction of the speech acts performed via the utterance of the clauses in question" (p. 111). Sweetser illustrates these distinctions with the following examples (p. 77):

(1) John came back because he loved her. (content)
(2) John loved her, because he came back. (epistemic)
(3) What are you doing tonight, because there's a good movie on. (speech act)

T. Sanders and Sweester (2009, p. 2) note that content causal relations, referred to by others as "ideational," "external," and "semantic" relations, relate causes to consequences due to their propositional content and are governed by real-world restrictions.[1] In these relations, the state of affairs described in the second segment is the cause of the state of affairs in the first one. For instance, in (1), John's loving her *caused* him to return. By contrast, epistemic causals indicate that the speaker's knowledge based on previous experience leads him/her to a conclusion, as in (2) where "the speaker's knowledge of John's return (as a premise) causes the *conclusion* that John loved her" (Sweetser, 1990, p. 77). In speech-act causal relations, Sweetser explains, "the *because*-clause gives the cause of the speech act embodied by the main clause" (p. 77). She suggests the following reading for (3): "I ask what you are doing tonight because I want to suggest that we go see this good movie" (p. 77). Furthermore, whereas epistemic causals involve conclusions that are inferred from facts presented as evidence (i.e., asserted) and therefore may be derived from semantic causal relations, as (1) and (2) illustrate, according to Sweetser, speech-act causal relations cannot be derived from the semantic meanings of the propositions.

Oversteegan (1997) discusses what it means for a connective to be interpreted pragmatically. She observes that earlier definitions of the pragmatic uses of connectives mentioned speech acts but that these also involve "internal acts of concluding" pertaining to Sweetser's epistemic domain (1997, p. 52). However, the pragmatic nature of both of these categories of causal relation seems to lie in the underlying implicatures they give rise to, which may be paraphrased, as Sweetser illustrates with a fourth example (1990, p. 79):

(4) The answer is on page 200, since you'll never find it for yourself.

Sweetser (1990) paraphrases and explains this utterance as follows: "I make this assertion because it gives you information which you can't acquire independently. A Gricean condition of informativeness is thus invoked as the cause of a statement" (p. 79). Both speech-act and epistemic causal relations appear to be characterized by the "paraphraseability" of the speaker's intentional meaning, that is, his/her implicature. However, Sweetser (1990) maintains that while conjunctions may be interpreted as pertaining to (at least) one of the three domains, "the choice of a 'correct' interpretation depends not on form, but on a pragmatically motivated choice between viewing the conjoined clauses as representing content units, logical entities, or speech acts" (1990, p. 78); and, furthermore, at times "only context can disambiguate the domain of conjunction" (p. 77), as Sweetser demonstrates with this example (p. 77):

(5) a. She went because she left her book in the movie theater last night.
    b. She went, because she left her book in the movie theater last night.
      (a) Semantic: Her intention to recover the lost book caused her to go.
      (b) Epistemic (logical conclusion): "I know she went (to the movies), because I discovered that she left her book in the movie theater".

Sweetser explains that these utterances could be read as an "assertion of a person's departure, followed by a real-world reason for the departure (intention to recover the lost book; 5a), or as a logical conclusion: I know she went (to the movies), because I discovered that she left her book in the movie theater" (5b).

But, she adds, "given sufficient context we can almost always force either a content-conjunction reading or an epistemic-conjunction reading on any pair of clauses conjoined with *because*; it is just harder to find reasonable contexts for some readings than for others" (pp. 77–78).

T. Sanders (1997) also addresses the potential ambiguity in meaning for causal relations such as the following (p. 128):

(6) The neighbors are not at home because there is a party downtown. (semantic or pragmatic?)

Here, the fact that there is a party downtown may be the semantic reason why the neighbors are not home, or the speaker's knowledge that there is a party downtown could serve as evidence leading him/her to conclude that the neighbors are not home. T. Sanders (1997) examines the relationship between the "source of coherence" (i.e., semantic or pragmatic) and the context to determine the extent to which the domain of a causal relation is clearer in context or is recognized independently of the context, and the extent to which the context plays a role in subjects' interpretations of ambiguous causal relations in Dutch. From his interpretation experiment, Sanders concludes, "when analysts are asked to judge relations which are ambiguous between a semantic and a pragmatic reading, they *are* influenced by the type of context in which the relation appears," and that, in ambiguous cases, "context strongly determines the interpretation of a relation" (p. 135). These findings highlight the importance of context in ascertaining causal domain.

Whereas speech-act uses of *because* provide reasons for saying, speaking, claiming, asking, requesting, commenting on, inviting, suggesting, and so on, epistemic uses convey reasons for the speaker's conclusion, supposition, or inference stated in the main clause. However, speech-act uses are more likely to refer to "the relevance or irrelevance of a state of affairs as causing or impeding the speaker's action" (Sweetser, 1990, p. 81). In other words, speech-act causal constructions explain why the speaker's utterance is *relevant* to the conversation. Nevertheless, both epistemic and speech-act relations are essentially justificational and the speaker is involved in construing these causal relations: In the former, the speaker provides an argument or justification for an inference or conclusion, whereas in the latter, s/he gives the motivation or justification for realizing the speech act expressed in the main clause.

Weaknesses in Sweetser's framework include the fact that some causal relations are hard to classify as clearly semantic, epistemic, or speech-act. Bardzokas (2012), in his study of Greek causal connectives, assesses Sweetser's framework noting, "reportedly, a large portion of real language data does not seem to support any one of the proposed delineations" (p. 19). Additionally, Sweetser's three categories do not always account for meaning distinctions among causal relations (see, e.g., Kitis, 2006; Bardzokas, 2012; Stukker & Sanders, T. 2012).

As our analysis of the *porque*-relations in both Spanish L2 learners' and native speakers' narratives reveals, some uses can have more than one interpretation and are difficult to classify by domain.

## Spanish *porque*

As early as 1847, the grammarian Bello (cited in Lapesa, 1978) offers examples with *porque* that correspond to the content and speech-act categories. Lapesa (1978) also presents "cause and effect" relations, which clearly correspond to Sweetser's content category, and others involving what Lapesa calls "el motivo o la premisa" ('the motive or the premise') and the consequence, which are in fact, epistemic and speech-act constructions. Lapesa identifies constraints on *porque*-constructions using syntactic tests and shows that sentences like the following may be inverted (pp. 182–183):

(7) a. Ha llovido, porque el suelo está mojado.
    It has rained, because the ground is wet.
    b. El suelo está mojado porque ha llovido.
    The ground is wet because it has rained.

Following Sweetser's domain approach, (7a) is epistemic, since the speaker explains why s/he knows or is able to conclude that it has rained; and (7b) is a content case of cause ('it rained') and effect ('the ground is wet'). These examples support the generalization regarding epistemic causals in English, mentioned earlier, namely, that epistemic causals like (7a) involve conclusions based on facts presented as evidence, and therefore they may be derived from semantic relations, as illustrated in (7b).

Jordan (1989) studies the use of conjunctions in Spanish discourse and analyzes some instances of *porque* in the corpus *El habla de la Ciudad de México* (1974, cited in Jordan, 1989). She identifies examples where speakers use *porque* to justify a preceding utterance and suggests that the speaker is "offering a cause for the possible effect his words may have had or may be about to have on the hearer" (p. 375). For instance, in the following exchange Jordan claims the informant (Inf.) "simply wants to justify not an external state of affairs but the fact that he makes a certain statement" (p. 376):

(8) Inf.: Pero vienes a cocinar.
    Otra persona: Pero usted me da todos los ingredientes y todo, ¿no, señora?
    Inf.: Bueno, los que estén en la casa, en el refrigerador más bien. *Porque* es importante que esté en el refrigerador. (*El habla...*: 78)
    Inf.: But you're coming to cook.
    Another person: But you're going to give me all the ingredients and everything, right, ma'am?

Inf.: Well, whatever is in the house, or rather in the refrigerator? Because it's important that it be in the refrigerator.

In Sweetser's domains approach, this use of *porque* would be classified as a speech-act connective.

Escandell Vidal (2006) examines discourse relations using Anscombre and Ducrot's (1983) argumentation theory, noting that argumentation involves the act of "adducing arguments in favor of a particular conclusion" (p. 92, our translation). She adds that speakers use various linguistic strategies to present utterances as arguments to support or justify a conclusion, in turn giving the addressee instructions to guide them in interpreting utterances (p. 96). Escandell Vidal refers to these linguistic means as "marcadores argumentativos" ('argumentative markers'; p. 97), which include epistemic uses of *porque*.

Briz (2001) proposes that connectives be analyzed at the sentence level as abstract syntactic units, and at the utterance level as units comprising speech acts, and that the function of a pragmatic connective is determined by the types of speech it connects and the context. Briz's "syntactic-propositional" *porque* corresponds to Sweetser's content category, whereas his "pragmatic" *porque* introduces an argument justifying the speaker's previous assertion. He illustrates these categories as follows (pp. 170–171, our translation):

(9)   Ha ido al médico *porque* está enfermo.
      EFECTO          CAUSA
      'He has gone to the doctor because he's sick.'
      EFFECT                    CAUSE
(10)  Está enfermo, *porque* ha ido al médico.
      AFIRMACIÓN    JUSTIFICACIÓN
      'He's sick, because he has gone to the doctor.'
      ASSERTION     JUSTIFICATION

Briz (2001) also observes that pragmatic *porque* can be used to reiterate a previous statement as in (11) (p. 171; our translation; / appears to indicate a pause):

(11)  Por eso muchas veces los que llaman/ *porque* les llaman por teléfono/ resulta que se quedan así un pocooo
      'That's why many times the ones who call/ because they call them on the phone/ it turns out that they're a littllle'

Briz presents syntactic tests showing how only semantic *porque* can be negated, questioned, or embedded in a larger context, as the (a)-utterances in (12), (13), and (14) reveal. However, when *porque* is used pragmatically, these transformations produce unacceptable sentences, as shown by the (b)-examples (p. 171, our translations; Briz uses * to indicate semantically illogical sentences), although, as one reviewer rightly noted, for (13b), if the question is changed to "¿Está enfermo?, porque ha ido al médico", it is perfectly correct):

(12) a. No ha ido al médico *porque* está enfermo.
'He hasn't gone to the doctor *because* he's sick.'
b. *No está enfermo, *porque* ha ido al médico.
*'He's not sick, *because* he has gone to the doctor.'
(13) a. ¿Ha ido al médico porque está enfermo?
'Has he gone to the doctor because he's sick?'
b. *¿Está enfermo, porque ha ido al médico?
*Is he sick, because he has gone to the doctor?'
(14) a. Juan dice que ha ido al médico *porque* está enfermo.
'Juan says that he has gone to the doctor because he's sick.'
b. *Juan dice que está enfermo, *porque* ha ido al médico.
*'Juan says that he's sick, because he has gone to the doctor.'

Briz also observes that a *porque*-relation can have a semantic interpretation or a pragmatic one, involving justification for a conclusion (pp. 172–173, our translation):

(15) Juan no viene a la fiesta *porque* está enfermo.
'Juan isn't coming to the party because he's sick.'

The fact that Spanish *porque*-constructions can describe both semantic relations of consequence-cause and pragmatic relations involving justification for the previous utterance, be it a conclusion, claim, or another speech act, indicates that Spanish *porque*-relations correspond to one or more of Sweetser's (1990) three domains. Furthermore, like English *because*-relations, Spanish *porque*-relations may be ambiguous, allowing either a semantic (consequence-cause) or a pragmatic (epistemic conclusion-argument) interpretation, as in (15). In addition, Briz (2001) provides a set of syntactic tests (negation, questioning, embedding, inversion), which may be useful in determining whether a causal relation with *porque* is pragmatic or semantic (see also Goethals, 2002, who identifies these and other criteria for distinguishing among causal connectives). Despite the fact that English and Spanish allow both semantic and pragmatic interpretations for *because* and *porque*-relations, we cannot assume automatic transfer from the L1 to the L2. Therefore, we examine both L2 learner and NS speech in order to ascertain whether learners make use of these functions in their L2 Spanish in the same ways that NSs do.

### Heuristic tests for causal relations

While determining causal domain in sentences in isolation seems straightforward, how can we identify the domain of causal relations in discourse? Sanders (1997) notes that in prototypical content relations, the events depicted "have already taken place" (p. 125), as in (16a, p. 122):

(16) a. Theo was exhausted because he had run to the university.
b. Theo was exhausted, because he was gasping for breath.
c. Theo was exhausted, because he told me so.

Example (16a) is clearly semantic, since its coherence is due to our world knowledge (e.g., "running causes fatigue," p. 122). Example (16b) is pragmatic because "the state of affairs in the second segment is not the cause of the state of affairs in the first segment, but the *justification* for making that utterance," although there is also a "'real world link' between a cause (being exhausted) and a consequence (gasping for breath)" (p. 122). However, in (16c) there is no real-world link between Theo's being exhausted and his telling me so (p. 122). Therefore, Sanders generalizes, pragmatic relations can be based on real-world connections, but need not be (p. 123).

To distinguish semantic and pragmatic relations in discourse, Sanders develops an analytical heuristic dubbed the "Basic Operation Paraphrase Test," which is summarized below (adapted from T. Sanders, 1997, p. 126):

1. Isolate the two segments that are connected by a coherence relation.
2. Strip all connectives from the sequence of segments.
3. Reconstruct the causal basic operation between the propositions P and Q... Paraphrase it using the formulations below and consider which formulation is the best expression of the meaning of the relation in this context.
    (i) a. the fact that P causes S[peaker]'s claim / advice / conclusion that Q
    (i) b. the fact that Q causes S's claim / advice / conclusion that P
    (ii) a. the fact that P causes the fact that Q
    (ii) b. the fact that Q causes the fact that P

According to Sanders, a relation is pragmatic if a type-(i) paraphrase corresponds to the relation as it was originally expressed, but semantic if a type-(ii) paraphrase corresponds to the relation, as he illustrates with the following examples (pp. 126–127).

(17) a. Theo was exhausted (P) because he had run to the university (Q).
b. Theo was exhausted (P), because he was gasping for breath (Q).

Unacceptable or at least questionable sentences are indicated by "?":

(18) (i) b. ?The fact that Theo had been running *causes my claim that* he was exhausted.
(ii) b. The fact that Theo had been running *causes the fact that* he was exhausted.
(19) (i) b. The fact that Theo was gasping for breath *causes my claim that* he was exhausted.
(ii) b. ?The fact that Theo was gasping for breath *causes the fact that* he was exhausted.

Paraphrase (18ii) accounts best for (16a), revealing that it is semantic, while (19i) corresponds best to (16b), providing evidence that it is pragmatic. However, isolating sequences from transcripts of spoken discourse to apply these paraphrases can be cumbersome. Therefore, we sought additional heuristic tests to classify *porque*-relations by causal domain.

Goethals (2010) proposes that content causal clauses may be interpreted as meaning "*the reason why this happened is that*"; epistemic causal constructions may be paraphrased as "*the reason why I think that this is true is that*"; and speech-act causals may be paraphrased as "*the reason why I say/ask/order/... this is that...*" (p. 2205, his italics). These paraphrases also served as viable tests for causal domain for the present study.

Another heuristic test is based on Reyes's (2002) proposal that *porque*, when pragmatic, is also "metapragmatic," conveying the speaker's reflection on his/her previous utterance, and may be viewed in Gricean terms as communicating more than its literal meaning, producing implicatures such as *lo digo porque...* ('I'm saying it because...'; p. 25). Blackwell (2016) analyzes *porque*-relations in oral film narratives produced by 30 native Peninsular Spanish speakers. In this study, the felicitous insertion of *y lo digo/y digo esto* ('and I'm saying it/and I'm saying this') before a *porque*-clause indicated that the relation pertained to the speech-act domain, as (20) illustrates; and, felicitous insertion of a similar phrase incorporating an epistemic verb of inferring or concluding, such as *y lo he concluido/inferido* ('and I concluded/inferred it', but literally, 'and I have concluded/inferred it'), revealed that *porque*-relations were epistemic, as in (21) (inserted metapragmatic phrases appear in curly brackets and italics; from Blackwell, p. 624):

(20)   ...estaba el señor de las peras, dando sus tirones al peral que a mí me hacía duelo {*y lo digo*} porque al peral hay que tratarlo como unas, ..., con un poco más de delicadeza.
'...the pear man was there, giving the pear tree his yanks and it pained me {*and I'm saying it*} because you have to treat the pear tree like some, ..., with a little bit more tenderness.

(21)   ...era como algu:no d'estos que se querían llevar las peras, como un ladronzuelo. Pero después yo he pensado que no. Que debía de ser el amo de la finca, {*y lo he concluido*} porque había otro señor que pasaba con una cabra, y: y he visto que no había pues un grito de decirle ¿y usted qué hace allí? Digo este señor será el amo.
'...he was like one of these types who wanted to take the pears, like a little thief. But later I thought no [i.e., no he wasn't]. That he must have been the owner of the farm, {*and I concluded it*} because there was another man who passed by with a goat, a:nd and I saw

that there wasn't well a shout to say to him, hey you what are you doing there? I say [i.e., thought] this man is probably the owner.'

However, insertion of these phrases into a semantic causal construction from the Peninsular Spanish narratives rendered a pragmatically odd sequence (indicated by #; pp. 624–625):

(22) a. ...apartan la piedra que hay en el camino, {#*y lo digo/*#*y lo he concluido*} *porque* el chico ha tropezao en aquella.
'...they m: move the rock that's in the road aside, {#*and I'm saying it*/#*and I concluded it*} *because* the boy has tripped over that.'

Application of both T. Sanders's (1997) and Goethals's (2010) paraphrase tests also confirms that the causal construction in (22) is semantic (Blackwell, 2016, p. 625):

(23) a. The fact that the boy tripped over the rock caused the fact that they moved it aside
b. The reason they moved the rock aside is that the boy had tripped over it.

This result is not surprising since the two events described in (22) are actions the speaker recalls as having taken place in the film. Furthermore, this semantic relation is reported more *objectively* than the speech-act and epistemic cases in (20) and (21), which are characterized by greater subjectivity, indicated by first-person references to the speakers and evaluative statements reflecting their interpretations of scenes in the film they are recounting. Not surprisingly, subjectivity has been identified as an important factor used in distinguishing causal relations (see, e.g., Pander Maat & Degand, 2001; Pander Maat & Sanders, 2000, 2001; Pit, 2003, 2006; J. Sanders & Spooren, 1997; T. Sanders & Sweetser, 2009; Stukker & Sanders, 2012).

In this section we have identified heuristic tests for causal domain, which were proposed in earlier studies to distinguish causal relations in English (T. Sanders, 1997) and Spanish (Blackwell, 2016; Goethals, 2010). These tests were also found to be effective in determining the domains of the *porque*-relations in both the NSs' and the L2 Spanish learners' narratives analyzed for the present study.

**L2 acquisition of causal relations**

Causal connectives have been the focus of numerous studies in child language development over the decades (e.g., Evers-Vermeul & Sanders, T. 2011; Orsolini, 1993; Vion & Colas, 2005); nonetheless, the investigation of their L2 acquisition has largely been ignored. Existing studies center on the pedagogical implications of connective use (or lack thereof), the effect of task type, or more recently, the comprehension of connectives. Motivated by the observation that Dutch-speaking learners of L2 French have difficulties using connectives, Lamiroy (1994) examined their writing and found that they fail to use French connectives where expected, use them inappropriately, or overuse them. She argues that this is because French and Dutch do not use connectives in the same way. Likewise, Kerr-Barnes (1998) discovered that English-speaking learners of L2 French, much like child L1 learners, overuse a small number of high-frequency connectives, but that more proficient learners expand their repertoire and use them for more complex semantic and pragmatic relations. In a comparison of child L1 and adult L2 French development, Benazzo (2004) revealed that whereas monolingual French children use causal relations to express the temporal succession of events, adult German and Polish learners of L2 French use them more often for marking cause and goals.

Research on the effect of task type on connective use has produced mixed results. Newton and Kennedy (1996) found that both NSs and L2 learners of English use more conjunctions (particularly *because*) when completing a task involving reason and persuasion than when merely exchanging information. In studies of NSs and L2 German learners, Neary-Sundquist (2008, 2013a, 2013b) found that higher proficiency level and simpler narrative tasks lead to greater use of subordinating conjunctions. By contrast, Michel (2013) found conflicting effects for task type. She explored the use of connectives by NSs and L2 learners of Dutch in cognitively simple and complex argumentative tasks and found that only *omdat* ('because') is affected by task complexity. Lastly, Degand and Sanders, T. (2002) examined the role causal connectives play in text comprehension and found that French and Dutch L1 and L2 speakers significantly improve their comprehension of texts when they contain explicit connectives. These results point to the important role connectives play in cognitive processing.

Thus far, research on discourse connectives has indicated that their L2 acquisition mirrors child L1 development to some extent in terms of frequency of use and cognitive and functional complexity and that their use is impacted by proficiency level and task type. The present study aims to fill a gap in our understanding of how L2 learners of Spanish develop and use the connective *porque*, and how different learner levels and narrative tasks affect this use. To this end, we pose the following research questions:

(1) How do NSs and L2 learners use pragmatic and semantic causal relations with *porque* in oral narratives?
(2) Does narrative task type impact this use?
(3) How do L2 learners at different levels differ from NSs in their use of *porque*?

## Method

In this study, we analyze *porque*-relations in NSs' and L2 Spanish learners' oral narratives in light of Sweetser's three causal domains. We distinguish pragmatic (epistemic and speech-act) *porque*-relations from semantic ones using heuristic tests for relation type while also examining the larger discourse context to determine the influence of narrative task-type and speaker level on *porque* usage.

### Participants

We examined 160 oral narratives by 30 L2 Spanish classroom learners from three levels and 10 native NSs from Mexico. The narratives come from the database of the *UAQ-UCD project for the study of Spanish as a foreign/ second language in Mexico and the US: The acquisition of discourse competence* (Lubbers-Quesada & Blake, 2003). There were 10 participants in each of the three learner groups. Group 1 was comprised of students at the end of their first year of college Spanish; eight of the 10 had studied Spanish in high school, but placement exams indicated a beginning level. Group 2 consisted of students enrolled in second-year college Spanish, and a third group were learners from upper-division undergraduate linguistics courses in their third or fourth year. None of the participants had studied abroad, and none were heritage speakers of Spanish. To corroborate learner level, an error analysis of verb morphology was conducted on the learners' narratives. The range of correct morphology for group 1 was 30–69% with a median score of 54%; the range for group 2 was 70–85% with a median of 81%; and group 3 had a range of 87–100% with a median score of 96%. The NSs comprising group 4 were monolingual undergraduate university students in Mexico.

### Narrative tasks

Each participant completed four oral narrative tasks: the retelling of a five-minute segment of a Charlie Chaplin film (*A Woman*); a personal description of an important person in their life; a narrative about the first time they fell in love; and a narrative describing their future plans. The learners were given instructions in English and asked to narrate in Spanish. For the film-retell the L2 participants were given basic Spanish vocabulary related to the film. The NSs received the instructions in Spanish but were not given any vocabulary. The narratives were digitally recorded and transcribed using conventional orthography, with periods and commas to indicate pauses with final (falling intonation) and continuing (slight rise or level) intonation contours, respectively.

### Methods of analysis

All instances of *porque* were identified using *WordSmith*, yielding 419 tokens, although 35 were eliminated due to being repetitions or abandoned utterances.

We analyzed the remaining 384 tokens of *porque* using the heuristic paraphrases proposed by T. Sanders (1997) and Goethals (2010) outlined in Section 2.3 (see examples 17–19 and 23) and Briz's (2001) syntactic tests for causal relations, which show that when *porque* is used semantically in a sentence, it may be negated, questioned, and embedded, but when a relation is pragmatic, it cannot pass these tests (see examples 12–14 above).

Application of T. Sanders's and Goethals's paraphrases below in (24a) and (24b), respectively, reveals that the *porque*-construction in (24) is semantic. In this excerpt, a NS explains why Chaplin gets wet in one scene from the film:

(24)      Chaplin que es—va caminando en el parque, también y todo y se moja *porque* va distraído...
         'Chaplin who is—goes walking along in the park, also and all and he gets wet because he's distracted...'

     a. (i) ?The fact that Charlie is distracted *causes my claim that* he gets wet. (?pragmatic)
         (ii) The fact that Charlie is distracted causes *the fact that* he gets wet. (semantic)
     b. (i) ?The reason why *I think it is true that/I say that* Charlie gets wet is that he is distracted. (?epistemic/?speech-act)
         (ii) The reason why Charlie gets wet is that he is distracted. (semantic)

Additionally, we tested each relation for domain through the insertion of metapragmatic phrases. As noted in Section 2.3, the felicitous insertion of epistemic phrases such as *y lo he concluido* ('and I concluded it') before *porque*-utterances reveals that a given relation is pragmatic, and more specifically, epistemic; and, felicitous insertion of *y lo digo* ('and I'm saying it') is possible for speech-act relations (Blackwell, 2016). For instance, insertion of these phrases before the *porque*-clause in (24) is infelicitous (indicated by #), demonstrating that a pragmatic interpretation is not possible:

(25)      Chaplin que es- va caminando en el parque, también y todo y se moja {#*y lo he concluido*/#*y lo digo*) *porque* va distraído...
         'Chaplin who is- goes walking along in the park, also and all and he gets wet {#*and I concluded it*/#*and I'm saying it*} because he's distracted...'

Conversely, felicitous insertion of the metapragmatic phrases into another *porque*-construction from a NS's film narrative reveals that it is epistemic:

(26)      ...pues resultó ser una ladrona, ¿no? {*y lo he concluido/y lo digo*) *porque* le quitó la cartera,...
         '...well she ended up being a thief, right? {*and I concluded it/and I'm saying it*} because she took his wallet...'

The felicitous use of both metapragmatic phrases before epistemic *porque* suggests that in epistemic relations speakers not only give reasons for reaching conclusions, but also provide justification for stating the conclusion or claim (i.e., the speech act) expressed in the main clause (cf. Blackwell, 2016).

The following *porque*-relation, also from a NS's narration of the Charlie Chaplin film, passes both metapragmatic insertion tests, suggesting an epistemic interpretation for (27a); however, it also passes Briz's (2001) syntactic tests (negation, questioning, embedding), demonstrating that it can also have a semantic consequence-cause interpretation (27b-d) (use of CAPS indicates prosodic stress):

(27)  a.  …y le roba su botella y quiere como vengarse, tomar venganza {*y lo he concluido/y lo digo*) *porque* él primero lo golpeó…
'…and he steals his bottle from him and he wants to like get even take revenge {*and I concluded it/and I'm saying it*} *because* HE hit him first…'
b. No quiere vengarse *porque* él primero lo golpeó. (negation)
'He doesn't want to get even *because* HE hit him first.'
c. ¿Quiere vengarse *porque* él primero lo golpeó? 
'Does he want to get even *because* HE hit him first?' (questioning)
d. Juan dice que quiere vengarse *porque* él primero lo golpeó. (embedding)
'John says that he wants to get even *because* HE hit him first.'

In other words, the *porque*-relation in (27a) may convey the speaker's interpretive inference or conclusion that Charlie wants to get even with another character who hit him earlier in the film, as suggested by the felicitous insertion of both metapragmatic paraphrases. At the same time, Briz's syntactic tests in (b-d) illustrate the potential for a semantic, stereotypical consequence-cause reading for (27): The reason why Charlie wants to get even is that HE hit Charlie first. However, these tests produced unacceptable or at least questionable sentences (indicated by ?) when *porque*-utterances were strictly pragmatic, as the following example from a NS's narrative of his future plans illustrates:

(28)   Bueno es ahorita mi meta a largo plazo, *porque* son cinco años de carrera.
'Well it's now my long-term goal, *because* it's a five-year degree.
a. ?No es ahorita mi meta a largo plazo, *porque* son cinco años de carrera. (negation)
?'It's not now my long-term goal, *because* it's a five-year degree.'
b. ?¿Es ahorita tu meta a largo plazo, *porque* son cinco años de carrera? (questioning)
?'Is it now your long-term goal, *because* it's a five-year degree?

c. ?Juan dice que es ahorita su meta a largo plazo, *porque* son cinco años de carrera.
  ?'John says that it's now his long-term goal, *because* it's a five-year degree

In (28), the speaker uses a *porque*-clause to justify his claim that his goal is long-term; as such, this relation was deemed a speech-act causal.

After applying these tests for causal domain, we analyzed the *porque*-relations in terms of task type, Spanish learner level, and linguistic features typically characterizing each domain of use.

## Results

The 40 transcribed texts rendered a total of 55,053 words. A summary of each group's total word count and instances of *porque* are presented in Table 1. Although total word counts increase according to speaker level, percentages of *porque*-tokens never reach more than .8% of the total words used by each group.

**Table 1.** Total word count and number/percentages of instances of *porque*

| participant group | total words | instances *porque* | percent *porque* |
|---|---|---|---|
| Group 4 (NSs) | 20,279 | 145 | .7% |
| Group 3 (upper division) | 16,232 | 131 | .8% |
| Group 2 (2nd year) | 11,036 | 70 | .6% |
| Group 1 (1st year) | 7,506 | 38 | .5% |
| total | 55,053 | 384 | .7% |

In the following sections, we present the results of our analysis in terms of domain (semantic, epistemic, and speech-act) and according to narrative task type and speaker group.

### Semantic domain

The use of semantic *porque* is highest among NSs for the personal descriptions (14.48% of the instances) followed by the film-retell and personal narratives, respectively (Table 2). For the learner groups, semantic *porque* occurs most frequently in the personal narratives of the participants in group 3, while lower level learners use it most often in the film-retell. The first-year learners use semantic *porque* with the same frequency in both the film-retell and personal descriptions.

**Table 2.** Frequency and percentage of semantic *porque* by text type and group

| text type | Group 4 (NS) | Group 3 (3rd+ year) | Group 2 (2nd year) | Group 1 (1st year) |
|---|---|---|---|---|
| film retell | 11 (8%) | 4 (3%) | 10 (14.29%) | 4 (11%) |
| personal narrative | 21 (14%) | 6 (5%) | 4 (6%) | 2 (5%) |
| personal description | 10 (7%) | 10 (8%) | 7 (10%) | 4 (11%) |
| future plans | 2 (1%) | 5 (4%) | 1 (1%) | 0 |
| total *N* and percentage | 44 (30%) | 25 (19%) | 22 (31.29%) | 10 (26%) |

### Speech-act domain

For the learners' use of *porque* is most frequent in the speech-act domain, comprising almost 53% of the *porque*-constructions produced by group 3 and almost 36% of those produced by group 2. Although the NSs use semantic *porque* more frequently, speech-act *porque* comprises about 28% of all instances of *porque* used by these speakers. The NSs and three learner groups used speech-act *porque* in the three personal texts but rarely, or not at all, in the film-retell (Table 3).

**Table 3.** Frequency and percentage of speech-act *porque* by text type and group

| text type | Group 4 (NS) | Group 3 (3rd+ year) | Group 2 (2nd year) | Group 1 (1st year) |
|---|---|---|---|---|
| film retell | 0 | 2 (2%) | 2 (3%) | 0 |
| personal narrative | 15 (11%) | 26 (20%) | 4 (6%) | 5 (13%) |
| personal description | 17 (12%) | 21 (16%) | 7 (10%) | 8 (21%) |
| future plans | 9 (7%) | 20 (15%) | 12 (17%) | 4 (11%) |
| total *N* and percentage | 41 (28%) | 69 (53%) | 25 (36%) | 17 (45%) |

### Epistemic domain

Epistemic *porque* is considerably less frequent for all groups than semantic and speech-act *porque*, although for the NSs it comprises almost 14% of their *porque*-relations. For group 1 there is only one epistemic token, while very few occur in the other learners' narratives (Table 4). Except for group 2, the participants tend to use epistemic *porque* for either the film-retell or personal narratives, although the NSs also use it for personal description and future plans.

**Table 4.** Frequency and percentage of epistemic *porque* by text type and group

| text type | Group 4 (NS) | Group 3 (3rd+ year) | Group 2 (2nd year) | Group 1 (1st year) |
|---|---|---|---|---|
| film retell | 8 (5.52%) | 2 (1.53%) | 0 | 1 (2.63%) |
| personal narrative | 3 (2.07%) | 4 (3.05%) | 0 | 0 |
| personal description | 5 (3.45%) | 1 (0.76%) | 1 (1.43%) | 0 |
| future plans | 4 (2.76%) | 0 | 5 (7.14%) | 0 |
| total *N* and percentage | 20 (13.80%) | 7 (5.34%) | 6 (8.57%) | 1 (2.63%) |

### Semantic and speech-act domain

In several instances, the analysis of *porque* passed both the semantic and speech-act tests for domain. In these cases, the speakers' *porque*-utterances could be interpreted as both giving the cause of an event or situation but also as providing justification for their preceding utterances. All groups used *porque* in this way, ranging from 18% for group 3 to almost one-fourth of the time for group 2 and the native speakers. However, semantic/speech-act *porque* occurs almost exclusively in the three personal texts (Table 5).

**Table 5.** Frequency and percentage of semantic/speech-act *porque* by text type and group

| text type | Group 4 (NS) | Group 3 (3rd+ year) | Group 2 (2nd year) | Group 1 (1st year) |
|---|---|---|---|---|
| film retell | 0 | 1 (0.76%) | 0 | 0 |
| personal narrative | 14 (9.65%) | 4 (3.05%) | 2 (2.86%) | 1 (2.63%) |
| personal description | 12 (8.28%) | 1 (0.76%) | 4 (5.71%) | 0 |
| future plans | 8 (5.52%) | 17 (12.98%) | 11 (15.71%) | 7 (18.42%) |
| total *N* and percentage | 34 (23.45%) | 23 (17.55%) | 17 (24.28%) | 8 (21.05%) |

### Semantic and epistemic domain

*Porque* was also used to introduce causes for consequences (semantic domain) and justification for conclusions (epistemic domain). However, these cases were infrequent and never occurred in the second-year learners' texts, making relating this category to text type difficult (Table 6).

**Table 6.** Frequency and percentage of semantic-epistemic *porque* by text type and group

| text type | Group 4 (NS) | Group 3 (3rd+ year) | Group 2 (2nd year) | Group 1 (1st year) |
|---|---|---|---|---|
| film retell | 3 (2.07%) | 2 (1.53%) | 0 | 0 |
| personal narrative | 1 (0.69%) | 2 (1.53%) | 0 | 0 |
| personal description | 0 | 1 (0.76%) | 0 | 1 (2.63%) |
| future plans | 2 (1.38%) | 2 (1.53%) | 0 | 1 (2.63%) |
| total *N* and percentage | **6 (4.14%)** | **7 (5.35%)** | **0** | **2 (5.26%)** |

## Discussion

We found that text type conditions the type of causal relations expressed by the participants. However, we also found some important differences among the groups. The most common relation used by the NSs was strictly semantic and was most common in their personal narratives where they report observable facts and past events. The following examples illustrate the use of strictly semantic (consequence-cause) *porque* by a NS, a group 3 participant, and a first-year learner (group 1):

(29) …Lo conocí *porque* llegó un día a saludar a uno de mis mejores amigos… (NS)
'…I met him *because* he came one day to say hello to one of my best friends…'

(30) …Nunca salía con mis amigos en bicicleta *porque* no sentía cómodo. (group 3)
'I never went out with my friends bike riding *because* I didn't feel comfortable…'

(31) …Y mis padres no me permitieron tuve, tener un novio *porque* no tuve dieciséis años… (group 1)
'…And my parents didn't let me had, have a boyfriend *because* I wasn't sixteen…'

These causal relations describe actions and situations that speakers report as having taken place, thus reflecting T. Sanders's (1997) generalization about semantic relations, namely, that in prototypical content relations, the events depicted "have already taken place" (p. 125; see section 2.3). While the NSs' use of semantic *porque* supports this generalization as revealed by the higher frequencies of semantic *porque* in their film-retell and personal narratives, which are, by definition, about events that have taken place, the two lower learner groups show this tendency only in their film-retell narratives, and the group 3 learners, only in their personal narratives. This result may be due to the fact that all learner groups used semantic *porque* less frequently than the NSs did.

The second most common causal relation for NSs is the strictly speech-act domain, seen mainly in the personal descriptions (justification for liking/wanting someone/something) but also in personal narratives (justification for describing past events). Whereas semantic *porque* is the most common type used by the NSs, it is the second most common for the learner groups, although not in their personal narratives. Speech-act causal relations, the type most frequently used by the learners, are often characterized by indicators of speaker involvement and subjectivity, which convey the perspective or viewpoint of the speaker (see e.g., J. Sanders & Spooren, 1997). These indicators include *tal vez* ('maybe'), *creo* ('I believe'), *no sé* ('I dunno'), and *¡ah!* ('oh'). Broadly speaking, speech-act *porque*-relations involved justification for a previous statement, as in (32), where a NS uses a *porque*-construction to explain why she has just mentioned her nephew:

(32) Un día me dijo mi sobrino, *porque* yo crecí con mis sobrinos en lugar que con mi hermano. Me dice... (NS)
'One day my nephew told me, *because* I grew up with my nephews instead of with my brother. He tells me...'

By contrast, the most common speech-act *porque*-constructions produced by the learners involved justification for evaluative personal claims. For instance, one group 2 learner justifies saying her father is important to her, while another gives a reason for why she expects to live in California in the future:

(33) a. ...mi padre es importante para mí *porque* él trabaja muy duro...
'...my father is important for me *because* he works very hard...'
b. ...yo uh viviré en el valle de centro California *porque* me gusta mi familia...
'...I uh will live in the valley of center California *because* I like my family...'

Similarly, two group 3 learners justify their personal evaluations of money (*importante*) and a past experience (*tan difícil* 'so difficult') using *porque*:

(34) a. ...el dinero es mucho importante a mí *porque* quiero dar todas las... todos oportunidades a mis niños.
'...money is a lot important to me *because* I want to give all the... all opportunities to my kids...'
b. ...fue tan difícil como pensé que habría sido antes de que pasó *porque* sabía que podía dolerme...'
'...it was so difficult as I thought that it would be before it happened *because* I knew that it could hurt me...'

These findings are in line with Sweetser's (1990) observation that speech-act causal relations typically explain why the speaker's preceding utterance is relevant (see section 2.1). Furthermore, both the NSs' and the learners' speech-act relations are characterized by indicators of subjectivity including first-person references (e.g., *porque yo crecí/quiero/me gusta* 'because I grew up/I want/I like') and evaluative language (e.g., *es importante... él trabaja muy duro* 'he's important...he works very hard'), which have been found to correspond to pragmatic uses of causal connectives cross-linguistically (e.g., Pander Maat & Degand, 2001; Pander Maat & Sanders, 2000, 2001; Pit, 2003). This generalization also helps explain why speech-act *porque* is so infrequently used in the film-retell narratives, since they focus on external, third-person actions and events (i.e., what happened in the film) instead of the speakers' personal experiences.

The learners tend to use *porque* in the semantic domain more often in their film-retell narratives and in their personal descriptions. Unlike the NSs, the learners use speech-act *porque* most often, although only the first-year group uses them in personal descriptions. Group 3 participants tend to use more instances of speech-act *porque* in their personal narratives (similar to the NSs), and the second-year participants tend to use it in their future plans to justify future desires.

Examples of *porque*-relations used by NSs, which could have both semantic and speech-act interpretations, include:

(35)  a. ...La quiero y también mucho *porque* ella ha estado en los momentos difíciles...
'...I love her and also a lot *because* she has been there in the difficult moments...'

b. ...Físicamente, no lo recuerdo muy bien, *porque* ya pasó mucho tiempo...
'...Physically, I don't remember him very well, *because* so much time has gone by...'

In both cases, there is a motivation for claiming or a cause for the subjective emotional state resulting from the speakers' liking, wanting, or perceiving events or states of affairs, which may explain why this type of *porque* is not observed in the film-retell narratives. Similarly, in the following examples from group 2 participants' descriptions and future plans, the speakers give reasons for their psychological states or reactions:

(36)  a. ...Sentí muy especial con él, *porque* siempre me tocaba mis pies, mis piernas, mis manos...
'...I felt very special with him, *because* he always touched my feet, my legs, my hands...

b. ...Y quiero vivir en California o Inglaterra, *porque* me gusta Inglaterra mucho...'
'...And I want to live in California or England, because I like England a lot...'
c. ...Quiero tener muchas gatos *porque* me encanta los gatos...
'...I want to have lots of cats because I love cats...'

The reasons for feeling special, wanting to live in California, and wanting many cats, given in the *porque*-clauses in (36), may be interpreted as semantic effect–cause-of-effect relations. At the same time, these speakers provide pragmatic justification for stating these emotions and desires.

*Porque*-relations that could have either a semantic or a speech-act reading are not used in the film-retell narratives by any participants, though they occur in the past narratives of the NSs, and in the future-plans narratives of the three learner groups. Although the NSs and learners distinguish themselves by using this ambiguous category of *porque*-relations for different text types, their expressions of this category of causal relation are similar in that they employ verbs of emotion, perception, volition, and mental activity. Specifically, they express a motivation or cause for subjective emotional states of liking or wanting something or someone, or for expressing a subjective evaluation of something or someone.

For all three learner groups there were very few instances of strictly epistemic *porque*. Although also a pragmatic causal relation, the epistemic domain involves inference and few of the learners appear capable of expressing this in their L2. Interestingly, studies on the L1 acquisition of causal categories report that, cross-linguistically, children acquire epistemic use of causals much later than speech-act and content uses, and that speech-act causal relations "are frequent even at a very early age" (Evers-Vermeul & Sanders, 2011, p. 1659; T. Sanders & Spooren, 2009, p. 220). The NSs use *porque* in this domain mostly in the film-retell task where they often infer the emotions and opinions of the film's protagonists. Examples of epistemic uses by the NSs when retelling the Charlie Chaplin film include:

(37) a. Pues resultó ser ladrona, ¿no? *Porque* le quitó la cartera.
'Well, it turned out—to be a thief, right? *Because* she took his wallet.'
b. ...ve a la señora ahí sentada sola e igual y le gustó *porque* pasa ahí le levanta la falda con el bastón...
'...he sees the lady there sitting alone and likewise and he liked her *because* he goes by there lifts up her skirt with the cane...'

In (37a) the speaker concludes that the woman in the film is a thief because she takes a man's wallet, and in (37b) the speaker infers that Charlie likes the woman on account of his lifting her skirt, revealing their reasoning from observable actions to probable causes. The only epistemic use of *porque* by a group 1 learner also occurred in the film-retell task when the speaker concludes that it does not matter that the man removes his blindfold because at that moment Chaplin strikes him:

(38)   ...se quita la, el pañuelo y, pero no importa *porque* Chaplin golpea el hombre con la bebida.
'...he takes off the, the blindfold and, but it doesn't matter *because* Charlie hits the man with the drink...'

A group 2 learner, in relating his/her future plans, concludes that working in the music industry is difficult based on his claim that it is competitive:

(39)   ... creo es difícil trabajar en la empresa de música *porque* so—es muy competitivo...'
'...I think it's difficult to work in the music business *because* so—it's very competitive...'

This speaker uses the epistemic verb *creo* ('I think') to introduce his conclusion. In each of the epistemic examples cited above, the speakers do not give reasons for why things happened; instead, they explain why they drew various inferences from the Charlie Chaplin film (37–38), and in (39), the speaker offers a logical reason for concluding that it is difficult to find a job in the music business. Each one is subjective, involving the speaker's interpretation of the situation being described.

There were also very few instances of *porque* that could have a semantic or an epistemic interpretation. Those used by the native speakers are mostly in the film-retell narratives, whereas those produced by the more advanced learners occur in all four text types. In the following example, a NS's *porque*-relation can have either a semantic or an epistemic reading:

(40)   ...Yo creo que el futuro es un poco incierto *porque* no depende completamente de nosotros...
'...I think that the future is a little uncertain *because* it doesn't depend completely on us...'

Similarly, a group 3 learner's *porque*-construction could have either interpretation:

(41)   ...y por esta razón ella me odia *porque* estoy muy ocupada con mis estudios...
'...and that's why she hates me *because* I'm very busy with my studies...'

In both cases, the speakers give reasons for tentative yet perceivable states of affairs in the world (e.g., 'the future is uncertain,' 'she hates me'), while also explaining the basis on which they reached these conclusions. The fact that such cases pass our heuristic tests for both semantic and epistemic relations lends empirical support for seeking a revised set of categories or domains of causal relation, which could better account for causal relations in naturally occurring discourse.

In terms of L2 acquisition, we can conclude that both the NSs and the L2 Spanish learners use the three types of *porque*-relations in their oral discourse. However, the learners use more speech-act *porque* (explaining why they say things), perhaps because it is cognitively less complex (as suggested by the findings from studies on L1 acquisition of causal relations), whereas the NSs use more semantic *porque*-relations, suggesting that they may be more complex to formulate for learners as these constructions require linking actions or events that are both causally related and have taken place, which are often expressed via past tense verbs. In addition, we can confirm that learners' use of *porque* is constrained by text type and causal relation but in different ways when compared with NS use. Whereas the NSs use semantic *porque* for relating past events, the non-NSs do not do so to the same extent. Finally, the learners in our study do not use *porque* to express epistemic relations to any great extent, again suggesting that the task of inferring or concluding is a complex and subtle cognitive/linguistic undertaking and a later-learned ability in L2 acquisition, as it is in L1 child acquisition (Evers-Vermeul & Sanders, 2011, p. 1659). This tentative conclusion is bolstered by the fact that, in an earlier study that examined the *porque*-relations in the oral film-retell narratives of 30 native Peninsular Spanish speakers, the majority were epistemic (57, or 45% of the 127 cases; Blackwell, 2016, p. 638), and several others could have semantic or epistemic readings (27, or 21% of the *porque*-relations; p. 634). As Blackwell (2016) reports, this finding was not surprising since the narrators were recalling and talking about a film they had just watched, which led them to give "reasons for events and situations in the film based on what they speculated, assumed, or inferred from often stereotypical or cultural expectations" (p. 647). In other words, this type of task (i.e., recalling and retelling a film under experimental conditions) lends itself to more subjective, interpretive expressions of epistemic causality by NSs, a conclusion not supported by the learner data examined in the present study.

## Conclusions and directions for future studies

Our findings reveal that semantic consequence-cause relations are less common in the Spanish L2 learners' oral production when compared with that of the NSs, suggesting that these relations may be more difficult for Spanish L2 learners to express. Furthermore, the fact that the learners produced relatively few instances of epistemic *porque* supports the hypothesis that such relations are cognitively more complex than the other two domains of causal relation, and thus, they are most likely learned and incorporated into learners' L2 repertoires at later stages in the language learning/acquisition process. Only more advanced learners' use of *porque* tends to reflect NS use, though in limited ways. Future studies might examine the spoken discourse of more advanced Spanish L2 learners to ascertain whether or not they use causal *porque* in the same ways as native speakers.

One limitation of the present study is the small number of participants in each learner level, and therefore our results may not be generalizable to all L2 Spanish learners and native speakers. Future studies should examine causal relations with both *porque* and other Spanish causal connectives (e.g., *como, ya que* 'since') in the speech of a larger number of participants, both native and non-native, and in a wider variety of discourse genres. Nonetheless, our findings have an important implication for the L2 classroom where communicative activities often center on the exchange of information. Instructors might better promote classroom tasks that involve learners in the discussion of topics that both require them to relate real-world cause and consequence relations, and encourage them to activate the more complex cognitive strategies needed for drawing inferences and justifying them in their second language.

### Notes

1   The terms *semantic* and *content* are used interchangeably in this paper to refer to the same category of causal relations.

### References

Anscombre, J.-C., & Ducrot, O. (1983). *L'argumentation dans la langue* [*Argumentation in language*]. Liege: Mardaga.

Bardzokas, V. (2012). *Causality and connectives: From Grice to relevance*. Amsterdam: John Benjamins.

Bardzokas, V. (2014). Linguistic constraints on causal content: The case of Modern Greek markers. *Journal of Pragmatics, 60*, 160–174.

Benazzo, S. (2004). L'expression de la causalité dans le discours narrative en français L1 et L2 [*The expression of causality in narrative discourse in L1 and L2 French*]. *Langages, 38*(155), 33–51.

Blackwell, S. E. (2016). *Porque* in Spanish oral narratives: Semantic *porque*, (meta) pragmatic *porque* or both? In A. Capone & J. L. Mey (Eds.), *Interdisciplinary studies in pragmatics, culture and society* (pp. 615–651). Dordrecht: Springer.

Briz, A. (2001). *El español coloquial en la conversación: Esbozo de pragmagramática* [*Colloquial Spanish in conversation: An outline of pragmagrammar*] (2nd ed). Barcelona: Ariel.

Couper-Kuhlen, E., & Kortmann, B. (Eds.). (2000). *Cause, condition, concession, contrast: Cognitive and discourse perspectives*. Berlin: Mouton de Gruyter.

Dancygier, B., & Sweetser, E. (2000). Constructions with *if, since*, and *because*: Causality, epistemic stance, and clause order. In E. Couper-Kuhlen & B. Kortmann (Eds.), *Cause, condition, concession, contrast: Cognitive and discourse perspectives* (pp. 111–142). Berlin: Mouton de Gruyter.

Degand, L, (2001). *Form and function of causation: A theoretical and empirical investigation of causal constructions in Dutch*. Leuven: Peeters.

Degand, L., & Fagard, B. (2012). Competing connectives in the causal domain: French *car* and *parce que*. *Journal of Pragmatics, 44*(2), 154–168.

Degand, L., & Sanders, T. (2002). The impact of relational markers on expository text comprehension in L1 and L2. *Reading and Writing, 15*(7–8), 739–758.

Escandell Vidal, M. V. (2006). *Introducción a la pragmática [Introduction to pragmatics]*. Barcelona: Ariel.

Evers-Vermeul, J., & Sanders, T. (2011). Discovering domains – On the acquisition of causal connectives. *Journal of Pragmatics, 43*, 1645–1662.

García, E. C. (1992). Por qué *como* o *porque* [Why *since* or *because*]. *Nueva Revista de Filología Hispánica, 40*(2), 599–621.

Goethals, P. (2002). *Las conjunciones causales explicativas españolas como, ya que, pues y porque: Un estudio semiótico-lingüístico* [The Spanish explicative causal conjunctions since, since, because and because: A semiotic-linguistic study]. Leuven: Peeters.

Goethals, P. (2010). A multi-layered approach to speech events: The case of Spanish justificational conjunctions. *Journal of Pragmatics, 42*, 2204–2218.

Jordan, I. (1989). Internal cohesive conjunction in spoken Spanish. *Hispania 72*(2), 374–377.

Kerr-Barnes, B. (1998). The acquisition of connectors in French L2 narrative discourse. *French Language Studies, 8*, 189–208.

Kitis, E. (2006). Causality and subjectivity: The causal connectives of Modern Greek. In H. Pishwa (Ed.), *Language and memory: Aspects of knowledge representation* (pp. 223–267). Berlin: Mouton de Gruyter.

Lamiroy, B. (1994). Pragmatic connectives and L2 acquisition: The case of French and Dutch. *Pragmatics, 4*(2), 183–201.

Lapesa, R. (1978). Sobre dos tipos de subordinación causal [On two types of causal subordination]. In *Estudios ofrecidos a Emilio Alarcos Llorach 3* [Studies in honor of Emilio Alarcos Llorach] (pp. 173–205). Oviedo, Spain: Universidad de Oviedo.

Lubbers-Quesada, M., & Blake, R. (2003). *The UAQ-UCD project for the study of Spanish as a foreign/second language in Mexico and the US: The acquisition of discourse competence*. University of California Institute for Mexico and the United States (UXMEXUS) and the Consejo Nacional de Ciencia y Tecnología de México (CONACYT), Grant No. CN0255.

Michel, M. (2013). The use of conjunctions in cognitively simple versus complex oral L2 tasks. *The Modern Language Journal, 97*(1), 178–195.

Neary-Sundquist, C. (2008). *The role of task type and proficiency level in second language speech production* (Unpublished doctoral dissertation). Purdue University, West Lafayette, IN.

Neary-Sundquist, C. (2013a). The development of cohesion in a learner corpus. *Studies in Second Language Learning and Teaching, 3*(1), 109–130.

Neary-Sundquist, C. (2013b). Task type effects on pragmatic marker use by learners at varying proficiency levels. *L2 Journal, 5*(2), 1–21.

Newton, J., & Kennedy, G. (1996). Effects of communication tasks on the grammatical relations marked by second language learners. *System, 24*(3), 309–322.

Orsolini, M. (1993). Because in children's discourse. *Applied Psycholinguistics, 14*(1), 89–120.

Oversteegan, L. E. (1997). On the pragmatic nature of causal and contrastive connectives. *Discourse Processes, 24*, 51–85.

Pander Maat, H., & Degand, L. (2001). Scaling causal relations and connectives in terms of speaker involvement. *Cognitive Linguistics, 12*(3), 211–245.

Pander Maat, H., & Sanders, T. (2000). Domains of use of subjectivity: The distribution of three Dutch causal connectives explained. In E. Couper-Kuhlen & B. Kortmann (Eds.), *Cause, condition, concession, contrast: Cognitive and discourse perspectives* (pp. 57–82). Berlin: Mouton de Gruyter.

Pander Maat, H., & Sanders, T. (2001). Subjectivity in causal connectives: An empirical study of language use. *Cognitive Linguistics, 12*(3), 247–273.

Pit, M. (2003). *How to express yourself with a causal connective: Subjectivity and causal connectives in Dutch, German and French*. Amsterdam: Rodopi.

Pit, M. (2006). Determining subjectivity in text: The case of backward causal connectives in Dutch. *Discourse Processes, 41*(2), 151–174.

Reyes, G., (2002). *Metapragmática: Lenguaje sobre lenguaje, ficciones, figuras* [Metapragmatics: Language about language, fiction, and figures]. Valladolid, Spain: Secretariado de Publicaciones e Intercambio Editorial, Universidad de Valladolid.

Sanders, J., Sanders, T., & Sweetser, E. (2012). Responsible subjects and discourse causality: How mental spaces and perspective help identifying subjectivity in Dutch backward causal connectives. *Journal of Pragmatics, 44*, 191–213.

Sanders, J., & Spooren, W. (1997). Perspective, subjectivity, and modality from a cognitive linguistic point of view. In W.-A. Liebert, G. Redeker, & L. Waugh (Eds.), *Discourse and perspective in cognitive linguistics* (pp. 85–112). Amsterdam: John Benjamins.

Sanders, T. (1997). Semantic and pragmatic sources of coherence: On the categorization of coherence relations in context. *Discourse Processes, 24*, 119–147.

Sanders, T., & Spooren, W. (2009). Causal categories in discourse—Converging evidence from language use. In T. Sanders & E. Sweetser (Eds.), *Causal categories in discourse and cognition* (pp. 205–246). Amsterdam: John Benjamins.

Sanders, T., & Spooren, W. (2013). Exceptions to rules: A qualitative analysis of backward causal connectives in Dutch naturalistic discourse. *Text and Talk, 33*(3), 377–398.

Sanders, T., & Sweetser, E. (2009). Introduction: Causality in language and cognition—What causal connectives and causal verbs reveal about the way we think. In T. Sanders & E. Sweetser (Eds.), *Causal categories in discourse and cognition* (pp. 1–18). Berlin, Germany: Mouton de Gruyter.

Stukker, N., & Sanders, T. (2012). Subjectivity and prototype structure in causal connectives: A cross-linguistic perspective. *Journal of Pragmatics, 44*, 169–190.

Sweetser, E. (1990). *From etymology to pragmatics: Metaphorical and cultural aspects of semantic structure*. Cambridge: Cambridge University Press.

Vion, M., & Colas, A. (2005). Using connectives in oral French narratives: Cognitive constraints and development of narrative skills. *First Language 25*(1), 39–66.

Zufferey, S. (2012). *"Car, parce que, puisque"* revisited: Three empirical studies on French causal connectives. *Journal of Pragmatics, 44*, 238–153.

Zufferey, S., & Cartoni, B. (2012). English and French causal connectives in contrast. *Languages in Contrast, 12*(2), 232–250.

# Perceptions of Spanish L2 Writing Quality: The Role of Discourse Markers and Sentence-level Phenomena

Mai Kuha
Lisa M. Kuriscak
Elizabeth M. Riddle
*Ball State University, USA*

*Discourse markers (DMs) help to organize written and spoken sequences by signaling connective relationships. Although most research on second language (L2) DMs has focused on English, work on L2 Spanish DMs has begun to emerge (e.g., Gánem-Gutiérrez & Roehr, 2011; Hernández, 2011; Lahuerta Martínez, 2009), primarily on DM functions and on their L2 acquisition and comprehension. This is in line with the focus over the last 40 years on discourse-level phenomena in teaching written and spoken communication. However, research on the influence of Spanish DM use versus grammatical correctness and sentence-level vocabulary choices on native speaker (NS) evaluation of writing quality is lacking. This chapter reports on an experimental study (utilizing an online survey) that investigated (a) whether presence versus absence of appropriate DMs in L2 writing affected participants' evaluation of the quality of the texts, (b) whether DMs or grammatical/lexical errors weigh more heavily in such evaluations, and (c) whether evaluations by native and near-native speaker Spanish instructors differ from non-instructor NSs. Our findings show that DMs did not influence all three participant groups' evaluations of learner writing in the same way, and the presence of an interaction effect with lexical/grammatical errors underlines a need for further research.*

## Introduction

This quantitative and descriptive study on the relative salience of discourse marker (DM) absence versus grammatical and lexical errors in second language (L2) writing in Spanish fits into two overlapping areas of L2 research. (In what follows, we will use "lexicon" and "lexical" to refer to lexical items other than DMs.) Most broadly, this study is situated within the field of interlanguage pragmatics (e.g., Kasper & Schmidt, 1996) in that it deals with how non-native speakers (NNSs) signal connections between ideas. Most interlanguage pragmatics studies have focused on speech acts. However, as Müller (2005), Bardovi-Harlig (2013), and Félix-Brasdefer and Koike (2015) point out, there are other areas of pragmatics that also merit researchers' attention (see other work by Bardovi-Harlig, 1995, 2010; Bohnacker & Rosén, 2008; Bouton, 1988; and Hartford, 1995, among others), and our study helps fill a gap by examining the effects of learners' DMs in writing. We draw from the tradition of research on native speaker (NS) perceptions of learner errors. Tyler's work (e.g., 1992) on how problems in the discourse structure of the speech of non-native English-speaking teaching assistants can have a big effect on comprehension by their students is pioneering in this regard. Much of the other research on the effect of learner errors on interlocutors/readers has focused on pronunciation in spoken English (e.g., Munro & Derwing, 2006) or on grammar/lexicon in writing. The present study combines attention to discourse structuring and the grammar/lexicon in planned writing rather than spontaneous or partially planned speech. We depart from previous research on Spanish DMs in the L2 context by not focusing on learner acquisition for either use or comprehension, but rather on the relative effect on NSs and near-native speakers (NrNSs)[1] of learners' use of DMs versus grammatical and other lexical choices in their writing. Specifically, we examine how the presence versus absence of appropriate DMs in L2 writing affected participants' evaluation of the quality of the texts, whether there is an interaction between DM presence/absence and grammatical/lexical errors, and whether any differences arise among the groups of participants. We begin with a theoretical framework, followed by presentation of the coding and instrumentation, discussion of the results, limitations, and conclusions.

## Theoretical framework

### Discourse markers

Because DMs carry a heavy communicative load in organizing discourse, it is unsurprising that their use by NSs in a number of languages has received much attention in pragmatics research (e.g., Blakemore, 1987; Fraser, 1988; James, 1973; Jucker & Ziv, 1998; Lakoff, 1973; Östman, 1981; Schiffrin, 1987; Schourup, 1985). In fact, a search of Linguistics and Language Behavior Abstracts with the keywords "Discourse Marker" produced 4,139 results on a variety of languages. The definition of DM itself has received significant attention. Müller (2005) notes the debate on what to consider a DM, and conversely what to call and how to group diverse words and phrases performing a multitude of functions relating more to interlocutor interaction and text organization than to basic content or strictly sentence-level phenomena. Many researchers (e.g., Blakemore, 1987, 2007) restrict the category to lexical items (including phrases) such as *subsequently, therefore, in contrast,* and *moreover,* which serve to organize discourse and signal sequencing, cause and effect, contrast, reinforcement, and other connective relationships among propositions. They consider attitudinal adverbs such as *remarkably, frankly,* and other pragmatic markers such as *well* and *just,* to form a separate category. Others (e.g., Fraser, 1988) make different distinctions. One would expect some variation in the definition across languages as well. Given that only the first type (i.e., organizing/connecting) is addressed in this paper, we adopt Blakemore's (2007) operationalization of DM for analytical purposes without making any claims about the status of attitudinal markers or the universality of the definition.

## Second language research and DMs

The acquisition and use of DMs by L2 learners of English has been studied by a number of researchers (e.g., Buysse, 2012; Groot, 2000; Hellermann & Vergun, 2007; H. Lee, 1999; Liu, 2013; Monassar, 2005; Müller, 2005; Romero Trillo, 2002; Tyler, 1992). For example, Buysse (2011) found that L2 learners favor some types of DMs and avoid others in their speech. However, research on the use of DMs by L2 learners of Spanish is very limited and mainly focuses on the range of functions and comprehension of DMs by L2 learners (e.g., Hernández, 2011; Jung, 2003; Lahuerta Martínez, 2009; Martí-Sánchez, 2008; Vande Casteele & Collewaert, 2013). Lahuerta Martínez (2009) shows that DMs have an important role in language learners' reading comprehension and suggests that this effect of DMs may interact with characteristics of the text (such as complexity and topic familiarity) as well as attributes of the learner, such as L2 proficiency and competency as a learner. Portolés (2005) argues that, given that written language aids memory for longer passages, DMs organize information in a more complex way in written Spanish than in spoken Spanish, so that certain DMs (*por el contrario, por una parte / por otra,* etc.) are unlikely to occur in spoken discourse but can convey information such as contrast or focus in written discourse, which has consequences for teaching. These are all important studies that have advanced the understanding of L2 DM use.

The present study takes a different direction in light of long-term trends in writing pedagogy where there has been a reaction for many years against the former focus on sentence-level phenomena such as grammar correctness and lexical choice, in favor of greater attention to discourse-level features, in both native composition teaching and foreign language (FL) writing instruction. This was aligned with the shift toward greater attention to the process of composing versus surface features of the written product, and related to the trend in communicative language teaching in general of prioritizing attention to global as opposed to local errors. In fact, research on L2 writing (e.g., Ferris, 2011) shows that, from the 1970s to the present, corrective feedback on grammatical errors has lost favor, regaining some recently but not at the former level.

Without a doubt, the attention to discourse-level phenomena has been useful, and the study of the functions and comprehension of DMs is well deserved. Yet there is a growing pedagogical trend prioritizing discourse over sentence-level characteristics. That is, many instructors consider discourse features to be more important to the final experience of reading the L2 written product than grammatical and other lexical features, which could imply that the appropriate use of DMs carries a higher functional load than the use of appropriate grammar and other types of vocabulary. It is easy to imagine how this could be true in extreme cases, such as with incoherent organization and argumentation, but it is an open question whether NSs and NrNSs reading L2 writing are more distracted by typical lacks in discourse structuring versus problematic grammar and vocabulary. Without significant research on NS reactions to the weight of grammatical/general vocabulary versus discourse problems of particular types, it is unclear how much priority should be given in the FL classroom to the process of composing as opposed to the product. In fact, we have found no research focusing on this issue for Spanish L2 writing, but studies on judgments of English can provide some guidance. For example, in a study of English L2 pronunciation, Munro and Derwing (2006) look at the functional load of different segments for intelligibility. Likewise, debate about the relative importance of grammatical feedback in the teaching of L2 writing is informative (e.g., Ferris, 2011; Hyland & Anan, 2006; Isaacs & Trofimovich, 2012; I. Lee, 2004).

It is thus an open question whether grammatical and general vocabulary problems are in fact less jarring to readers than failure to use DMs. To begin to fill this gap, we designed an exploratory study focusing on the relative weight given to appropriate DM use as opposed to grammar and non-DM vocabulary in the evaluation of L2 Spanish paragraphs by NSs and near-native Spanish language teachers. In addition, although there has been increased focus in the FL classroom on discourse structure in writing instruction, Fung and Carter (2007) state that the teaching of DMs has generally been neglected, also citing Romero Trillo (2002) and Müller (2005) on this point. For these reasons, we isolated DMs as the single discourse feature to be investigated. Given the aforementioned communicative load of DMs, it makes sense to consider the relative weight that addressees might give to presence or absence of correct DMs versus grammatical and lexical errors in L2 production. Learner writing is read primarily by instructors, but ideally instructors would like to help prepare their students to interact well with NSs who are not instructors. For this reason, we included a group of non-instructor NSs. In examining raters' perceptions of learner writing with and without DMs and with more versus fewer grammatical/lexical errors, we were interested in what variation might exist within the rater group and how that would affect the ratings. A number of studies have shown that rater characteristics, such as being an instructor or a NS of the language in question, can influence how raters judge learner production. For example, Galloway (1980) found that high school Spanish instructors focused more on grammatical errors, whereas non-instructors focused more on content and gave high ratings when L2 learners made a visible effort to communicate. In contrast, linguistically "naïve" participants in Barnwell's (1989) study rated learner writing more harshly than trained raters did. Indeed, Lim (2009) concluded from a review of studies on training raters to evaluate learner writing that such training does not necessarily have the same impact on all trainees. Similarly, in another review of research, Erdosy (2004) notes that instructors and non-instructors have been found to rate writing differently and that the direction of the difference is not consistent across studies. An instructor's field of academic experience also matters: Instructors who normally teach composition to English NSs are likely to react more negatively to learner errors than English as a Second Language teachers accustomed to features of L2 writing (Erdosy, 2004). Furthermore, NS instructors have been found to rate learner production less severely than NNS instructors do (Hyland & Anan, 2006). Overall, previous research shows that a rater's professional status as an instructor can be expected to make a difference, but we cannot yet predict how. Therefore, we wanted to include raters' professional status and raters' NS status as variables, as the research outlined above establishes that they are likely to have an impact on ratings.

In sum, our study is informed by research in interlanguage pragmatics and NS perceptions of learner production, without adhering to a single theoretical approach. It is intended to contribute to the literature by looking at how NS instructors, NS non-instructors, and NrNS instructors rate learner texts in four conditions, as will be described in the next section. We examine their reactions to texts written by Spanish L2 learners at a U.S. university. As will be described in greater detail subsequently, these texts were written in a class context and were both narrative and reflective in style. Specifically, we looked at how the presence/absence of DMs versus grammatical/lexical errors might affect readers' perceptions of quality in these texts. The following research questions guided this study:

1. What are the effects of the presence versus absence of accurately used DMs in L2 writing on participants' evaluations of the quality of the texts?
2. Which weighs more heavily in such evaluations: the appropriate use of DMs or accurate grammar and lexicon?
3. Is there a difference in the evaluations of trained NS and NrNS Spanish instructors versus non-instructor NSs?

## Method

### Participants

The data were collected from 50 participants (17 men and 33 women) with an average age of 48 years (range: 26 to 67) in two broad groups: (a) instructors of Spanish at U.S. colleges and universities who were NSs (N=8) or NrNSs (N=14) of Spanish, and (b) NSs of Spanish who were not university instructors of Spanish (N=28). There is some overlap in their traits that allows us to compare the participants in terms of profession and language background—namely, although instructors and non-instructors are mutually exclusive groups, the trait of NS applies to all non-instructors and to a subset of the instructors. Thus, we can look at differences in how NS instructors, NS non-instructors, and NrNS instructors responded to the texts. The university instructors were employed at various U.S. institutions concentrated primarily in the Midwest. Within this group, the NSs were from a number of Spanish-speaking regions, including Spain, Puerto Rico, Venezuela, Cuba, and Argentina. The majority of the non-instructor NSs lived in northern or central Spain. Of those who were instructors of Spanish, most did not teach composition classes frequently. That said, many Spanish classes from the 200-level[2] and higher involve some writing component, so we can presume that even though the majority of instructors may not teach a composition class frequently, they are still involved in reading and evaluating learner writing.

### Instrumentation and procedures

To create the instrument, we selected texts written by Spanish L2 learners (L1=English) enrolled in 300-level composition/grammar classes at a large midwestern university (see endnote 2). The texts were reflective and narrative in style and came from a writing prompt in which students were instructed to venture into unfamiliar contexts where they would feel out of their comfort zone and then describe and reflect on those experiences in their Spanish essays. Given that the typical essay length was between 350 and 450 words and that we wanted to present the participants with a variety of texts without overtaxing them, we excerpted shorter segments of these essays for our survey. They ranged in length from 170 to 207 words (average=186 words). The texts were blinded of all identifying information and were modified to fit one of the four combinations shown in Table 1.

**Table 1.** Matrix of text types

|  |  | grammatical/lexical errors | |
|---|---|---|---|
|  |  | many | few |
| discourse markers | present | + + | + − |
|  | absent | − + | − − |

The modifications involved standardizing the texts as much as possible for type and frequency of grammatical/lexical errors and for presence/absence of DMs, which sometimes meant adding or removing errors and/or DMs, depending on the text; and all DMs were appropriately used. For those with *more* grammatical/lexical errors, there were between 19 and 25 errors per text dealing with agreement (gender and number in noun phrases as well as subject-verb agreement), aspect (preterite/imperfect), mood (subjunctive/indicative), tense, verb form (e.g., using a gerund where an infinitive is needed), lexical choice other than DMs (verb confusions between, e.g., *saber/conocer*, false cognates, etc.), and the need to add or omit a word. For those with *fewer* grammatical/lexical errors, eight or fewer errors (of the same types) were present in each text. These particular error types were chosen because of their frequency in learner texts at this level (i.e., from a larger survey of learners' writing in Spanish composition classes at this level). For the DMs, we established a range of four to nine tokens per text for "presence" of DMs and zero for absence.[3]

In deciding which types of DMs to manipulate, we considered the naturalness of the usage according to one of the authors as a NS and one as a NrNS Spanish professor, and also reviewed Spanish composition textbooks to choose relevant DMs for the context. Most of these were in the students' original paragraphs. The list of DMs appears in Table 2. Our labeling of DM categories is compatible with the categorization by Portolés (1998); we have partitioned further his category "conectores consecutivos" (consecutive connectors), as we wanted to make sure to include in our stimulus texts DMs conveying the cause-and-effect and purpose distinctions that this category encompasses. Some of the DMs in Table 2 have more than one function, but we have identified the function(s) used in our stimulus texts.

**Table 2.** DMs included in stimulus texts

| categories | DMs included in the texts | glosses |
|---|---|---|
| illustration | *por ejemplo* | for example |
| verifactive | *en realidad* | actually |
| organization | *primero, a continuación* | first, next |
| reformulation | *o sea, en otras palabras* | that is, in other words |
| summarizing | *en resumen* | in sum |
| contrast | *sin embargo, aunque, a pesar de (que)* | however, although, in spite of |
| cause and effect | *por lo tanto, por eso, por consiguiente, como, a medida (de) que, así que, como resultado* | therefore, as a result, as, so |
| purpose | *para que, a fin de que* | so that, in order to |

The two resulting sets (A and B) of eight texts had equal representation of the four text types in Table 1 (i.e., two of each type per set).[4] Two sample texts follow; for the convenience of the reader, we have italicized DMs and underlined grammatical errors here. In Appendix C, the texts are shown as they were presented to our participants.

### With grammatical errors and without DMs
Mucha gente cree que hay igualdad en nuestro país porque ha mantenido un fundación de este concepto para casi cincuenta años, o hasta el movimiento de _ derechos civiles. Me encanta la idea de _ igualdad de toda _ gente que abrazan los americanos. Muchos de _ problemas se han fijados, pero todavía _ tiempos de separación y de querer conformarse a los modos de _ sociedad para ser cómodo. Yo asistí _ mi primera reunión de Los Mujeres Negras en la universidad _ dos semanas pasadas, y no sabía _ esperar. Llegué al reunión un poco tarde, y veía inmediatamente que yo fui una de dos personas blancas del grupo entero—que consistía de casi treinta personas. Me sentí muy nerviosa, incómoda, y aprensiva; no voy a mentir. Probablemente era sólo de mi mente, pero podía sentir todos los ojos de otros en mí, especialmente cuando tuvimos que presentarnos al grupo. Yo sé que ellos probablemente no estaban juzgando_ a mí, pero todavía me sentí incómoda. Pasaba un poco de tiempo de conocer _ nuevos amigos y comentar los estereotipos, yo empecé _ sentir más cerca de ellos.

Many people believe that there are equal rights in our country, because it has had this concept at its foundation for fifty years, until the Civil Rights movement. I love the idea of equal rights for everyone that Americans embrace. Many problems have been fixed, but there are still times of separation and wanting to conform to society in order to be comfortable. I attended my first Black Women's meeting at the university two weeks ago, and I didn't know what to expect. I arrived a bit late and saw immediately that I was one of two white people in the entire group, which consisted of nearly thirty people. I felt very nervous, uncomfortable, and apprehensive; I won't lie about it. It was probably all in my mind, but I felt everyone's eyes on me, especially when we had to introduce ourselves to the group. I know they probably weren't judging me, but I felt uncomfortable all the same. A little time went by and I made new friends and discussed stereotypes, I started to feel closer to them.

### With fewer grammatical errors and with DMs
Decidí trabajar de voluntaria en un hogar para ancianos. Lo primero que vi al entrar fue a un señor en su silla de ruedas. Fue la primera vez que realmente pensé en lo que tendría que hacer en el hogar y me dio

miedo. Abrí la puerta de la entrada y él me miró, *así que* le sonreí pero su expresión nunca cambió; *o sea*, era una expresión en blanco. Si participo como voluntaria en el "programa de actividades" sería donde tendría mayor interacción con los ancianos. Esto es lo que más me pondría a prueba y *por eso* fue lo que escogí. La encargada que me dio la solicitud me dijo que la podía llenar en el comedor del hogar. Una anciana me siguió hasta el comedor y se paró donde llenaba mi solicitud. *En realidad*, le iba a empezar a hablar cuando una de las enfermeras la llamó y la alejó de mi mesa. Llené la solicitud, se la di a la secretaria, y salí del hogar. Vi a la anciana detrás de la puerta, viéndome ir, y alguien la llamó y se fue.

I decided to do volunteer work in a nursing home. The first thing I saw when I got there was a man in a wheelchair. It was the first time that I really thought about what I would be doing in the nursing home and I got nervous. I opened the front door and he looked at me, so I smiled at him but his expression never changed; that is, it was a blank expression. If I work as a volunteer in the "activities program" it would be where I would have the most interaction with the seniors. This is what would test me and that was why I chose it. The administrator who gave me the application form said that I could fill it out in the dining room of the nursing home. One of the older ladies followed me to the dining room and stopped where I was filling out my form. Actually, I was going to start to talk to her when one of the nurses called her and moved her away from my table. I filled out the form, I gave it to the secretary, and I left the nursing home. I saw the same older lady by the door, watching me go, and someone called to her, and she left.

Each participant received either Set A or B, and through the Qualtrics survey software's[5] randomization, branching, and embedded-data features, we were able to ensure equal, random distribution of the sets among the instructor/non-instructor participants. In addition to the questions dealing with the texts, participants were also asked a few basic demographic questions (e.g., age, sex, and languages spoken); see the Participants section for a summary.

We informed the study participants of the general topic of the writing task and also told them that the texts were written by learners of Spanish who had completed two years of Spanish at the university. Participants received a link to the Qualtrics survey via email and, after completing the Informed Consent electronically, were able to access the survey items. The survey was distributed entirely in Spanish. Participants were not allowed to go back to previous pages because we wanted to get their spontaneous reaction and try to standardize their reading process as much as possible. They first responded to the text items described above, followed by the demographic questions. Each text was presented separately (on its own screen), and they were asked to read it only once and without taking too long.[5] On the next screen, they were presented with two items to judge the overall quality of each text (using a 7-point Likert-scale) and to indicate two reasons for their judgments (using two drop-down response items with the same six options for each one). An example of one text with its two corresponding questions, a translation of these two Likert questions, and all the stimulus texts can be found in the appendices.

### Coding system and analyses

We averaged the two text type measures into one measure of each type. That is, we paired up the texts in Set A with their counterparts in Set B such that the texts in Set A that had more grammatical errors and no DMs were paired with texts in Set B with those same traits, and so forth for the other three combinations in the matrix (see Table 1). We also created a variable to distinguish our three subgroups of participants: 1 (instructor NrNSs), 2 (instructor NSs), and 3 (non-instructor NSs).

For our analyses of the overall text ratings (i.e., participants' answers to the item "Please indicate your impression of the quality of the writing sample that you just read." 1 [very deficient] to 7 [outstanding]), we chose a three-way ANOVA using the factors of group (non-instructor NSs, instructor NSs, and NrNS instructors), grammatical/lexical errors (more vs. fewer), and DMs (presence vs. absence).

Participants had six options to indicate the reasons for their evaluations (see the English translation and the original Spanish version in the appendices). These options grouped nicely into two broad categories—namely, those dealing with grammar/lexicon and those dealing with discourse-level phenomena. Therefore, we collapsed the grammar and vocabulary response options because the types of vocabulary and grammar errors in our stimulus texts were both local, and we did the same with the coherence, organization/development, and connections between ideas, as they dealt more with discourse-level phenomena (and omitted the "other" category, given its low response rate). Given the sample size, this choice to focus on the broader groupings also increased the likelihood of obtaining more interpretable results from the chi-square tests of associations to determine if there was an overall association between the reasons and whether participants were NSs (vs. NrNSs) or instructors (vs. non-instructors).

## Results

In this section, we discuss the results for our three research questions, which investigated (1) the effects of the presence/absence of appropriate DMs in L2 writing on how participants' evaluated the quality of the texts, (2) whether these evaluations by NSs were more influenced by the DMs or by grammatical/lexical errors, and (3) if evaluations by NS and NrNS instructors differed from those of non-instructor NSs. Descriptive statistics of text type by participant group are shown in Table 3, and discussion of the inferential analyses follows.

**Table 3.** Descriptive statistics (averages) for the overall rating item "Please indicate your impression of the quality of the writing sample that you just read." (1=very deficient; 7 = outstanding)

| text type | NrNS instructors | NS instructors | NS non-instructors |
|---|---|---|---|
| Type 1 (+DM, more gram/lex errors) | 4.00 | 3.75 | 3.36 |
| Type 2 (+DM, fewer gram/lex errors) | 5.71 | 6.06 | 5.29 |
| Type 3 (-DM, more gram/lex errors) | 3.68 | 4.06 | 3.59 |
| Type 4 (-DM, fewer gram/lex errors) | 4.93 | 5.63 | 5.64 |

From these descriptive statistics (averages), we can see that overall the three groups appear to have some patterns in common, albeit not consistently. For example, with the exception of Type 1 texts (+ DMs and more grammatical/lexical errors), NS instructors rated the texts higher than their NrNS (instructor) counterparts; and with the exception of Type 4, where they match NS instructors, NS non-instructors rated the texts lower than other participants did. These trends are only suggestive, however, prompting us to carry out inferential analyses utilizing a three-way ANOVA that revealed two significant outcomes: one interaction effect between DMs and participant group (allowing us to answer research question #1) and one main effect for grammatical/lexical errors (allowing us to answer research question #2), as shown in Table 4. We focus our discussion on these two questions because, as will be noted at the end of this section, the results are insufficient to allow us to answer research question #3 with confidence.

First, the significant interaction effect shows that DMs affected one or more groups differently. Interestingly, there was not a significant interaction effect for grammatical/lexical errors by group. Another interaction effect approached (but did not reach) significance: grammatical/lexical errors by DMs. Although not statistically significant, the pattern suggests that DMs did not affect ratings in the presence of grammatical/lexical errors. However, in the *absence* of the distraction of such errors, the presence of DMs was correlated with higher ratings. These results indicate that the group differences that emerged in the descriptive statistics are best understood in conjunction with other variables rather than in isolation. Post hoc analyses (estimated marginal means) revealed that (a) NrNS instructors gave higher ratings when DMs were present (4.857) than when they were absent (4.304); (b) DMs did not seem to impact NS instructors' ratings (4.907 with DMs and 4.844 without); and (c) NS non-instructors gave higher ratings when DMs were absent (4.616) than when they were present (4.321), as shown in Figure 1. Therefore, we can say that, in answer to research question #1, the effects of DMs on participants were variable, depending in particular on whether the NSs formed part of the instructor or non-instructor group.

Table 4. Three-way ANOVA

| source | type III sum of squares | df | Mean square | F | p | partial $\eta^2$ | noncent. parameter | observ. power[a] |
|---|---|---|---|---|---|---|---|---|
| GramLex | 126.111 | 1 | 126.111 | 213.886 | <.000 | .820 | 213.886 | >.999 |
| GramLex*group | 2.508 | 2 | 1.254 | 2.127 | .131 | .083 | 4.254 | .415 |
| error (GramLex) | 27.712 | 47 | .590 | | | | | |
| DMs | .445 | 1 | .445 | .805 | .374 | .017 | .805 | .142 |
| DMs*group | 6.752 | 2 | 3.376 | 6.104 | .004 | .206 | 12.207 | .867 |
| error(DMs) | 25.998 | 47 | .553 | | | | | |
| GramLex*DMs | 1.278 | 1 | 1.278 | 3.583 | .065 | .071 | 3.583 | .458 |
| GramLex*DMs*group | 1.584 | 2 | .792 | 2.221 | .120 | .086 | 4.441 | .431 |
| error (GramLex*DMs) | 16.761 | 47 | .357 | | | | | |

[a] computed using alpha=.05

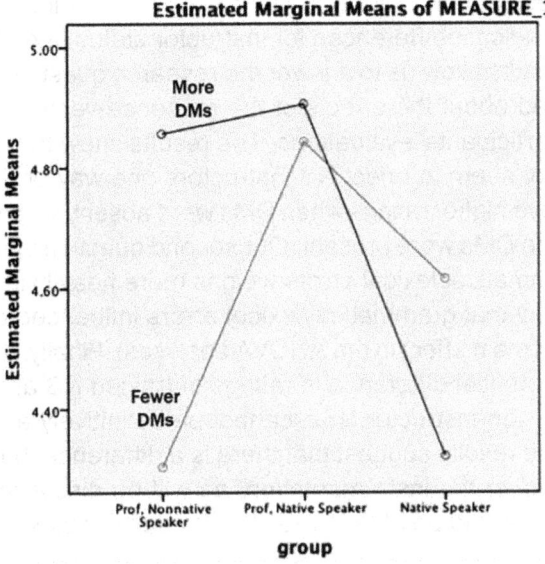

**Figure 1.** Post-hoc analyses of DMs by group

In addition to the effect of group membership, the ANOVA results also show that grammatical and lexical errors themselves make a difference in how participants (in all groups) evaluated the texts, independent of other variables. A similar main effect for DMs across all groups, however, was not found and therefore the answer to research question #2 is that grammatical/lexical errors weigh more heavily in evaluations of learner writing. Overall, average rating scores were higher when there were fewer grammatical and lexical errors (as would be expected: 5.543 fewer errors vs. 3.740 more errors), and there were no differences for presence or absence of DMs across the board unless we take into account other variables.

For research question #3, given that the analyses showed variation in how participants evaluated the texts, we wanted to examine in greater detail the reasons given for these evaluations. Therefore, we carried out chi-square tests of association to compare the observed and expected frequencies of the reasons given for each text: NS status (yes or no) and whether they selected grammar/lexicon as one of the reasons for their evaluation, as well as instructor status (yes or no) and whether they selected grammar/lexicon as one of the reasons for their evaluation on each item. As noted in the Coding section, we collapsed the six response options into two broad groups (grammar/lexicon vs. discourse-level phenomena) to see first if any patterns would emerge. The results only reached statistical significance for one of the 16 texts (Pearson Chi-Square 6.750; $N=.027$)—that is, in only one text was there a significant difference whereby NSs reported paying less attention to grammar/lexicon than their NrNS counterparts. There were no significant differences for instructor status and reason.

In sum, the results allow us to answer the research questions as follows. Our first question asked about the effects of the presence versus absence of DMs in L2 writing on participants' evaluations. The results show that this depends on group: DMs did not seem to affect NS instructors one way or the other, but NS non-instructors gave higher ratings when DMs were absent, whereas NrNSs gave higher ratings when DMs were present. Our second question asked if DMs or the distraction of grammatical/lexical errors weighs more heavily in ratings, and our results clearly show that grammatical/lexical errors influenced the ratings more (by their significant main effect in the ANOVA analyses). Finally, our third question, dealing with the potential difference in ratings of trained NS and NrNS Spanish instructors versus non-instructor NSs, cannot be definitively answered with our current dataset; the results suggest that there is a difference, but more data and some modifications to the instrumentation, as will be discussed subsequently, will likely be necessary to be able to examine these variables in greater detail.

## Discussion

The variation in participants' responses to texts with more or fewer DMs does not appear to be due to chance alone (given the statistically significant interaction effect described above for research question #1) but rather suggests that the results may be indicative of other processes at work. It may be that the NrNS instructors rated texts with DMs more highly because some attention to DMs is part of the curriculum and therefore, as instructors who in their own language learning would have learned DMs consciously, they are more attuned to their use by learners.

NS non-instructors, on the contrary, rated texts without DMs higher than those with DMs, which is more difficult to interpret but could indicate unmeasured expectations about the text type or learner production at this level.[6] Lahuerta Martínez (2009) suggests that DMs help readers understand texts on unfamiliar topics, and in our stimulus materials, which describe relatively common interactions, DMs may not have been as necessary for perception of text organization as they could be in more complex texts. This group's stronger rejection of grammatical/lexical errors is certainly in line with previous research; for example, Sweedler-Brown's (1993) raters unfamiliar with typical L2 features were influenced more by sentence-level errors than by rhetorical features.

The fact that the NS instructors' evaluations showed no real difference for the presence or absence of DMs places them between the two other participant groups; nativeness and professorial role influence the ratings of this in-between group. In Kobayashi and Rinnert (1996), evaluations of learner writing suggested a preference for the rhetorical structure associated with raters' L1, and it was also found that many interrelated factors influence evaluations; taken together, these two points suggest that our NS instructors may have found sufficient cues to meet their implicit expectations for text organization.

Given the finding by Tyler, Jeffries, and Davies (1988, as cited in McCarthy, 1998) that spoken discourse by NNS instructors was less comprehensible to listeners when DMs were infrequent (i.e., showing that DMs are helpful in understanding speech and presumably also written text), it seems striking that our participants' ratings were influenced so much more by grammatical errors than by the presence of DMs (i.e., research question #2), and furthermore, that the NS non-instructors actually gave *higher* ratings when DMs were *absent*, as discussed above. Perhaps our participants, unlike students listening to a NrNS instructor's lecture, were more focused on evaluating the writers' grammatical accuracy, so that the connections within the content of the passages became a secondary concern for them. Alternatively, we might also speculate whether our participants, in the process of reading about the events described in passages lacking DMs, could have filled in causal and textual connections that made sense to them, without having a way to detect that these connections may or may not have been what the writer intended. In this way, communicative failure would not necessarily result in lower ratings.

The findings of the chi-square tests (i.e., only 1 of the 16 texts reached statistical significance) imply that there were largely no differences between NSs and NrNSs as to whether they paid more attention to grammar/lexicon versus the discourse-level phenomena (research question #3). This points to the difficulty of constructing an instrument with categories narrow enough to allow us to differentiate with sufficient granularity the reasons for participants' ratings and the interactions between those ratings and yet still broad enough to avoid explicitly directing their attention to our topic of study. A think-aloud protocol would be the next step to try to meet both needs.

Finally, the perception of DMs in L2 discourse has potential for important communicative and social repercussions. As Stubbs (1983) points out, a missing DM in a learner's speech may lead to a negative evaluation of the speaker's social skills or personality; a learner's writing may be evaluated as "stylistically poor" (p. 92). Furthermore, our study could also have implications for research on L2 pragmatic development, especially when considering the existing emphasis on separating grammatical and pragmatic development and the growing interest in examining their relationship (Bardovi-Harlig, 2010).

Future research could expand upon the present study by making several adaptations in research design. In terms of the participant pool, it would be of interest to include participants who speak other languages, Spanish NS instructors of other subjects, and instructors who teach Spanish to NSs of English in study abroad programs where the instructors are local NSs. Increasing sample size is beneficial in any study, but it is of particular interest here in order to further investigate trends that did not reach statistical significance with the current sample size, to increase the predictive power that would come with a larger sample size (i.e., although the results reached statistical significance, with a larger sample size for each of the three subgroups we would be more confident that the results could be generalized to a larger population and replicated in other studies), and to include additional variables, as described below. Future instrumentation should include think-aloud protocols to provide more detailed information about the reasons for participants' ratings as well as longer, more complex passages for participants to judge in order to show DMs in even more varied contexts. It is possible that DMs would have a more crucial role in establishing coherence in longer texts (e.g., readers may be able to rely on other cues in shorter passages) as well as in texts of a different genre (e.g., texts that are more argumentatively complex as opposed to the narrative/reflective texts of the present study). Furthermore, NS-generated texts could be included as a control element. Our instrument also includes a series of background items in which we asked participants how much personal experience they had with language learning as well as how much contact they had with NNSs of Spanish. We thought these variables might affect how the participants responded to the student essays. The data gleaned, however, were not sufficient to include these variables in the inferential analyses. A future study would benefit from asking participants a more detailed battery of questions related to their own language learning background, their attitudes toward NNSs, the frequency with which those who are instructors teach composition classes as well as any special training they have had for L2 writing instruction.

## Conclusions

Our participants' responses show that the influence of DMs on ratings of L2 writing depends on the participant group. DMs did not seem to affect the ratings given by Spanish NSs who are instructors, but NSs with other occupations gave higher ratings when DMs were absent, and NrNSs gave higher ratings when DMs were present. This result could be due to different expectations and familiarity regarding writing in an academic context. Not surprisingly, grammatical errors in student writing had a greater impact on ratings than DMs did; at the same time, the significant interaction effect of DMs by group shows that there is more work to be done to understand the way DMs, grammatical/lexical errors, and readers' characteristics interact.

### Notes

1   Because the term non-native speakers (NNSs) is typically associated with students or language learners, we use the term near-native speakers (NrNSs) to refer to instructors of Spanish with extremely high proficiency and to distinguish them as people who use Spanish professionally.

2   Classes at the 200 and 300 levels at this university are usually taken by students in their second or third year of college, who typically have an intermediate level of proficiency (by the American Council on the Teaching of Foreign Languages' [ACTFL] guidelines), although some reach the advanced level.

3   The learner texts featured instances of *probablemente* ("probably") and *obviamente* ("obviously"), sentence adverbs indicating the writer's evaluation of the information presented. In keeping with Blakemore's (2007) definition of DM, we did not count these as DMs.

4   A pilot study was not conducted, but the texts were carefully reviewed by two of the researchers: One speaks Spanish as one of her L1s and the other is a NrNS whose recent ACTFL Oral Proficiency Interview (OPI) score was Superior, and therefore we felt confident that the use of DMs in the texts was appropriate. We would like to underscore that the omission of the DMs was not intended to make the texts unreadable or seriously hamper comprehensibility. Rather, we were interested in how the L2 learners were perceived and what kind of impression they made through their writing, as a function of the presence versus absence of DMs in an otherwise coherent text, vis-à-vis the relative weight given to grammatical and lexical errors. This is why the wording of the Likert item following each text was "…your impression of the quality of the writing."

5   Some participants may have taken longer than others to read and evaluate the texts and this unmeasured variable could have affected the results, but limiting the time frame and still maintaining other Qualtrics features was not feasible. Therefore, we chose to emphasize to the participants in the email invitation and the survey instructions that they should read the texts only once and without taking too long, as a way to attempt to standardize the survey administration. Informal conversations with a number of the participants after they completed the survey suggest that there was reasonable compliance with our instructions.

6   We also considered the possibility that the results could be due to variation among NS non-instructors on the basis of the amount of time they report spending interacting with language learners. However, no effects involving time spent with learners were found to be statistically significant in a 4-way ANOVA. It is also possible that the results could be due to variation in the backgrounds of NSs; as noted previously, they were from several Spanish-speaking regions. We cannot discount this possibility, but given that most of them lived in northern or central Spain, we suspect that other factors besides regional background may play a larger role in the results. Finally, the type of writing may also have influenced the outcomes in that there may be less variation in academic writing than in other genres.

# References

Bardovi-Harlig, K. (1995). A narrative perspective on the development of the tense/aspect system in second language acquisition. *Studies in Second Language Acquisition, 17*(2), 263–291.

Bardovi-Harlig, K. (2010). Pragmatics and second language acquisition. In R. Kaplan (Ed.), *The handbook of applied linguistics* (2nd ed., pp. 232–243). Oxford: Oxford University Press.

Bardovi-Harlig, K. (2013). Developing L2 pragmatics. *Language Learning, 63*(Suppl. 1), 68–86.

Barnwell, D. (1989). "Naïve" native speakers and judgements of oral proficiency in Spanish. *Language Testing, 6*(2), 152–163.

Blakemore, D. (1987). *Semantic constraints on relevance.* Oxford: Blackwell.

Blakemore, D. (2007). Discourse markers. In L. R. Horn & G. Ward, (Eds.), *The handbook of pragmatics.* (pp. 221-240). Oxford: Blackwell.

Bohnacker, U., & Rosén, C. (2008). The clause-initial position in L2 German declaratives: Transfer of information structure. *Studies in Second Language Acquisition, 30*(4), 511–538.

Bouton, L. (1988). A cross-cultural study of ability to interpret implicatures in English. *World Englishes, 7,* 183–196.

Buysse, L. (2011). The business of pragmatics: The case of discourse markers in the speech of students of business English and English linguistics. *ITL International Journal of Applied Linguistics, 161,* 10–30.

Buysse, L. (2012). So as a multifunctional discourse marker in native and learner speech. *Journal of Pragmatics, 44*(13), 1764–1782.

Erdosy, M. U. (2004). *Exploring variability in judging writing ability in a second language: A study of four experienced raters of ESL compositions.* TOEFL Research Reports 70. Princeton, NJ: Educational Testing Service.

Félix-Brasdefer, J. C., & Koike, D. A. (2015). Perspectives on Spanish SLA from pragmatics and discourse. In M. Lacorte (Ed.), *The Routledge handbook of Hispanic applied linguistics* (pp. 25–43). New York, NY: Routledge.

Ferris, D. R. (2011). *Treatment of error in second language student writing.* Ann Arbor: University of Michigan Press.

Fraser, B. (1988). Types of English discourse markers. *Acta Linguistica Hungarica, 38*(1–4), 19–33.

Fung, L., & Carter, R. (2007). Discourse markers and spoken English: Native and learner use in pedagogic settings. *Applied Linguistics, 28*(3), 410–439.

Galloway, V. (1980). Perceptions of the communicative efforts of American students of Spanish. *Modern Language Journal, 64*(4), 428–434.

Gánem-Gutiérrez, G. A., & Roehr, K. (2011). Use of L1, metalanguage, and discourse markers: L2 learners' regulation during individual task performance. *International Journal of Applied Linguistics, 21*(3), 297–318.

Groot, I. (2000). *The use of conjunctions in English as a second language (ESL): Students' oral narratives* (Unpublished doctoral dissertation). Ball State University, Muncie, IN.

Hartford, B. (1995). Zero anaphora in nonnative texts: Null hyphen object anaphora in Nepali English. *Studies in Second Language Acquisition, 17*(2), 245–261.

Hellermann, J., & Vergun, A. (2007). Language which is not taught: The discourse marker use of beginning adult learners of English. *Journal of Pragmatics, 39*(1), 157–179.

Hernández, T. A. (2011). Re-examining the role of explicit instruction and input flood on the acquisition of Spanish discourse markers. *Language Teaching Research, 15*(2), 159–182.

Hyland, K., & Anan, E. (2006). Teachers' perceptions of error: The effects of first language and experience. *System, 34*(4), 509–519.

Isaacs, T., & Trofimovich, P. (2012). Reconstructing comprehensibility: Identifying the linguistic influences on listeners' L2 comprehensibility ratings. *Studies in Second Language Acquisition, 34*(3), 475–505.

James, D. M. (1973). *The syntax and semantics of some English interjections* (Doctoral dissertation). Available from ProQuest Dissertations and Theses database. (UMI No.7415763)

Jucker, A., & Ziv, Y. (1998). Discourse markers: Introduction. In A. Jucker & Z. Yael (Eds.), *Discourse markers: Description and theory* (pp. 1–12). Amsterdam: John Benjamins.

Jung, E. H. (2003). The role of discourse signaling cues in second language listening comprehension. *The Modern Language Journal, 87*(4), 562–577.

Kasper, G., & Schmidt, R. (1996). Developmental issues in interlanguage pragmatics. *Studies in Second Language Acquisition, 18*(2), 149–169.

Kobayashi, H., & Rinnert, C. (1996). Factors affecting composition evaluation in an EFL context: Cultural rhetorical pattern and readers' background. *Language Learning, 46*(3), 397–437.

Lahuerta Martínez, A. C. (2009). Empirical study of the effects of discourse markers on the reading comprehension of Spanish students of English as a foreign language. *International Journal of English Studies, 9*(2), 19–43.

Lakoff, R. (1973). Questionable answers and answerable questions. In B. B. Kachru, R. B. Lees, Y. Malkiel, A. Pietrangeli, & S. Saporta (Eds.), *Issues in linguistics: Papers in honor of Henry and Renée Kahane* (pp. 453–467). Urbana: University of Illinois Press.

Lee, H. (1999). The acquisition of colloquial English features by Korean Americans. *Journal of Pan-Pacific Association of Applied Linguistics, 3*, 71–87.

Lee, I. (2004). Error correction in L2 secondary writing classrooms: The case of Hong Kong. *Journal of Second Language Writing, 13*(4), 285–312.

Lim, G. S. (2009). *Prompt and rater effects in second language writing performance assessment* (Unpublished doctoral dissertation). University of Michigan, Ann Arbor.

Liu, B. (2013). Effect of first language on the use of English discourse markers by L1 Chinese speakers of English. *Journal of Pragmatics, 45*(1), 149–172.

Martí-Sánchez, M. (2008). *Los marcadores en español L/E: Conectores discursivos y operadores pragmáticos* [Markers in Spanish L/E: Discursive connectors and pragmatic operators]. Madrid, Spain: Arco Libros.

McCarthy, M. (1998). *Spoken language & applied linguistics.* Cambridge: Cambridge University Press.

Monassar, H. M. (2005). *Cohesion and coherence: Contrastive transitions in the EFL/ESL writing of university Arab students* (Unpublished doctoral dissertation). Ball State University, Muncie, IN.

Müller, S. (2005). *Discourse markers in native and non-native English discourse.* Amsterdam: John Benjamins.

Munro, M. J., & Derwing, T. M. (2006). The functional load principle in ESL pronunciation instruction: An exploratory study. *System, 34*(4), 520–531.

Östman, J. (1981). *You know: A discourse-functional approach.* Amsterdam: John Benjamins.

Portolés, J. (1998). *Marcadores del discurso* [Discourse markers]. Barcelona: Editorial Ariel, S.A.

Portolés, J. (2005). La escritura y los marcadores del discurso [Writing and discourse markers]. In J. A. Moya Corral (Ed.), *Pragmática y enseñanza de la lengua española: Actas de las X jornadas sobre la enseñanza de la lengua española* [Pragmatics and teaching of the Spanish language: Proceedings of the 10th conference on the teaching of the Spanish language] (pp. 37–53). Granada: Editorial Universidad de Granada.

Qualtrics Research Suite [Computer software]. Provo, UT: Qualtrics.

Romero Trillo, J. (2002). The pragmatic fossilization of discourse markers in nonnative speakers of English. *Journal of Pragmatics, 34*(6), 769–784.

Schiffrin, D. (1987). *Discourse markers.* Cambridge: Cambridge University Press.

Schourup, L. (1985). *Common discourse particles in English conversation.* New York, NY: Garland.

Stubbs, M. (1983). *Discourse analysis: The sociolinguistic analysis of natural language.* Chicago, IL: University of Chicago Press.

Sweedler-Brown, C. O. (1993). ESL essay evaluation: The influence of sentence-level and rhetorical features. *Journal of Second Language Writing, 2*(1), 3–17.

Tyler, A., Jefferies, A., & Davies, C. (1988). The effect of discourse structuring devices on listener perception of coherence in non-native university teachers' spoken discourse. *World Englishes, 7,* 101–110.

Tyler, A. (1992). Discourse structure and the perception of incoherence in international teaching assistants' spoken discourse. *TESOL Quarterly, 26*(4), 713–729.

Vande Casteele, A., & Collewaert, K. (2013). The use of discourse markers in Spanish language learners' written compositions. *Procedia-Social and Behavioral Sciences, 95,* 550–556.

# Appendix A: One stimulus text and associated questions, as shown to participants

A continuación le presentaremos muestras de la escritura de estudiantes de español; o sea, son pasajes extraídos de ensayos más largos. Los estudiantes estaban en una clase de Composición y todos ya habían completado dos años de estudios del español en la universidad. Para esta tarea, les pedimos que buscaran situaciones o contextos nuevos donde se sentirían fuera de lugar y que luego escribieran sobre esas experiencias, con lo cual los temas de los textos varían bastante.

En las siguientes páginas le aparecerán 8 párrafos en total y después de cada párrafo habrá dos preguntas para indicar su evaluación de la escritura. Le pedimos que lea los párrafos sólo una vez y sin tardar demasiado.

Mucha gente cree que hay igualdad en nuestro país porque ha mantenido un fundación de este concepto para casi cincuenta años, o hasta el movimiento de derechos civiles. Me encanta la idea de igualdad de toda gente que abrazan los americanos; sin embargo, aunque muchos de problemas se han fijados, todavía tiempos de separación y de querer conformarse a los modos de sociedad para ser cómodo. Yo asistí mi primera reunión de Los Mujeres Negras en la universidad dos semanas pasadas, y no sabía esperar. Llegué al reunión un poco tarde, y veía inmediatamente que yo fui una de dos personas blancas del grupo entero—que consistía de casi treinta personas. En otras palabras, me sentí muy nerviosa, incómoda, y aprensiva; no voy a mentir. Probablemente era sólo de mi mente, pero podía sentir todos los ojos de otros en mí, especialmente cuando tuvimos que presentarnos al grupo entero. Yo sé que ellos probablemente no estaban juzgando a mí, pero todavía me sentí incómoda. Sin embargo, a pesar de eso, a medida que pasaba un poco de tiempo de conocer nuevos amigos y comentar los estereotipos, yo empecé sentir más cerca de ellos.

**Figure.** One stimulus text and associated questions, as shown to participants.

Usando la siguiente escala, indique su impresión de la calidad de la escritura.

| | 1. Deficiente | 2. | 3. | 4. Aceptable | 5. | 6. | 7. Sobresaliente |
|---|---|---|---|---|---|---|---|
| La calidad de la escritura | ○ | ○ | ○ | ○ | ○ | ○ | ○ |

¿Cuáles eran los rasgos que le llevaron a calificar la escritura así? Indique los dos rasgos que influyeron MÁS en su decisión.

Rasgo #1 [                    ]
Rasgo #2 [                    ]

**Figure (continued).** One stimulus text and associated questions, as shown to participants.

# Appendix B: Translation of the rating question

Using the following scale, indicate your impression of the quality of the writing sample that you just read.
Very deficient 1 2     3     4     5     6     7     Outstanding

What were the traits or elements of the sample that led you to rate it as you did? Mark the two options that most influenced your decision.
 - vocabulary

- grammar
- coherence in general
- organization/development of ideas in general
- connections between ideas
- something else [text box]

## Appendix C: All stimulus texts

### Set A

**A.1**

Mucha gente cree que hay igualdad en nuestro país porque ha mantenido un fundación de este concepto para casi cincuenta años, o hasta el movimiento de derechos civiles. Me encanta la idea de igualdad de toda gente que abrazan los americanos; sin embargo, aunque muchos de problemas se han fijados, todavía tiempos de separación y de querer conformarse a los modos de sociedad para ser cómodo. Yo asistí mi primera reunión de Los Mujeres Negras en la universidad dos semanas pasadas, y no sabía esperar. Llegué al reunión un poco tarde, y veía inmediatamente que yo fui una de dos personas blancas del grupo entero—que consistía de casi treinta personas. En otras palabras, me sentí muy nerviosa, incómoda, y aprensiva; no voy a mentir. Probablemente era sólo de mi mente, pero podía sentir todos los ojos de otros en mí, especialmente cuando tuvimos que presentarnos al grupo entero. Yo sé que ellos probablemente no estaban juzgando a mí, pero todavía me sentí incómoda. Sin embargo, a pesar de eso, a medida que pasaba un poco de tiempo de conocer nuevos amigos y comentar los estereotipos, yo empecé sentir más cerca de ellos.

**D.2**

Cuando empecé a asistir a las reuniones, me sentí como una minoría. Sin embargo, como mi asistencia incrementó, mi comprensión de sentirme como una minoría comenzó a cambiar lentamente. El objetivo principio de mi tiempo con el "Grupo de Conversación entre Estudiantes Internacionales" era comprender mejor a las personas que yo pensaba que eran diferentes a mí. Este grupo enfatizó la necesidad de la conversación para poder conocer a otras personas, especialmente las personas de otras culturas. Esto se hace dando a cada grupo una serie de preguntas. Obviamente, los grupos no se limitan a comentar sólo estas temas. A pesar de esto, mi grupo y yo siempre sentimos obligados a hablar más de las preguntas que otras temas. Como resultado, empecé a entender a la gente y su cultura mejor. Por ejemplo, una estudiante de Corea del Sur dijo que todo estaba más orientado al trabajo en los EE.UU. que en su país. Dijo que su ciudad en particular era una ciudad turística, lo que significa que todo lo que había que hacer era ir a fiestas con amigos.

### G.3
Me interesa cómo simple es hacer amigos con personas más jóvenes. Adolescentes usualmente son conocidos ser sentencioso con sus compañeros. Más la gente de la iglesia tiene la reputación a ser poco receptivo de personas quien tienen ideas diferentes de su mismo. Me sorprendió mucho que los adolescentes de la iglesia me invitaron a ir al restaurante con ellos. Era la conclusión de la misa y Eric, un chico de quizás 16 años me dijo que el grupo de los jóvenes estaban yendo a comer juntos porque la misa era a las 6:30 hasta la 8:00 y mucha de la gente no tenía tiempo comer antes. Decidí a ir con ellos. Seguí allí y me sentí con ellos. Empezaron a preguntarme sobre mi vida. Este me hacía un poco nervioso porque había escondido mucha de mi vida para no atrajera atención a mí. Quería ser una cara en la multitud y nada más. Me preguntaron de la escuela, mi padres y amigos, y lo que quería hacer con mi vida. No dijeron nada de la religión. Me sorprendió mucho.

### J.4
Decidí trabajar de voluntaria en un hogar para ancianos. Lo primero que vi al entrar fue a un señor en su silla de ruedas. Y fue la primera vez que realmente pensé en lo que tendría que hacer en el hogar y me dio miedo. Abrí la puerta de la entrada, él me miró, y le sonreí pero su expresión nunca cambió, era una expresión en blanco. Si participo como voluntaria en el "programa de actividades" sería donde tendría mayor interacción con los ancianos. Esto es lo que más me pondría a prueba y fue lo que escogí. La encargada que me dio la solicitud me dijo que la podía llenar en el comedor del hogar. Una anciana me siguió hasta el comedor y se paró donde llenaba mi solicitud. Le iba a empezar a hablar cuando una de las enfermeras la llamó y la alejó de mi mesa. Llené la solicitud, se la di a la secretaria, y salí del hogar. Vi a la anciana detrás de la puerta, viéndome ir, y alguien la llamó y se fue.

### C.1
Este fin de semana pasada, mi amiga me invite a cenar para celebra su cumpleaños con otros amigos también. Quería que todos sus amigos asistan la celebración en su restaurante favorito. Cuando mi hija y yo llegamos al restaurante, vi mi amiga con cuatro otras personas. Inmediatamente estaba nerviosa porque era la única persona con un niño. Al principio todos estaban en la barra pero como yo tenía mi hija (y la regla no permite a menores en la barra), teníamos que cambiáramos de sitio y nos sentáramos en otra zona, por lo tanto me sentía mal y quería que voy porque estaba avergonzada. Mientras comíamos todo parecía que iba bien, pero todavía me sentía un poco extraño e incómoda. Creo que sabían que me sentía incómodo porque sonrieron, tratando de ser agradable. A continuación, mi hija empezó a llorar y me llevé rápidamente nuestras cosas y salió el restaurante aunque todos me querían para volver pero

yo estaba demasiado avergonzada. No me arrepiento ser madre, pero cuando estoy con otros de mi edad que no tiene hijos me siento como un extraterrestre.

### *E.2*

A lo largo de este proyecto, he querido evaluar los efectos de género en mis propios relaciones porque no había pensado mucho antes de empezar este investigación. Por lo tanto, decidí charlar con mi novio para aprender de su percepción de los efectos de los estereotipos en nuestra comunicación a fin de que podamos mejorarlo. Reconoció varias diferencias en la comunicación entre hombres y mujeres que afectan nuestra comunicación. Primero, reconoció que hay diferencia en la manera de presentar la información. Por ejemplo, cuando estoy contando una historia añado demasiados detalles y él se confunde. Yo supongo que no ha estado escuchando y, por consiguiente, me hago frustrada con él. Sin embargo, en realidad no ha entendido la importancia de mi historia porque en su opinión los detalles no son necesarios para hablar del problema. Cree que los chicos prefieren concentrarse en el problema y por eso los he percibido como impacientes. Pensamos en varias maneras para ser más comprensivos para que no nos enfademos o nos hagamos daño. Por ejemplo, cuando cuento historias trato de identificar los detalles más importantes para evitar la confusión pero también él tiene que ser paciente cuando está escuchándome.

### *H.3*

Durante las semanas pasadas, he conocido pocas personas incapacitadas. Conocí a una chica que se llama Sydney. Ella tiene un amigo común conmigo, Dylan. Ellos me invitaron a cenar con ellos. Nosotros hablamos de nuestras vidas, cenamos, y comemos un pastel. Supe que ella es cristiana y hablamos de las iglesias que asistimos. Le pregunté a Sydney, "¿Qué es tu condición?" y me dijo que ella es parapléjica. La condición parapléjica significa que la mitad inferior de su cuerpo está paralizada. Las piernas no funcionan en movimiento. Ella usa una silla de ruedas porque ella no puede caminar. Otra día conocí a un estudiante que se llama Dustin. Hablé con él de su vida y me dijo sus pasatiempos como mirar deportes y pasar tiempo con amigos. Supe que Dustin nació desfigurado y que su condición hace que sus huesos sean muy frágiles. Me preguntó si le podía ayudar a ponerse su suéter, porque iba afuera. Le ayudé. Al principio pensaba que me sentiría incómodo durante mis conversaciones con ellos, y sentía poco incómodo pero no era difícil hablar con ellos. Me sorprendió que no les molesta hablar de sus discapacidades.

### *F.4*

El haber visitado el templo hindú antes me hizo entender un poco más a las personas que son de la minoría religioso. La última vez fue durante el tiempo más ocupado, el viernes por la mañana. Visitar el viernes me sirvió para observar mejor los rituales y las costumbres. Pero, los viernes hay muchos creyentes y no tuve oportunidad de hablar con Anika sobre lo que se hace allí. Esta vez decidí visitar el templo lunes para poder observar en otras circunstancias y hablar con Anika. Decidí sentarme y contemplar lo que estaba sintiendo por un momento. El templo se sentía calmante y me relajaba fácilmente. Empecé a ver los imágenes de los dioses que estaban adornadas de flores y telas preciosas. Traté de ser de mente abierta, pero mi instinto me ganó y empecé a juzgar las imágenes. Me parecían extrañas, unas con cabeza de elefante, y otras con serpientes en el cuello. Me pregunté ¿qué pensaría un hindú si visitara una iglesia católica? Tal vez pensaría que rezarle a un hombre en una cruz con poca ropa y sangre era ilógica. Me volví a dar cuenta de algo que ya sabía; todos somos iguales.

## Set B

*B.1*
Gente dice que la manera al corazón de un hombre es a través del estómago. Pienso que esto se aplica a todo el mundo porque mucha gente le gusta la comida. La asociación de estudiantes asiáticos (AASA) dedicó una reunión a la comida asiática. El consejo explicó mucha comida, incluyen arroz frito, un plato con fideos, y un plato de pollo. Después podíamos probar la comida y hablar con la gente en la reunión. Yo no había asistido todas las reuniones, así que no quería comer. Esperaba en el parte de atrás por mi amiga cuando un miembro me dijo, "¡come, come, hay demasiada comida!" Me ayudó sentir como parte del grupo. A pesar de que esto evento no pareció grande, me afectó mucho. Sabía que AASA me quería estar allí. Después de obtuve mi comida, me senté con gente desconocida. Nos presentamos y hablamos por un rato hasta que tenía que salir. En resumen, me gustaba mucho esta reunión. Me sentí que podía hablar con cualquier miembro. Los miembros la trataron a la gente nueva como miembros. De verdad estaban felices que estábamos allí. Querían estar seguro que nos divertíamos en la reunión y que no necesitábamos nada.

*F.2*
El haber visitado el templo hindú antes me hizo entender un poco más a las personas que son de la minoría religioso. La última vez fue durante el tiempo más ocupado, el viernes por la mañana. Visitar el viernes me sirvió para observar mejor los rituales y las costumbres. Sin embargo los viernes hay muchos creyentes y por lo tanto no tuve oportunidad de hablar con Anika sobre lo que se hace allí. Así que esta vez decidí visitar el templo lunes para poder observar en otras circunstancias y hablar con Anika. Decidí sentarme y contemplar lo que estaba sintiendo por un momento. El templo se sentía calmante y me relajaba fácilmente. Empecé a ver los imágenes de los dioses que estaban adornadas de flores y telas preciosas. Traté de ser de mente abierta, pero mi instinto me ganó y empecé a juzgar las imágenes. Por ejemplo, me parecían extrañas, unas con cabeza de elefante, y otras con serpientes en el cuello. Me pregunté ¿qué

pensaría un hindú si visitara una iglesia católica? Tal vez pensaría que rezarle a un hombre en una cruz con poca ropa y sangre era ilógica. Y como resultado me volví a dar cuenta de algo que ya sabía; todos somos iguales.

### A.3
Mucha gente cree que hay igualdad en nuestro país porque ha mantenido un fundación de este concepto para casi cincuenta años, o hasta el movimiento de derechos civiles. Me encanta la idea de igualdad de toda gente que abrazan los americanos. Muchos de problemas se han fijados, pero todavía tiempos de separación y de querer conformarse a los modos de sociedad para ser cómodo. Yo asistí mi primera reunión de Los Mujeres Negras en la universidad dos semanas pasadas, y no sabía esperar. Llegué al reunión un poco tarde, y veía inmediatamente que yo fui una de dos personas blancas del grupo entero—que consistía de casi treinta personas. Me sentí muy nerviosa, incómoda, y aprensiva; no voy a mentir. Probablemente era sólo de mi mente, pero podía sentir todos los ojos de otros en mí, especialmente cuando tuvimos que presentarnos al grupo. Yo sé que ellos probablemente no estaban juzgando a mí, pero todavía me sentí incómoda. Pasaba un poco de tiempo de conocer nuevos amigos y comentar los estereotipos, yo empecé sentir más cerca de ellos.

### D.4
Cuando empecé a asistir a las reuniones, me sentí como una minoría. Mi asistencia incrementó y mi comprensión de sentirme como una minoría comenzó a cambiar lentamente. El objetivo principio de mi tiempo con el "Grupo de Conversación entre Estudiantes Internacionales" era comprender mejor a las personas que yo pensaba que eran diferentes a mí. Este grupo enfatizó la necesidad de la conversación para poder conocer a otras personas, especialmente las personas de otras culturas. Esto se hace dando a cada grupo una serie de preguntas. Obviamente, los grupos no se limitan a comentar sólo estas temas. Mi grupo y yo siempre sentimos obligados a hablar más de las preguntas que otras temas. Empecé a entender a la gente y su cultura mejor. Una estudiante de Corea del Sur dijo que todo estaba más orientado al trabajo en los EE.UU. que en su país. Dijo que su ciudad en particular era una ciudad turística, lo que significa que todo lo que había que hacer era ir a fiestas con amigos.

### G.1
Me interesa cómo simple es hacer amigos con personas más jóvenes. Adolescentes usualmente son conocidos ser sentencioso con sus compañeros. Más la gente de la iglesia tiene la reputación a ser poco receptivo de personas quien tienen ideas diferentes de su mismo, así que me sorprendió mucho que los adolescentes de la iglesia me invitaron a ir al restaurante con ellos. Era la conclusión de la misa y Eric, un chico de quizás 16 años me dijo que el grupo de los jóvenes estaban yendo a comer juntos porque la misa era a las 6:30 hasta la

8:00 y como resultado mucha de la gente no tenía tiempo comer antes. Decidí a ir con ellos. Seguí allí y me sentí con ellos. Empezaron a preguntarme sobre mi vida. Este me hacía un poco nervioso porque había escondido mucha de mi vida para no atrajera atención a mí. En otras palabras, quería ser una cara en la multitud y nada más. Me preguntaron de la escuela, mi padres y amigos, y lo que quería hacer con mi vida, sin embargo no dijeron nada de la religión y por lo tanto me sorprendió mucho.

### J.2

Decidí trabajar de voluntaria en un hogar para ancianos. Lo primero que vi al entrar fue a un señor en su silla de ruedas. Fue la primera vez que realmente pensé en lo que tendría que hacer en el hogar y me dio miedo. Abrí la puerta de la entrada y él me miró, así que le sonreí pero su expresión nunca cambió; o sea, era una expresión en blanco. Si participo como voluntaria en el "programa de actividades" sería donde tendría mayor interacción con los ancianos. Esto es lo que más me pondría a prueba y por eso fue lo que escogí. La encargada que me dio la solicitud me dijo que la podía llenar en el comedor del hogar. Una anciana me siguió hasta el comedor y se paró donde llenaba mi solicitud. En realidad, le iba a empezar a hablar cuando una de las enfermeras la llamó y la alejó de mi mesa. Llené la solicitud, se la di a la secretaria, y salí del hogar. Vi a la anciana detrás de la puerta, viéndome ir, y alguien la llamó y se fue.

### C.3

Este fin de semana pasada, mi amiga me invite a cenar para celebra su cumpleaños con otros amigos también. Quería que todos sus amigos asistan la celebración en su restaurante favorito. Cuando mi hija y yo llegamos al restaurante, vi mi amiga con cuatro otras personas. Inmediatamente estaba nerviosa porque era la única persona con un niño. Al principio todos estaban en la barra pero yo tenía mi hija (y la regla no permite a menores en la barra), y teníamos que cambiáramos de sitio y nos sentáramos en otra zona. Me sentía mal y quería que voy porque estaba avergonzada. Mientras comíamos todo parecía que iba bien, pero todavía me sentía un poco extraño e incómoda. Creo que sabían que me sentía incómodo porque sonrieron, tratando de ser agradable. Mi hija empezó a llorar y me llevé rápidamente nuestras cosas y salió el restaurante. Todos me querían para volver pero yo estaba demasiado avergonzada. No me arrepiento ser madre, pero cuando estoy con otros de mi edad que no tiene hijos me siento como un extraterrestre.

### E.4

A lo largo de este proyecto, he querido evaluar los efectos de género en mis propios relaciones porque no había pensado mucho antes de empezar este investigación. Decidí charlar con mi novio para aprender de su percepción de los efectos de los estereotipos en nuestra comunicación y poder mejorarlo.

Reconoció varias diferencias en la comunicación entre hombres y mujeres que afectan nuestra comunicación. Reconoció que hay diferencia en la manera de presentar la información. Cuando estoy contando una historia añado demasiados detalles y él se confunde. Yo supongo que no ha estado escuchando y me hago frustrada con él. En realidad no ha entendido la importancia de mi historia porque en su opinión los detalles no son necesarios para hablar del problema. Cree que los chicos prefieren concentrarse en el problema y los he percibido como impacientes. Pensamos en varias maneras para ser más comprensivos y no enfadarnos o hacernos daño. Cuando cuento historias trato de identificar los detalles más importantes para evitar la confusión pero también él tiene que ser paciente cuando está escuchándome.

# The Interactional Establishment of the Membership Category "Nonnative Speaker" in Gatekeeping Encounters

Louise Tranekjær
Katherine Kappa
Roskilde University, Denmark

*This paper examines how the membership category* nonnative speaker *is interactionally established and initiated by the* native speaker *interviewers during internship interviews between Danish employers and born abroad[1] candidates. The analysis is based on 16 recorded internship interviews and related to studies that demonstrate how membership categories are fundamentally indexical of the context of interaction (Day, 2006; Drew & Heritage, 1992; Mondada, 2004). By taking a membership categorization analysis (MCA) approach and utilizing conversation analytic (CA) tools, this paper shows three different ways in which the interviewers orient to and establish the candidate as a member of the category nonnative speaker without performing other-repair. Thus, the paper focuses on orientations to proficiency that are not related to linguistic errors or repair-sequences. The direct address of the interviewers' orientations to the candidates' proficiency in our data is noteworthy as it is in stark contrast to previous research that shows that other-repair is rarely initiated by native speakers in native/nonnative speaker settings. We argue that language-related membership categorization processes are problematic in institutional settings, such as the interviews analyzed here, as they contribute to the gatekeeping effect of the speech situation by reproducing asymmetrical power relations.*

## Introduction

### Nonnativeness as interactionally constituted

Within the disciplines of Conversation Analysis (Jefferson, 1992; Sacks, 1972b; Schegloff, 2007a), Cultural Studies (Hall, 1997) and Discursive Psychology (Billig, 1996; Potter & Wetherell, 1987), membership categories or "identities" (Antaki & Widdicombe, 1998) are not given properties of individuals. Rather, they are contingent, in the sense that they are available as interpretative and interactional resources that can be produced and oriented to by interactants engaging in particular actions and activities. However, processes of categorization are enabled and limited by the linguistic and interactional resources of interactants and by the way in which actions and utterances are interpreted, heard, and perceived by others. As such, categorization processes are gatekeeping processes that are enabled and limited by speakers and hearers alike.

Individuals learning a target language will inevitably engage in target language speaking contexts where their utterances will be interpretable as second language talk; and where the category nonnative speaker is potentially more salient than other categories with which they might be affiliated. Rampton (1990, p. 98) very aptly problematizes this by arguing that the relevance of learning a language to a native speaker level only becomes relevant in a social context to the extent that the target language speaking society chooses to make it so.

This study examines native speaker orientations towards nonnative speakers' language behaviors that are gatekeeping in the way they construct another as deviant from their expected norms of the language spoken. From an interactional perspective, the aim is to show how the negotiation and establishment of nonnative speakers' linguistic membership and knowledge within institutional interactions introduces a hierarchical relation between categories and category members, which presents a challenge for the candidates that has to be addressed and solved interactionally.

The research question addressed in this paper is when and how one becomes recognizable and visible as *nonnative speaker* (Britzman, Santiago-Válles, Jiménez-Múñoz, & Lamash, 1993), and to what degree nonnativeness is oriented to or "let to pass" (Garfinkel, 1967; Goffman, 1963). This relates to a broader issue of how relations of power and ideology play a central role in enabling or preventing processes of language learning (Blackledge, 2005; Norton, 2000).

### Establishing nonnative speaker in interaction

The study of categories related to second language talk makes relevant an entire field of L2 research and requires clarification of our positioning in relation to the central discussions of terms such as native speaker (a speaker for whom the target language is their L1), nonnative speaker (a speaker for whom the target language is not their L1 but rather their Ln), and proficiency. However, beyond the definitions of these, the intricate relationship between how each "speaker" is viewed in relation to the other is important with regard to linguistic asymmetries in gatekeeping encounters.

The notion of native speaker is based on the idea that native speakers are the ideal models and ultimate authorities on the use of the target language, maintenance, and direction (Benati, 2009; Davies, 2003). As such, nonnative speakers are from this perspective seen as lacking in this "state of assumed perfection" (Davies, 2003). The identity of a nonnative speaker is thus established in relation to a native speaker (Park, 2007).

Underlying this perspective on native and nonnative speakers is the assumption of linguistic asymmetry among people, according to which native speakers are seen as the masters of a target language while the nonnative speakers' abilities need to be measured in terms of proficiency. We see this asymmetry, rooted in ideas about proficiency, as a social construction that can, for various reasons, be oriented to and made relevant by participants during particular interactions (Davies, 2003).

Although proficiency is also considered as an interactional product, it is a notion that has a history of academic controversy. Proficiency has thus far defied a commonly agreed upon definition (Davies, 2003, p. 173; Hulstijn, 2011). Nevertheless, in broad terms, proficiency in nonnative speakers can differ from native speakers along the lines of phonology, grammar, semantics, comprehension, and performance in a target language (Davies, 2003, p. 93, 174). What we argue in this paper is precisely that the orientation towards nonnativeness involves an interpretation of the candidate's language use as non-proficient without any specification of the nature of the deviance. Such specification is a researcher's concern rather than a participant's or, in ethnomedological terms, a "member's" concern. The key concern of any interactant is to communicate and to co-accomplish particular activities on the basis of whatever language resources the participants have at their disposal. This involves the interpretation and evaluation of another as a co-participant and as part of that the assessment of whether participants who are hearable as nonnative speakers satisfy the culturally established expectations associated with this category.

The notion of proficiency has already previously been challenged by interactional sociolinguists, who have argued that what is of importance for nonnative speakers in interaction with native speakers is not just their knowledge of lexis, syntax, and grammar but their ability to build a coherent interaction (Campbell & Roberts, 2007; Davies, 2003; Roberts & Campbell, 2005; Roberts & Moss, 2004). Gumperz's (1982) work is exemplary in showing how in intercultural interactions, where a nonnative interactant is linguistically fully proficient in the target language, miscommunication can still occur due to nonnative speakers not meeting the expected communicative norms within the majority-defined language setting. He refers to this as "parallel tracks which don't meet" (Gumperz, 1982,

p. 185), pointing to the relevance of nonnative speakers' discursive proficiency as much as linguistic proficiency. Similarly, Davies (2003) argues that native speakers take both linguistic and paralinguistic features (facial expressions, body movements and distance) for granted among other native speakers. These "taken-for-granted" expectations of behavior in interaction point to underlying membership categorization processes in the sense that, "membership means acceptance of and an agreement to use certain norms of behavior" (Davies, 2003, p. 203). The failure to comply with them has a negative impact on an individual's membership acceptance. Benati (2009) shows in a study of native speakers' ability to distinguish between native and near-native speakers upon listening, that while the majority of the native judges asserted that they are always able to make the distinction, in reality they often failed to distinguish between the two. Benati (2009) concluded that "the [native] speaking judges unconsciously admitted that such features as body language, gestures, race and appearance are important determiners for them when judging [individuals]" (pp. 161–162). Such findings suggest the need to study the interactional sense-making practices wherein inferences and categorizations are made about proficiency, nonnativeness, and related categories.

This paper adopts a membership categorization analysis (MCA) approach and utilizes tools from conversation analysis (CA) to explore orientations to nonnative speaker categorization. Previously, interactional studies on nonnative/native interactions were predominantly focused on other- or self-repair, but now a vast amount of interactional studies exist that seek to describe other aspects of interactions involving non-native speakers (Gardner & Wagner, 2004). While other- or self-initiated repair demonstrate one way in which interactants show an orientation towards nonnativeness and/or deviations from an expected norm, the salience of the category nonnativeness cannot merely be understood with reference to repairs or repairable talk but must be understood as something reflexively constituted with reference to a range of different category predicates. This paper opens up the scope of orientations to nonnativeness to include any kind of orientations to language proficiency of a participant that are not exclusively related to linguistic errors and repairs. Park (2007) comes closest to our research interest in that she demonstrates how native speaker/nonnative speaker categories are a locally established phenomenon and relates to invoking of linguistic asymmetry among participants, yet she also only focuses on repair sequences of various kinds.

Others have focused on characterizing second language talk (Gardner & Wagner, 2004) or language proficiency (Brown, 2003; Fogtmann, 2007; Kasper & Ross, 2007; Okada, 2010; Ross, 2007) as an interactional phenomenon. The studies of oral proficiency interviews are, however, less focused on category-work and the distribution of roles and rights between participants, and instead address the power dimension of such interactions as manifested in how interviewers facilitate or hinder "proficient" language performances. Within a Nordic context, we find a study by Sundberg (2004) which, in line with the present paper, addressed power and asymmetry as related to not only linguistic behavior but to roles and rights defined by linguistic, institutional, and cultural memberships. This is confirmed by Svennevig's (2004, 2005, 2013) studies of social worker interactions that demonstrate how native Norwegian speaking social workers' use of repetitions orients towards an asymmetric power relation to the nonnative speaking client which is rooted in a context of language ideology as well as institutionality. Even closer in perspective to the present study of nonnativeness is the study of workplace interactions by Day (1998), which shows how interactants at a multi-ethnic workplace orient to and resist ethnic differentiation through membership categorization practices (see also Higgins 2009; Nishizaka 1995, 1999 in broadcast media). What is highlighted in Day's study as well as in this paper is how differences in relation to ethnicity and language background are produced interactionally but simultaneously bear witness to established power relations and ideologies.

**Redefining gatekeeping**

Within institutional interactions such as job interviews, service encounters, and medical interactions, the categorization and evaluation of individuals in relation to perceived norms and deviances have potentially greater consequences for interactants with different ethnic and language backgrounds from that of the majority group. Such interactions have been described as *gatekeeping* encounters first by interactional sociolinguists Gumperz, Roberts, Erickson and Schultz (Erickson & Schultz, 1982; Gumperz, Roberts, & Jupp, 1979; Roberts & Sarangi, 1999) and later by other disciplines and researchers (Baptiste & Seig, 2007; Holmes, 2007; Kasper & Ross, 2007; Kerekes, 2006, 2007a, 2007b; Komter, 1991; Tranekjær, 2015; Trinch, 2007). The term *gatekeeping* itself refers to all interactions where one of the participants has the right, authority, and obligation to make decisions about another participant, and where the outcome of the interaction has direct and concrete consequences for the latter.

Gatekeeping processes have previously been described and documented by comparing patterns in the selection or success of some candidates or clients and explaining gatekeeping as a result of misunderstandings and communicative differences (Akinnaso & Seabrook Ajirotutu, 1982; Auer, 1998; Auer & Kern, 2001; Baptise & Seig, 2007; Erickson & Schultz, 1982; Gumperz et al., 1979; Kasper & Ross, 2007; Kerekes, 2006, 2007a, 2007b; Scheuer, 2001). However, while these studies document how differences in linguistic and interactional resources can result in the systematic differentiation between candidates, interviewees, and clients, they do not focus on describing the establishment of difference as such from a micro-analytical perspective. There is a need to, in order words, illuminate the actual processes of categorization in which differences and similarities between categories and interlocutors, as members of categories, become relevant and significant for ongoing talk and interactional development. Such processes constitute the core of gatekeeping (Tranekjær, 2015).

With this in mind, the present paper examines processes of gatekeeping as the maintenance of majority defined norms of linguistic behavior that manifest in the categorization of particular linguistic behaviors as noticeably different or treated as deviant by the interactants. This paper emphasizes how processes of gatekeeping unfold in the very categorization of nonnative speakers and nonnative speech in institutional interactions. This MCA approach to the notion of gatekeeping suggests a process broader in scope than discriminatory institutional evaluation processes. What is suggested is rather that gatekeeping includes any process of categorization that involves a hierarchical categorical order and the (re)production of asymmetrical relations between categories and members of those categories (Tranekjær, 2015).

## Method

### Membership Categorization Analysis (MCA)

MCA was introduced by Sacks (1972a; 1972b) to allow for the systematic account of how interlocutors make sense of one another in interaction by organizing themselves in relation to various membership categories (Lepper, 2000). These categories are culturally organized into so-called membership category devices (MCDs; Sacks, 1972a, 1972b) such as family, race, language, and so forth, which are linked to particular actions and behaviors through a shared, cultural *common sense* (Garfinkel, 1967).

As individuals interact with each other, they reflexively constitute various categories by employing certain predicates and by implicitly or explicitly highlighting certain characteristics, traits, or descriptors as part of the ongoing talk. Other individuals within or outside of the present interaction who can be said to have such characteristics, including specific actions or behavior, are in this way implicitly or explicitly ascribed to the categories that are made relevant. The categorical and sequential aspects of interaction are fundamentally interdependent (Hester & Eglin, 1997; Watson, 1997) which means that in order to understand the organization of second language talk, one has to engage with the categories that such talk makes relevant. Processes of membership categorization are thus influenced by the principle of indexicality (Heritage, 1984b; Schegloff, 2007a) and by fact that actions are *category-bound* (Sacks, 1995), which means interactants hear and interpret actions as directly bound to and indicative of a particular category membership. The most famous example of this, explained by Sacks (1972b), is when we see a baby cry, which is seen as the category predicate of babies and then also when a woman picks the baby up, in which the woman is assumed and interpreted to be the mother of the baby since the action of *picking up a baby* is culturally linked to the category *mother*.

The internship interviews analyzed here offer many possibilities of membership categorization in relation to the participants, and yet they reveal patterns in the foregrounding of some categories and the backgrounding of others. Such patterns should be investigated and questioned, since they inform and reveal the structures of meaning and common sense that constitute individuals' membership knowledge and can in this way potentially constitute a barrier for alternative categorizations and meanings. It should be stressed here that similar to traditions within CA, the categorization is not imposed by the researcher but rather based on the orientations of the participants themselves.

In short, processes of membership categorization constitute a window to contextually specific understandings of how a given social reality is organized, and to the way that this organization is intimately tied to the processes in which normativity and deviance are established and reproduced.

## Data

The study is based on audio recordings of 16 internship interviews.[2] The 16 interviews come from nursing homes (10), schools (3), an orchard, an NGO, and a home health company.

All of the internship candidates, except for one, were women from non-western countries, most of them Muslim and many of them visibly identifiable as such on account of their clothing. The workplaces involved were mainly nursing homes, since this line of work was the focus of one of the larger job-counselling programs providing data for the study.

The cases presented in this paper are part of a larger study of 40 cases found in a study of 16 internship interviews reported on in Tranekjær (2015). The interviews presented are introductory interviews between different second language speaking internship candidates (IN) and native-speaking employers (HO) at a variety of different work-places. Also present was a job consultant (CO) responsible for the various job training programs that the internship candidates were undertaking. The job consultant facilitates the planning of the internship and the interview and sets up the interview and makes initial inquiries about the possibilities of establishing an internship with the candidates. The interviews are in this way a situation where it is to be decided if and how the internship can be arranged and agreed upon between the parties involved. Some of the interviews also included an employee (EM) who has specific knowledge of the line of work to which the intern will be assigned and who assists the employer in the interviewing.

These situational identities (Zimmerman, 1998) constitute the membership categories of the particular context, and they are categorically ordered in a particular way by the participants as they establish the meaning of this context through their activities (Hester & Eglin, 1997, p. 28).

In some cases, this job-counseling program is integrated with a second language teaching program, but in all cases employers have been informed that the internship candidates are migrants and nonnative speakers. The candidates had all completed or nearly completed their obligatory second language training programs and some were undertaking additional work-specific language training as part of their job counselling.

## Analysis

### Orientations to *nonnative speaker* membership category in internship interviews

In the following analysis, we focus on how nonnativeness and proficiency are locally accomplished, reflexively constituted, and interactionally negotiated. We argue that the categorizations of linguistic otherness involve gatekeeping, not in the sense that the candidate is denied the internship, but in the way that ideas and expectations about proficiency in and of themselves become interactional obstacles and barriers.

Language-related membership categories were made relevant explicitly by the employers in various ways throughout our data. Interestingly enough, this did not occur in the form of orientations towards or corrections of particular grammatical or lexical mistakes. In a CA-focused study of nonnative speech qualities (i.e., grammar), Kurhila (2005) indeed shows that there are often no corrections from the native speakers' side in institutional encounters. Only the nonnative speaker can be seen self-repairing or making initiations for help in repair from the native speaker. Kurhila (2005) argues that this phenomenon can be explained by the native speakers' orientation "to the turns by the NNSs with reference to their institutional relevance and not to their grammatical correctness. By only minimally orienting to the form of the NNSs' utterances, the NSs avoid 'doing being second language teachers' and maintain the relevance of their [institutional] role" (p. 156). The frequency of self-repair over other-repair has also been documented by Gardner and Wagner (2004). From this it follows that conversations between native and nonnative speakers should be seen as "normal conversations" in terms of conversational organization found in native speaker interactions where linguistic proficiency is rarely oriented to in terms of repair (Hosoda, 2006, p. 28; Wagner & Gardner, 2004).

While the cases presented show that there are features of the candidates' talk that makes it identifiable as second language talk, the characterization of such features is not of key interest here. Rather, we wish to illuminate the category constitutive process that is triggered by the orientation towards nonnativeness and the pattern in categorical order manifested in this constitutive process. The examples presented reveal the boundaries of normativity related to language use and language ideologies in the given speech situation.

The first example is from an interview with a female internship candidate (IN1) who is being interviewed for an internship at a nursing home. We enter the interaction towards its beginning, when the participants are getting acquainted and have been talking about a training program that IN1 will be doing after completing the internship. The extract begins with the job consultant (CO1) asking the employer (HO1) at the nursing home to share his experience and knowledge about this program. HO1 is male and CO1 is female.

**Extract 1**

```
60      CO₁:    du kender det godt ik os stig
                you know that well not also Stig
                you do know it right Stig
(0.4)
61      CO₁:    det s- det det det grundforløb der↑ på
                that s- that that that basic course there in
62              skolen
                the school
                that basic course in that school

63      HO₁:    .hh jeg [kender] jo: jeg kender lidt til det
                .hh I    know    yes: I  know  little about it
                I know yeah, I know a little bit about it

64      CO₁:            [ja]
                         yes

65      HO₁:    jeg [kender] det jeg [kender] det ikke vældigt
                I    know    it  I    know    it  not  mighty
66              godt
                well
                I know it, I don't know it too well

67      CO₁:            [ja]                [ja]
                         yes                 yes
(.)
68      IN₁:    o:[kay
                o:kay

69      HO₁:    [men øh jeg kender lidt til det
                 but eh I   know little about it
                 but eh I know a little bit about it

70      IN₁:    °ja°
                yes

71      HO₁:    ja
                yes
(0.5)
```

72  HO₁:    øh og når jeg siger jeg kender lidt til det
            eh and when I say  I  know little about it

73          så er det fordi øøh .hhh jeg kend- jeg har
            then it is because eh    I   kno-  I have

74          sådan set studieordningen og f- og v- kender
            so  seen study description and f- and v- know

75          sådan teorien i det kan man sige ik
            so theory  in that can one say not
            and when I say I know a little bit about
            it then it is because eh I am familiar
            with the study description and know the
            theory around it you could say, right

76  IN₁:    °o:[kay°
            o:kay

77  HO₁:    [.hh øh [og] så har vi e- en øh en øh: en
            eh and then have we o- one eh one eh: one
78          i praktik
            in iternship
            eh and then we have one doing and internship

79  IN₁:            [nå]
                     oh

80  HO₁:    her øh som .hh som er på det særlige
            here eh who    who is on the special

81          grundforløb
            basic course
            here who is doing the special basic course

82  IN₁:    °nå ['kay°
            oh 'kay

83  HO₁:        [så]
                 so

84  HO₁:    me[n det] men det [de- det] den erf- det
            but that  but that tha- that the exp-

85          den erfaring
            this experience
            but that's the experience

```
86   IN₁:      [det godt]         [heh. he.]
               that good
               that's good

87   HO₁:      jeg har med det så det jo ikke meget
               I have with it so that you know not much
               I have with it so it's not much isn't it

88   IN₁:      °ja°
               yes
(.)
89   HO₁:      .hh [nej] .hh er det svært f- øh kan du
                    no       is it difficult f- eh can you

90             forstå
               understand
               no, is it difficult, do you understand

91   IN₁:      ['kay]
                'kay

92   HO₁:      hvad jeg siger
               what I   say
               what I'm saying

93   IN₁:      £JA↑AA£
               YE:ES

94   HO₁:      >£det godt£<
               that good
               that's good

95   IN₁:      h[hundrede procent heh. heh. he. jah.]=
                 hundred   percent                yeah

96   HO₁:      [heh. heh. he. he. he.              ]

97   IN₁:      =[heh. heh. .hhhh]

98   CO₁:      [IN er god til dansk]
                IN is good at Danish
```

In this extract, we find the employer's (HO1) orientation towards the proficiency of the candidate (IN1) in lines 89, 90, 92. As he inquires about the understanding of the candidate, he is orienting to IN1's prior responses as displays of language problems. With this question, he simultaneously dissociates IN1 from the category *native speaker* and assigns her the category *nonnative speaker*. From an employer perspective, his inquiry represents a necessary move in determining the premise of the interview but also the basis of the potential internship, where the candidate will be working with elderly and sick people who are likely to need to be able to communicate and be understood. From an ethnomethodological perspective, what is interesting is how the proficiency (or lack hereof) of the candidate is made relevant and addressed by the participants, but not least how particular boundaries of normativity and deviance related to language and language learning manifest in the participants' behaviors and orientations.

Looking at IN1's responses, which are all minimal responses, they do not show direct displays of incomprehension, but there are aspects about them that reveal that IN1 is not a native speaker of Danish, in addition to the fact that IN1's pronunciation is also hearable to the participants as non-standard.

First, the "okay" uttered in line 68 is slightly off as a response to HO1's dispreferred, hesitant, and mitigated expression of limited knowledge about the school. A different and more acceptable response to HO1's admitted limitation in knowledge could be a display of surprise or change of state (Nå ok/oh right with rising intonation), disappointment (nå ok/oh okay with falling intonation) or acceptance (nej nej/no no; Heritage, 1984a).

Similarly, IN1's "yes" in line 70 does not align with the dispreferred formatting of HO1's response, nor with the change formulated in epistemic positioning, which could have been more meaningfully oriented to with a change of state token (nå okay/oh right; Heritage, 1984a). However, one could say that by formatting her response in low voice, IN1 shows an orientation to the difficulty of responding meaningfully to the indeterminacy and insecurity of HO1's answers, which would be a difficult task even for native speakers. The meaning and formatting of HO1's utterances are not easy to respond to because they offer a dispreferred claim to a lack of knowledge. Furthermore, they are primarily responding to and addressing the job consultant, which creates ambiguity around whether a response is even required or expected from the candidate. The contribution of IN1 in line 70 could, in a different context, have gone unnoticed, but within this particular sequential context and setting, it contributes to IN1's display of nonnativeness for the participants. The same can be said about the third response by IN1, another low voice "okay" in line 76, which follows a further account by HO1. While this response is again placed at the end of HO1's turn and could be considered a meaningful epistemic marker in relation to the new information provided by HO, the low voice, the hesitating stretch in vowels, and not least its appearance as part of a series of ambiguous and hesitant responses from IN1, makes it salient as a display of comprehension difficulties. As formulated by Sacks (1972a, 1972b), it follows from the hearers' maxim that if an action can be seen or heard as related to a given category, then it should be heard that way. This principle can be said to provide for the hearing of IN1's utterances as linked to and a predicate for the category of nonnative speaker. It is possible that the continual overlaps by HO1 of IN1's response are action manifestations of his "hearing" of IN1 as less than proficient, since they work to disregard their possible function as sites of turn-shifting. In any case, the overlaps represent an orientation towards IN1 as having a peripheral position in this particular sequence, whether this is related to an institutional categorization of her as an internship candidate, a nonnative speaker, or both.

Another hearable display of nonnativeness can be found in IN1's overlapping "nå'"('oh') in line 79, which is the relevant epistemic marker that could have been meaningfully used earlier and which works as a receipt of new information. However, here the placement is slightly off in that it is delayed as a response to HO1's previous utterance, and too early to relate to the ongoing utterance, considering that HO1 has not yet supplied any additional information but merely taken an in-breath and said "eh." This is yet another display of problems with understanding which is reinforced by the use of the change of state token (Heritage, 1984a) "nå" in line 82, because it constitutes a simultaneous display of understanding and lack of understanding. One could say that the efforts made by IN1 to claim understanding and participation are undermined by her subtle displays of incomprehension.

The indications of nonnativeness do not stop there, however. After HO1 has finished his turn in line 81, and after a 0.2 second pause, IN1 supplies another "oh" followed directly by a "kay," which can be seen as a follow-up and correction of the previous, prematurely placed "oh." Though this displays understanding, it is once again uttered in a low voice. Once more, HO1 overlaps the second half of her "oh kay," this time with a "so," which indicates that HO1 has finished his turn and is giving the floor to the other participants. However, he continues immediately with a closing utterance in lines 84, 85, and 87 that summarizes his previous turns. IN1 overlaps this closing utterance in line 86 with "that's good" and some laughter which can be said to display orientation to HO's previous "so" and its projection of a closing. Nevertheless, she still does not take the opportunity to carry on the conversation in the already established "small talk" format, which can be seen as a misalignment similar to the intercultural miscommunication cases found in Gumperz' and Roberts' gatekeeping studies (Gumperz et al., 1979; Roberts & Campbell, 2005, 2006).

Finally, the clearest indication of nonnativeness can be found in line 88, where IN1 responds with a "yes" to a declaration by HO1, which projects a negative polarity response. HO1 sidesteps this mistake in line 89, in accordance with Kurhila's (2005) findings on native speakers keeping to institutional roles, by supplying the correct response, "no," at the beginning of his next utterance, immediately following an in-breath. This analysis shows how, within the particular context in question, IN1's utterances are heard and understood as predicates of the category nonnative speaker, not on account of their being minimal but because they in various ways contribute to the participants potentially treating them as slightly deviant from the expected interactional norm, which is also what ensues

What is central here, is that the employer orients to these very subtle deviances in behavior as displays of nonnativeness, and he consequently categorizes her as a nonnative, non-proficient speaker. Since HO1's account of his epistemic status and access to the training program in question is at no point addressed directly to IN1, her minimal uptake and response to this issue could have had little effect on the interactional development, if not for this orientation towards proficiency. IN1's less than "perfect" display of understanding could have been "allowed to pass" and the nonnativeness of IN1 could have been less foregrounded. What happens instead is that HO1 addresses the issue of understanding directly, which makes IN1's language membership and non-membership an issue to be defended explicitly by IN1, resulting in a topical side-tracking. We see this in line 93 where IN1 responds to HO's question with a strong positive affirmation that she does indeed understand, which shows an orientation to the challenge that HO1's question represents. Being marked as a nonnative speaker poses an institutional and interactional challenge for IN1 because her proficiency in the target language is central to claiming both equal participation in the interaction, and to presenting herself as a competent future intern.

While it is clear from the analysis of Example 1 that IN1's responses are hearable to the participants as second language talk, IN1's self-defense challenges the established link between nonnative talk and lack of understanding. What is negotiated in this interaction is the meaning of the category nonnative speaker and whether the predicates of this category are lack of proficiency and understanding. What we wish to argue, then, is that the gatekeeping taking place here is not only or even primarily of an institutional nature, such as it is described in previous gatekeeping studies. Rather, it is a gatekeeping related to granting or preventing category membership. While IN1's responses could, in her native-speaking, monolingual context, have been understood or heard as hesitant and withholding responses to a marginal position within an institutional participation framework and in this particular interactional sequence, the participants' orientation to the setting as a linguistic and cultural encounter allows for their hearing of IN1's responses as indications of nonnativeness. This hearing, and the resulting explicit orientation towards IN1 as the nonnative speaker within the context, reproduces an asymmetric relation between the categories *native speaker* and *nonnative speaker*, informed by a monolingual ideology (Karrebæk, 2013) and cultural norm.

The "gates" of monolingual normativity are not only visible in the explicit orientation by HO1 towards a potential lack of understanding, but also in IN1's attempts to comply with the normative expectations of her response tokens. The normative "model" response is heard in her responses as much as her failure to comply adequately with this norm in order to pass. A final point to be made in relation to Example 1 is how IN1's defense leaves the other participants to remedy the flow of the interaction – HO1 orients to it by saying 'that's good' in a fast pace and smile voice. Most interesting, however, is how the job consultant (CO1) steps in to assist IN1's defense with a positive evaluation of her Danish speaking skills in line 39. This works to not only confirm the co-construction of IN1 as a nonnative speaker but also to establish the asymmetry between membership categories, institutional and linguistic alike.

This example thus shows how an explicit inquiry about the candidate's level of comprehension reveals a normative common sense distinguishing between the categories of native speaker and nonnative speaker on the basis of a particular language behavior, that is, ways of showing comprehension rather than grammatical differences. Davies (2003) has also argued that native speakers "expect interaction to be intelligible" in their target language and when faced with responses that do not fit with that expectation, they tend to assume intelligibility is the issue (p. 201). Thus, the same scenario could just as well have been enacted among native speakers, but the addition of 'is it difficult' to the question on comprehension in line 89 actually points to an assumption of lack of proficiency on behalf of the candidate.

In sum, the very idea of non-proficiency becomes an even bigger challenge and obstacle for the nonnative speaker than the challenges of communicating in a second language. We see this challenge manifest itself again in the following example where the problem is not that of assumed miscommunication but of categorization. What is clear is that the essence of the gatekeeping involved in processes of membership categorization is that the candidates are, from the onset, heard and evaluated on the basis of assumptions about a lack in proficiency. This gives reason for the participants to emphasize misunderstanding or lack of understanding which has to be defended and accounted for by the candidate.

In the following example, which is taken from the very beginning of another encounter at a nursing home, the orientation towards the candidate (IN2) as a nonnative speaker gets established without any indication of communicative misunderstandings between the participants. We have included this very beginning of the interaction (lines 1–25) in order to show the nature of the candidate's linguistic behavior, in light of which the employer's direct line of questioning stands out in stark contrast to the otherwise unhindered flow of the interaction. In this interview all participants are female.

## Extract 2

```
1   IN₂:      det første gang jeg kommer i plejehjem
              the first time I come in nursing home
              jeg (blevet) (.) mmhehehmm
2                I became

3   EM/CO₂:   forvirret
              confused

4   IN₂:      (på) mig jah (.) hhe he
              on me yeah
              for me yes

5   EM/CO₂:   hheh

(0.2)

6   HO₂:      har du aldrig set et plejehjem [før]=
              ((very articulated))
              have you never seen a nursing home before

7   IN₂:                                     [nej]
                                              no

8   HO₂:      =alle[rede] på [pleje]hjem
              already in nursing home

9   IN₂:           [nej]      [nej]
                    no          no
(.)
10  HO₂:      nej
              no

(0.3)

11  IN₂:      papir til dig eller til mig
              paper to you or    to me
              is this paper for you or me
(.)
12  HO₂:      det ved jeg ikke
              that know I not
              that I don't know

13  IN₂:      he [he he
```

```
14   HO₂:       [det finder vi lige ud af
                that find we   just out
                let's see if we can find that out

15   IN₂:      °njah°
               myeah

(0.5)((sounds of shuffling paper))

16   HO₂:      nå (.) det er nok det ik' til mig
               well   that is probably that not for me
               well that's probably not for me

17   IN₂:      okay det til mig °jah°
               okay that for me yes
               okay that's for me then

18   HO₂:      det det tror jeg ikke [det er] i hvert fald
               that that think I not   it is  in any case
               at least I don't think that's the case

19   IN₂:                            [jah]
                                     yeah
(.)

20   HO₂:      det det kan du ikke snakke med dem om du ude
               that that can you not talk to them if you out
21             på skolen (0.2) eller undervisningscenteret
               in school         or    teaching center
22             der hvor du går
               there where you go
               could you not talk to them about it at school
               or at the teaching center that you go to

23   IN₂:      jahh (.)°jo°
               yeah    sure
(0.4)

24   HO₂:      øm:
               erm

(0.2)((sounds of pouring water))

25   HO₂:      °jah°
               yeah
```

```
        (.)

26  HO₂:    forstår du alt hvad jeg siger
            ((very articulated))
            understand you everything what I say
            do you understand everything I say
        (.)
27  IN₂:    jah
            yeah

28  HO₂:    det [gør] du
            that do you
            you do

29  IN₂:        [jahh]
                yeahh

30  HO₂:    [fint]
            fine
            good

31  IN₂:    [hhe h]e he

32  HO₂:    ja de- det faktisk rimelig vigtigt at v[ide]
            yes th-that actually fairly important to know
33          fordi
            because
            yes, that's actually quite important to know
            because

34  IN₂:                                            [ja]
                                                    Yes

35  IN₂:    når jeg ikke forstå så spørger jeg °hhe hhe°
            when I not understand then ask I
            when I don't understand I will ask

36  HO₂:    jah
            yeah

37  IN₂:    °ja°
            yes
```

As we can see in this extract, IN2 displays substantial "proficiency" and confidence by opening the interaction with an utterance that works as small talk (line 1) and also works as an immediate disclaimer for whatever non-standard behavior might follow. The completion of IN2 utterance by EM2/CO2 in line 3 can be argued to represent the first orientation towards IN2 as a nonnative speaker, but it does not disrupt the following exchange between the participants nor does it prevent IN2 from continuing to assert herself as an active interlocutor in what follows, where she is not only responsive (line 7 and 9) to HO2's question about her previous encounters with nursing homes (line 6) but also initiates talk about the proper procedures of the paper work (line 11). As in the previous example, HO2's following inquiry about comprehension seems again evoked by assumptions and ideas about nonnativeness and proficiency rather than by the actual communicative and linguistic resources of the candidate.

In this extract, the question of understanding raised by HO2 in line 26 is formatted slightly differently than in the previous example, in that it is stated without hesitation or restarts and with an emphasis on the extent of IN2's understanding rather than on her potential difficulties in understanding. The predicates assigned to IN2, which reveal an orientation to the category of nonnative speaker, are that the candidate understands some, but perhaps not all, of what HO2 says. However, similar to the previous example, the categorization which this entails, of IN2 as a nonnative speaker, is one that cannot be challenged with an affirmative claim of complete understanding, or even with a display of proficiency, whatever that would constitute. Even if the question presents an opportunity to claim, display, and assert proficiency, the mere formulation of the question reveals that the language membership of the candidate is already heard as or expected to be non-standard by the other participants. This is partly due to the institutional particularity of the setting and the monolingual particularity of the broader cultural context. This highlighted "otherness" of IN2 cannot be altered by the response of the candidate, though as we show in the previous and present example, it can be oriented to and challenged.

In this extract, we see how IN2 without any hesitation produces a very clear "yes", which has the same assertive function as the stress, high pitch, and "hundred percent" utterance in the previous example. Regardless, HO2 restates the question in a different formatting in line 28, which works to not only double-check, but also question the response by IN2, who overlaps it with a second "yes." IN2 produces a few laughter particles, once again similar to the previous example, and works to challenge and "ridicule" (Billig, 2005) the question together with its categorical implications by suggesting a contrary "common sense" (Tranekjær, in press). That is, that the candidate is a proficient Danish speaker who otherwise would not participate in the interview in Danish. HO2 acknowledges and responds to this challenge by accounting for and justifying her direct line of questioning. The account "that's actually quite important to know because" (line 32–33) again points to an expectation of communicative problems as the basis of her orientation towards the candidate and the context.

However, this is overlapped and cut off by IN2 with a "yes" in line 34 and with the statement in line 35 that she will ask if she does not understand. Again, we have two laughter particles that on the one hand work to counter and "laugh off" the suggested lack of proficiency, but on the other mitigate the assertive challenge of IN1's response. With this she has claimed her right to be seen as a competent future employee based on target language proficiency. This assertion is accepted by HO2 in line 36.

This example shows how a native speaker can also ascribe the category nonnative speaker to someone without any indication of interactional difficulties. As a result, HO2 establishes a linguistic asymmetry between those participants, who are expected to understand all that she says, and the candidate, who is expected to not fully understand. Although this expectation might be meaningful and valid within the given context, the benefits of clearing up misunderstandings and communication are potentially outweighed by the interactional challenge that the question presents. With HO2's challenge, IN2 has to defend her target language proficiency in order to be seen as a competent employee without overstepping institutional boundaries.

The final example, taken from another nursing home interview, shows a case where the orientation towards nonnativeness is not even related to determining a basis of understanding between the participants, since it is taken from the very end of the interaction. Even though the candidate's expected lack of proficiency is not addressed as a matter of understanding, an understanding of a "problem with proficiency" is here being clearly formulated by HO3. In this example, the central issue is how the candidate should work on improving her proficiency, which reveals not only the monolingual ideology at play but the ideological hierarchization of the categories *Danish* and *migrant*. The participants are all female.

**Extract 3**

```
473    EM₃:   er din mand også fra i:ran((very articulated))
              is your husband also from Iran

474    IN₃:   ja
              yes

475    EM₃:   ja↑
              yes

476    IN₃:   ja=
              yes

477    EM₃:   =[.tsk]

478    ( )    [.hja]
              hyeah

479    EM₃:   så skal i begge [to lære £dansk£=
              ((very articulated))
              then must you both learn Danish
              then you both have to learn Danish

480    IN₃:                   [han kommer (ja/her)=
                              he comes (yes/here)

481    EM₃:   =[sk.ha]    [( )]

482    IN₃:   =[ja] ha ha  [ha ]=

483    CO₃:   [nej han har ]boet her i mange år
              no he has lived here many years
              no he has been living here for many years

484    IN₃:   =[ja::        ]
              ye::s
```

In this extract, it is the employee (EM3) that initiates the "othering" of IN3 by asking whether her husband is also Iranian (line 473), which foregrounds the non-Danishness of the candidate as well as potentially that of the husband. IN3 responds affirmatively with no delay in line 474, which is followed by a rising intonation confirmation token produced by EM3 (line 475) which coveys no indication of surprise. "Ja" as an epistemic marker of information receipt works as a confirmation request by virtue of being produced with rising intonation. The rising intonation works to invite further elaboration from IN3, but instead she merely reconfirms with another "yes' (line 476) that signals a closing of the topic.

EM3 pursues the topic further with another "yes," immediately followed by a clicking sound of the tongue .tsk., which can be seen as an evaluative expression (line 477). The sound is overlapped by another confirmation from IN3 who once again renounces the opportunity to elaborate. At this point, EM3 makes a categorical link between the category membership of *Iranian* and the predicate "having to learn Danish," expressed in the turn-initial particle "so" in line 479 which naturalizes the relation between the category memberships of *Iranian*, *non-Danish*, and *nonnative speaker*. Thus, here, as well as in Example 2, the category nonnative speaker is not brought forward due to any particular interactional complications or ambiguous displays of understanding.

Also similar to Example 2, EM3 makes a point of thoroughly articulating her questions, which can be interpreted as an implicit orientation towards IN3 as a non-proficient and nonnative speaker. As IN3 is made aware in line 479 that the topic addressed by EM3 in line 473 was not fully covered by providing the nationality of the husband, she initiates a further elaboration of their history of migration "he comes yes/here" (line 480). This is formulated in overlap with the final part of EM3's utterance and thereby cut off. Even though IN3 may not have understood that what she is implicitly being told to do is learn Danish, she responds affirmatively to EM3 by providing a few laughter particles, which may be seen as an orientation to the awkwardness of being explicitly told "to do" something by a stranger, let alone being told to learn Danish.

In this example, much as in Example 1, the job consultant orients to the categorization made by EM3 as well as to the imposition and challenge of the demands that she makes. Her response in line 483 that "he has lived here for many years" works to challenge the implication that the husband does not speak Danish simply because he is from Iran. However, the defense that CO3 provides does not challenge the categorization of IN3 as a nonnative speaker which was implied in EM3's linking of nationality and lack of target language proficiency. Though CO3's assertion that the husband has lived here for many years helps to establish that he in fact does already speak Danish, this does not undo the orientation towards the lack of proficiency and the implied otherness of IN3 which EM3's question brought to bear.

Similar to the previous examples, what the extract shows is that the candidates, despite their ability to conduct the interviews in Danish, are oriented to as nonnative speakers with language difficulties, which creates an interactional challenge in that it prevents the foregrounding of alternative co-memberships between the participants in relation to, for example, professional categories.

## Conclusion

This paper has illustrated how nonnative speaker is a membership category that is interactionally established among participants and related to native speakers' expectations and assumptions in terms of the born abroad candidates' target language proficiency. We exemplified cases where the orientation towards a candidate's language-related behavior was brought forward by the interviewers interpreting the candidates' behavior as linguistically non-standard and which point to naturalized, common sense perceptions of a particular language behavioral standard as the preferred and expected norm. As Fukuda (2006) has formulated, it is the native speakers who claim ownership of a language and which in turn points to underlying normative expectations that allow native speakers to evaluate, accept and disapprove of the language use by nonnative speakers (Fukuda, 2006).

The current study suggested a critical focus on the nature of such language norms and the monolingual ideologies that define them. This is because the orientation towards nonnativeness involves a problematic "othering" of the nonnative speaker, which is counterproductive to the candidates' otherwise meaningful and relevant contributions to the ongoing institutional interaction. In line with Kerekes' (2006) findings, the establishment of non-membership, such as othering a candidate on the basis of language proficiency, can serve to hinder the success of the interview for the interviewee, as it is the very establishment of co-membership that works in favor of candidates' success. Kerekes defines success in employment terms, that is whether the candidate is granted a placement. In contrast, the present study emphasizes interactional success or failure as locally constituted in the ongoing talk because the candidates have already been chosen for the position. The internship interviews are thus a mere formality where candidates and employers meet to discuss the internship. Such an interactional focus on institutional encounters has larger implications for the way that candidates have to navigate othering categorization processes during employment interviews, and which in turn can have implications for the success of the interview as a whole.

Thus, the aim of this paper was not to characterize second language talk or showcase instances where candidates failed to be granted an employment placement, but to highlight how the orientation towards a candidate's proficiency works to establish and reinforce asymmetries between interactants and membership categories. Common sense ideas and norms of proficiency, native language, and second language inform this process in ways that make processes of categorization into processes of gatekeeping. We will return to this argument shortly.

In all three examples, linguistic errors or interactional deviances from the expected norm are not oriented to by the interviewers in the form of repairs (Kurhila, 2005; Schegloff, 2000). This can be considered a paradox in light of the degree of explicitness and forwardness exhibited by the employers and employees in relation to proficiency. Nevertheless, in all cases, linguistic asymmetry between the participants is assumed and made explicit by the interviewer, which leaves the candidates to defend their proficiency. In this light, the extended sequence of talk in relation to topicalizing the candidate's proficiency works to sustain the established linguistic asymmetry (Park, 2007, p. 342).

In sum, the cases examined show a pattern in the way that explicit orientation towards a candidate's language proficiency entails a normative presumption of a lack in proficiency purely based on the candidate being foreign born. In this light, the making salient of the presumed linguistic asymmetry works to put a social hierarchy in place in which the "Danishness" of some of the participants and the "otherness" of the candidate on linguistic grounds involves an uneven distribution of knowledge, rights, and status, which in turn is part and parcel of gatekeeping.

Day (1998) argued that ascriptions to specific ethnic groups (e.g., Pakistani or Swedish) may present an interactional problem for the person being categorized and that interactants employ different resistance strategies to the ethnification taking place. Fukuda (2006) presents a similar research perspective yet focuses on moments of "exoticization" in native and nonnative Japanese speaker interactions. The study reminds us that it is the ideological assumptions and particular common sense that underline utterances which work to exoticize another and thereby assert asymmetrical power relations with respect to being a native or nonnative speaker. More importantly, by assuming a certain inferiority of proficiency in the case of a nonnative speaker and thereby constructing them as an other, it is the native speaker who embodies the ideology of asymmetry rather than the nonnative speaker with his/her demonstration of proficiency (Fukuda, 2006, p. 452). Along the lines of this argument, Nishizaka (1995, 1999) observes that the various characteristics of an individual are socially constituted but also act as resources for establishing someone as not belonging or, in this instance, as a nonnative speaker. It is a participant choice to topicalize certain perceived or assumed deviations, whereby the choice to do so has considerable implications for the trajectory that an interaction can subsequently take. We wish to argue that the systematic foregrounding of language proficiency also represents examples of "ethnification" or "exoticization" and that the defenses by candidates and job consultants alike reveal that gatekeeping processes are central to the language categorizations illuminated here.

Our analysis of how the membership category of nonnative speaker is established and made relevant in three different ways showed how orienting to the candidate as a nonnative speaker posed a bigger challenge for the candidates than the interview conducted in a nonnative language itself. This orientation worked to make the linguistic asymmetry in the speech setting salient and underlined the gatekeeping nature of the encounters. We have also shown how sense-making practices about nonnativeness are informed by culturally established asymmetries between broader membership categories that are linked to but not solely defined by an institutional order.

Thus, in this paper we presented gatekeeping as an intrinsic part of categorization processes rather than merely an institutional phenomenon. As suggested by the examples presented here, gatekeeping is at play in the establishment and reproduction of relations between categories, predicates, and actions, which work to uphold a hierarchical organization of categories and members. While such processes can be linked to the interactional constitution of institutional membership categories and contexts, they are also intimately linked with the asymmetries established within a broader cultural and categorical context.

This broader cultural and categorical context is drawn upon by participants by way of the inferences that interactants make about one another, which are informed by their knowledge and expectations of a particular category and in turn set up expectations of behavior from others. In this sense, gatekeeping is quite fundamentally an essential part of the cultural processes in which boundaries of normativity and deviance are established and maintained (Tranekjær, 2015). The central argument of this paper with regards to gatekeeping is that the establishment and negative valorization of difference through processes of membership categorization in relation to target language proficiency is what constitutes the barrier for candidates who are seen to fall outside established boundaries of language-related normativity. Gatekeeping is thus not only or even primarily of an institutional nature, but related to granting and preventing category membership on linguistic grounds as well.

### Notes

1 The recordings have been transcribed following a simplified version of the transcription conventions developed by Gail Jefferson as described by Atkinson & Heritage (1984) and Hutchby & Wooffitt (1998). These are described in the Appendix.
2 *Born abroad* is a term to indicate migrants and refugees who are not born in Denmark but have come to Denmark during their adulthood. It is a term used by Roberts and Campbell (2006) in their study of job interviews in Britain.

## References

Akinnaso, F. N., & Seabrook Ajirotutu, C. (1982). Performance and ethnic style in job interviews. In J. Gumperz (Ed.), *Language and social identity* (pp. 119–144). Cambridge: Cambridge University Press.

Antaki, C., & Widdicombe, S. (Eds.). (1998). *Identities in talk*. London: Sage.

Atkinson, J. M., & Heritage, J. (1984). *The structure of social action. Studies in conversation analysis*. Cambridge: Cambridge University Press.

Auer, P. (1998). Learning how to play the game: An investigation of role-played job interviews in East Germany. *Text, 18*, 7–38.

Auer, P., & Kern, F. (2001). Three ways of analysing communication between East and West Germans as intercultural communication In A. D. Luzio, S. Günthner, & F. Orletti (Eds.), *Culture in communication: Analyses of intercultural situations* (pp. 89–116). Philadelphia, PA: John Benjamins.

Baptise, M. C., & Seig, M. T. (2007). Training the guardians of America's gate: Discourse-based lessons from naturalization interviews. *Journal of Pragmatics, 39*, 1919–1941.

Benati, A. (2009). *Issues in second language proficiency*. London: Continuum.

Billig, M. (1996). *Arguing and thinking: A rhetorical approach to social psychology.* Cambridge: Cambridge University Press.

Billig, M. (2005). *Laughter and ridicule. Towards a social critique of humour.* London: Sage.

Blackledge, A. (2005). *Discourse and power in a multilingual world.* Amsterdam: John Benjamins.

Britzman, D. P., Santiago-Válles, K., Jiménez-Múñoz, G., & Lamash, L. M. (1993). Slips that show and tell: Fashioning multicultural as a problem of representation In C. McCarthy & W. Crichlow (Eds.), *Race, identity and representation in education* (pp. 188–200). New York, NY: Routledge.

Brown, A. (2003). Interviewer variation and the co-construction of speaking proficiency. *Language Testing, 20,* 1–25.

Campbell, S., & Roberts, C. (2007). Migration, ethnicity and competing discourses in the job interview: Synthesizing the institutional and personal. *Discourse & Society, 18,* 243–271.

Davies, A. (2003). *The native speaker myth and reality.* Clevedon: Multilingual Matters.

Day, D. (1998). Being ascribed, and resisting, membership of an ethnic group. In C. Antaki & S. Widdicombe (Eds.), *Identities in talk* (pp. 151–171). London: Sage.

Day, D. (2006). Ethnic and social groups and their linguistic categorization. In K. Buehrig & J. T. Thie (Eds.), *Beyond misunderstanding, the linguistic analysis of intercultural discourse* (pp. 217–244). The Hague: John Benjamins.

Drew, P., & Heritage, J. (Eds.). (1992). *Talk at work: Interaction in institutional settings.* Cambridge: Cambridge University Press.

Erickson, F., & Schultz, J. (1982). *The counselor as gatekeeper: Social interaction in interviews.* New York, NY: Academic Press.

Fogtmann, C. (2007). *Samtaler med politiet* [Conversations with the police]. (Doctoral thesis, University of Copenhagen).

Freeman-Larsen, D., & Long, M. (1991). *An introduction to second language acquisition research.* London: Longman.

Fukuda, C. (2006). Resistance to being formulated as cultural other: The case of a Chinese student in Japan. *Pragmatics, 16,* 429–456.

Gardner, R., & Wagner, J. (2004). *Second language conversations. Studies of communication in everyday settings.* London: Continuum.

Garfinkel, H. (1967). *Studies in ethnomethodology.* Englewood Cliffs, NJ: Prentice-Hall.

Goffman, E. (1963). *Stigma. Notes on the management of spoiled identity.* Englewood Cliffs, NJ: Prentice-Hall.

Gumperz, J. J. (Ed.). (1982). *Language and social identity.* Cambridge: Cambridge University Press.

Gumperz, J. J., Roberts, C., & Jupp, T. C. (1979). *Crosstalk: A study of cross-cultural communication.* London: National Centre for Industrial Language Training in association with BBC.

Hall, S. (1997). *Representation cultural representations and signifying practices.* London: SAGE in association with The Open University.

Heritage, J. (1984a). A change-of-state token and aspects of its sequential placement. In J. M. Atkinson & J. Heritage (Eds.), *Structures of social action. Studies in conversation analysis* (pp. 299–346). Cambridge: Cambridge University Press.

Heritage, J. (1984b). *Garfinkel and ethnomethodology.* Cambridge: Polity Press.

Hester, S., & Eglin, P. (1997). The reflexive constitution of category, predicate and context. In S. Hester & P. Eglin (Eds.), *Culture in action. Studies in membership categorization analysis* (pp. 25–49). Washington, DC: International Institute for Ethnomethodology and Conversation Analysis & University Press of America.

Higgins, C. (2009). "Are you Hindu?:" Resisting membership categorization through language alternation. In H. t. Nguyen & G. Kasper (Eds.), *Talk-in-interaction: Multilingual perspectives* (pp. 111–136). University of Hawai'i: National Foreign language Resource Center.

Holmes, J. (2007). Monitoring organisational boundaries: Diverse discourse strategies used in gatekeeping. *Journal of Pragmatics, 39*, 1993–2016.

Hosoda, Y. (2006). Repair and relevance of differential language expertise in second language conversations. *Applied Linguistics, 27*, 25–50.

Hulstijn, J. (2011). Language proficiency in native and nonnative speakers: An agenda for research and suggestions for second-language assessment. *Language Assessment Quarterly, 8*, 229–249.

Hutchby, I., & Wooffitt, R. (1998). *Conversation analysis.* Cambridge: Polity.

Jayyusi, L. (1984). *Categorization and the moral order.* Boston, MA: Routledge.

Jefferson, G. (Ed.). (1992). *Harvey Sacks. Lectures on Conversation* (5th ed.). Malden, MA: Blackwell.

Karrebæk, M. S. (2013). "Don't speak like that to her!" Linguistic minority children's socialisation into an ideology of monolingualism. *Journal of Sociolinguistics, 17*, 355–375.

Kasper, G. (2004). Participant orientations in German conversation-for-learning. *The Modern Language Journal, 88*, 551–567.

Kasper, G., & Ross, S. J. (2007). Multiple questions in oral proficiency interviews. *Journal of Pragmatics, 39*, 2045–2070.

Kerekes, J. A. (2006). Winning an interviewer's trust in a gatekeeping encounter. *Language in Society, 35*, 27–57.

Kerekes, J. A. (2007a). The co-construction of a gatekeeping encounter: An inventory of verbal actions. *Journal of Pragmatics, 39*, 1942–1973.

Kerekes, J. A. (2007b). Introduction to the special issue "High stakes gatekeeping encounters and their consequences: Discourses in intercultural institutional settings." *Journal of Pragmatics, 39*, 1891–1894.

Komter, M. (1991). *Conflict and cooperation in job interviews: A study of talk, tasks, and ideas.* Amsterdam: John Benjamins.

Kurhila, S. (2004). Clients or language learners—being a second language speaker in institutional interaction. In R. Gardner & J. Wagner (Eds.), *Second language conversations* (pp. 58-74). London: Continuum.

Kurhila, S. (2005). Different orientations to grammatical correctness. In K. Richards & P. Seedhouse (Eds.), *Applying conversation analysis* (pp. 143-158). Basingstoke: Palgrave Macmillan.

Lepper, G. (2000). *Categories in text and talk.* London: Sage Publication.

Mondada, L. (2004). Ways of 'doing being plurilingual' in international work meetings. In R. Gardner & J. Wagner (Eds.), *Second language conversations* (pp. 18-39). London: Continuum.

Nishizaka, A. (1995) The interactive constitution of interculturality: How to be a Japanese with words. *Human Studies, 18*, 301-326.

Nishizaka, A. (1999) Doing interpreting within interaction: The interactive accomplishments of a "Henna Gaijin" or "Strange Foreigner". *Human Studies, 22*, 235-251.

Norton, B. (2013). *Identity and Language Learning (2nd ed.): Extending the Conversation.* Harlow: Longman.

Okada, Y. (2010). Role-play in oral proficiency interviews: Interactive footing and interactional competencies. *Journal of Pragmatics, 42*, 1647-1668.

Park, J. (2007). Co-construction of nonnative speaker identity in cross-cultural interaction. *Applied Linguistics, 28*, 339-360.

Potter, J., & Wetherell, M. (1987). *Discourse and social psychology. Beyond attitudes and behaviour.* London: Sage Publications.

Rampton, M. (1990). Displacing the "native Speaker": Expertise, affiliation, and inheritance. *ELT Journal, 44*, 97-101.

Roberts, C., & Campbell, S. (2005). Fitting stories into boxes: Rhetorical and textual restraints on candidates' performances in British job-Interviews. *Journal of Applied Linguistics, 2*, 45-74.

Roberts, C., & Campbell, S. (2006). *Talk on trial: Job-interviews, language and ethnicity.* Leeds: Corporate Document Services.

Roberts, C., & Moss, B. (2004). Presentation of self and symptoms in primary care consultations involving patients from non-English speaking backgrounds. *Communication and Medicine, 11*, 159-170.

Roberts, C., & Sarangi, S. (Eds.). (1999). *Talk, work and institutional order: Discourse in medical, mediation and management settings.* Berlin: Mouton de Gruyter.

Ross, S. J. (2007). A comparative task-in-interaction analysis of OPI backsliding. *Journal of Pragmatics, 39*, 2017-2044.

Sacks, H. (1972a). An initial investigation of the usability of conversational data for doing sociology. In D. Sudnow (Ed.), *Studies in social interaction* (pp. 31-74). New York, NY: The Free Press.

Sacks, H. (1972b). On the analyzability of stories by children. In J. Gumperz & D. Hymes (Eds.), *Directions in sociolinguistics* (pp. 329-345). New York, NY: Holt, Rinehart & Winston.

Sacks, H. (1995). "We"; Category-bound activities, Spring 1966. In G. Jefferson (Ed.), *Lectures on conversation* (pp. 333–340). Cambridge: Blackwell.

Schegloff, E. (1997a). Practices and actions: Boundary cases of other-initiated repair. *Discourse Processes, 23*, 499–545.

Schegloff, E. (1997b). Third turn repair. In G. R. Guy, C. Feagin, D. Schiffrin, & J. Baugh (Eds.), *Towards a social science of language 2* (pp. 31–41). Amsterdam: John Benjamins.

Schegloff, E. (2000). When "others" initiate repair. *Applied Linguistics, 21*, 205–243.

Schegloff, E. (2007a). *Sequence organization in interaction: A primer in conversation analysis 1*. Cambridge: Cambridge University Press.

Schegloff, E. (2007b). A tutorial on membership categorization. *Journal of Pragmatics, 39*, 462–482.

Schegloff, E., Jefferson, G., & Sacks, H. (1977). The preference for self-correction in the organization of repair in conversation. *Language, 73*, 361–382.

Scheuer, J. (2001). Recontextualization and communicative styles in job interviews. *Discourse Studies, 3*, 223–248.

Sundberg, G. (2004). Asymetrier och samförstånd i rekryteringssamtal med andraspråkstalare [Asymmetries and mutual understanding in employment interviews with second language speakers]. Stockholm: Almqvist & Wiksell International.

Svennevig, J. (2004). Other-repetition as display of hearing, understanding and emotional stance. *Discourse Studies, 6*, 489–516.

Svennevig, J. (2005). Repetisjon og reformulering som forståelsesstrategier i andrespråkssamtaler [Repetition and reformulation as understanding strategies in second language conversations]. In S. E. A. Lie (Ed.), *MONS 10 Utvalde artikler frå det tiande Møte om norsk språk I Kristiansand 2003* [Selected papers from the tenth meeting on the Norwegian language in Kristiansand 2003]. Kristiansand, Norway: Høyskoleforlaget.

Svennevig, J. (2013). Reformulation of questions with candidate answers. *INterantional Journal of Bilingualism.* 17(2) 189-204.

Tranekjær, L. (2015). *Interactional categorisation and gatekeeping: Institutional encounters with otherness*. Clevedon: Multilingual Matters.

Tranekjær, L. (in press). Laughables as an investigation of co-membership through the negotiation of epistemics. In D. V. D. Mieroop & S. Schnurr (Eds.), *Identity struggles at work*. Amsterdam: John Benjamins.

Trinch, S. (2007). Deconstructing the "stakes" in high stakes gatekeeping interviews: Battered women and narration. *Journal of Pragmatics, 39*, 1895–1918.

Watson, R. (1997). Some general reflections on "categorization" and "sequence" in the analysis of conversation. In S. Hester & P. Eglin (Eds.), *Culture in action: Studies in membership categorization analysis* (pp. 49–75). Washington, DC: International Institute for Ethnomethodology and Conversation Analysis & University Press of America.

Wong, J. (2000). Delayed next turn repair initiation in native/non-native speaker English conversation. *Applied Linguistics, 21*, 244–267.

Zimmerman, D. H. (1998). Identity, context and interaction. In C. Antaki & S. Widdicombe (Eds.), *Identities in talk* (pp. 87–106). London: Sage.

## Appendix: Transcription notations

| | |
|---|---|
| (.) | Just noticeable pause or micro-pause (less than 0.2 seconds) |
| (2.6) | Pauses timed in seconds |
| [nå] | denotes overlapping talk |
| hh. | In-breath |
| hh | Out-breath |
| ja- | Dash denotes sharp cut-off |
| wha:t | Colon denotes extension or stretching of the preceding sound |
| (word) | Brackets around words denotes a guess at what might have been said if unclear |
| ja=<br>=nå | Equal sign denotes that there is no discernible pause between two speakers' turns or, if put between two sounds within a single speaker's turns, shows that they run together |
| word | Underlined sounds are stressed |
| WORD | Words or sounds in capitals are spoken in loud voice |
| °word° | Material between "degree signs" is spoken in low voice |
| >word< | Inwards arrows show faster speech |
| £word£ | Material between pound signs are spoken in "smile" voice |
| ↑word | Upwards arrow denotes a rising intonation |

# Research in Pedagogical Contexts

# Effects of Metapragmatic Instruction on the Production of Compliments and Compliment Responses: Learner–learner Role-plays in the Foreign Language Classroom

Maria Hasler-Barker
Sam Houston State University, USA

The compliment-compliment response sequence has a great deal of social utility for building solidarity (Haverkate, 2004) and as a social lubricant (Wolfson, 1983). This chapter reports the effects of metapragmatic instruction of this sequence on intermediate learners of Spanish as a foreign language. Though there is research on both compliments and compliment responses, as well as on instruction of speech acts, this study not only analyzes both acts in the compliment-compliment response sequence together, but also looks at intermediate-level learners rather than advanced learners. The role-play data come from 26 learners of Spanish across three conditions (explicit instruction, implicit instruction, and a control group) and from two groups of native speakers. Instructed learners participated in awareness activities and cross-cultural analysis using authentic language samples, and had an opportunity for controlled and guided practice. Pretest, posttest, and delayed posttest role-plays were transcribed and analyzed for compliment and compliment response strategies. Learner production was compared to both native speaker groups, across testing times, and between learner groups. The results show advantages for learners in both instructional conditions over the control group, indicating that intermediate-level learners can benefit from instruction, and that both types of instruction are advantageous and may be combined for pedagogical success.

## Introduction

Previous research has indicated that pragmatics is both teachable and beneficial to learners (e.g., Bardovi-Harlig, 1999a; Félix-Brasdefer & Cohen, 2012; Ishihara & Cohen, 2010; Kasper & Rose, 2002; Olshtain & Cohen, 1990; Rose, 2005; Tatsuki & Houck, 2010). Much of this research has focused on learners at advanced levels, though mixed results at lower levels of proficiency leave questions about the effectiveness of instruction for beginning and intermediate learners. Based on the findings of these and other studies, researchers have made recommendations for teaching pragmatics in the classroom. They propose that pragmatic instruction should include awareness activities, authentic language samples, input prior to interpretation (Bardovi-Harlig & Mahan-Taylor, 2003; Félix-Brasdefer, 2008; García, 1996), cross-cultural analysis (Cohen, 2005; Félix-Brasdefer, 2008; García, 2001; Takahashi, 2001), form-focused instruction, controlled and guided practice, and communication strategies (Ishihara & Cohen, 2010; Tatsuki & Houck, 2010).

The present study operationalizes the activities suggested above in order to teach compliments and compliment responses to intermediate-level learners of Spanish as a foreign language (FL). These speech acts are important because they frequently occur as openers or continuers in interaction and help to build solidarity. In essence, they function as social lubricants (Wolfson, 1983). Because compliments and compliment responses have such great social utility, they are important for learner pragmatic development and can even lead to enhanced interaction with native speakers (NSs; Billmyer, 1990).

This paper analyzes the effects of pedagogical intervention on compliment and compliment response production. The study also highlights the need to engage more than one method of analysis to better understand learner production. Section 2 addresses relevant theoretical constructs and identifies gaps in the previous research. The method, including participant information, data collection procedures, and pedagogical treatment, is presented in section 3. Results are described in section 4. The discussion in section 5 includes pedagogical implications, as well as limitations and areas for future research. Section 6 consists of concluding remarks.

## Theoretical framework

### Previous research on L2 pragmatic instruction

Interlanguage pragmatics, or the "pragmatics of language learners" (Bardovi-Harlig, 1999a, p. 678), forms a central component of learners' communicative competence. Unfortunately, this area is frequently neglected in language teaching, as well as in teacher training programs, despite learner-demonstrated need and even desire for this type of metapragmatic instruction (Bardovi-Harlig,

2001; Bardovi-Harlig & Mahan-Taylor, 2003; Pearson, 2006). This need is exacerbated in FL learning environments where authentic input in the target language is minimal or nonexistent. In fact, research has demonstrated that, regardless of the learning context, metapragmatic instruction is more beneficial than input alone (Kasper, 1996; 2001; Kasper & Rose, 2002; Olshtain & Cohen, 1990; Roever, 2009; Rose, 2005), and that explicit metapragmatic instruction is the most effective type of instruction (e.g., Cohen, 1996; 2005; 2009; Koike & Pearson, 2005). The present study contributes to the growing body of research on metapragmatic instruction in languages other than English and adds to our knowledge of developmental pragmatics (Bardovi-Harlig, 2013). The present examination of the effects of instruction on learner–learner role-play data highlights the complexity of acquiring new pragmatic structures and the need for pedagogical intervention to aid in the process.

Current research suggests that metapragmatic instruction should incorporate many components: awareness activities, authentic language samples, input preceding interpretation (Bardovi-Harlig & Mahan-Taylor, 2003; Félix-Brasdefer, 2008; García, 1996), cross-cultural comparison (Cohen, 2005; Félix-Brasdefer, 2008; García, 2001; Takahashi, 2001), form-focused instruction, and controlled and guided practice (Ishihara & Cohen, 2010; Tatsuki & Houck, 2010). These elements are firmly grounded in second language acquisition (SLA) theory, including input (Krashen, 1985), awareness (Schmidt, 1990; 1993a; 1993b), and communicative competence (Canale, 1983; Celce-Murcia, 2008). By providing metapragmatic instruction, FL teachers provide the opportunity to "raise learners' pragmatic awareness and to give them choices about their interactions in the target language" (Bardovi-Harlig & Mahan-Taylor, 2003, p. 5).

## Compliment and compliment responses

Compliments and compliment responses are expressive speech acts (Searle, 1976). The two speech acts are inextricably intertwined and must be considered together in order to understand their function in interaction (see Félix-Brasdefer, 2014, for a discussion of speech act sequences). Compliments and compliment responses function primarily to reinforce positive face and emphasize solidarity (Haverkate, 2004). They are social lubricants that can mitigate criticism, extend or open conversation, and smooth apologies (Wolfson, 1983). In both English and Spanish, compliments and compliment responses are strikingly formulaic, comprising only a few syntactic (compliments) or semantic (compliment responses) formulas (see Figures 1 and 2). The crucial interactional features, social utility, and relatively simple formulas of this speech act sequence makes it an ideal target for Spanish FL instruction, particularly at early stages of language acquisition.

**American English**

85% of all compliments follow three syntactic patterns:
- NP {is/looks} (really) ADJ
  (e.g., *Your hair looks nice*)
- I (really) {like/love} NP
  (e.g., *I really like those shoes*)
- PRO is (really) (a) ADJ NP
  (e.g., *That is a nice jacket*)

**Spanish**

60-80% of compliments follow seven syntactic patterns
- ¡Qué + Adj + Noun + (VP)!
  (e.g., *¡Qué bonito vestido!*; What a pretty dress!)
- ¡Qué + Adv + Verb {estar/ser/verse/quedar/andar} + (NP)!
  (e.g., *¡Qué padre está tu playera!*; What a cool t-shirt!)
- VP + (Intensifier) Adj + (Noun)
  (e.g., *Tienes bonitos ojos*; You have pretty eyes)
- (Pro) {verse/quedar/andar} Adj/Adv (NP)
  (e.g., *Te queda bien*; It suits you)
- (Tu) + (Noun) + VP + Adj/Adv + (Noun)
  (e.g., *Tu trabajo estuvo muy bien*; your work was really well done)
- PRO + {gustar/encantar/fascinar} + NP
  (e.g., *Me gusta tu casa*; I like your house)
- (Noun) VP + NP
  (e.g., *Eres un ángel*; You're an angel)

**Figure 1.** Most frequent compliment formulas in English and Spanish (Félix-Brasdefer & Hasler-Barker, 2012; Hernández-Herrero, 1999; Kryston-Morales, 1997; Manes & Wolfson, 1980; Nelson & Hall, 1999; Placencia & Yepez, 1999).

**American English**

Compliment responses are semantically formulaic
- Acceptance
- Agreement
- Upgrade
- Self-praise
- Downgrade
- Reassignment of praise
- Returns

**Spanish**

Compliment responses are semantically formulaic
- Acceptance
- Agreement
- Upgrade
- Downgrade
- Reassignment of praise
- Returns
- Lend/give
- Expansion/Confirmation

**Figure 2.** Most frequent compliment response formulas in English and Spanish (Lorenzo-Dus, 2001; Pomerantz, 1978; Valdés & Pino, 1981; Wierzbicka, 2003)

For NSs of English learning Spanish, two compliment formulas can be problematic. First, NSs of Spanish tend to produce *¡Qué+ADJ/ADV+Noun/Verb!* more frequently than other types of compliments. The corresponding strategy in English, *How/What+ADJ/ADV+Noun/Verb* occurs very infrequently in Wolfson's (1983) American English data. Furthermore, Spanish FL learners are taught *Me gusta/encanta+(NP)* (I like+NP; NP is pleasing to me) early and often. This compliment type roughly corresponds to the frequent English strategy, *I like+NP*. However, this strategy is infrequent among NSs of Spanish. Together, these two cross-linguistic factors, combined with the one-to-one principle (Andersen, 1984), may contribute to learners rarely, if ever, producing *¡Qué+ADJ/ADV+Noun/Verb!* and heavily overproducing *Me+gusta/encanta+NP*. It is possible that interlocutors may not recognize compliments as such when producing forms that are cross-culturally different.

In addition to these potentially problematic compliment formulas, learners need to be made aware of semantic differences in compliment responses. In American English, speakers may respond by offering some sort of self-praise (e.g., "I worked really hard on my project"). This strategy is not attested in previous research on Spanish compliment responses (Lorenzo-Dus, 2001; Valdés & Pino, 1981). Meanwhile, NSs of Spanish may seek expansion or confirmation (i.e., fishing for a compliment) of the original compliment. These strategies are not attested in the research on American English compliment responses and, in fact, may be considered rude (Pomerantz, 1978; Wierzbicka, 2003). In particular, the cross-cultural differences between compliment response types have potential for confusion or embarrassment for the interlocutors, which could lead to pragmatic failure (Thomas, 1995).

The present study operationalizes the suggestions made by previous researchers (Bardovi-Harlig & Mahan-Taylor, 2003; Cohen, 2005; Félix-Brasdefer, 2008; García, 1996; 2001; Ishihara & Cohen, 2010; Takahashi, 2001; Tatsuki & Houck, 2010) in order to test the effectiveness of metapragmatic instruction on compliment and compliment response production. It also seeks to understand whether instruction has an effect on learners' ability to engage their pragmatic knowledge to make choices in their interactions (Bardovi-Harlig & Mahan-Taylor, 2003). Role-plays were chosen for this study because they permit researchers to test learners' interaction while still maintaining some control over variables that allow for comparison (Félix-Brasdefer, 2010).

The study was guided by the following research questions:

- Does the frequency of production of compliments and compliment responses in learner–learner role-plays change following metapragmatic instruction?
- Do learners become more variable in their production of compliment and compliment response types following instruction, thus taking advantage of the choices they have in interaction?

# Method

## Participants

Participants in the present study included three intact classes of fourth-semester Spanish, divided across three learning conditions (explicit instruction, implicit instruction, and control group; see Table 1). The instructors were three NSs of English, all with 4+ years of teaching experience, 10+ years of formal Spanish language study, and 6+ months of residency in a Spanish-speaking country. The initial group of learners included 60 fourth-semester students (38 female; 22 male). A total of 26 learners (17 female; 9 male) completed all components of the study, as described in the following sections, and were included in the analysis.

**Table 1.** Fourth-semester learners of Spanish, demographic information.

| condition | participants | age (M) | years studying Spanish (M) |
|---|---|---|---|
| explicit | 9 (6 F; 3 M) | 19.7 (19–21 years) | 5.2 (3–10 years) |
| implicit | 10 (6 F; 4 M) | 19.9 (19–21 years) | 5.6 (1.5–14 years) |
| control | 7 (5 F; 2 M) | 20.0 (19–21 years) | 4 (2–5 years) |
| total | 26 (17 F; 9 M) | 19.9 (19–21 years) | 4.9 (1.5–14 years) |

In addition to the instructor and learner populations, a NS of English group and a NS of Spanish group served as a baseline. The NS of English group consisted of 33 students aged 18–21 years while the NS of Spanish group consisted of FL instructors. The latter group, which comprised 21 NSs of Spanish, ranging in age from 24–47 years, from several Spanish-speaking countries (Argentina, Colombia, Costa Rica, Mexico, Peru, Puerto Rico, Spain, and US-born bilingual), was selected because they were language instructors in the language department of the learners' university and were the most likely candidates to provide NS input for the learner group.

### Data collection procedures

Role-plays were conducted in learner–learner dyads. The learners participated in a pretest three weeks prior to receiving any treatment. They then completed a posttest the class period following open role-play practice (one to two days later). Finally, four weeks following the posttest, participants completed a delayed posttest.

Participants were instructed to interact for as long as they felt comfortable during the role-play, generally between 30 seconds to two minutes. Participants had 20 minutes[1] to complete seven role-play scenarios (one distractor and six compliment-compliment response scenarios). The interactions were audio recorded.

### Instructional treatment

Instruction closely followed suggestions made by Bardovi-Harlig and Mahan-Taylor (2003), Ishihara & Cohen (2010), and Tatsuki and Houck (2010), including awareness activities, cross-cultural comparisons, authentic language samples, input preceding interpretation, form-focused instruction, and controlled and guided practice. Instructors had not taken linguistics courses and were not trained in teaching pragmatics; rather they were provided with detailed scripts for the approximately 50 minutes of total instruction time[2] (20 minutes for compliments, 20 minutes for compliment responses, and 10 minutes for role-play practice). Instruction on compliments was presented to the learners first and, due to course scheduling, compliment responses were presented 10 days later. In the next class period (two days following the compliment response module), learners in all three groups participated in controlled and guided practice through open role-plays.

In both the implicit and explicit instruction groups, learners were introduced to the concept of communicative actions (Félix-Brasdefer, 2015), thus raising their awareness of metapragmatic concepts. Learners in the control group did not receive this introduction.

All groups, including the control group, then saw and heard the same input in the form of recorded dialogues in both English in Spanish (Cohen, 2015; Félix-Brasdefer, 2015). Though recorded, planned dialogues are not as authentic as spontaneous natural speech; they were used in the present study because they contained simplified oral language that was accessible to intermediate learners. Prior to interpreting any aspect of the dialogues, learners in all groups listened to or watched the input twice.

The instructed learners' attention was drawn to metapragmatic aspects of the dialogues (e.g., complimented attribute). Learners in the control group focused on the content of the dialogues (e.g., the name of the participants) rather than on metapragmatic aspects.

Participants in the instructional groups did a cross-cultural comparison of Spanish and English compliments and compliment responses. Both instructional groups then did activities to focus their attention on the form of compliments/compliment responses. In the explicit instruction group, they were provided patterns (e.g., compliment-compliment response types) with which to analyze a set of speech acts, while the implicit instruction group derived patterns from the same set of speech acts.

Following the two 20-minute instructional modules, all learners participated in 10 minutes of role-play practice. They were provided with four scenarios in which they could practice giving and responding to compliments in a controlled environment. Ten role-plays were created for the study, four for practice and six for data collection. All were designed with two crucial characteristics in mind. First, learners never had to play a role that they would not normally have held, such as teacher or doctor (Hudson, Detmer, & Brown, 1995). Second, interlocutor characteristics were clearly identified to encourage participants to imagine the same interlocutor (see Figure 3 for an example of a role-play description; Bardovi-Harlig, 1999b). The role-play scenarios were created based on situations described in the previous literature and informal interviews with NSs of Spanish.

**PARTNER A**
You have been in (*Spanish-speaking country of your choice*) for the entire summer and it is now time to return home. You have been looking for months for the perfect souvenirs to take home to your family. You have been able to find a souvenir for everyone except for your father. He is very difficult to shop for and always tells you that you do not need to bring him anything. However, you want to find something you know he will love. You have shopped in nearly every store in the city you live in and haven't found what you're looking for yet. You enter a store that you have never been to and find exactly what you want in a display case at the front of the store. As the salesperson rings up your purchase, you notice that he/she is wearing lime green sneakers with red soles and shoelaces. Give the salesperson a compliment on his/her shoes.

**PARTNER B**
You have worked at a tourist shop in (*Spanish-speaking country of your choice*) for the entire summer and only have a few weeks left before returning to the university for the fall. You have enjoyed your job because it has allowed you to meet people from all over the world. You also met several co-workers who have become your friends. One of your co-workers has a good sense of style and has taught you a few things about choosing high quality, interesting clothes. Today you are wearing a new pair of sneakers that you recently purchased. They are unusual because they are lime green with red laces and soles. A customer arrives in the shop at the end of a long day of work. You notice that you are about the same age. After looking around for a few minutes, the customer identifies an item that he/she wants to buy. You have a brief conversation as you ring up the purchase.

**Figure 3.** Role-play prompt. This type of prompt was used in role-play practice as well as in the pretest, posttest, and delayed posttest.

## Data analysis

Role-play data were transcribed using Jefferson's (2004) transcription conventions; the transcriptions were then checked for accuracy by another researcher. All instances of compliments and compliment responses were counted in order to have a complete overview of this speech act sequence in context. Data were coded for compliment and compliment response type and were also checked by another researcher. Interrater reliability for both transcription and coding was 90%. All cases were resolved after a discussion between the two coders/transcribers. In addition to coding for overall compliment frequencies, a type analysis was conducted for each learner in order to tease out individual results. Compliment and compliment response types were tallied for each participant. These counts were also averaged to identify group trends. The results of the study are presented in the following sections.

## Results

Results are presented here by each of the research questions that guide this study. The results are supplemented by a sequential analysis presented at the end of this section.

### Research question #1: Effects of instruction on frequency of compliments and compliment responses

Research question #1 asked whether metapragmatic instruction had an effect on the frequency of production of compliments and compliment responses in learner–learner role-plays. The results are discussed here in terms of distribution and frequency of compliment and compliment response strategies.

## Distribution and frequency of compliment strategies

Table 2 presents overall frequency results for the pretest, posttest, and delayed posttest by treatment condition (i.e., explicit, implicit, and control) alongside the NS baseline data. The results are presented first by percentage of total compliments (%): (320 compliments produced by 26 learners in six roleplay scenarios per testing period; 166 compliments produced by 26 NS in six roleplays), followed by a token count (*n*). Token counts are totaled at the bottom of the table while percentage totals can be assumed to be approximately 100%. Though all results are presented here, three compliment strategies are highlighted: *Me gusta/encanta+(NP)* (I like+NP; NP is pleasing to me), *NP(PRO)+ser/estar* (to be)*+ADJ*, and *Qué+ADJ/ADV* (How/What+ADJ/ADV).

Learners in the explicit condition (*N*=9) produced *Me gusta/encanta+(NP)* (I like+NP; NP is pleasing to me) 44.4% (12 tokens) of the time; learners in the control condition (*N*=7) produced it 31.3% (10 tokens) of the time, and learners in the implicit condition (*N*=10) produced this strategy 26.7% (16 tokens) of the time. They also frequently produced *NP(PRO)+ser/estar* (to be)*+ADJ*, with learners in the explicit condition producing it 22.2% (6 tokens) of the time, learners in the implicit condition producing it 36.7% (22 tokens) of the time, and learners in the control condition producing it 34.4% (11 tokens) of the time. *Qué+ADJ/ADV* (How/What+ADJ/ADV) was not produced by learners in the explicit condition prior to treatment. In both the implicit and control conditions, learners produced one token of this compliment type accounting for 1.7% and 3.1%, respectively. Immediately following instruction, learners in the explicit condition reduced production of *Me gusta/encanta+(NP)* (I like+NP; NP is pleasing to me) from 44.4% (12 tokens) to 38.5% (10 tokens), which was in the targeted direction. This change was maintained through the delayed posttest (38.2%, 13 tokens). The learners in the explicit condition slightly decreased their production of *NP(PRO)+ser/estar* (to be)*+ADJ*, which was not in the targeted direction, from the pretest (22.2%, 6 tokens) to the posttest (19.2%, 5 tokens), though this increased to 23.5% (8 tokens) by the delayed posttest. These learners did not produce any tokens of *Qué+ADJ/ADV* (How/What+ADJ/ADV) at any testing time.

Learners in the implicit condition reduced production of *Me gusta/encanta+(NP)* (I like+NP; NP is pleasing to me) from the pretest (26.7%, 16 tokens) to the posttest (17.8%, 8 tokens), which was in the targeted direction, increasing again at the delayed posttest (26.7%, 12 tokens). They also slightly decreased their production of *NP(PRO)+ser/estar* (to be)*+ADJ* from 36.7% (22 tokens) on the pretest to 33.3% (15 tokens), a level which was maintained on the delayed posttest (33.3%, 15 tokens). This change was toward the frequency produced by NSs of Spanish in this study. These learners produced only one token of *Qué+ADJ/ADV* (How/What+ADJ/ADV) on the pretest.

**Table 2.** Pretest, posttest, delayed posttest compliment type frequency by condition.

| compliment form | explicit condition (n=9) | | | implicit condition (n=10) | | | control (n=7) | | | Spanish NS (n=14) | English NS (n=12) |
|---|---|---|---|---|---|---|---|---|---|---|---|
| | pretest | posttest | delayed | pretest | posttest | delayed | pretest | posttest | delayed | | |
| | (N) % | | | | | | | | | | |
| me gusta/encanta + (NP) (I like + NP; NP is pleasing to me) | (12) 44.4 | (10) 38.5 | (13) 38.2 | (16) 26.7 | (8) 17.8 | (12) 26.7 | (10) 31.3 | (11) 34.4 | (7) 36.8 | (15) 15.8 | (9) 12.7 |
| NP (PRO) + ser/estar + ADJ (NP + is + ADJ) | (6) 22.2 | (5) 19.2 | (8) 23.5 | (22) 36.7 | (15) 33.3 | (15) 33.3 | (11) 34.4 | (9) 28.1 | (5) 26.3 | (28) 29.5 | (24) 33.8 |
| qué + ADJ/ADV (how/what + ADJ) | (0) 0.0 | (0) 0.0 | (0) 0.0 | (1) 1.7 | (0) 0.0 | (0) 0.0 | (1) 3.1 | (1) 3.1 | (0) 0.0 | (7) 7.4 | (1) 1.4 |
| PRO/NP + VP (+NP) + ADJ (+NP) | (3) 11.1 | (1) 3.9 | (3) 8.8 | (3) 5.0 | (3) 6.7 | (1) 2.2 | (4) 12.5 | (2) 6.3 | (2) 10.5 | (5) 5.3 | (18) 25.4 |
| PRO/NP (+ADV) + VP +ADV | (1) 3.7 | (3) 11.5 | (0) 0.0 | (0) 0.0 | (1) 2.2 | (1) 2.2 | (1) 3.1 | (1) 3.1 | (1) 5.3 | (4) 4.2 | — |
| PRO + quedarse + ADV/ADJ (PRO + suits you + ADV/ADJ) | (0) 0.0 | (0) 0.0 | (0) 0.0 | (0) 0.0 | (0) 0.0 | (0) 0.0 | (0) 0.0 | (0) 0.0 | (0) 0.0 | (3) 3.2 | — |
| PRO + verse/mirarse + ADV/ADJ you/that look(s) + ADV/ADJ | (1) 3.7 | (0) 0.0 | (0) 0.0 | (7) 11.7 | (4) 8.9 | (7) 15.6 | (4) 12.5 | (0) 0.0 | (1) 5.3 | (7) 7.4 | (4) 5.6 |
| (intensifier) + ADJ (+NP) | (1) 3.7 | (2) 7.7 | (2) 5.9 | (8) 13.3 | (8) 17.8 | (4) 8.9 | (0) 0.0 | (3) 9.4 | (2) 5.3 | (8) 8.4 | (3) 4.2 |
| question | (2) 7.4 | (4) 15.4 | (6) 17.6 | (3) 5.0 | (6) 13.3 | (5) 11.1 | (4) 12.5 | (1) 3.1 | (2) 10.5 | (7) 7.4 | (7) 9.9 |
| other (includes gratitude, sarcasm, speaker-oriented) | (1) 3.7 | (1) 3.9 | (2) 5.9 | (0) 0.0 | (0) 0.0 | (0) 0.0 | (1) 3.1 | (4) 12.5 | (2) 10.5 | (11) 11.6 | (5) 7.0 |
| total (100%) | (27) | (26) | (34) | (60) | (45) | (45) | (32) | (32) | (19) | (95) | (71) |

Following exposure to input, learners in the control group increased their production of *Me gusta/encanta+(NP)* (I like+NP; NP is pleasing to me) from 31.3% (10 tokens) to 34.4% (11 tokens) on the posttest and to 36.8% (7 tokens) on the delayed posttest. Learners in this condition reduced production of *NP(PRO)+ser/ estar* (to be)+*ADJ* from 34.4% (11 tokens) on the pretest to 28.1% (9 tokens) on the posttest and to 26.3% (5 tokens) on the delayed posttest. Though these learners produced a token of *Qué+ADJ/ADV* (How/What+ADJ/ADV) on the pre- and posttests, they produced no tokens of this strategy on the delayed posttest.

## Distribution and frequency of compliment response strategies

We turn now to an analysis of compliment response frequency. Table 3 presents overall frequency results for the pretest, posttest, and delayed posttest by treatment condition (i.e., explicit, implicit, and control) alongside the NS baseline data. The results are presented first by percentage of total compliment responses (%) (414 compliment responses produced by 26 learners in six roleplay scenarios per testing period; 236 compliment responses produced by 26 NS in six roleplays), followed by a token count (*N*). Token counts are totaled at the bottom of the table while percentage totals can be assumed to be approximately 100%. Though all results are presented here, the discussion focuses on four strategies: Appreciation, Agreement, Comment/Upgrade, and Self-praise, which were the most frequently produced by all speaker groups, as well as Fishing, which is attested in the literature for NSs of Spanish (Kryston-Morales, 1997; Lorenzo-Dus, 2001; Valdés & Pino, 1981).

At the time of the pretest, learners in all groups favored Comment/Upgrade, with learners in the implicit condition (*n*=10) producing this strategy 46.0% (23 tokens) of the time, learners in the control condition (*n*=7) producing it 40.5% (17 tokens) of the time, and learners in the explicit condition (*n*=9) producing it 40.0% (10 tokens) of the time. They also frequently produced Appreciation, with learners in the explicit condition producing it 36.0% (9 tokens) of the time, learners in the control condition producing it 33.3% (14 tokens) of the time, and learners in the implicit condition producing it 30.0% (15 tokens) of the time. Learners in the explicit condition produced Agreement 16.0% (4 tokens) of the time, with learners in the implicit condition producing it 14.0% (7 tokens) of the time, and those in the control condition producing it 11.9% (5 tokens) of the time. Production of Self-praise was low among the learners at the time of the pretest. Learners in the control condition produced 3 tokens (7.1%), those in the implicit condition produced 2 tokens (4.0%), with learners in the explicit condition producing no tokens of Self-praise. Each of the learner groups had a single token of Fishing at the time of the pretest.

**Table 3.** Pretest, posttest, delayed posttest compliment response type frequency by condition.

| compliment form | explicit condition (n=9) | | | implicit condition (n=10) | | | control (n=7) | | | Spanish NS (n=14) | English NS (n=12) |
|---|---|---|---|---|---|---|---|---|---|---|---|
| | pretest | posttest | delayed | pretest | posttest | delayed | pretest | posttest | delayed | | |
| | (N) % | | | | | | | | | | |
| appreciation | (9) 36.0 | (16) 51.6 | (20) 39.2 | (15) 30.0 | (19) 28.8 | (23) 34.9 | (14) 33.3 | (15) 37.5 | (15) 34.9 | (39) 25.8 | (22) 25.9 |
| agreement | (4) 16.0 | (2) 6.5 | (7) 13.7 | (7) 14.0 | (14) 21.2 | (8) 12.1 | (5) 11.9 | (7) 17.5 | (5) 11.6 | (17) 11.3 | (10) 11.8 |
| comment/upgrade | (10) 40.0 | (10) 32.3 | (14) 27.5 | (23) 46.0 | (21) 31.8 | (19) 28.8 | (17) 40.5 | (11) 27.5 | (10) 23.3 | (47) 31.1 | (25) 29.4 |
| fishing for compliment | (1) 4.0 | (0) 0.0 | (0) 0.0 | (1) 2.0 | (2) 3.0 | (0) 0.0 | (1) 2.4 | (1) 2.5 | (2) 4.7 | (8) 5.3 | (0) 0.0 |
| self-praise | (0) 0.0 | (2) 6.5 | (6) 11.8 | (2) 4.0 | (3) 4.6 | (6) 9.1 | (3) 7.1 | (3) 7.5 | (2) 4.7 | (14) 9.3 | (16) 18.8 |
| disagree | (0) 0.0 | (0) 0.0 | (0) 0.0 | (0) 0.0 | (1) 1.5 | (0) 0.0 | (0) 0.0 | (0) 0.0 | (0) 0.0 | (3) 2.0 | (0) 0.0 |
| downgrade | (0) 0.0 | (0) 0.0 | (0) 0.0 | (0) 0.0 | (0) 0.0 | (0) 0.0 | (0) 0.0 | (1) 2.5 | (0) 0.0 | (6) 4.0 | (1) 1.2 |
| transfer | (10) 4.0 | (0) 0.0 | (0) 0.0 | (0) 0.0 | (3) 4.6 | (4) 6.1 | (0) 0.0 | (0) 0.0 | (3) 7.0 | (10) 6.6 | (6) 7.1 |
| return | (0) 0.0 | (0) 0.0 | (1) 2.0 | (1) 2.0 | (0) 0.0 | (2) 3.0 | (1) 2.4 | (0) 0.0 | (4) 9.3 | (0) 0.0 | (1) 1.2 |
| offer | (0) 0.0 | (0) 0.0 | (0) 0.0 | (1) 2.0 | (0) 0.0 | (0) 0.0 | (0) 0.0 | (0) 0.0 | (0) 0.0 | (4) 2.7 | (2) 2.4 |
| other | (0) 0.0 | (1) 3.2 | (3) 5.9 | (0) 0.0 | (0) 0.0 | (4) 6.1 | (1) 2.4 | (2) 5.0 | (2) 4.7 | (3) 2.0 | (2) 2.4 |
| total (100%) | (25) | (31) | (51) | (50) | (66) | (66) | (42) | (40) | (43) | (151) | (85) |

Immediately following instruction, learners in the explicit condition reduced their overall relative production of Comment/Upgrade from 40.0% (10 tokens) to 32.3% (10 tokens). This downward trend continued through the delayed posttest (27.5%, 14 tokens) toward levels produced by the NSs of Spanish and English. These learners increased their production of Appreciation from 36.0% (9 tokens) to 51.6% (16 tokens) on the posttest. This dropped to 39.2% (20 tokens) by the time of the delayed posttest, which moved away from the NS norm. Production of Agreement dropped from 16.0% (4 tokens) to 6.5% (2 tokens) on the posttest, but increased to 13.7% (7 tokens) by the delayed posttest, which was in the hoped for direction. Production of Self-praise increased from 0.0% to 6.5% (2 tokens) to 11.8% (6 tokens), bringing learners to a frequency level between that of NSs of Spanish and English. After the pretest, these learners produced no cases of Fishing.

Learners in the implicit condition also reduced their production of Comment/Upgrade, from 46.0% (23 tokens) to 31.8% (21 tokens), which continued through the delayed posttest (28.8%, 19 tokens). Like the explicit condition, this group of learners approached the NS norm. They slightly decreased the relative frequency of Appreciation from 30.0% (15 tokens) to 28.8% (19 tokens), though this increased to 34.9% (23 tokens) by the delayed posttest, which was away from the NS norm. Agreement became more frequent in this group, increasing from 14.0% (7 tokens) to 21.2% (14 tokens), though this level fell to 12.1% (8 tokens) on the delayed posttest, which was toward the NS norm. These learners increased their production of Self-praise from 4.0% (2 tokens) to 4.6% (3 tokens) to 9.1% (6 tokens), which was in the hoped for direction. Fishing increased from the pretest (2.0%, 1 token) to the posttest (3.0%, 2 tokens), but did not occur on the delayed posttest.

In the control group, learners decreased production of Comment/Upgrade from the pretest (40.5%, 17 tokens) to the posttest (27.5%, 11 tokens), which continued through the delayed posttest (23.3%, 10 tokens). Their production frequency was below the NS norm. Appreciation increased slightly among these learners from the pretest (33.3%, 14 tokens) to the posttest (37.5%, 15 tokens), with a small drop on the delayed posttest (34.9%, 15 tokens). Agreement became more frequent among these learners, increasing from 11.9% (5 tokens) on the pretest to 17.5% (7 tokens) on the posttest, but dropping back to 11.6% (5 tokens) on the delayed posttest. These learners remained stable in their production of Self-praise from the pretest (7.1%, 3 tokens) to the posttest (7.5%, 3 tokens), decreasing on the delayed posttest (4.7%, 2 tokens). The learners in the control group also remained stable in their production of Fishing from the pretest (2.4%, 1 token) to the posttest (2.5%, 1 token), though they increased frequency by a token on the delayed posttest (4.7%, 2 tokens).

The frequency analysis shows that instructed learners in both conditions moved toward a strategy distribution like that of the NSs of Spanish while participants in the control group did not. Explicit instruction had a positive effect on increasing overall production of compliment responses, though its effect was not as strong on compliments. Meanwhile, learners in the implicit condition decreased compliment production while also increasing compliment response productions.

In addition to understanding whether instruction had an effect on the distribution and overall frequency of compliments and compliment responses, learner variability in strategy choice was also tested. A type analysis was conducted to do this and is presented in the following section.

### Research question #2: Effects of instruction on variability of compliment and compliment response types.

Research question #2 asked whether learners would become more variable in their production of compliment and compliment response types following instruction, thus taking advantage of the choices they have in interaction. The results for compliment and compliment response strategy types are presented together.

Table 4 shows individual type counts from all learning conditions for compliments and compliment responses, as well as averages for each learner group. Learners are identified by a letter corresponding to their instructional group and a number. An increase in number of types indicated that learners were experimenting with different types of compliment or compliment response strategies, while remaining stable or decreasing the number of types produced indicated a lack of experimentation.

**Table 4.** Individual learner type counts.

| | explicit instruction group | | | | | |
|---|---|---|---|---|---|---|
| | compliments | | | compliment responses | | |
| participant | pretest | posttest | delayed | pretest | posttest | delayed |
| E1 | 5 | 3 | 5 | 2 | 2 | 4 |
| E2 | 2 | 3 | 2 | 2 | 1 | 3 |
| E3 | 1 | 2 | 1 | 3 | 2 | 3 |
| E4 | 4 | 0 | 2 | 1 | 3 | 3 |
| E5 | 4 | 3 | 3 | 2 | 2 | 5 |
| E6 | 2 | 2 | 3 | 2 | 4 | 4 |
| E7 | 1 | 5 | 3 | 2 | 0 | 1 |
| E8 | 0 | 2 | 3 | 0 | 1 | 3 |
| E9 | 1 | 1 | 2 | 1 | 3 | 4 |
| average | 2.2 | 2.3 | 2.7 | 1.7 | 2.0 | 3.3 |

**Table 4 (continued).** Individual learner type counts.

| | implicit instruction group | | | | | |
|---|---|---|---|---|---|---|
| | compliments | | | compliment responses | | |
| participant | pretest | posttest | delayed | pretest | posttest | delayed |
| I1 | 3 | 0 | 4 | 2 | 3 | 0 |
| I2 | 6 | 4 | 3 | 4 | 4 | 1 |
| I3 | 5 | 7 | 3 | 2 | 2 | 2 |
| I4 | 4 | 0 | 3 | 3 | 4 | 4 |
| I5 | 5 | 3 | 5 | 3 | 8 | 1 |
| I6 | 6 | 4 | 4 | 3 | 4 | 2 |
| I7 | 4 | 3 | 1 | 2 | 3 | 3 |
| I8 | 3 | 2 | 3 | 2 | 0 | 2 |
| I9 | 2 | 4 | 2 | 2 | 5 | 1 |
| I10 | 4 | 2 | 4 | 2 | 4 | 1 |
| average | 4.3 | 2.9 | 3.2 | 2.5 | 3.7 | 1.7 |

| | control group | | | | | |
|---|---|---|---|---|---|---|
| | compliments | | | compliment responses | | |
| participant | pretest | posttest | delayed | pretest | posttest | delayed |
| C1 | 3 | 3 | 3 | 2 | 3 | 3 |
| C2 | 5 | 4 | 2 | 1 | 4 | 5 |
| C3 | 3 | 0 | 2 | 4 | 2 | 3 |
| C4 | 1 | 3 | 2 | 4 | 3 | 2 |
| C5 | 3 | 5 | 0 | 2 | 4 | 5 |
| C6 | 4 | 4 | 5 | 4 | 5 | 3 |
| C7 | 3 | 2 | 1 | 2 | 4 | 3 |
| average | 3.1 | 3.0 | 2.1 | 2.7 | 3.6 | 3.4 |

In the explicit instruction group, the average number of compliment types remained essentially equal between the pretest (2.2 types, range 0–5) and the posttest (2.3 types, range 0–5). However, the average increased slightly by the delayed posttest (2.7 types, range 1–5). From the pretest to the posttest, four learners increased compliment types (E2, E3, E7, and E8) while the remaining learners showed no change or a decrease. From the posttest to the delayed posttest, five of nine participants increased compliment types (E1, E4, E6, E8, E9).

These learners increased in the number of compliment response types from the pretest (1.7 types, range 0–3) to the posttest (2.0 types, range 0–4). This increase continued through the delayed posttest (3.3 types, range 1–5). Individual results corroborated the group results with four learners increasing types from the pretest to the posttest (E4, E5, E8, E9) and seven increasing types from the posttest to the delayed posttest (E1, E2, E3, E5, E7, E8, E9).

Though learners in the implicit condition started the study with higher production levels of compliment types, they decreased average production from the pretest (4.3, range 3–6) to the posttest (2.9, range 0–7), rebounding somewhat by the delayed posttest (3.2, range 1–5). In fact, only two learners increased the number of compliment types from the pretest to the posttest (I3, I9), while five of the learners in this group (I1, I4, I5, I8, I10) increased the number of types of compliments that they produced on the delayed posttest.

Immediately following instruction, learners in the implicit instruction group increased from 2.5 compliment response types (range 2–4) on the pretest to 3.7 types (range 0–8) on the posttest, decreasing to 1.7 types (range 0–4) on the delayed posttest. From the pretest to the posttest, seven learners (I1, I4, I5, I6, I7, I9, I10) increased compliment response type production. On the delayed posttest, only one learner (I8) increased compliment type production.

The control group remained stable in their production of compliment types from the pretest (3.1 types, range 1–5) to the posttest (3.0 types, range 0–5), decreasing to 2.1 (range 0–5) on the delayed posttest. Two learners (C4, C5) increased production of compliment types from the pretest to the posttest and only one learner increased production (C6) from the posttest to the delayed posttest.

This group of learners increased compliment response types from the pretest (2.7, range 1–4) to the posttest (3.6, range 2–5), and remained relatively stable on the delayed posttest (3.4, range 2–5). From the pretest to the posttest, five learners (C1, C2, C5, C6, C7) increased the number of types of compliment responses they produced. On the delayed posttest, three learners (C2, C3, C5) increased the number of types of compliment responses they produced.

These results indicate that learners in the two instructed groups became more variable in the types of strategies that they produced following instruction, though there was still very little variation in comparison to NSs. Explicit instruction had a delayed positive effect on the variety of both compliment and compliment response strategies produced, while implicit instruction had an immediate positive effect only on compliment responses strategies.

### Sequential analysis

The changes demonstrated in the quantitative results presented above were also reflected in the qualitative sequential analysis. We focus now on Alicia and Sarah,[3] female learners in the explicit instruction condition.

Example 1 reflects overall patterns identified among learners prior to instruction, including rigid adjacency pairs, overuse of *Me gusta/encanta+(NP)* (I like+NP; NP is pleasing to me), and simple compliment responses such as

Agreement. These strategies highlight the lack of pragmalinguistic resources among learners prior to instruction.

**Example 1.** Pretest compliment-compliment response sequence, learner–learner role-play

1 Sarah: *Hola (1.0) muchacha*
Hi (1.0) girl
2 Alicia: *hola*
hi
3 Sarah: *me gusta su su zapatos*
I like your your shoes
4 Alicia: *sí*
yes
5 Sarah: *me encanta el color de los zapatos*
I love the color of your shoes
6 Alicia: *es verde y rojo*
it is green and red
7 Sarah: *mucho verde y el rojo es el color de mi pelo*
a lot of green and the red is the color of my hair
8 Alicia: (laughter) *sí*
(laughter) yes

After opening with a greeting sequence (lines 1 and 2), Sarah offers Alicia a *Me gusta/encanta*+NP (I like/love+NP) compliment (lines 3 and 5). Alicia responds with Agreement (line 4) and Comment/Upgrade (line 6), though she only produces one compliment response per turn. It is interesting to note that Sarah intensifies the compliment by using *Me encanta* (I love) in the second compliment that she gives (line 5). Intensification of compliments was a feature present in many of the role-play interactions among NSs and learners. Following Alicia's confirmation of Sarah's comment (line 7), the learners change topic and the remaining turns are omitted for the sake of space.

Though the posttest role-play in Example 2 is short, it still clearly shows overall instructed learner tendencies. Learners continued to use rigid adjacency pairs and to overproduce *Me gusta/encanta*+NP (I like/love+NP), but they were more likely to produce expanded compliment responses.

**Example 2.** Posttest compliment-compliment response sequence, learner–learner role-play

1 Sarah: *Me gusta la cosa en su (1.0) en tu mano es muy*
I like the thing on your (1.0) on your hand it's very
2 Alicia: *gracias um me compro la uh tienda de anti::gas*
thanks um, I buy myself the uh anti::que store

3   Sarah:   *lo cuesta mucho dinero?*
             it cost a lot of money?

Sarah opens the sequence with a compliment (line 1). Instead of responding with "*sí*" (yes), as she did on the pretest (Example 1, line 4), Alicia's produces an expanded compliment response, incorporating two strategies, Appreciation and Comment (line 2). This combination of strategies was highly frequent among both NS groups. Her expanded compliment response demonstrates an increase in pragmalinguistic competence.

Example 3 demonstrates features of instructed learner compliment-compliment response sequences on the delayed posttest, four weeks following instruction. Learners still overproduced *Me gusta/encanta*+NP (I like/love+NP), though they tended to produce more expanded compliment and compliment response sequences in their interactions.

**Example 3.**   Delayed posttest compliment-compliment response sequence, learner–learner role-play

1   Sarah:   *Hola, uh, me suuu me gusta sus zapatos de verde*
             Hi, uh, I your I like your green shoes
2   Alicia:  hold on one second
             hold on one second
3   Sarah:   we've done these already[4]
             we've done these already
4   Alicia:  *gracias*
             thanks
5   Sarah:   *uh, ¿dónde comprarlos?*
             uh, where did you buy them?
6   Alicia:  *uh, uh, pequeño tienda en la ciudad*
             uh, uh, small store in the city
7   Sarah:   *oh, me gusta la tienda*
             oh, I like the store
8   Alicia:  *sí, uh tu* (3.0) (unintelligible)
             yes, uh tu (3.0) (unintelligible)

Sarah again opens the sequence with a compliment (line 1). After the learners have determined that they have role-played the scenario before (lines 2–3), Alicia picks back up and thanks Sarah for the compliment (line 4), Sarah responds with a follow-up question about where the shoes were purchased (line 5). Questions frequently served as a part of compliments among NSs; their appearance in learner compliment-compliment response sequences reflect enhanced pragmalinguistic competence. Alicia answers Sarah's question (line 6) and Sarah responds with an additional comment about the store (line 7). Alicia agrees with her (line 8) and the interaction ends.

These compliment-compliment response sequences reflect the increased pragmalinguistic competence among instructed learners. They were better able to perform expanded sequences, bringing them closer to NS norms following instruction. These positive gains were maintained or continued even after instruction was ceased.

## Discussion

Unlike the findings of previous research on compliments and compliment responses, which focused primarily on only one of the two speech acts (e.g., Hernández-Herrero, 1999; Lorenzo-Dus, 2001; Nelson & Hall, 1999; Placencia & Yépez, 1999), the present study elicited multi-turn speech act sequences (e.g., Félix-Brasdefer, 2014). Role-play interactions were a minimum of three turns long (a greeting followed by a compliment-compliment response sequence), though some were much longer, up to 35 turns. Speakers consistently produced multiple instances of either compliments or compliment responses in a single turn (e.g., I like your sweater; it looks really nice on you). The following sections consist of a discussion of the results of the present study, guided by the research questions.

### Research question #1: Effects of instruction on frequency of compliments and compliment responses

*Me gusta/encanta+(NP)* (I like+NP; NP is pleasing to me) was frequently overproduced by all learner groups at the time of the pretest. Instruction was designed to reduce the frequency of this strategy in the learners' repertoire by downplaying it while highlighting other strategies. For example, because *Qué+ADJ/ADV* (How/What+ADJ/ADV) is the most frequent strategy attested in previous literature, instruction heavily favored it in an attempt to increase its relative production among learners.

Despite efforts to curtail production of *Me gusta/encanta+(NP)* (I like+NP; NP is pleasing to me), the posttest showed that learners in all groups still produced it well above the levels produced by the NSs of Spanish in this study and far above the levels attested in the previous literature (Félix-Brasdefer & Hasler-Barker, 2015; Hernández-Herrero, 1999; Kryston-Morales, 1997; Nelson & Hall, 1999; Placencia & Yépez, 1999). NSs of Spanish produced *me gusta/ encanta+(NP)* (I like+NP; NP is pleasing to me) at a level not attested in any of the previous literature. Because this compliment strategy distribution is unusual, two potential factors should be taken into account. First *Me gusta/encanta+(NP)* (I like+NP; NP is pleasing to me) frequently occurred in conjunction with another compliment (e.g., *Qué bonito suéter, me gusta* (What a pretty sweater, I like it), which increased its frequency. Second, the NSs of Spanish had lived in the United States as graduate students and had taught Spanish courses to NSs of English learning Spanish. It is possible that English-language exposure had an effect on this group of NSs. Nevertheless, learners in the explicit instruction group reduced production of this strategy and maintained that reduction through the delayed posttest. Learners in the implicit instruction group also reduced production of this strategy, though this was not maintained through the delayed posttest. These changes indicate a positive effect for the instructional modules.

Learners also produced a high level of *NP(PRO)+ser/estar* (to be)*+ADJ* throughout the study. Given that this is a highly frequent strategy in the literature (Wolfson, 1983) and was also frequent among the NSs of English in the baseline group for this study, this result is not surprising. In fact, learners in the implicit condition favored this strategy even above *Me gusta/encanta+(NP)* (I like+NP; NP is pleasing to me), reducing production slightly between the pretest and the posttest. Though the NSs of Spanish also produced this strategy quite frequently, this is not true of the findings of previous literature (Félix-Brasdefer & Hasler-Barker, 2015; Hernández-Herrero, 1999; Kryston-Morales, 1997; Nelson & Hall, 1999; Placencia & Yépez, 1999).

The 26 participants in the study produced only three tokens of *Qué+ADJ/ADV* (How/What+ADJ/ADV) across all testing times. Because this strategy was heavily favored in the instruction, this was not the hoped for result. It is likely that, while 20 minutes of instruction may have helped learners to reduce overproduction of *Me gusta/encanta+(NP)* (I like+NP; NP is pleasing to me), it simply was not enough time to help learners to produce *Qué+ADJ/ADV* (How/What+ADJ/ADV) during role-play testing.

NSs of Spanish and English were remarkably similar in the distribution of compliment response strategies. In theory, learners would have had to reduce production of Self-praise and increase production of Fishing to become more like NSs of Spanish. The reality was that, at the time of the pretest, all of the learners overproduced Comment/Upgrade and Appreciation when compared to the NSs of Spanish and English, indicating a phase of interlanguage pragmatic development unrelated to their L1 or to the L2. They also produced Agreement frequently, though more in line with NS levels. They produced very few tokens of Self-praise or Fishing on the pretest.

Appreciation (*Gracias* [Thank you]) is a very simple, transparent, single word response strategy (Koike, 1989). Thus, it is not surprising that learners produced this strategy frequently across all three testing times. Comment/Upgrade is a syntactically and pragmatically more complicated strategy, requiring learners to add additional commentary to the initial compliment. Their overproduction of this complex strategy is somewhat surprising. However, that learners at the intermediate level were already prepared to do this speaks to their preparedness for this type of instruction.

Learners in all conditions adjusted their production toward that of the NSs of Spanish on the posttest by reducing their production of Comment/Upgrade, though learners in the control group fell below NS levels of production on the posttest. By the delayed posttest, all learner groups produced Comment/Upgrade less than NSs of English or Spanish, although the instructed learners were closer to the NS norm giving them a slight advantage over uninstructed learners for this strategy.

In the explicit instruction group, learners increased their production of Self-praise from the pretest to the posttest, which continued through the delayed posttest. The learners in the implicit instruction group shared the same movement toward the NS norm, producing this strategy at a level that approached that of the NSs of Spanish by the delayed posttest. Learners in the control group, meanwhile, reduced their overall production of this strategy by the time of the delayed posttest. Learners in the instructed groups had an advantage over the control group participants.

Only the learners in the implicit condition reduced production of Appreciation toward NS levels, though they then increased to a level above their pretest levels by the delayed posttest. Both the learners in the explicit instruction and control groups produced this strategy above the nearly identical NS Spanish and English levels, though learners in the control group were more stable in their production levels. Learners in the implicit condition had a clear advantage in becoming more like NSs for this strategy; regrettably the change did not maintain through the delayed posttest.

Unfortunately, the target strategy of Fishing did not approach NS levels for any of the learner groups. It is possible that this strategy was underproduced because it is not attested to in the previous literature on American English compliments (Pomerantz, 1978; Wierzbicka, 2003) and is generally considered rude by NSs. It is clear that this strategy needed additional instruction for learners to feel comfortable in producing it.

In sum, there are some obvious advantages for instructed learners in terms of compliment and compliment response distribution and frequency. However, it is difficult to determine which type of instruction was the most advantageous. In fact, it appears that both types of instruction, explicit and implicit, have advantages for bringing learners of Spanish toward the NS norm for this speech act sequence and that the two modes of instruction should be combined for best results. This will be discussed in detail in the pedagogical implications (section 5.3) below.

## Research question #2: Effects of instruction on variability of compliment and compliment response types.

As previous researchers have discussed (Bardovi-Harlig & Mahan-Taylor, 2003), the goal of metapragmatic instruction is to give learners choices about the language they choose to use in interaction. Because learners come to the table with previous knowledge about L1 pragmatics (Kasper, 1996; 2001), they need help to use those preconceived notions in conjunction with metapragmatic instruction in order to have the resources to make choices in their interactions in the target language. By assessing changes in the number types of compliments and compliment responses produced by learners, we can gain a better understanding of the effects of instruction.

Learners in the explicit instruction condition did not immediately show positive effects for instruction on compliment types, though they did on compliment response types. There were delayed instructional effects for this group as they continued to increase variability in the types of compliment and compliment response strategies that they produced. Implicit instruction had an immediate negative effect on production of compliment types, though this was somewhat rectified by the delayed posttest. These learners increased compliment response type variability from the pretest to the posttest, though they did not maintain this effect. In fact, they decreased variability from the posttest to the delayed posttest. Control group learners were stable in compliment type production from the pretest to the posttest; they then decreased type variability from the posttest to the delayed posttest. Compliment responses were more variable on the posttest than the pretest for the control group, though they showed no change from the posttest to the delayed posttest.

In short, learners who received metapragmatic instruction became more variable in their production of compliments and compliment responses. Learners in the explicit instruction condition were the most successful at increasing type variability, though there were some positive effects for learners in the implicit condition. As with the frequency and distribution results, there is evidence that the two types of instruction might be more effective when presented together. This is discussed in the following section.

## Pedagogical implications

The present study operationalized research-based suggestions for metapragmatic instruction (Bardovi-Harlig & Mahan-Taylor, 2003; García, 1996, 2001; Ishihara & Cohen, 2010; Tatsuki & Houck, 2010). Like previous work (e.g., Félix-Brasdefer, 2008; García 2001), learners were presented with complete interactions in the target language in the form of role-plays. FL textbooks that do include metapragmatic information typically offer decontextualized phrases to the learners instead of the rich context of complete interactions. Exposing learners to the full conversational context of the speech act sequence is crucial to their ability to understand how and when compliments and compliment responses are deployed in interaction.

Previous researchers have emphasized the importance of cross-cultural comparisons in metapragmatic instruction, whether between target cultures (e.g., García, 2001) or between the target culture and the native culture (e.g., Félix-Brasdefer, 2008; Takahashi, 2001). The present study adds weight to the argument that learners must have the opportunity to formally examine their own pragmatic competence (Kasper, 1996, 2001) in order to take advantage of both L1 and L2 interactional resources, as the instructed learners who did this moved toward the NS of Spanish norm and increased the variety of strategies that they produced.

An additional consideration is the reaction of both instructors and learners, who made unsolicited comments about how much they enjoyed participating in the instructional modules and testing for this experiment. Students commented that they felt like they were learning something practical and that they were able to practice interacting without feeling foolish. Instructors indicated that they appreciated the opportunity to expose their students to practical intercultural information.

Finally, by conducting both a frequency/distribution analysis as well as a type analysis, it is clear that a combination of implicit and explicit metapragmatic instruction would likely be the most effective instructional approach for enhancing learner production of compliments and compliment responses. It is possible that learners could approach NS frequency/distribution, while also increasing variability in the types of strategies that they produced. This is certainly a fruitful area for future research, which will be discussed along with limitations of the study in the following section.

## Limitations and areas for future research

The present study has its limitations. Its principal limitation is the small data set, limiting analysis to descriptive statistical comparisons between groups, which was a result of multiple factors. First, attrition played a major role in limiting the number of participants. If a learner did not participate in all instructional modules and all three testing periods, that learner was excluded from the data set. Second, role-plays are not as tightly controlled as other methods of data collection. Learners did not always produce the desired speech act sequence, further reducing the number of tokens that were counted in the present study. Third, the time constraint set by the research institution limited how many role-plays could be completed. A 20-minute testing session was not always adequate to ensure that all learners were able to produce the desired speech act sequence. Finally, learners at the intermediate level may not have been advanced enough to produce the structures required for complex compliment-compliment response sequences, thus relying on transparent structures (Koike, 1989) such as Appreciation (*Gracias* [Thank you]). This may have been compounded by the tendency to associate one form, such as *Me gusta/encanta+(NP)* (I like+NP; NP is pleasing to me), with one function (Andersen, 1984).

A further limitation of the study was the restricted timeframe for metapragmatic instruction. Only 40 minutes were allotted for the instructors to present the materials to their classes. Despite this, instructed learners still demonstrated advantages over the control group participants, reflected in both the quantitative data analysis and in the qualitative sequential analysis. It is possible that additional focus on this speech act sequence would further enhance the effects seen here.

In spite of these limitations, the present study offers important information about the effects of pragmatic instruction on learner production of the compliment-compliment response sequence. Furthermore, learners were given the opportunity to learn about and practice interaction in a safe context, free from real world consequences (Bardovi-Harlig & Mahan-Taylor, 2003).

In the future, a more in-depth sequential analysis of the role-plays produced by learners would prove beneficial for understanding the effects of instruction and the passage of time on co-construction of interaction. It is also crucially important to more fully understand what monolingual NSs of Spanish do in producing compliments and compliment responses. The NS Spanish group in this study is unique precisely because they are not monolingual. However, a significant portion of the previous research on compliments and compliment responses in monolingual Spanish (e.g., Hernández-Herrero, 1999; Lorenzo-Dus, 2001; Nelson & Hall, 1999; Placencia & Yepez, 1999; Valdés & Pino, 1981) has relied on participants' recall or written questionnaires rather than more reliable oral data (Félix-Brasdefer, 2010; see Félix-Brasdefer & Hasler-Barker, 2015, and García, 2012 for exceptions). Gathering authentic oral compliment and compliment response data from monolingual Spanish speakers will provide researchers and instructors with crucial information for developing appropriate pedagogical materials.

## Conclusion

The conclusions afforded by this research are multifaceted. They add to the growing body of FL pedagogical research indicating that explicit metapragmatic instruction is not only effective, but gives learners an advantage over input alone. They provide evidence that implicit metapragmatic instruction also has positive effects and should be explored as a companion to explicit instruction. This study adds to our ever increasing knowledge about the effects of metapragmatic instruction on FL learners of languages other than English. Furthermore, while much previous research in FL metapragmatic instruction has focused on advanced learners, the results of this study indicate that learners in even intermediate-level FL classrooms are able to learn to produce a variety of compliment and compliment response strategies with appropriate instruction.

### Notes

1. This 20-minute time limit was set by the research institution.
2. The 50-minute limit for teaching was set by the research institution.
3. Learner names are pseudonyms.
4. Learners completed the same role-play scenarios on the pretest, posttest, and delayed posttest for the sake of comparison. The order was randomized, but some learners still noticed that the prompts were the same

# References

Andersen, R. (1984). The one to one principle of interlanguage construction. *Language Learning, 34*(4), 77–95.

Bardovi-Harlig, K. (1999a). Exploring the interlanguage of interlanguage pragmatics: A research agenda for acquisitional pragmatics. *Language Learning, 49*(4), 677–713.

Bardovi-Harlig, K. (1999b). Researching method. In L. Bouton (Ed.), *Pragmatics and language learning* (Vol. 9; pp. 273–264). Urbana: University of Illinois at Urbana-Champaign.

Bardovi-Harlig, K. (2001). Evaluating the empirical evidence: Grounds for instruction in pragmatics? In K. Rose & G. Kasper (Eds.), *Pragmatics in language teaching* (pp. 13–32). Cambridge, : Cambridge University Press.

Bardovi-Harlig, K. (2013). Developing L2 pragmatics. *Language Learning, 63*(1), 68–86.

Bardovi-Harlig, K., & Mahan-Taylor, R. (2003). Introduction. In K. Bardovi-Harlig & R. Mahan-Taylor (Eds.), *Teaching pragmatics* (pp. 1–13). Washington, DC: US Department of State.

Billmyer, K. (1990). *The effects of formal instruction on the development of sociolinguistic competence: The performance of compliments* (Unpublished doctoral dissertation). The University of Pennsylvania, Philadelphia.

Canale, M. (1983). From communicative competence to communicative language pedagogy. In J. Richards & R. Schmidt (Eds.), *Language and communication* (pp. 2–27). New York, NY: Longman.

Celce-Murcia, M. (2008). Rethinking the role of communicative competence in language teaching. In E. Alcón-Soler & M. Safont-Jordà (Eds.), *Intercultural language use and language learning* (pp. 41–57). Dodrecht, The Netherlands: Springer.

Cohen, A. (1996). Developing the ability to perform speech acts. *Studies in Second Language Acquisition 18*, 253–267.

Cohen, A. (2005). Strategies for learning and performing L2 speech acts. *Interlanguage Pragmatics, 2*(3), 275–301.

Cohen, A. (2009). Comprehensible pragmatics: Where input and output come together. In M. Pawlak (Ed.), *New perspectives on individual differences in language learning and teaching* (pp. 256–265). Poznań-Kalisz: Adam Mickiewicz University Press.

Cohen, A. (2015). Dancing with words: Strategies for learning pragmatics in Spanish. Retrieved from http://www.carla.umn.edu/speechacts/sp_pragmatics/home.html

Félix-Brasdefer, J. C. (2008). Teaching Spanish pragmatics in the classroom: Explicit instruction of mitigation. *Hispania, 91*(2), 477–492.

Félix-Brasdefer, J. C. (2010). Data collection methods in speech act performance: DCTs, role-plays, and verbal reports. In A. Martínez-Flor & E. Usó-Juan (Eds.), *Speech act performance: Theoretical, empirical and methodological issues* (pp. 41–56). Amsterdam: John Benjamins.

Félix-Brasdefer, J. C. (2014). Speech act sequences. In K. Schneider & A. Barron (Eds.), Pragmatics of discourse (*Handbooks of Pragmatics*, Vol. 3, pp. 323–352). Berlin: Mouton de Gruyter.

Félix-Brasdefer, J. C. (2015). Discourse pragmatics: Language and culture resources for instructors, students and researchers of Spanish linguistics. Retrieved from http://www.indiana.edu/~discprag/spch_acts.html

Félix-Brasdefer, J. C., & Cohen, A. D. (2012). Teaching pragmatics in the foreign language classroom: Grammar as a Communicative Resource. *Hispania, 95*(4), 650–669.

Félix-Brasdefer, J. C., & Hasler-Barker, M. (2012). Complimenting and responding to a compliment in the Spanish FL classroom: From empirical evidence to pedagogical intervention. In L. Ruíz de Zarobe & Y. Ruíz de Zarobe (Eds.), *Speech acts and politeness across languages and cultures* (pp. 241–274). Bern: Peter Lang.

Félix-Brasdefer, J. C., & Hasler-Barker, M. (2015). Complimenting in Spanish in a short-term study abroad context. *System, 48*, 75–85

García, C. (1996). Teaching speech act performance: Declining an invitation. *Hispania 79*(20), 267–279.

García, C. (2001). Perspectives in practices: Teaching culture through speech acts. In V. Galloway (Ed.), *Teaching the cultures of the Hispanic world: Products and practices in perspective* (pp. 95–112). Boston, MA: Thomson Learning.

García, C. (2012). Complimenting professional achievement: A case study of Peruvian Spanish speakers. *Journal of Politeness Research, 8*, 223–244.

Haverkate, H. (2004). El análisis de la cortesía comunicativa: Categorización pragmalingüística de la cultura española [Analysis of communicative politeness: Pragmalinguistic categorization of the Spanish culture]. In D. Bravo & A. Briz (Eds.), *Pragmática sociocultural: Estudios sobre el discurso de cortesía en español* [Sociocultural pragmatics: Studies on discourse of Spanish politeness] (pp. 60–70). Barcelona: Ariel.

Hernández-Herrero, A. (1999). Analysis and comparison of complimenting behavior in Costa Rican Spanish and American English. *Kañina, 23*, 121–131.

Hudson, T., Detmer, E., & Brown, J. (1995). *Developing prototypic measures of cross-cultural pragmatics*. Honolulu: University of Hawai'i Press.

Ishihara, N., & Cohen, A. (2010). *Teaching and learning pragmatics: Where language and culture meet*. New York, NY: Longman.

Jefferson, G. (2004). Glossary of transcript symbols with an introduction. In G. Lerner (Ed.), *Conversation analysis: Studies from the first generation*, (pp. 13–23). Amsterdam: John Benjamins.

Kasper, G. (1996). *Can pragmatic competence be taught?* Paper presented at the 1997 TESOL Convention Plenary Speech. Retrieved from http://www.nflrc.hawaii.edu/networks/NW06/default.html

Kasper, G. (2001). Classroom research on interlanguage pragmatics. In K. Rose & G. Kasper (Eds.), *Pragmatics in language teaching* (pp. 33–60). Cambridge, UK: Cambridge University Press.

Kasper, G., & Rose, K. (2002). *Pragmatic development in a second language.* Malden, MA: Blackwell.

Koike, D. (1989). Pragmatic competence and adult L2 acquisition: Speech acts and interlanguage. *Modern Language Journal, 73*(3), 279–289.

Koike, D., & Pearson, L. (2005). The effect of instruction and feedback in the development of pragmatic competence. *System, 33*, 481–501.

Krashen, S. (1985). *The input hypothesis: Issues and implications.* New York, NY: Longman.

Kryston-Morales, C. (1997). The Production of compliments and responses in English by native Spanish speakers in Puerto Rico: An intercultural pragmatics study. (Unpublished doctoral dissertation). New York: New York University.

Lorenzo-Dus, N. (2001). Compliment responses among British and Spanish university students: A contrastive study. *Journal of Pragmatics, 33*(1), 107–127.

Manes, J., & Wolfson, N. (1980). The compliment formula. In Florian Coulmas (Ed.), *Conversational routine* (pp. 115–132). The Hague: Mouton.

Nelson, G., & Hall, C. (1999). Complimenting in Mexican Spanish: Developing grammatical and pragmatic competence. *Spanish Applied Linguistics, 3*(1), 91–121.

Olshtain, E., & Cohen, A. (1990). The learning of complex speech act behavior. *TESL Canada Journal, 7,* 45–65.

Pearson, L. (2006). Teaching pragmatics in Spanish L2 courses: What do learners think? In K. Bardovi-Harlig, J. C. Félix-Brasdefer, & A. Omar (Eds.), *Pragmatics and language learning* (Vol. 11, pp. 165–197). Honolulu: University of Hawai'i Press.

Placencia, M., & Yépez, M. (1999). Compliments in Ecuadorian Spanish. *Lengua, 9,* 83–121.

Pomerantz, A. (1978). Compliment responses: Notes on the co-operation of multiple constraints. In J. Schenkein (Ed.), *Studies in the organization of conversational interaction* (pp. 79–112). New York, NY: Academic Press.

Roever, C. (2009). Teaching and testing pragmatics. In M. Long & C. Doughty (Eds.), *The handbook of language teaching* (pp. 560–577). Oxford, : Oxford University Press.

Rose, K. (2005). On the effects of instruction in second language pragmatics. *System, 33*(3), 385–399.

Schmidt, R. (1990). The role of consciousness in language learning. *Applied Linguistics, 10*(2), 129–158.

Schmidt, R. (1993a). Awareness and second language acquisition. *Annual Review of Applied Linguistics, 13*(1), 206–226.

Schmidt, R. (1993b). Consciousness, learning and interlanguage pragmatics. In G. Kasper & S. Blum-Kulka (Eds.), *Interlanguage pragmatics* (pp. 21–42). Oxford, : Oxford University Press.

Searle, J. (1976). A classification of illocutionary acts. *Language in Society, 5,* 1–23.

Takahashi, S. (2001). The role of input enhancement in developing pragmatic competence. In K. Rose & G. Kasper (Eds.), *Pragmatics in language teaching* (pp. 171–199). Cambridge: Cambridge University Press.

Tatsuki, D., & Houck, N. (2010). *Pragmatics: Teaching speech acts*. Alexandria, VA: TESOL.

Thomas, J. (1995). *Meaning in interaction*. London: Longman.

Valdés, G., & Pino, C. (1981). Muy a tus órdenes: Compliment responses among Mexican-American bilinguals. *Language and Society, 10*(1), 53–72.

Wierzbicka, A. (2003). *Cross-cultural pragmatics: The semantics of human interaction* (2nd ed.). Berlin: Walter de Gruyter.

Wolfson, N. (1983). An empirically based analysis of complimenting in American English. In N. Wolfson & E. Judd (Eds.), *Sociolinguistics and language acquisition* (pp. 82–95). London: Newbury House.

# Challenges Facing Mexican EFL Learners: Disagreement and Local Pragmatic Practices

Gerrard Mugford
Universidad de Guadalajara, Mexico

*In this paper, I focus on how users of English as a Foreign Language (EFL) in Mexico express disagreement in potentially uncomfortable and unfriendly situations. Current research examines disagreement in terms of pragmatics, discourse and conversation analysis, and socio-cultural practices with a focus on appropriate and acceptable strategies. However, learners also need to develop politeness and disagreement strategies that give them choices when negotiating difficult situations. I study politeness strategies in terms of Scollon and Wong Scollon's (1995) solidarity, deference, and hierarchical politeness as interlocutors consider their relationship with their addressee(s). Following Walkinshaw (2009), I describe the disagreement strategies in terms of high involvement disagreement, conciliative involvement, and suppression. To carry out the research, 31 participants responded to a discourse completion task (DCT) containing 10 potentially difficult and antagonistic situations that reflected negative/misguided comments concerning themselves and their country. The questions invited participants to take into consideration aspects such as the status of speaker and social distance and the degree of importance given the disagreement. Results indicate that there is a strong prevalence for conciliative involvement and a lack of variety when using of mitigating devices. This suggests that participants need to employ a much broader range of pragmalinguistic resources.*

## Introduction

Users of English as a Foreign Language (EFL) are often judged on their ability to follow target-language practices while disagreeing in the target language

(TL). When disagreeing, interlocutors face choices ranging from outright or "aggravated" disagreement and direct disagreement to less antagonistic partial disagreement and "token agreement" (Brown & Levinson, 1987, p. 113). I follow Bardovi-Harlig and Salsbury (2004) and define disagreement as oppositional turns where interactants are trying to express contrary views. Current literature in interlanguage pragmatics (ILP) focuses on the pragmatic and discursive resources for selecting a given disagreement strategy in order to downplay or soften potential antagonism (Bardovi-Harlig, 2010; Kasper & Rose, 2002). However, I argue it is also important that EFL users know how to react appropriately to potentially hostile situations and that they are also made aware of the implications of the choices that they make. Within the context of ILP (Bardovi-Harlig, 2010, 2013; Félix-Brasdefer & Koike, 2014; Kasper & Rose, 2002), I examine how EFL users in Guadalajara, Mexico, reacted to intimidating and unfriendly situations by administering Discourse Completion Tasks (DCTs) and analyzing the pragmalinguistic resources and strategies employed in order to negotiate antagonism.

The paper is structured as follows: In the theoretical section, I discuss definitions of disagreement before looking at different approaches to understanding and examining disagreement practices and strategies. I then specifically examine how disagreement has been approached in the teaching of English as a foreign language and the challenges with regard to learning and "doing" disagreement in the target language. I argue that responses to antagonistic situations depend on the EFL user's level of involvement, interpersonal and transactional relationships, and the importance of disagreeing in a given context. Finally, I offer the pedagogical implications of the study and how they can help develop EFL learner's pragmatic production.

## Theoretical framework

Disagreement can be understood in different ways, pragmatically, discursively, and conversationally, all of which are relevant to the teaching and learning of English as a foreign language. They lead to a working definition of this speech act. Such insights allow me to understand the choices that EFL users make regarding how they want to disagree in antagonistic situations. These include strong disagreement, mitigation or softened disagreement, and message abandonment (Maíz-Arévalo, 2014b). Classroom input and activities such as student judgment tasks, discourse completion tasks, and role-plays can help raise learners' awareness of disagreement practices as they are given opportunities to notice how disagreement is expressed in the target language.

### Defining disagreeing

Definitions regarding disagreeing focus on the lack of cooperation between interlocutors in "denoting any non-supportive previous turn within that immediate talk exchange" (Kleinke, 2010, p. 206). Furthermore, disagreement can undermine conversational harmony as expressed by Malamed: "Disagreement is a conflicting view offered as a response to an expressed view of a previous speaker" (2010, p. 202). Just like the native speaker, the EFL user needs to decide in a given interaction whether to cooperate with his/her interlocutor and, if not, how this lack of cooperation is to be communicated. This may be expressed by the participant going on record and voicing disagreement. Bond, Žegarac, and Spencer-Oatey (2000) underscore the public aspect to disagreement in that "some participant or participants in a situation of communication communicate(s) some belief or beliefs which are partly or fully inconsistent with some other belief or beliefs publicly held by another participant (or participants) in the same situation" (p. 62). Interlocutors need the pragmalinguistic resources to adopt a publicly-stated contrary position towards the assessments and statements of others. Conflicting views may be expressed in multiple ways: explicitly, implicitly, directly, indirectly, hedged, aggressively, and so forth. Therefore, any definition of disagreement needs to capture a sense of non-supportiveness, taking a public stance, and negotiating conflict. Following the work of Bardovi-Harlig and Salsbury (2004), along with Kleinke (2010), Bond, Žěgarac, and Spencer-Oatey (2000), and Malamed (2010), I define disagreement as openly expressing, both verbally and non-verbally, an oppositional stance towards the opinions, comments, and assertions of other interlocutors. However, since disagreement can be analyzed in different ways, I now briefly review different approaches to disagreement with the aim of understanding what interlocutors want to achieve and how they can go about achieving that objective.

### Approaches to disagreement

The study of disagreement can be approached through pragmatics (Brown & Levinson, 1987; Leech, 1983), relational work (Locher, 2004), discourse and conversation analysis (Pomerantz, 1984), and socio-cultural practices (Sifianou, 2012). Each approach offers its own insights into the enactment of disagreement patterns and practices that are especially relevant in the EFL teaching and learning context. Furthermore, disagreement can be studied as either a dichotomy between agreement and disagreement or an accepted and even encouraged social practice. While this paper primarily focuses on EFL users (i.e., English-language learners in Mexico), I will also make reference to ESL users (i.e., English-language learners in the United States).

A pragmatic approach to disagreement can be described in terms of avoidance strategies (e.g., Brown & Levinson's [1987] face-threatening acts [FTAs]), Leech's (1983) Politeness Principles, and relational work (Locher, 2004). In keeping with conventional approaches towards disagreement, Brown and Levinson (1987) and Leech (1983) follow the line that outright and antagonistic disagreement should be avoided. Brown and Levinson offer four sub-strategies for avoiding disagreement: token agreement, pseudo agreement, white lies, and hedging opinions (pp. 113–117). These sub-strategies aim to avoid conflict with the hearer. In a similar vein, Leech lists in his Politeness Principles the Agreement Maxim which calls on interactants to

(a) Minimize disagreement between *self* and *other*
[(b) Maximize agreement between *self* and *other*]
(1983, p. 132, emphasis added, brackets in the original)

Leech (1983) argues for the avoidance of disagreement and says "partial disagreement is often preferable to complete disagreement" (p. 138). Further, he states, "there is a tendency to exaggerate agreement with other people, and to mitigate disagreement by expressing regret, partial agreement, etc." (p. 138).

In contrast, disagreement may be seen as accepted and even preferred behavior. For instance, Locher (2004) examines disagreement in terms of relational work and situated context. She focuses on the interactants themselves rather than on purely examining interactional practices and patterns. She argues that disagreeing is not always purely negative as speakers may "even enjoy the exchange of verbal disagreement because it is part of the expected speech" (p. 94). Seeing disagreement in terms of participants and interaction offers an interpersonal dimension to disagreement, and "[t]his *relational* view allows us to focus not only on the content of the disagreement, the interactional order of exchange, and the linguistic forms in which disagreement is rendered, but also on how disagreement is used to negotiate relationships through relational work (Locher & Watts, 2005)" (Angouri & Locher, 2012, p. 1550). Disagreement as preferred social behavior has been documented in both culturally-focused and socially-related studies. For instance, Kakava (2002), Sifianou (2012), and Tannen and Kakava (1992) argue that disagreement is ubiquitous in Greek society. In social contexts, disagreement is an expected form of behavior in business meetings (Angouri & Locher, 2012; Locher, 2004) and academic debate (Angouri & Tseliga, 2010; Tannen, 2002).

A structural approach to disagreement is found in conversation analysis and in the work of Pomerantz (1984) who focuses on preferred and dispreferred assessments. In examining disagreement, Pomerantz argues that there are two main courses of action: agreement preferred and agreement dispreferred. In agreement preferred, interlocutors avoid outright disagreement: "When a conversant hears a coparticipant's assessment being completed and his or her own agreement / disagreement is relevant and due, he or she may produce delays, such as 'no talk,' requests for clarification, partial repeats, and other repair initiators, turn prefaces, and so on. Incorporating delay devices constitutes a typical turn shape for disagreements when agreements are invited" (Pomerantz, 1984, p. 70). Such actions offer EFL users non-antagonistic ways of dealing with disagreement. Disagreement may subsequently come across as strong or weak as in "agreement-plus-disagreement" types (Pomerantz, 1984, p. 74).

An examination of disagreement in terms of pragmatics, relational work, socio-cultural practices, and conversation analysis can shed light on the resources that ESL interlocutors need to access. Brown and Levinson (1987) and Leech (1983, p. 2014) offer pragmalinguistic resources for mitigating disagreement. Locher (2004) offers a relational view as interlocutors negotiate disagreement. Other studies show how disagreement is an expected form of cultural and social behavior. In conversation analysis, Pomerantz provides a structural approach to disagreement through preferred and dispreferred responses. I will now examine the teaching and learning of disagreement in the EFL context following Scollon and Wong Scollon (1995) theoretical approach.

## Disagreement in EFL teaching

Studies on TL disagreement patterns and practices have increased considerably in recent years with a focus on developing EFL user's disagreement strategies (e.g., Hidalgo, Hidalgo, & Downing, 2014; Walkinshaw, 2009), the identification of desirable and undesirable EFL disagreement practices (e.g., Kreutel, 2007; Maíz-Arévalo, 2014a), and the appropriateness of disagreement strategies (e.g., Bell 1998; Maíz-Arévalo, 2014b; Zhu & Boxer, 2012). Studies on disagreement have also been carried out in ESL (e.g., Bardovi-Harlig & Salsbury, 2004) that are also relevant to EFL. I will argue however, little research has been conducted on providing EFL users with the appropriate resources to disagree in potentially uncomfortable and unfriendly situations.

Analyzing turn-taking in natural conversation, through a longitudinal study based on conversational interviews, Bardovi-Harlig & Salsbury (2004) studied the disagreement strategies of ESL users interacting with MA linguistics students enrolled in a graduate second language acquisition course. The results show that interaction with native speakers helped ESL students to develop indirect disagreement strategies as they increased their amount of talk, included agreement along with disagreement components, delayed the expression of disagreement within a turn, and expressed disagreement across several turns. Hidalgo et al. (2014), through adopting a role-play eliciting procedure, examine the EFL users' thought processes when expressing disagreement, among other speech functions, in English and Spanish. Analyzing the use of indirectness and mitigation strategies, Hidalgo et al. argue that ESL users have a wider range in Spanish, while in English they tend to use conventionalized forms of disagreement.

Employing a combination of student judgment tasks, discourse completion tasks and role-plays, Walkinshaw (2009) carried out a cross-cultural study of Japanese learners of English with New Zealand speakers of English. While accepting Brown and Levinson's (1987) view of politeness, Walkinshaw (2009) examines possible cross-cultural differences in expressing disagreement in Japanese and English. In conducting the part of the study that related to production, Walkinshaw divided disagreement strategies into four categories:

explicit disagreement; hedged disagreement; implied disagreement; and avoidance, that is, no disagreement (p. 137). Although the results indicated that the Japanese learners of English showed some similarities with New Zealand speakers of English, there was a "noted trend toward using more explicit and direct disagreement strategies in situations where the JLEs did not know their native speaker interlocutor..." (Walkinshaw, 2009, p. 163).

Evaluating the performance of ESL users when disagreeing, Kreutel (2007), using discourse completion tasks, and Maíz-Arévalo (2014a), employing text analysis of student work and explicit instruction, identify desirable and undesirable disagreement practices. Kreutel lists desirable disagreement features as token agreement, hedges, requests for clarifications, explanations, expressions of regret, and positive remarks. Meanwhile, undesirable features include message abandonment, total lack of mitigation, use of the performative *I disagree*, use of the performative negation *I don't agree*, use of the bare exclamation *no*, and the blunt statement of the opposite (Kreutel, 2007, p. 5). She argues that in this study EFL users engage in "desirable, mitigating features significantly less frequently than native speakers" (p. 19). Furthermore, she says they should be encouraged to evade avoidance strategies and potentially rude replies.

Examining through classroom observation the appropriateness of student interaction when disagreeing with each other, Bell (1998) compared the expression of disagreements with requests and suggestions among high-beginning Korean learners of English. She identified the expression of disagreement as "linguistically well-formed" and "linguistically simple." The participants demonstrated a strong preference for an indiscriminate use of negative politeness strategies (Brown & Levinson, 1987) regardless of context. She also found that L1 factors such as status and age influenced the use of TL disagreement responses. Meanwhile, Maíz-Arévalo (2014b) examined the expression of disagreement in English as a lingua franca through text analysis of students' written production and in particular those norms and patterns the EFL users adhere to. She concludes that "participants with a high linguistic proficiency closely follow the same strategies native speakers do in order to avoid face-threat (not only toward their interlocutors' face but also to their own)" (p. 220). Maíz-Arévalo (2014b) argues that the participants "followed the common rules of the native variety they all shared: Standard British English. This allowed them to discuss and negotiate more comfortably according to common rules that avoided pragmatic failure and facilitated a satisfactory fulfilment of their group task" (pp. 220–221). Therefore, adherence to TL norms and practices can be seen as providing common ground and understandings.

By recording natural conversations, Zhu and Boxer (2012) also examined disagreement behavior in English as a lingua franca. Studying Mandarin speakers of English, they found that interlocutors tended to overuse strong disagreement, perhaps influenced by L1, and consequently ran the risk of coming across inappropriately since there is little interaction with native TL speakers.

Whereas research into disagreement has generally examined disagreement in terms of resources, interaction patterns, and cultural and social behavior, studies in EFL have focused more on whether learners follow target-language norms and practices, especially with regard to strong / weak disagreement and the use of mitigation as well as appropriateness. Less research has focused on disagreement as an acceptable practice, especially when EFL users face difficult and uncomfortable situations.

In the present study, I investigate the following overarching research question: What pragmalinguistic resources do Mexican EFL users employ to express disagreement in difficult or antagonistic situations? My specific research question is: Do EFL students follow conventional target-language practices and patterns of use to express disagreement in the target language? If they do not, this may be problematic if EFL users are not aware of how they come across of the pragmatic force of their chosen disagreement strategy. I am conducting qualitative research that examines the range of pragmalinguistic resources employed rather than their frequency.

## Method

In this section, I outline data collection methods and describe the participants, the empirical setting, and the use of DCTs for conducting research.

### Participants

The 31 students who participated in this research were in the final year of their BA at a public university in Guadalajara, Mexico. There were 18 women and 13 men, aged between 18 and 24 years old, and they came from middle-class urban backgrounds. They have advanced levels of English and they have been achieving scores of over 500 points in Test of English as a Foreign Language (TOEFL) in their final year of study – a university requirement to graduate from the program. Although most students had visited the United States, Canada, and the United Kingdom, usually on holiday, they largely learned their English in Mexico in the public school systems or at private language institutes.

### Research instrument: The use of DCTs

Discourse completion tasks have been subjected to scrutiny with regards to their reliability in collecting data in pragmatics research. Indeed, research into EFL and ESL disagreement practices have often used naturally occurring conversation (e.g., Bardovi-Harlig & Salsbury, 2004; Bell, 1998), protocols (e.g., Hidalgo et al., 2014), or computer-mediated communication (CMC; e.g., Maíz-Arévalo, 2014a, 2014b). DCTs were used by Kreutel but she admits she uses "the written mode to elicit speech act data that we assume to represent spontaneous reactions in the oral mode" (2007, p. 20). Therefore, she accepts that "naturally occurring conversations or oral activities such as role-plays" (p. 20) might have offered different results.

As Leech (2014) remarks, "[o]f all the methods of pragmatic data collection, the discourse completion test (DCT) has been the most prevalent, but it has also lent itself to a great deal of controversy" (p. 252). He outlines the limitations of this research instrument by noting that "the DCT is strictly constrained in eliciting a response to a particular scenario, which specifies details of the interlocutor and the context" (p. 252). Furthermore, focusing on written questionnaires, Leech (2014) argues that

...the DCT has traditionally and typically been delivered in the form of a written questionnaire, containing a number of items, which can be as many as twenty or so. Thus the respondent (a) has a limited amount of white space to fill and (b) may also be subject to time constraints; further fatigue may set in, so in practice responses will be fairly short. (p. 252)

DCTs have also been criticized because they lack authenticity and fail to record what participants would actually say. Bardovi-Harlig (2013) argues that DCTs lack individuality and interaction. Furthermore, because interlocutors have time to reflect, discourse completion tasks lack spontaneity and, in the case of disagreement, a failure to capture on-the-spot reaction to antagonistic situations. Indeed, reflection may result in interlocutors producing more mitigation than in real-life conversations (for discussion, see Kasper, 2000, 2008).

DCTs have limitations in that they may lack spontaneity and more often than not reflect intuition rather than actual language use (see, e.g., Kasper, 2008) and fail to capture the sociopragmatic dimensions. However, I am more interested in examining the range of pragmalinguistic resources EFL users employ when disagreeing and DCTs offer one way to study those resources.

**Discourse completion task**

To answer the research question, I asked 31 students to respond to a discourse completion task (DCT), which they had to complete in the classroom. They were not given a time limit. Participants were asked to respond to situations in writing. The potentially difficult and antagonistic situations had been previously collected, though oral interviews, at the beginning of the semester from experiences that the students from another group had confronted in and outside of Mexico:

Research participants were given a range of situations in which they had to respond to negative / misguided comments concerning themselves and their country (i.e., Mexico). The questions invited participants to take into consideration aspects such as status of speaker and their potential power (e.g., teacher and father / mother of a host family), the degree of *face* threat (e.g., the student being accused of not paying attention or being told that they are wrong in front of the whole class), social distance (e.g., classmates and strangers), and the degree of importance given the disagreement (e.g., the location of Guadalajara or whether Mexicans are lazy). Situations included the EFL classroom in Mexico, study abroad contexts, staying with a host family, and traveling by plane. Fuller details of these situations are presented in the Appendix.

The different settings are summarized as in Table 1 to reflect situation, context, the politeness dimension, and interactional factors. Situations reflect possible negative / antagonistic circumstances that are potentially uncomfortable and unfriendly for the EFL learner. Context introduces relational considerations such as social distance, status, and so forth. The politeness dimension focuses on the type of politeness system: solidarity politeness (–P,–D), deference politeness (–P, +D) or hierarchical politeness (+P, +D). Interactional factors summarize the nature of the incident in transactional and interpersonal terms and whether it is a public or closed event.

**Table 1.** Antagonistic and difficult contexts + politeness system

| situation | context | politeness system | factors |
|---|---|---|---|
| 1 | teacher says that there will be a class on a public holiday | hierarchical +P +D | transactional misinformation |
| 2 | teacher tells a student that he/she has not been paying attention | hierarchical +P +D | transactional allegation |
| 3 | teacher tells a student he/she is wrong in front of the whole class | hierarchical +P +D | public allegation |
| 4 | classmate gives the wrong location of Guadalajara | solidarity –P –D | peer's interpersonal misinformation |
| 5 | Canadian classmate says that Mexicans are lazy | solidarity –P –D | peer's serious interpersonal allegation |
| 6 | Canadian classmate insists that Mexicans speak Mexican | solidarity –P –D | peer's interpersonal misinformation |
| 7 | host family father/mother insists that Mexicans are lazy | deference –P +D | serious transactional allegation |
| 8 | host family father/mother insists that Mexicans speak Mexican | deference –P +D | transactional misinformation |
| 9 | fellow passenger insists that Mexicans are lazy | deference –P +D | stranger's serious allegation |
| 10 | fellow passenger insists that Mexicans speak Mexican | deference –P +D | stranger's misinformation |

All the participants answered in English. The participants were given no instructions on how to respond to the situations and were free to express agreement or disagreement. As the results will show, the vast majority of participants responded through expressing disagreement.

## Descriptive categories

In determining how to express disagreement in a given situation, interlocutors need to take into consideration the closeness / distance in the relationship, the need to openly demonstrate personal respect for other interlocutors, and possible acknowledgement of social status. These aspects reflect the interpersonal degree of involvement when disagreeing. Scollon and Wong Scollon (1995) have categorized them in terms of solidarity politeness (−P,−D), deference politeness (−P, +D) or hierarchical politeness (+P, +D) where P stands for power and D for distance. Solidarity politeness reflects a high level of involvement between interlocutors who see themselves as equals. With deference politeness participants see themselves as equals but show mutual respect for one another. Meanwhile, hierarchical politeness recognizes socially inequal relationship as one interlocutor "lowers" him/herself to the other, and in response the other adopts an independent stance which underscores social distance.

To understand how Scollon and Wong Scollon's (1994) politeness systems can be seen in foreign-language users' disagreement strategies, I examine whether participants are engaged in high involvement, conciliative involvement or suppression. High involvement, or explicit disagreement (Walkinshaw 2009), reflects the intensity of an interlocutor's participation in a given situation where the interest is in expressing disagreement rather than in attending to the relationship. It shows a lack of concern for closeness or respect for other interlocutors. High involvement may be expressed through aggravated / unmodulated and direct disagreement. Conciliative involvement, or hedged and implied disagreement (Walkinshaw, 2009), shows that an interlocutor is concerned about the relationship which may be demonstrated by showing closeness, by exhibiting respect for other interlocutors, or by ratifying the addressee's social status. Conciliative involvement can be expressed through indirect and softened disagreement such as hedging.

Given the potential face-threatening immensity of the disagreement itself or its effect on the interlocutor, participants may decide to suppress any attempt at disagreement and undertake avoidance, that is, no disagreement (Walkinshaw, 2009). Suppression of disagreement suggests that an interlocutor disagrees but resists voicing his/her dissent, which is mirrored in Brown and Levinson's "Don't do the FTA" (1987, p. 69). An interlocutor has choices: He/she may agree for the sake of agreeing, "token agreement" (Brown & Levinson, 1987, p. 113); avoid making any comment and change the topic of conversation (e.g., avoidance; delay making any comment, postponement); or remain quiet and in silence. These strategies are illustrated in Table 2:

**Table 2.** Disagreement strategies

| disagreement strategy | importance of defending point of view | focus on relationship | strategy | example (student response to teacher about paying attention in class) |
|---|---|---|---|---|
| high involvement / explicit disagreement | + | — | aggravated / unmodulated and direct disagreement | Mmm, but I was paying attention, I even took notes. |
| conciliative involvement, or hedged and implied disagreement | — | + | indirect and softened disagreement e.g., hedging | I'm sorry you think that I was actually paying attention. |
| suppression of disagreement | — | + | token agreement; change topic; delay making any comment; remain quiet | silence |

## Results

In the following section, I examine whether findings from the 31 participants who responded to the 10 DCTs help answer the research question regarding the resources that Mexican EFL users employ to express disagreement in difficult or antagonistic situations in terms. I look at whether the learners expressed high involvement (aggravated or unmodulated disagreement, direct disagreement), conciliative disagreement (indirect disagreement and softened disagreement), and suppression (token agreement, avoidance, postponement and silence). I then analyze disagreement practices in terms of solidarity politeness (–P, –D), deference politeness (–P, +D) and hierarchical politeness (+P, +D).

### Overall results of strategy use

A summary of the results, presented in Table 3, demonstrates how the three politeness systems are expressed in terms of high involvement, conciliative involvement, and suppression by the participants in the study:

The overall findings indicate that respondents sought to use high and conciliative involvement and avoid suppression and token agreement and avoidance. However, conciliative involvement (i.e., indirect / hedged disagreement) was used extensively and, to a large degree, independently of the situation or the context (62% or 192/310 strategies). These results suggest that EFL students need to have a wider range of strategies to match differing and contrasting situations.

**Table 3.** Summary of overall results: Use of politeness and disagreement strategies

| politeness system | situations | use of high involvement (explicit disagreement) | use of conciliative involvement (indirect / hedged disagreement) | use of suppression (token agreement / avoidance) | other | total |
|---|---|---|---|---|---|---|
| hierarchical politeness | 1–3 | 24 | 64 | 4 | 1 | 93 |
| solidarity politeness | 4–6 | 43 | 46 | 3 | 1 | 93 |
| deference politeness | 7–10 | 32 | 82 | 9 | | 124 |
| totals | | 99 (32%) | 192 (62%) | 16 (5%) | 3 (1.0%) | 310 |

## Specific use of politeness and disagreement strategies

In order to illustrate the strategies used in individual situations, Table 4 shows a summary of each context in terms of situation, politeness parameters, and strategies employed (e.g., high involvement, conciliative involvement, and suppression). I then provide the findings for each of the individual situations.

The summary of the individual situations indicates that conciliative involvement (192 responses), in terms of indirectness (82 responses) and softeners (110 responses), was the preferred strategy when dealing with disagreement. These results suggest a strategy of avoiding direct conflict while disagreeing.

Hierarchical politeness (+P, +D) reflects the need to take into consideration the status of addresses as seen in the teacher-student contexts: context 1 (Teacher says that there will be a class on a public holiday), context 2 (Teacher says to a student that he/she has not been paying attention), context 3 (Teacher tells a student he/she is wrong in front of the whole class). The student would be expected to recognize status inequality in the relationship.

**Table 4.** Summary of individual situations: Use of politeness and disagreement strategies

| | situation | politeness system | high involvement aggravated / unmodulated | high involvement direct | conciliative involvement indirect | conciliative involvement softened | suppression token agreement / avoidance / postponement / silence | other | total strategies used |
|---|---|---|---|---|---|---|---|---|---|
| 1 | teacher says that there will be a class on a public holiday | hierarchical +P +D | 2 (6%) | 1 (3%) | 20 (65%) | 7 (23%) | 0 | 1 (3%) | 31 |
| 2 | teacher tells a student that he/she has not been paying attention | hierarchical +P +D | 0 | 18 (58%) | 1 (3%) | 11 (36%) | 1 (3%) | 0 | 31 |
| 3 | teacher tells a student he/she is wrong in front of the whole class | hierarchical +P +D | 1 (3%) | 2 (6%) | 16 (52%) | 9 (29%) | 3 (10%) | 0 | 31 |
| 4 | classmate gives the wrong location of Guadalajara | solidarity −P −D | 2 (7%) | 8 (26%) | 2 (6%) | 18 (58%) | 0 | 1 (3%) | 31 |
| 5 | Canadian classmate says that Mexicans are lazy | solidarity −P −D | 10 (32%) | 7 (23%) | 2 (6%) | 10 (32%) | 2 (6%) | 0 | 31 |
| 6 | Canadian classmate insists that Mexicans speak Mexican | solidarity −P −D | 11 (36%) | 5 (16%) | 9 (29%) | 5 (16%) | 1 (3%) | 0 | 31 |
| 7 | host family father/mother insists that Mexicans are lazy | deference +P −D | 1 (3%) | 4 (13%) | 5 (16%) | 18 (58%) | 3 (10%) | 0 | 31 |
| 8 | host family father/mother insists that Mexicans speak Mexican | deference +P −D | 1 (3%) | 4 (13%) | 11 (36%) | 13 (42%) | 1 (3%) | 1 (3%) | 31 |
| 9 | fellow passenger insists that Mexicans are lazy deference | deference +P −D | 4 (13%) | 7 (23%) | 5 (16%) | 11 (36%) | 4 (13%) | 0 | 31 |
| 10 | fellow passenger insists that Mexicans speak Mexican | deference +P −D | 8 (26) | 3 (10%) | 11 (36%) | 8 (26%) | 1 (3%) | 0 | 31 |
| | total | | 40 | 59 | 82 | 110 | 16 | 3 | 310 |

In context one, participants were asked to respond to the teacher's announcement that there would be a class the following Friday, which was in fact a public holiday. Given the teacher's status, students could be expected to engage in hierarchical politeness (+P, +D) and express conciliative involvement. Perhaps recognizing the teacher's position and trying to avoid threatening the teacher's *face*, the majority of participants (65%) opted for indirect disagreement, such as *But I think that day is a public holiday* and *Teacher, I'm afraid there are no courses next Friday*. The answers reflect hierarchical politeness where the participants recognize rank (e.g., with the use of *teacher* and impersonal structures reflecting independent strategies). None of the participants agreed to go to class. Indirect disagreement was expressed through asking questions as in *Next Friday? Isn't it a holiday?* and *Teacher, do we have to come even if it's a public holiday?* Softened disagreement (23%) was expressed through the use of such hedges as *I'm afraid* (2), *sorry* (1), *I think* (1) and *but* (1), and by employing the modals *may* and *might*. In the "other" category, one participant said that he would just laugh.

In context two, the participants were accused by the teacher of not paying attention in class. Taking into consideration the status of the teacher, students could be expected to demonstrate hierarchical politeness (+P, +D). However, in this instance, the participants' *face* is being directly threatened and they may not have felt so conciliatory. Since the situation is *face-threatening*, 18 participants (58%) were highly involved, ignored the interpersonal dimension, and defended themselves against the teacher's allegations. They directly challenged the teacher with such replies as: *I was teacher. Why do you think so, teacher?* and *Yes I was, ask me something*. In contrast, 11 participants (36%) appeared to recognize the status of the teacher and demonstrated softened disagreement. They employed softeners such as *Sorry, but I was paying attention* and *I'm sorry you think that, I was actually paying attention*. There was a significant use of hedges such as *I'm afraid* (3), *but* (2), *well* (1), *just* (1), and *actually* (1), along with the use of the modal *might* and the filler *mmm*.

In context three, the participants were told in front of the whole class that they were wrong. In this situation, the participants' *face* is being directly threatened by a higher authority in front of an audience, that is, the rest of the class. They have the option of saving their public *face* or engaging in hierarchical politeness (+P, +D) and respecting the teacher's status. Due to the nature of the public FTA, one might have expected participants to have reacted in more aggravated and direct ways. However, 16 respondents (52%) opted for conciliatory involvement with expressions such as *Could you explain why it's wrong?* and *Why you say so?* Indirect disagreement was often expressed through asking questions (13 participants). Meanwhile, nine participants (29%) chose softened disagreement with expressions such as *Well, I thought I was correct* and *Well, you have a point there. However, I think I gave the right response*. The following hedges were used:

*think* (4), *sorry* (2), and *well*, (1) along with the use of the modals *may* and *would* and the filler *mmm*. These respondents were presumably aware of the status difference between themselves and the teacher and were unwilling to confront the teacher. In the case of the students who suppressed disagreement, two said that they would talk to the teacher later, perhaps reflecting Pomerantz's delayed disagreement, and a third would try rephrasing what he had originally said with the aim of the teacher saying that he was correct.

Solidarity politeness (−P,−D) is focused on the nature of the relationship since neither power nor distance play key roles in determining the politeness strategy, as can be seen in context 4 (Classmate gives the wrong location of Guadalajara), context 5 (Reacting to a Canadian classmate who says that Mexicans are lazy), and context 6 (A Canadian classmate insists that Mexicans speak Mexican),

In context four, the participants were in a business course in Canada when a classmate gave the wrong location of Guadalajara. As peers, the relationship between the interlocutors shows both reduced power and social distance (−P,−D) and offers an opportunity to engage in solidarity politeness. Furthermore, the misinformation and inaccuracy may not be considered as particularly serious. The majority of respondents adopted a conciliatory position by engaging in solidarity politeness. Taking into account *face* considerations, they expressed softened disagreement (58%), such as *I see why you think that but it is not exactly in the south* and *I don't think so, I think it's more*. A closer examination of the softening devices reveals the use of a wide range of mitigating devices: *actually* (6), *well* (5), *I think* (4), *but* (2), *I'm afraid* (2), *I'm sorry* (1), *I see* (1), and *kind of* (1). Eight participants felt that it was important to correct the classmate and used expressions such as *That's not true* and *No, no. That's not right*. One participant said that he would just laugh.

In context five, the respondents were faced with the situation where a classmate claims that Mexicans are lazy. While the situation reflects a lack of power and social distance (−P,−D) between peers, the assertion is particularly *face* threatening. In contrast to context four where the location of Guadalajara might not have been seen as that important, context five directly attacks the *face* of the respondents and perhaps *national face* (Magistro, 2011). One would expect to see a high level of involvement and indeed 10 respondents (32%) expressed aggravated / unmodulated disagreement (e.g., *Well thanks to Mexicans you have fruit on your table, so I don't think Mexicans are lazy* and *Of course not. I am Mexican and I'm not lazy*) and seven (23%) direct disagreements (e.g., *I totally disagree!* and *I don't agree with you*). These respondents were willing to adopt a hard-hitting stance towards the classmate while others used softening expressions such as *I don't think so. I'm a Mexican and don't feel I'm so lazy* and *Well, of course there are some but most are hard-working*. The following hedges were used: *I think* (3), *well* (2), *but* (2), *feel* (1), *kind of* (1), and *I'm afraid* (1). Such a stance would appear to be overly conciliatory and may reflect the desire to avoid argument and conflict.

In context six, a Canadian classmate insists that Mexicans speak Mexican. The situation, reflecting a lack of power and social distance (–P,–D) between peers, highlights a lack of knowledge or, at worst, ignorance. The participants can engage in solidarity politeness and try to correct the misperception or outright rejecting the comment. The idea that a Canadian student does not know that Mexicans speak Spanish provoked a high involvement response from the participants with 11 respondents (36%) opting for aggravated / unmodulated disagreement (e.g., *You can't be serious* and *Of course not! We speak Spanish*). The need to correct such a misperception may be a matter of national pride and undermines national face. Indirect disagreement tended to be hostile (e.g., *What is exactly Mexican to you?* and *Mexican is not a language, you know*). Only two softeners were used: *well* (4) and *but* (3). One respondent expressed token agreement: *That is true*.

Deference politeness is concerned with demonstrated respect for other interlocutors that can be employed with hosts and strangers. This can be seen in context 7 (Host family father/mother insists that Mexicans are lazy), context 8 (Host family father/mother insists that Mexicans speak Mexican), context 9 (Fellow passenger insists that Mexicans are lazy) and context 10 (Fellow passenger insists that Mexicans speak Mexican).

In context seven, the father/mother of a host family in the United States insists that Mexicans are lazy. In this situation, there is a need to show deference (–P, +D) to the family with whom the participants are staying. The family may merit respect even if they do not have social power. In contrast to context five when the respondents were interacting with a peer, in this situation the participants are staying with a host family where it may be more difficult to express open disagreement, especially given the nature of the relationship: paying guests staying in someone's home. Eighteen participants (58%) adhered to conciliative involvement and adopted a softened approach with expressions such as *Well, there are some but…* and *Well, perhaps some are, but I feel I most are hard-working people*. A closer examination of the softening devices reveals limited use of mitigating devices: *but* (5), *I think* (4), *well* (3), *I'm afraid* (3), and *I'm sorry* (3).

In context eight, the respondents are staying with a host family when the father / mother insists that Mexicans speak Mexican. Similar to situation seven, there is a need to show politeness deference (–P, +D) to the family with whom the participants are staying but, at the same time, the participants need to evaluate the importance of voicing disagreement over this misperception. In contrast to situation 6 where a peer was insisting that Mexicans speak Mexican, the participants have to consider the degree of deference that should be shown to the host family. Reflecting conciliative agreement, the majority of respondents opted for indirect disagreement (36%; e.g., *You think so?, Why?,* and *You mean*

Spanish don't you?) and softened disagreement (42%; e.g., *Well, maybe you mean Spanish* and *I see your point but we speak Spanish as any other Latin country*). There was a wide range of hedges including *well* (4), *actually* (3), *maybe* (2), *but* (1), *I think* (1), *you know* (1), *I see* (1), and *I'm afraid* (1). The use of hedges suggests that the respondents were sensitive to the situation.

In context nine, the participants' *face* is being directly threatened by a stranger who insists that Mexicans are lazy in front of an audience (i.e., fellow passengers on a plane in the United States). The participants can react by demonstrating deference politeness (–P, +D) given that there is a lack of power and a casual relationship. Contexts five and seven examined how a peer and host family viewed Mexicans as lazy. In context nine, respondents had to react to a group of fellow passengers who, for all intents and purposes, were strangers. The respondents' level of involvement would not appear to have been governed by an ongoing relationship. Despite the level of *face* threat, the majority of participants adhered to conciliative involvement (52%): indirect (16%) and softened disagreement (36%;e.g., *I'm sorry you think that way, but not all of them are like that*, and *Well, not all of us*). There were a variety of hedges used including *but* (4), *I think* (3), *well* (2), *sorry* (1), and *kind of* (1).

In context ten, a fellow passenger on the plane insists that Mexicans speak Mexican. Given the transitory nature of the encounter, the participants do not have a close relationship but may want to show respect and engage in deference politeness (–P, +D). The respondents adopted a variety of approaches, suggesting different levels of involvement. High involvement was expressed through aggravated/unmodulated agreement (25%), as in *No, we don't. How about looking for some information about it* and *Of course not. You're wrong*, and through direct disagreement (10%). Perhaps given the unlikelihood of meeting the fellow passenger again, the respondents might have been expected to extensively employ aggravated / unmodulated disagreement. However, the majority of participants (51.5%) opted for conciliative agreement: Indirect disagreement (36%) was reflected in the use of questions such as *What do you mean by Mexican?* and *Where did you get that information?* Meanwhile, softeners included *I'm sorry if I disagree, there are many hard working people* and *I'm afraid we don't. Don't you mean Spanish?* The following hedges were employed: *but* (4), *well* (1), *sorry* (1), *a little bit* (1), *I believe* (1), *I see* (1), and *I'm afraid* (1) along with the use of the modal *would*.

## Discussion

The discussion section centers on whether findings from the 31 participants who responded to the 10 DCTs helped to answer the research question regarding the resources that Mexican EFL users employ to express disagreement in difficult or antagonistic situations in terms. An analysis of the results reveals that solidarity politeness (–P,–D), deference politeness (–P, +D), and hierarchical politeness

(+P, +D; Scollon and Wong Scollon, 1995) were evident in the answers. However, the range of answers was limited and there was strong preference for conciliatory agreement even when high involvement may have called for aggravated / unmodulated and direct disagreement (Walkinshaw, 2009).

With regards to hierarchical politeness (+P, +D), in context one where the teacher says there will be a class on a public holiday, the participants had to decide between engaging in a face threatening act and their ongoing relationship with the teacher (+P, +D). EFL students need to have at their disposal a range of appropriate disagreement strategies (Kreutel, 2007; Maíz-Arévalo, 2014a). Learners who opted for high involvement (i.e., aggravated or direct disagreement) need to be made aware of the ramifications of expressing strong disagreement in an institutional context. Most participants employed conciliative involvement and pedagogical intervention needs to introduce a wider range of softeners. Again, with regard to hierarchical politeness, in context two where the teacher says to a student that he/she has not been paying attention (+P, +D), the participants were especially willing to challenge the teacher with the "do not agree" structure as in *I'm afraid I don't agree* and *I can't agree with you*. As Carter & McCarthy (2006) argue, the verb *disagree* is rarely used in everyday conversational English. Students need to weight up the desire to defend their own face against going on record and unwittingly attacking the face of the teacher. Following Leech (1983), students may want to consider the advantages of minimizing disagreement between *self* and *other* (p. 132) in ongoing hierarchical institutional relationships. Hierarchical politeness is relevant to context three where the teacher tells a student he/she is wrong in front of the whole class, the student's public face is threatened. In such instances, learners need to think about consequences of voicing disagreement. If a student feels that he/she is being attacked, open disagreement may only lead to heightened tensions and conflicts. Instead students need to consider whether disagreement can be achieved in a more measured and controlled way over a series of turns (Bardovi-Harlig & Salsbury, 2004) rather than through single-turn aggravated or unmodulated disagreement. In this context participants opted for conciliative disagreement but there was still a lack of softeners. At the same time, EFL students need to take into account that other students are participating in the interaction whether it be as ratified side participants or unratified bystanders or overhearers (Kádár & Haugh, 2013, p. 1). Their very presence will influence the subsequent development of and reaction to disagreement.

Solidarity politeness reflects the need to consider the interpersonal dimension of interacting with peers. In context four where a classmate gives the wrong location of Guadalajara, participants had to consider how to interact with classmates. Options can be examined in terms of Walkinshaw's (2009) disagreement strategies: explicit disagreement, hedged disagreement, implied disagreement, and avoidance (i.e., no disagreement). Their selected strategy will depend on the need to disagree and, if so, how this will be carried out. It may not be necessary to contradict or voice disagreement with every opinion or statement if its relevance or importance is not particularly significant. Students need to reflect on the effectiveness of strong disagreement strategies in this context. Also reflecting possible solidarity politeness, in context five where a Canadian classmate says that Mexicans are lazy, there is a greater need to come across forcefully and dispute the statement, especially since national *face* is also at stake. Students need a range of ways of expressing strong disagreement, for example, Walkinshaw's (2009) explicit disagreement strategies. This is especially challenging for the EFL teacher since pedagogic materials aim to soften or avoid disagreement. Students may benefit from analyzing TL speakers' strategies when disagreeing in order to see the options available to them (Maíz-Arévalo, 2014a). In context six, where a Canadian classmate insists that Mexicans speak Mexican, students need to think about how to react to this misperception. Rather than adopt an aggravated or direct strategy, students may wish to be more conciliatory and reflect about whether everyone should really know that Mexicans speak Spanish. Direct confrontation may not be the best way to inform or instruct people. In this study, there was little difference in how participants reacted to Mexicans being called lazy and Mexicans speaking "Mexican." I would argue that students need help in assessing the seriousness and significance of different misperceptions and consequently how they should react.

Deference politeness reflects perceived equality between interlocutors along with mutual respect for one another. In context seven where a host family father / mother insists that Mexicans are lazy, participants need to balance the nature of their transactional relationship (i.e., paying "guests" with the interpersonal relationship they have with the family). Nevertheless, the comment is a direct attack on the participants' face and national face while students chose conciliative disagreement. Although Locher (2004) has examined interpersonal aspects regarding disagreement, within the EFL literature itself the interpersonal disagreement dimension in transactional situations has not been actively considered. Classroom teaching needs to present the available options and discuss the implications of taking a given course of action, especially when trying to disagree from a potentially weaker position. In context eight where the host family father/mother insists that Mexicans speak Mexican, participants need to weigh up the benefits of disagreeing over a misperception in a transactional situation. Direct disagreement with a peer, as in context six, might only have interpersonal consequences. Disagreement is a much more sensitive undertaking with a host family where the need for deference is an important consideration. Most participants engaged in conciliative disagreement using indirectness and softeners. Appropriate use can be reinforced pedagogically by asking students to reflect on desirable and undesirable disagreement practices (Kreutel, 2007; Maíz-Arévalo, 2014a). In context nine, where a fellow passenger on a plane insists that Mexicans are lazy, participants are confronted with a direct face threat from a stranger. There is no ongoing relationship and participants may have more options in coming across forcefully and disputing the statement. Since EFL materials do not provide sufficient guidelines for engaging in overt disagreement, learners may be able to refer to resources from their first language (Hidalgo et al., 2014) and evaluate their applicability in the target language. Respondents appeared to be divided between using high involvement and conciliatory agreement and need to reflect on the implications of each strategy. In context ten, where a fellow passenger on a plane insists that Mexicans speak Mexican, participants need to consider their choices when interacting with strangers. Similar to context nine, participants may feel that they can be more assertive given the transitory nature of the relationship. At the same time, interlocutors should consider whether there is really a need to disagree and whether vehement disagreement will help them achieve their objective. Once again, learners may be able to call on resources from their first language (Hidalgo et al., 2014). As with fellow students, there was little difference in how interlocutors reacted to a passenger calling Mexicans lazy and another interlocutor thinking that Mexicans speak Spanish. Again, I would argue that students need help in assessing the seriousness of the misperception and consequently how they should react.

Discussion of the results reveals that the interpersonal-transactional dimension is an important consideration when examining ways of disagreeing in the target language. While participants are aware of the sociolinguistic considerations in a given context, they do not consider the importance of topic, the possible need to disagree, and the options available to them. Furthermore, the strong prevalence for conciliative involvement and the lack of variety in the use of mitigating devices indicate that participants need to access a broader range of pragmalinguistic resources.

## Pedagogical implications

Pedagogical approaches to pragmatics range from examining speech acts (e.g., Rose & Kasper, 2001) and employing pragmalinguistic and sociopragmatic knowledge (e.g., O'Keeffe, Clancy, & Adolphs, 2011) to teaching formulaic routines (e.g., Bardovi-Harlig & Vellenga, 2012) and engaging in conversation analysis (Felix-Brasdefer, 2006). For a review of teaching pragmatics in the ESL classroom, see, for instance, Felix-Brasdefer & Cohen (2012), Ishihara & Cohen (2010), and O'Keeffe, Clancy, & Adolphs (2011). Despite the wide range of approaches, a pedagogical consensus has centered on the need to find appropriate examples, for example, using corpus data (e.g., Bardovi-Harlig, Mossman & Vellenga, 2015); make students aware of/notice the use of pragmatics in the target language (e.g., Ishihara, 2010); teach the selected pragmatic item; and offer students opportunities for further practice. For example, in identifying short-term and long-term teaching goals, O'Keeffe et al. (2011) describe the following activities: raising awareness, noticing strategies, and building receptive pragmatic strategies and developing productive pragmatic competence (p. 143). Bardovi-Harlig, Mossman, and Vellenga (2015) argue for an approach that involves "selecting the corpus, identifying expressions, extracting examples, preparing corpus examples for teaching, developing noticing activities, and developing production activities" (p. 3).

A significant amount of attention has been paid to constructing awareness-raising and noticing exercises (e.g., Hasler-Barker, this volume; Ishihara & Cohen, 2010). However, less consideration has focused on developing production activities, which are often carried out through role-plays and controlled practice (e.g., Bardovi-Harlig et al., 2015; Cohen, 2010; O'Keeffe, Clancy & Adolphs, 2011). Research outlined in this paper offers a complementary approach based on giving EFL learners choices in how they want to react and what they want to say. In giving students scenarios taken from real-life experiences and perhaps possible future situations, the first decision focuses on how to react rather than on purely practicing pragmatic routines. EFL users have pragmalinguistic and sociopragmatic resources and knowledge on how to disagree from their first language but they may not have the necessary competence to do so in the target language. Therefore, learners should decide how they want to react in a given situation as seen in context 5 (*You are in conversation with classmates in the United States when someone insists that Mexicans are lazy. What would you say to them all?*) or in context 6 (*You are speaking individually with a classmate who insists that Mexicans speak Mexican. What would you say to him or her?*). For instance, it must be more important to voice strong and robust disagreement about pejorative remarks regarding Mexicans in comparison to correcting misperceptions regarding the language spoken in Mexico. However, it is the individual language user's choice. He/she has to decide on a stance: high involvement, conciliative involvement, or suppression (Walkinshaw, 2009). After deciding on a disagreement strategy, learners then need to consider the available resources that convey their position, for example, direct disagreement (high involvement), indirect and softened disagreement (conciliative disagreement) and token agreement, avoidance, postponement, or silence (suppression), and whether the chosen strategy reflects solidarity politeness, deference politeness, or hierarchical politeness. Such an approach follows Widdowson's (1978) dictum that learning should help to produce "meaningful communicative behavior" rather than demonstrating "instances of correct English usage" (p. 3).

## Conclusion

In this paper, I have argued that responses to antagonistic situations depend on the EFL user's level of involvement, interpersonal and transactional relationships, and the context. I have reported that participants used a range of approaches when disagreeing. The results indicate that conciliatory agreement appears to be overused while high involvement is often avoided even when its use would be appropriate (e.g., when calling Mexicans lazy). Learners did not appear to fully exploit the high involvement choices available to them, which include outright or "aggravated" disagreement and direct disagreement.

Pedagogical intervention has an important role to play in making learners aware of how to disagree forcefully and how to achieve a balance between interpersonal and transactional considerations (see Hasler-Barker, this volume). Current EFL pedagogy focuses on teaching and practicing hedged disagreement and softeners (Pomerantz, 1984; Walkinshaw, 2009) and ignores how students should achieve strong disagreement, for example, employing solidarity politeness, deference politeness, and hierarchical politeness (Scollon & Wong Scollon, 1995). Investigation needs to examine how students can further be given additional opportunities and practice to respond appropriately in difficult and antagonistic situations.

## References

Angouri, J., & Locher, M. A. (2012). Theorising disagreement. *Journal of Pragmatics, 44*(12), 1549–1553.

Angouri, J., & Tseliga, T. (2010). "You have no idea what you are talking about!" From e-disagreement to e-impoliteness in two online fora. *Journal of Politeness Research. Language, Behaviour, Culture, 6*(1), 57–82.

Bardovi-Harlig, K. (2010). Exploring the pragmatics of interlanguage pragmatics: Definition by design. In A. Trosborg (Ed.), *Pragmatics across languages and cultures* (Vol. 7 of *Handbook of Pragmatics*; pp. 219–259). Berlin: Mouton de Gruyter.

Bardovi-Harlig, K. (2013). Developing L2 pragmatics. *Language Learning, 63*(s1), 68–86.

Bardovi-Harlig, K., Mossman, S., & Vellenga, H. E. (2015). Developing corpus-based materials to teach pragmatic routines. *TESOL Journal, 6*, 499–526.

Bardovi-Harlig, K., & Salsbury, T. (2004). The organization of turns in the disagreements of L2 learners: A longitudinal perspective. In D. Boxer & A. D. Cohen (Eds.), *Studying speaking to inform second language learning* (pp. 199–227). Clevedon, England: Multilingual Matters.

Bardovi-Harlig, K., & Vellenga, H. E. (2012). The effect of instruction on conventional expressions in L2 pragmatics. *System, 40*(1), 77–89.

Bell, N. (1998). Politeness in the speech of Korean ESL learners. *Working Papers in Educational Linguistics, 14*(1), 25–47.

Bond, M. H., Žegarac, V., & Spencer-Oatey, H. (2000). Culture as an explanatory variable: Problems and possibilities. In H. Spencer-Oatey (Ed.), *Culturally speaking* (pp. 47–71). New York, NY: Continuum.

Brown, P., & Levinson, S. (1987). *Politeness: Some universals in language usage*. Cambridge: Cambridge University Press.

Carter, R., & McCarthy, M. (2006). *Cambridge grammar of English*. Cambridge: Cambridge University Press.

Cohen, A. (2010). Approaches to assessing pragmatic ability. In N. Ishihara & A. D. Cohen (Eds.), *Teaching and learning pragmatics*, (pp. 264–285) Harlow, England: Longman.

Félix-Brasdefer, J. C. (2006). Teaching the negotiation of multi-turn speech acts. Using conversation-analytic tools to teach pragmatics in the classroom. In K. Bardovi-Harlig, C. Félix-Brasdefer, & A. Omar (Eds*.), Pragmatics and language learning* (Vol. 11, pp. 165–197). Honolulu: National Foreign Language Resource Center, University of Hawai'i at Mānoa.

Félix-Brasdefer, J. C., &. Cohen. (2012). Teaching pragmatics in the foreign language classroom: Grammar as a communicative resource. *Hispania 95*(4), 650–669.

Félix-Brasdefer, J. C., & Koike, D. (2014). Perspectives on Spanish SLA from pragmatics and discourse. In M. Lacorte (Ed.) *Handbook of Hispanic applied linguistics* (pp. 25–43). New York, NY: Routledge.

Hidalgo, L., Hidalgo, R., & Downing, A. (2014). Strategies of (in)directness in Spanish speakers' production of complaints and disagreements in English and Spanish. In M. A. Gómez González, F. J. Ruiz de Mendoza Ibáñez, F. Gonzálvez-García, & A. Downing (Eds.), *The functional perspective on language and discourse* (pp. 262–283), Philadelphia, PA: John Benjamins.

Ishihara, N. (2010). Theories of language acquisition and the teaching of pragmatics. In N. Ishihara & A. D. Cohen (Eds.), *Teaching and learning pragmatics* (pp. 99–122). Harlow, England: Longman.

Ishihara, N. & Cohen, A. D. (2010). *Teaching and learning pragmatics*. Harlow, England: Longman.

Hasler-Barker, M. (this volume). Effects of metapragmatic instruction on the production of compliments and compliment responses: Learner–learner role-plays in the foreign language classroom. In K. Bardovi-Harlig & J. C. Félix-Brasdefer (Eds.), *Pragmatics and language learning* (Vol. 14.). Honolulu: National Foreign Language Resource Center, University of Hawai'i at Mānoa.

Kádár, D. Z., & Haugh, M. (2013). *Understanding politeness*. Cambridge, England: Cambridge University Press.

Kakava, C. (2002). Opposition in Modern Greek discourse: Cultural and contextual constraints. *Journal of Pragmatics, 34*, 1537–1568.

Kasper, G. (2000). Data collection in pragmatics research. In H. Spencer-Oatey (Ed.), *Culturally speaking: Culture, communication and politeness theory* (pp. 316–341) London: Continuum.

Kasper, G. (2008). Data collection in pragmatics research. In H. Spencer-Oatey (Ed.), *Culturally speaking: Managing rapport through talk across cultures* (2nd ed., pp. 279–303). London: Continuum.

Kasper, G., & Rose, K. R. (2002). *Pragmatic development in a second language*. Malden, MA: Blackwell.

Kleinke, S. (2010). Interactive aspects of computer-mediated communication. In S-K. Tanskanen, M-L. Helasvuo, M. Johansson, & M. Raitaniemi (Eds.), *Discourses in interaction* (pp. 195–222). Amsterdam: John Benjamins.

Kreutel, K. (2007). "I'm not agree with you." ESL Learners' expressions of disagreement. *TESL-EJ, 11*, 1–35.

Leech, G. (1983). *Principles of pragmatics*. London: Longman.

Leech, G. (2014). *Pragmatics of politeness*. Oxford: Oxford University Press.

Locher, M. A. (2004). *Power and politeness in action: Disagreements in oral communication*. New York, NY: Mouton de Gruyter.

Locher, M., & Watts, R. (2005). Politeness theory and relational work. *Journal of Politeness Research, 1*(1), 9–33.

Magistro, E. (2011). National face and national face threatening acts: Politeness and the European constitution. In B. Davies, M. Haugh, & A. Merrison (Eds.), *Situated politeness* (pp. 232–252). London: Continuum.

Maíz-Arévalo, C. (2014a). "I'm sorry I don't agree with you": Can we teach nonnative students pragmatic competence when expressing disagreement? *Revista Español de Lingüística Aplicada, 27*(2), 433–453.

Maíz-Arévalo, C. (2014b). Expressing disagreement in English as lingua franca: Whose pragmatic rules? *Intercultural Pragmatics, 11*(2), 199–224.

Malamed, L. (2010). Disagreement: How to disagree agreeably. In A. Martínez-Flor & E. Usó-Juan (Eds.), *Speech act performance: Theoretical, empirical and methodological issues* (pp. 199–216). Philadelphia, PA: John Benjamins.

O'Keeffe, A., Clancy, B., & Adolphs, S. (2011). *Introducing pragmatics in use*. Abingdon, England: Routledge.

Pomerantz, A. (1984). Agreeing and disagreeing with assessments: Some features of preferred / dispreferred turn shapes. In J. M. Atkinson & J. Heritage (Eds.), *Structures of social action* (pp. 57–101). Cambridge: Cambridge University Press

Rose, K., & Kasper, G. (2001), *Pragmatics in language teaching*. Cambridge: Cambridge University Press.

Scollon, R., & Wong Scollon, S. (1995). *Intercultural communication: A discourse approach*. Oxford: Blackwell.

Sifianou, M. (2012). Disagreements, face and politeness. *Journal of Pragmatics, 44*, 1554–1564.

Tannen, D. (2002). Agonism in academic discourse. *Journal of Pragmatics, 34*, 1651–1669.

Tannen, D., & Kakava, C. (1992). Power and solidarity in Modern Greek conversation: Disagreeing to agree. *Journal of Modern Greek Studies, 10*, 11–34.

Walkinshaw, I. (2009). *Learning politeness: Disagreement in a second language*. Oxford, England: Lang.

Widdowson, H. G. (1978). *Teaching language as communication*. Oxford: Oxford University Press.

Zhu, W., & Boxer, D, (2012). Disagreement and sociolinguistic variables: English as a lingua franca of practice in China. In J. C. Félix-Brasdefer & D. A. Koike (Eds.), *Pragmatic variation in first and second language contexts: Methodological issues* (pp. 113–140). Philadelphia, PA: John Benjamins.

# Appendix

1. You are studying English in Mexico and you have to speak in English in class. Your teacher says that there is a class next Friday when in fact it is a public holiday. What would you say to him or her?
2. You are studying English in Mexico and after class your teacher asks you in English why you were not paying attention when in fact you were. What would you say?
3. You are studying English in Mexico and you have to speak English in class. In front of the whole class, you give an answer to a question which the teacher says is wrong. You feel that it is right. What would you say to him or her at that moment?
4. You are studying a business course in Canada and are having a conversation with your classmates outside the classroom when someone says that Guadalajara is south of Mexico City. What would you say to them?
5. You are in conversation with classmates in the United States when someone insists that Mexicans are lazy. What would you say to them all?
6. You are speaking individually with a classmate who insists that Mexicans speak Mexican. What would you say to him or her?
7. You are staying with a host family in the United States when, during the evening meal with everyone present, the father/mother insists that Mexicans are lazy. What would you say to them all?
8. You are staying with a host family in the United States and chatting alone with the father/mother when he/she insists that Mexicans speak Mexican. What would you say to him or her?
9. You are speaking to a group of fellow passengers on a plane in the United States when someone insists that Mexicans are lazy. What would you say to them all?
10. You are chatting with a fellow passenger on the plane who insists that Mexicans speak Mexican. What would you say to him or her?

# Playful Performances of Russianness and L2 Symbolic Competence

Maria Shardakova
Indiana University, USA

*This paper reports on an exploratory classroom study that focuses on spontaneous humorous performances of Russianness by university-level students with varying proficiency levels in Russian enrolled in an intensive summer program at a large Midwestern university. Approaching the students' performances from the language socialization standpoint (Schieffelin & Ochs,1986; Ochs, 1993), the study investigates whether the playful double-voicing can provide opportunities for the development of symbolic competence (Kramsch, 2006; Kramsch & Whiteside, 2008). In agreement with previous research (Broner & Tarone, 2001; Bushnell, 2009; Cook, 2000; Pomerantz & Bell, 2011), this study confirms the beneficial role of spontaneous performances of Russianness in the students' acquisition of new voices and semiotic resources. However, the role of such performances in the students' ability to access target culture social memories, discourses, and scripts is problematized. The study highlights the key role of the instructor in the students' acquisition of symbolic competence. The paper outlines directions for future research.*

## Introduction

This paper focuses on spontaneous humorous performances of Russianness as a means of honing symbolic competence in a foreign language (FL) Russian language classroom. The phenomenon under scrutiny – the playful pretense of being someone else and inventing a voice for this imaginary persona – has been addressed in second language acquisition (SLA) as ludic language play (Cook, 2000). A common practice among FL learners, it has been shown to promote second language (L2) acquisition and sociocultural competence (Broner

& Tarone, 2001; Bushnell, 2009; Cook, 2000; Pomerantz & Bell, 2011). This study investigates whether the playful double-voicing can also provide opportunities for the development of symbolic competence. It is argued that the adoption of target culture personas and identities may facilitate acquisition of new semiotic resources and afford access to target culture social memories, discourses, and scripts.

### Symbolic competence and second language learning

This paper defines symbolic competence as the ability to access contextually relevant social memories and symbols, including social roles and identities (Back, 2013; Kramsch, 2006; Kramsch & Whiteside, 2008), and regards the development of symbolic competence as one of the primary goals of FL teaching. Kramsch and Whiteside (2008) distinguish the following four dimensions of symbolic competence: subjectivity, historicity, performativity, and reframing. The authors analyze brief multilingual conversations between immigrants at several small grocery stores in San Francisco. Participants are shown to employ various linguistic resources, even those of which they have only limited command, to express a range of personal meanings and to secure advantageous self-positioning. They construct desired identities (cf., Bucholtz & Hall, 2005; Cutler, 2008; Rampton, 1998) and invoke personal and cultural histories (Kramsch & Whiteside, 2008). Ultimately, participants were able to reframe the very nature of interaction, moving away from the default position of "the linguistically challenged immigrant" (Back, 2013, p. 384) to asserting their symbolic power (Kramsch & Whiteside, 2008).

Further adapting the notion of symbolic competence to her analysis of an L2 Quichua learner's integration within the target community, Back (2013) focuses on the reactions of the target community members to the learner's display of L2 symbolic competence. The researcher argues that the learner's inability to access relevant L2 social histories and construct an appropriate L2 identity triggered negative reactions among the target community members and ultimately led to the learner's being ostracized from the community.

### Humorous role-playing and symbolic competence

Humor and humorous role-playing seem to be particularly conducive to displaying and constructing symbolic competence in a new language. Humor can enable students to "position themselves inside the discourse of others" (Kramsch, 2011, p. 359) and to practice the four key components of symbolic competence. Humor and play, argues Derrida (1978), shift the established symbolic order and destabilize habitual perspectives because they always imply the possibility of a "not." By cancelling or suspending the first culture perspective, humor reframes the very context and the meaning of interaction, creating affordances for manipulating reality. In the context of the L2 classroom, through humor and humorous play students have been shown to transform rigid pedagogical tasks to meaningful social interactions (Bell, 2009; Broner & Tarone, 2001; Bushnell, 2009; Pomerantz & Bell, 2011), to restructure power relations between instructors and themselves (Forman, 2011; Pomerantz & Bell, 2011; Sullivan, 2000; van Dam, 2002), to resist certain classroom practices that they perceived as oppressive, demeaning, or boring (Blackledge & Creese, 2009; Gutierrez, Rymes, & Larson, 1995; Norrick & Klein, 2008; Pomerantz & Bell, 2011; Rampton, 2006), and to construct desired identities and subject positions (Belz, 2002; Belz & Reinhardt, 2004; Lytra, 2007; Rampton, 1998, 2006).

Humor is often seen as involving incongruity of scripts that are simultaneously activated (Attardo, 1994). In this, layered simultaneity (or historicity) – another constituent of Kramsch and Whiteside's (2008) symbolic competence – is an essential component of humorous discourse. In their study of humor in an advanced L2 Spanish conversation class, Pomerantz and Bell (2011) show how each time learners engaged in humor, they accessed divergent genres, identities, and discourses, some of which were synchronous with the situation at hand, while others linked to processes that extended into the past or forestalled the future.

Performativity, the fourth component of symbolic competence, is regarded as "the capacity to use the various codes to create alternative realities" (Kramsch & Whiteside, 2008, p. 666). A similar outcome – the creation of alternative realities – is usually produced by humor and ludic language play (Broner & Tarone, 2001; Carter, 2004; Cook, 2000; Warner, 2004).

The functions of humor (i.e., destabilization, double-voicing, script opposition, and creation of alternative realities) make it a powerful resource for developing symbolic competence. The study seeks to answer the following questions: Does participation in humorous performances of Russianness create opportunities for the development of symbolic competence? Are students able to construct culturally valid and socially recognizable L2 identities in their performances? Do students access relevant social, political and historical meanings associated with the target language? What changes, if any, are observed in the students' symbolic development as a function of their linguistic proficiency?

## Theoretical framework

In its conceptualization of performance, this paper draws on two traditions: linguistic anthropology and general pragmatics. The former advances the notion of performance as a "specially marked way of speaking" that opens itself up to audience scrutiny (Bauman, 1987, p. 8). In this sense, it is possible to perform ethnicity, gender, or other subjectivities. In general pragmatics, the notion of performativity refers to utterances that do/perform an action by the sheer act of uttering (Austin, 1962). It is precisely in this sense that Kramsch and Whiteside (2008) use the notion of performativity: "Utterances not only perform some role or meaning, but they bring about that which they utter, that is, they are performatives" (p. 666). Thus, students' playful pretense of being Russian was analyzed as both a conscious act put on display for the audience's appreciation and as a way of creating a new reality.

The paper approaches the students' spontaneous performances of Russianness from the language socialization standpoint. According to this approach, learning a language is inseparable from becoming a member of a particular speech community, acquiring not only communicative competence, but also certain dispositions, identities, and behaviors considered normative by the group (Garrett & Baquedano-López, 2002; Ochs, 1993; Schecter & Bayley, 1997; Schieffelin & Ochs, 1986). Duff (2007) posits,

> "Language socialization" refers to the process by which novices or newcomers in a community or culture gain communicative competence, membership, and legitimacy in the group. It is a process that is mediated by language and whose goal is the mastery of linguistic conventions, pragmatics, the adoption of appropriate identities, stances (e.g., epistemic or empathetic) or ideologies, and other behaviors associated with the target group and its normative practices (p. 310)

Experts deploy both explicit and implicit means to socialize learners. For instance, explicit feedback may take the form of correction, explanation, or praise. Implicit socialization refers to situations when experts and learners routinely participate in "semiotically mediated practices" (Ochs & Schieffelin, 2012, p. 12). The instructional L2 setting may be viewed as a favorable environment for language learning, with instructors acting as sympathetic and understanding experts, which natural settings often do not offer (Back, 2013; Kinginger, 2009; Polanyi, 1995). On the other hand, isolated from real life, the instructional L2 setting limits interactional opportunities, actual L2 use, and identity options available to students (Duff, 2007).

The present study explores the effect of classroom socialization – particularly the instructor's responses to students' humorous performances of Russianness – on the development of symbolic competence.

## Method

This classroom-based study was conducted in an intensive eight-week summer program at a large public university located in the midwest of the United States. Data came from three Russian FL groups: elementary, intermediate, and advanced (henceforth first-, second-, and third-year). The classes met daily for 6 hours Monday through Thursday and for 4 hours on Friday. At each level, the classroom hours were divided into listening (1 hour/4 times a week), phonetics (1 hour/4 times a week), speaking (1 hour/5 times a week), and grammar practice (3 hours/5 times a week). Each subject was taught by a different instructor, and therefore each group of students worked with four different instructors. The composition of the instructional staff is captured in Table 1.

**Table 1.** Instructional staff

| class | 1st year | 2nd year | 3rd year |
|---|---|---|---|
| grammar | NNS female grad. student | NNS male grad. student | NS female grad. student |
| speaking | NNS male instructor | NS female grad. student | NNS female instructor |
| listening | NS female grad. student | NS female grad. student | NS female grad. student |
| phonetics[1] | NS female grad. student | NS female grad. student | NS female grad. student |

note. NNS=non-native speaker; NS=native speaker

Forty-eight learners participated in the study (Table 2). The average age of the participants varied across levels, with 18.4 years in the first-year group, 19.3 years in the second-year group, and 26.5 years in the third-year group. At the time of the study, participants were enrolled as both undergraduate (77%) and graduate (23%) students at different U.S. universities. Most of the undergraduate students were Russian majors or minors. The majority of the graduate students were pursuing degrees in Russian literary studies.

**Table 2.** Distribution of students across study groups

| gender | 1st year | 2nd year | 3rd year | total |
|---|---|---|---|---|
| female | 9 | 2 | 8 | 19 |
| male | 15 | 9 | 5 | 29 |
| total | 24 | 11 | 13 | 48 |

All participants (except for the first-year group) took the placement test. The second-year group scored intermediate-low and the third-year group scored intermediate-mid. These scores were based on the ACTFL proficiency scale (ACTFL, 2012).

The study drew on several sources, including ethnographic field notes, interviews, and 84 hours of audio recordings of classroom interaction. From these recordings spontaneous humorous performances of Russianness in whole-class interactions were transcribed to create a corpus of 128 mini-polylogues, that is, short playful exchanges carried over several turns and united by a common topic. The performances were considered spontaneous even when prompted by instructors; the main criteria were that roles or speech behaviors were not predetermined or scripted.

## Analysis

Qualitative and quantitative methods were used to analyze the data. Discourse analysis was used to describe qualitative changes in students' performances and to discern the broader cultural discourses and ideologies that affected constructed personas and identities. The data were analyzed quantitatively along the following lines: number of performances of Russianness compared with other spontaneous speech events initiated by students, use of the target language in performances of Russianness, number and type of performed personas, linguistic devices employed, and type of instructor reactions.

## Results and discussion

Over the course of the study, students often engaged in spontaneous performances of Russianness that were usually framed as humorous, and participation increased exponentially as students gained in L2 proficiency (Table 3). The performances also grew in length and complexity and were predominantly executed in the target language.

**Table 3.** Performances of Russianness across study groups. The proportion of performances of Russianness in relation to the overall number of spontaneous interactions initiated by students, including one-line interjections.

| level/ year | spontaneous performances of Russianness | spontaneous interactions initiated by students, including performances of Russianness | use of Russian language in performances of Russianness |
|---|---|---|---|
| | N (%) | N | % |
| 1st | 13 (8) | 157 | 26 |
| 2nd | 32 (18) | 201 | 89 |
| 3rd | 79 (16) | 486 | 98 |
| total | 128 (15) | 844 | 87.5 |

In what follows, examples of classroom interaction will be examined. The examples were selected based on their prototypicality of the groups' interactional practices, that is, they represent characteristic performances of each group.

The exchange in (1) took place at the beginning of a grammar class in the first-year group taught by a female American graduate student. One of the students (S-1) was late and used the back door to get into the classroom. When she plopped into her chair, she startled the student next to her (S-2) who called her a Russian spy for being sneaky. This playful name-calling was typical in this group and to a great extent inspired by the instructor who often made references to Russian villains of American pop culture (e.g., Whiplash in *Iron Man 2* or Ivan Drago in *Rocky IV*), taught her students jokes about Russians, and referred to her classroom as a Russian labor camp. She playfully embodied the persona of a Soviet authority, often referring to herself as "big sister" and making allusions to other popular representations of Soviet Russia (e.g., Orwell's *Nineteen Eighty-*

*Four, The Animal Farm* cartoon of the namesake book, Gulag, and KGB). Strict and implacable, she demanded hard work from her students: "Stop whining, it's a Russian class, do as I say or you will be punished." The students adored this instructor and played along, pretending to be obedient Soviet laborers, spies, or villains (Table 4). The speakers' original language, including errors, is preserved in all examples.

**Excerpt (1)**  "In Soviet Russia, television watches you," first-year group. S-1, S-2, S-3 – students; I – instructor

```
01   S-1:   izvinite ia snuck up on you
             sorry, I snuck up on you

02   S-2:   russki spies (.) eto russki spies vezde
             Russian spies. There are Russian spies
             everywhere

03   S-1:   da::h (.) eto russki klass
             yes, it is a Russian class

04   S-3:   po sovetskoi Rossii
             in Soviet Russia

05   S-1:   ty net vidish televizor
             you don't see a television (set)

06   S-3:   [televizor vidit tebia] ((the entire
             class laughs))
             the television (set) sees you

07   I:     [televizor vidit tebia]
             the television (set) sees you
```

**Table 4.** Performed personas across study groups (for more, see Appendix)

| personas performed (in all three levels or above 5%) | 1st year | 2nd year | 3rd year | frequency across all groups (percent) |
|---|---|---|---|---|
| drunk | 3 | 7 | 3 | 13 (10.5%) |
| Soviet-obedient-activist | 2 | 1 | 19 | 22 (17.7%) |
| victim |  | 5 | 5 | 10 (8.1%) |
| Stalin |  | 1 | 7 | 8 (6.4%) |
| total | 13 | 32 | 79 | 124 (100%) |

In (1) the innocuous excuse "Sorry, I snuck up on you" (line 1) receives a new, playfully malignant meaning when uttered in a Russian language class because it ignites well-known American stereotypes about Russians being spies (line 2).

In addition to equating Russianness with conspiratorial activity, the students and the instructor also perform Russianness as membership in a surveillance society when they collaboratively recite the formulaic joke[2] "In Soviet Russia, you do not watch television, television watches you" (lines 4–7). The joyful collaboration between the instructor and the students testifies to the high alignment of their symbolic competencies that are based on the shared L1 culture. In this jointly constructed humorous polylogue, the students and the instructor mold and display their symbolic competencies by creating particular subject positions and identities, evoking cultural myths and social memories, and ultimately reframing the typical classroom interaction (Richards, 2006). The mocking pretense of being Russian spies or members of a surveillance society allows the students to take advantageous subject positions both in relation to the target culture and within the classroom. On one hand, using negative stereotypes and constructing Russianness in opposition to one's native culture allows the students assume superior subject positions vis-à-vis the target culture (Said, 1979; Tomi, 2001). Portraying the other as different and non-contemporaneous has been implicated as a common technique of symbolic domination (Fabian, 1983; Shi-xu, 1994). On the other hand, engaging the instructor in their play, the students reduce the power imbalance in the classroom. Furthermore, drawing on the stereotypes and cultural myths, including literary and cinematic dystopias that go as far back as the Cold War era, the students expand the timescale of their classroom and demonstrate historical and cultural awareness. This evocation of shared social memories and symbols reframes the typical classroom interaction, allowing the students and the instructor to bond, while reconfirming their cultural loyalties and reconfiguring participatory roles, temporarily suspending the power imbalance between the instructor and the students.

Excerpt (2) comes from the second-year group taught by a male American graduate student who adopted a distinct teaching style by concentrating on the exchange of linguistic information, rarely discussing cultural beliefs or values. The instructor's formal disposition, nevertheless, did not curtail students' playful performances, which almost tripled in comparison to the first-year class. The students in the second-year group not only considerably expanded their repertoire of Russian personas, they were also able to index the intended personas and identities by employing a diverse range of linguistic means (e.g., statements of interest [lines 1, 13]; self-descriptions [lines 8, 11]; references to authentic realia [lines 4–5]), rather than overtly labeling themselves as their first-year peers did (e.g., "there are Russian spies" in [1]). The differences between each group's ability to signal intended identities by using indirect versus direct linguistic strategies reached statistical significance. Low-proficiency students preferred direct strategies, as compared to higher-proficiency students who opted for indirect strategies in their performances of Russianness, $X^2 (2, N = 230) = 23$, $p<.000$ (Table 5).

**Table 5.** Primary linguistic means of signaling performed personas across groups

| year/level | direct identification | indirect strategies ||||| total |
| --- | --- | --- | --- | --- | --- | --- |
| | | speech acts | lexicon | syntax/ grammar | references to authentic realia | |
| 1st | 6 | 3 | 2 | 1 | 2 | 14 |
| 2nd | 28 | 7 | 9 | 0 | 9 | 53 |
| 3rd | 32 | 68 | 34 | 25 | 4 | 163 |
| total | 66 | 78 | 45 | 26 | 15 | 230 |

In their performances, the second-year students usually positively oriented towards performed Russian personas, claiming them as their own, which was different from typical performances of the first-year group who "deauthenticated" (Chun, 2009; Coupland, 2001, p. 347) the voices of performed Russian personas from their own voices, often overtly ridiculing the performed personas as they did in (1). Another distinct characteristic of the second-year students' performances of Russianness was their avoidance of stereotypes and recourse to personal experience, however cursory it was. Some of the students had Russian immigrant acquaintances (18%), others took Russian civilization courses (45%), yet others collected information on their own (54%), which imbued their performances with personal histories and mementos (the exchange in [2] illustrates this). The exchange in (2) features two students' playful performance occasioned by the instructor's prompt to talk about interests and desired occupations using the instrumental case.

**Excerpt (2)** "I am a rodeo businessman in Siberia," second-year group

```
01   S-1:   ia interesuius' loshatei (.) poetomu ia
02          zhivu na ferme
            I am interested in horses, therefore
            I live on a farm

03   I:     vy navernoe zhivete v Kentuki
            you probably live in Kentucky

04   S-1:   net (.) ia zhivu v Sibiri (.)
05          ochen' kholodno vsegda
            no, I live in Siberia. It is always
            very cold

06   S-2:   how do I say animal doctor

07   I:     veterinar
            veterinarian

08   S-2:   ia veterinarom i rabotaiu nad zhivotnym
            I am a veterinarian and work with animals

09   S-1:   how to say peasant person

10   I:     krestianin (.) vy krestianin da
            peasant. You are a peasant, aren't you

11   S-1:   net (.) ia russky biznesmenom rodea
12          v Sibiri
            no, I am a Russian rodeo businessman
            in Siberia

13   S-2:   da (.) on vsegda dumaet nad reklamirovat'
14          rodeo s krestianinom ((laughs))
            yes. He always thinks about advertising
            rodeo among peasants
```

This exchange exemplifies what could be called a co-construction of partial second symbolic competence, when the instructor accepts symbols and identities that are not fully authentic. Upon learning that one of the students loves horses and lives on a farm (lines 1–2), the instructor deduces that the student resides in Kentucky (line 3), thus anchoring the conversation in American reality and linking horse farming with the state known for horse breeding. Through this deduction, the instructor displays his own symbolic competence, positioning himself as someone with intimate knowledge of American culture, including regional specialization. The student, however, retorts that he lives in Siberia where "[i]t is always very cold" (line 5). When the student later asks for a Russian equivalent of the word "peasant" (line 9), the instructor inquires if the student is a peasant himself (line 10) and the student explains that he is "a rodeo businessman" (line 11), with his peer further clarifying that his friend "always thinks about advertising rodeo among peasants" (lines 13–14). The performance is intended to impress and entertain the instructor and the other students, and it is also meant as a display of symbolic competence and knowledge of the target culture. The students construct advantageous subject positions, claiming membership in the target speech community. They imbue their performance with multiple historical layers and symbols traceable both to their native and second cultures. Drawing on their own cultural memories, the students mention living on a farm, working as veterinarians or rodeo businessmen. They also conjure up recognizable second culture identities, if somewhat anachronous ones. When calling their Siberian countrymen "peasants," the students did not realize that the word "peasant" indexes not contemporary Russian farmers but pre-revolutionary rural workers. Nevertheless, the students are able to "recreate environments from other scales of space and time, produce fractals of patterns from one timescale to another" (Kramsch & Whiteside, 2008, p. 666). The students corroborate their performance by selecting Siberia as a place of residence (the reference to severe Siberian climate authenticates the students' Russianness), by referencing famous Siberian horses, and also by the insistence on authentic Russian vocabulary (e.g., *krestianin* 'peasant' instead of "farmer"), which they perceive as an Americanism. Despite obvious oxymoronic clashes (e.g., rodeo in Siberia, peasants and advertisement), this performance is not intended to be what Kramsch and other SLA researchers call transgressive activities, when learners create absurd utterances with unexpected meanings (Kramsch, 2009; Laviosa, 2014); instead, it was meant as a showcase of expertise. As one of the students related in a post-field interview, he saw an American documentary film about Siberian horses and thought of using these horses in rodeo competitions. Thus, the students positioned themselves as legitimate members of the target speech community.

By supplying the students with Russian translations and not commenting on obvious cultural oddities (there are no rodeos in Siberia, nor do Russians use the word "peasant" to index those working in the agricultural sector), the instructor ratifies the students' performance, confirming their second culture expertise and accepting their more powerful participatory roles. While refraining from comments on the cultural inaccuracies, the instructor misses the opportunity to advance the students' second symbolic competence. In his post-field interview, the instructor explained that he was not sure about the contemporary uses of the word "peasant" but, more importantly, he did not want to diverge from his lesson plan. The instructor believed that his primary responsibility was to teach the students grammar, because they could learn about culture in Russian civilization courses. This instructor's position illustrates well every FL teacher's dilemma and explains why, despite increasing calls to include broad cultural exploration in foreign language instruction (MLA, 2007; National Standards, 2006), the mainstream FL classroom continues to focus primarily on the development of morphosyntactic knowledge (Warford & White, 2012; Wong, 2005).

The next two examples come from the third-year group. The instructor in (3) was a Russian female graduate student who espoused a very engaging teaching style, attending to all the students' verbal and nonverbal behaviors, including playful performances of Russianness. As the instructor explained in her post-field interview, there were no off-task behaviors in the classroom. When reacting to the students' performances of Russianness, this instructor employed two distinct, though often combined, techniques – she partook in the performance, playing along with students or making explicit comments about linguistic and other types of indexicality (e.g., gestures or attire; lines 2, 7–8, 13), as well as the cultural, social, historical, or political significance of the performed personas (lines 14–16, 24–25). Students in this group had a rather extensive and diverse list of Russian social types and identities, often supplying these performed personas with appropriate linguistic repertoires, speaking like a Russian grandmother, a WWII veteran, or a nagging wife among others (Tables 4 & 5). Most performed personas were easily recognizable by native speakers (the researcher and an assistant). The students drew on their personal study-abroad experiences (e.g., when performing over-protective Russian host-mothers or *babushkas* who insisted that their American guests not drink milk from the refrigerator so as to avoid catching a cold) or their academic research (e.g., when performing Soviet stamp orators who proposed toasts to the Communist Party, Soviet leadership, and the spread of communism) for constructing easily recognizable Russian social types and identities. The third-year students were aware of the symbolic potential of their new language and were able to use other semiotic means, such as gestures, body postures, and elements of attire, to help them evoke various cultural memories (Kramsch & Whiteside, 2008, p. 665). Unlike their peers in the first- or second-year groups, the third-year students were able to access a range of Russian social references, including the Napoleonic war, Soviet collectivization, and present day events (e.g., the Pussy Riot scandal).

The exchange in (3) took place during a grammar class dedicated to indefinite pronouns and adverbs. True to her teaching method, the instructor explained to the students how these linguistic forms can index particular social types and identities.

## Excerpt (3) "I am Pushkin," third-year group

```
01   S:   dozhd' perestan'te
          rain, stop!

02   I:   vy kak poet (.) govorite so stikhiiami
          as a poet - you talk to elemental forces

03   S:   da (.) ya Pushkin
          yes. I am Pushkin

04   I:   izvinite Aleksandr Sergeevich (.) ya vas
05        ne uznala
          I am sorry, Aleksander Sergeevich,
          I didn't recognize you

06   S:   nichego
          it's okay

07   I:   a pochemu vy k dozhdiu na vy a k moriu
08        na ty (.) proshchai svobodnaia stikhia
          and why do you address rain formally and
          the sea informally 'farewell, unfettered
          element!'

09   S:   ia uvazhaiu dozhdia bolshe
          I respect rain more

10   I:   nu vot (.) teper' more obiditsia
          well, now the sea will take offence

11   S:   ia emu napishu (.) i izviniaus'
          I will write to it and apologize

12   I:   vy uzh napishite pozhaluista (.) vse-taki
13        my russkie so stikhiiami i bogom na ty
          you do that please. After all we Russians
          are on a first-name basis with elements and god

...  ((some fifteen minutes later))

14   I:   on poet (.) nebozhitel' (.) emu nevazhno vse
15        zemnoe (.) poetomu on v chem-to ispanskom
16        i chem-to norvezhskom
          he is a poet, a heaven's resident. He is not
          interested in anything earthly that is why he is
          in something Spanish and something Norwegian

17   S:   ia tozhe poet
          I am also a poet

18   I:   my vse pomnim ob etom
          we all remember about it
```

```
19  S:  ia sizhu na chem-to stule (.) govoriu o
20      chem-to russkoe (.) dumaiu o chem-to vazhy
        I sit on some chair, talk about
        something Russian, think about something
        important

21  I:  vot chto znachit nastoyashchi poet
        this is what it means [to be] a real poet

... ((some three minutes later))

22  I:  nu (.) kto takoi russki poet
        so, what is a Russian poet

23  S:  nash Ben (.) on Pushkin
        (it is) our Ben. He is Pushkin

24  I:  poet (.) on znaet istinu ili khotia by
25      zdorovalsia s nei
        poet knows Truth or at least said 'hello'
        to it
```

This example of playful teasing between a student and the instructor extends over multiple turns and is maintained throughout a 50-minute class. The exchange starts with a student talking out of turn, appealing to the heavy rain outside the classroom window, asking the rain to stop (line 1). The instructor teases the student, calling him a poet because he talks to the elemental forces. A lighthearted tease on the surface, it teaches about cultural perceptions, social identities, and semiotic means for indexing these identities (line 2). The student engages in this play and announces himself as Pushkin, a renowned Russian poet (line 3). The instructor playfully apologizes for not recognizing the greatest Russian poet and calls the student by the name and patronymic of the poet, adhering to cultural conventions (lines 4–5). The student, speaking from the assumed position, accepts her apology (line 6). In lines 7–8, the instructor inquires why the poet/student addresses the rain formally, when on a different occasion he used an informal address when talking to the sea, at which point the instructor recites a line from the famous Pushkin's "Farewell to the Sea" that features an informal address to the sea. The student/poet retorts that he respects the rain more (line 9). Then, the instructor suggests that the sea will take offence (line 10), the student promises to write an apology letter to the sea (11), and the instructor approves this gesture (12). In this brief light-hearted exchange, the instructor validates the student's symbolic competence while helping him calibrate his performance, first by framing his behavior as poetic, implicitly conveying to the student and the rest of the class who witness this exchange that addresses to the elemental forces are perceived as poetic in Russian culture; then by reciting Pushkin's poem with an example of the direct address to the sea; and finally by explaining that it is customary to use informal language when talking to the elements or God in Russian (line 13).

The playful exchange rekindles some 15 minutes later when the instructor presents a poetic text to exemplify the use of indefinite pronouns. Turning a routine grammar instruction into an exciting multimedia cultural exploration (the instructor shows a YouTube video with a theatrical performance of the verse), the instructor further explains that through the use of indefinite pronouns one can position oneself as a poet, that is, a person who, according to a common Russian perception, is dismissive of the mundane and expresses this uncertainty through indefinite linguistic forms, like Severyanin did in the quoted verse (lines 14–16). The student immediately puts this instruction to practice and creates a free-verse poem punctuated with indefinite pronouns (lines 19–20). His effort is appreciated, as the instructor validates his identity as a "true poet" (line 21). In 24–25, the instructor returns to her explanation of what it means to be a poet in Russian culture. She tells the students that Russian poets are intimately familiar with Truth[3] or at least are on the nodding terms with it.

This exchange illustrates how symbolic competence can be taught in a foreign language classroom, even when the focus is on grammatical structures. The instructor skillfully fills her teaching with relevant cultural symbols both as planned activities (incorporation of Severyanin's poem into the presentation of indefinite pronouns) and as reactions to students' spontaneous interjections (the instructor frames the student's appeal to the rain as poetic and the student himself as a poet, explaining that this is what Russians believe poets do). Unlike in previous examples, the student and the instructor are working together to co-construct shared symbolic competencies and culturally recognizable identities. The student also draws on his first culture practices and symbols, as well as his personal academic history, when he uses poetic intonation and rhythmically arranges his utterance, alternating iambic and dactylic feet. This ability to use linguistic resources for social indexing distinguishes third-year students from their first- and second-year peers.

The exchange in (4) was observed during the conversation class taught by a female American instructor who had extensive experience living and working in Russia. This class produced the highest number of performances of Russianness, as part of both the curriculum and spontaneous exchanges. The role-play topics were usually proposed by the students themselves and ranged from job interview scenarios to family vacation planning, marriage proposals, formal banquet speeches, participation in talk shows, and political debates. While explaining her teaching methods in a post-field interview, the instructor emphasized that she saw her role in encouraging the students to discover Russia for themselves. She also wanted the students to find their own authentic voices that would resonate with Russian native speakers. To this end, this instructor employed various explicit and implicit techniques, ranging from offering the students models of self-expression to tacit ratification of their contributions. This instructor adopted practices of pedagogical engagement similar to those of her Russian colleague in the grammar class, for example, she often participated in the students' performances of Russianness, while also providing them with an explicit explanation of the connection between social identities and their linguistic representations (lines 23–24, 30–31). This instructor distinguished herself from her colleagues by offering the students models of linguistic behavior associated with particular social stances and identities.

**Excerpt (4)**  "You should not speak sincerely," third-year group

```
01   S1:   kak vy nashli nashu kompaniiu
            how did you find our company

02   S2:   ia videla gazetu s vashei informatsiei
            I saw a newspaper with your information

03   S3:   ((in a sing-song voice)): ia dumal eto
04         znak ot boga (.)
            I thought it was a sign from God.

05   I:    oni mogut sprosit o religii (.) esli vy v
06         Rossii
            they can ask about religion if you are in
            Russia
...

19   S1:   chto vy mechtaete
            what do you dream (about)

20   S2:   ia mechtaiu o deti
            I dream about children

21   I:    nikogda ne govorite ob etom
            never speak about that

22   S2:   eto pravilny (.) ia mechtau o deti
            it is true. I dream about children

23   I:    net (.) ((affectedly)) dlia menia samoe
24         vazhnoe kariera ((switches to her authentic
25         voice)) nel'zia govorit' iskrenne
            no. for me career is the most important
            (thing). You should not speak sincerely

26   S2:   chto iskrenno
            what is 'sincerely'
```

```
27   I:    pravdu to est'
           it means (to speak) the truth

28   S3:   ((dramatically)) zashchita nashikh detei
29         samaia vazhnaia zadacha nashego obshchestva
           protection of our children is the most
           important task of our society

30   I:    ((in a dramatic voice)) khotite sem'iu (.)
31         net (.) ya l'ubl'u tol'ko rabotu ((switches
32         to her authentic voice)) nado vyuchit' otvety
33         naizust' (.) no nado delat' vid chto
34         spontanno
           Do you want a family? No. I love only my job.
           You must learn your answers by heart but you
           have to pretend that they are spontaneous

35   S2:   kak v Amerike
           as in America

36   I:    v Rossii oktryto govoriat (.) davaite naimem
37         zhenshchinu (.) potomu chto u zhenshchin
38         malen'kaia zarplata
           in Russia they openly say let's hire a
           woman. Because women have small salaries
```

This exchange imitates a job interview and starts with a company's hiring manager's question about how the interviewee has found out about the position (line 1). While the student playing the interviewee offers a standard answer about finding a job (i.e., thanks to an ad in the newspaper [line 2]), another student jumps in to the conversation alluding to the divine intervention that made the interviewee find this job (lines 3–4). Potentially disruptive, the student's contribution is nevertheless acknowledged by the instructor as valid when she clarifies that questions about one's religion may come up during a job interview in Russia (lines 5–6). The role play, then, unfolds according to the standard script of a job interview shared by both American and Russian contemporary cultures until line 20 when the interviewee naively confesses that she dreams about having children. At this point, the instructor (a) warns the students against breaching the conventions of a job interview that do not favor childbearing aspirations (line 21); (b) offers linguistic models, including intonation patterns, to express an appropriate stance during the job application process (lines 23–24); (c) explains target culture conventions regarding job interviews (lines 5–6, 25, 32–34); (d) offers tacit criticism of the hypocrisy of job interview conventions (lines 25, 27); (e) helps students discover similarities between the target and native cultures with regard to job interview conventions and expectations (line 35); (f) overtly criticizes Russian society for its discriminatory practices against women (lines 36–38); and (g) presents a linguistic portrayal of the discriminators (lines 36–38). All of this is done on record as a reaction to the official role-playing that took place. However, it is worth noting that the instructor provides implicit ratification of playful contributions by student 3 whose contributions on two occasions (lines 3–4 and 28–29) noticeably enrich the exchange, and thus add important overtones to this mock interview. The references to the preordained nature of the interviewee's finding out about the job (lines 3–4) evoke notorious superstitiousness permeating Russian everyday life (Popov, 2011), while at the same time hinting at similar native sentiments. His reference to God, as the student confirmed in a post-field interview, also allowed him to "slip a comment on the Russian obsession with God" as evidenced by various literary and artistic works. In his second contribution (lines 28–29), the student draws on the Russian official/bureaucratic discourse that proclaims the protection of children to be the most important task of the society. The student's critical intent is amplified by the juxtaposition of this populist slogan alongside the instructor's admonition about mentioning children while participating in a job interview. Thus, the student supports the instructor's critique of the hypocrisy of contemporary society – be it in Russia or the US.

In (3) and (4), the observed collaboration between the students and the instructors reframes the classroom interaction as well as standard participatory roles, allowing the students to creatively engage with the target language, access diverse (American and Russian) discourses and social memories, construct sustainable subject positions, and "transportable identities" – i.e., identities that are claimable on the basis of cultural significance and sustainable in various contexts, providing the intersubjective foundation for social activities (Zimmerman, 1998, p. 91). The examples illustrate the key role of instructors in helping students mediate between the two worlds and gain participatory legitimacy in their target communities.

Students at all proficiency levels engaged in playful, spontaneous performances of Russianness, which they deployed for both displaying and constructing their symbolic competency. The students' ability to take on various subject positions noticeably changed as they gained L2 proficiency, which in turn affected the range of social histories and symbols that students were able to access. As a result, each group constructed different student-instructor relationships, some of which reinforced old cultural allegiances, while others allowed the students to build new alliances.

The first-year students were mostly confined to their native language and culture, which became apparent in the Russian personas they evoked, the subject positions they assumed, the linguistic means they employed to index their stances and social identities, the social histories they accessed, and the ideologies they reproduced. The most performed Russian personas in the first-year group were those of a Russian spy, an obedient Soviet citizen living under state surveillance, a villain, and a drunk. The students clearly differentiated themselves from the performed Russian personas by openly ridiculing the portrayed personas and/or assuming the position of cultural superiority (Example 1). The indexical means that the first-year students were able to deploy for signaling their assumed Russian personas and identities were both limited (often, the students simply identified themselves in English, e.g., "I am Russian bear," Table 5) and at odds with the native speaker symbolic repertoire (in [1], though delivered in Russian, the premade joke is a translation from English and is not known in Russia). The disjunction between the symbolic repertoires of the native speaker and the learners stemmed from the learners' inability to access relevant Russian social histories, discourses, and scripts.

The second-year students differed from their first-year peers on all counts: the number and types of Russian personas they performed, subject positions they took in relation to both the target speech community and their local community of practice (peers and instructors in the second-year group), indexical means they deployed for signaling their stances and identities, social histories, discourses, and scripts they accessed, and participatory roles they constructed for themselves within their community of practice. The second-year group began incorporating new personas inspired by their personal experiences as in (2) when the students performed a rodeo businessman and a veterinarian, drawing on their personal knowledge about life on a farm. The second-year students often positioned themselves as legitimate members of the target speech community, and it was often impossible to separate the invented voices of the performed personas from the students' authentic voices. Despite this unidirectional diglossia (Rampton, 1998), the second-year students were not able to access authentic Russian social histories, scripts, and discourses; nor were the students able to use culturally meaningful linguistic signs to index their identities and stances. As a result, the performed Russian personas were often markedly foreign (rodeo-businessman in Siberia). The second-year students' linguistic behavior revealed much about how they conceived cultural and linguistic differences. As the above example shows, the students asked the instructors for Russian equivalents of English words designating certain personas. This behavior testifies that students believed in "one-to-one correspondence between languages," without realizing that "[e]ach language operates a different discourse system" and "refers not only to observable objects and actions, but to ideas and opinions that need to be deduced and imagined" (Morgan & Cain, 2000, pp. 5–6).

Most significant changes in how the students performed their symbolic competence were observed in the third-year group. The students in this group began to draw on the target culture discourses, scripts, stereotypes, and expressive means. This shift from the local to the target culture references and symbols was affected by the students' personal experiences studying abroad (77%) as well as their academic explorations as graduate students at various Slavic and area studies programs (92%). The students significantly broadened their repertoire of social types and personas, most of which represented authentic Russian stereotypes (e.g., bureaucrats taking bribes, Soviet stump orators, jaded war veterans, dissidents, and the like) or evoked students' personal experiences (e.g., host mother, a grandmother who is nostalgic for Stalin). The students were also able to index their adopted personas through culturally recognizable means, including intonation, lexical items, grammatical structures, speech acts, as well as paralinguistic means (gestures, attire, and demeanor). They did not emphasize their outsider status by ridiculing "the Russian way of life," nor did they claim an unproblematic membership in the target community; instead, they tried to negotiate complex subject positions appropriate for their learner identities. Examples 3 and 4 illustrate how the students expressed their new stances and identities and how they indexed these identities with L2 means.

One of the questions this study sought to answer was how interaction with instructors affected the students' gains in symbolic competence. In the absence of direct contact with native speakers, classrooms serve as miniature target communities in which instructors shape not only students' linguistic development, but also their mastery of socio-pragmatic conventions, and the adoption of appropriate identities and stances, as well as beliefs and ideologies.

Through explicit or implicit means, instructors either ratify or ban certain linguistic and other types of behaviors, thus conferring or suspending students' membership and legitimacy in the group and guiding their development. The instructors in this study used various strategies to hone the students' second symbolic competence: That is, they suggested roles and personas for students to role-play; provided semiotic means to index certain stances and identities; conferred particular stances and orientations (positive/negative, sympathetic/derisive); ratified or dismissed the students' performances, stances, and identities; and exemplified dispositions, personas, and identities. Examples 1–4 illustrate the instructors' common strategies across the study groups. Some instructors influenced the students' developing second symbolic competence by drawing on American stereotypes of Russia and Russians and setting a particular interpretive frame, as observed in (1). Even though ridiculing the target culture helped the instructor and the students establish strong bonds as American citizens, these practices prevented the students from acquiring second symbolic competence and seeing the world from the target culture's lens.

The most common instructor reactions to the students' spontaneous performances were implicit and explicit ratifications; the former refers to situations when the instructor listened to the students' performances, sometimes sharing a laugh (first part of [1]), while the latter includes situations when the instructor provided Russian translations requested by students or gave other forms of feedback (as in [2]). Practices when the instructors played off the students' performances and taught the students new authentic voices and identities were mostly observed in the third-year group (as in [3] and [4]). In the first- and second-year groups, the instructors usually ratified the students' performances without engaging in the construction of new identities or furnishing these identities with indexical means. Table 6 illustrates these divergent instructor practices.

**Table 6.** Instructor strategies when dealing with students' spontaneous performances of Russianness

| instructor's participation | 1st year (13) | | 2nd year (32) | | 3rd year (79) | |
|---|---|---|---|---|---|---|
| | C1 | C2 | C1 | C2 | C1 | C2 |
| ignores | 1 | 1 | 1 | | | |
| rejects | 1 | 1 | 1 | | | |
| ratifies implicitly | 5 | | 17 | | 5 | 16 |
| ratifies explicitly | 1 | | 3 | 1 | 3 | 38 |
| teaches new identities/stances | | | 1 | 1 | 1 | 1 |
| teaches new identities & expressive means | 1 | 2 | 4 | 3 | 1 | 14 |
| total | 9 | 4 | 27 | 5 | 10 | 69 |

note. C1=performances inspired by American culture; C2=performances inspired by Russian culture

Finally, sometimes the instructors rejected the students' performances because they did not share symbolic capital with the students (e.g., on one occasion when a first-year student compared himself with Vasily Zaitsev, a Soviet WWII sniper featured in a 2001 war film *Enemy at the Gates*[4] but not well-known to Russians, his Russian phonetics instructor did not recognize the name and dismissed his performance) or thought that these performances contradicted reality (e.g., when a second-year student, who performed a Russian parent, told his kids not to play in the streets, his Russian conversation instructor corrected him, telling that Russian children are allowed to play in the streets[5]). On three occasions the instructors ignored the students' performances because they did not hear the students, as revealed in post-field interviews.

## Conclusion

Recent educational research of classroom interaction advocates the benefits of "off-task" behaviors for students, including humor as a way of promoting learning (Belz & Reinhardt, 2004; Blackledge & Creese, 2009; Broner & Tarone, 2001; Bushnell, 2009; Canagarajah, 2004; Cook, 2000; Gutierrez et al., 1995; Kramsch & Sullivan, 1996; Lantolf, 1997; Markee, 2005; Pomerantz & Bell, 2007, 2011; Pratt, 1991; Rampton, 2006; Sullivan, 2000; Tarone, 2006). This study investigates one form of such "off-task" behaviors, that is, spontaneous humorous student performances of Russianness as a way of fostering symbolic competence. The questions that guided this study were Do spontaneous humorous performances of Russianness allow students to access the target culture's identities, discourses, and social memories? Are these performances instrumental to the students' self-positioning in relation to the target culture as well as to their construction of new subject positions and identities? What is the relationship between the students' L2 proficiency and their second symbolic competence? What are typical instructor reactions to the students' performances and how do these reactions affect the students' development of symbolic competence?

This study shows that students used spontaneous performances both to display and to hone their symbolic competence. The performances facilitated the acquisition of new roles and identities, moving beyond those prescribed by the textbooks and classroom rules (Richards, 2006; van Lier, 1996). Most performed personas prompted the students to seek new semiotic means and to reflect on the connection between language and social meaning. The humorous pretense of being someone else also affected the learners' authentic identities and subject positions as they negotiated their membership in the local speech communities of their classrooms and in the imaginary communities of native speakers, gradually moving from skeptical outsiders to legitimate members with distinct voices.

L2 proficiency proved to be a major factor in the students' symbolic development, which was evidenced in the number of performed personas, the ability to access the target culture's social histories and relevant discourses, the ability to use L2 to index stances and identities, and the ability to express culturally relevant subject positions and construct valid authentic identities by aligning one's own notions of social meanings with those of the target community. While low-proficiency students in the first- and second-year groups were constrained by their native language and culture and were unable to use L2 for social indexing, their more advanced classmates were able to evoke culturally recognizable types by performing relevant stances and appropriate L2 discourses, scripts, and social histories. The third-year group was able to deploy a broad range of L2 devices for social indexing, ranging from derivational morphology to speech acts and lexical stylization. As a result, this group effectively aligned their symbolic competence with that of native speakers.

It is necessary to note that L2 proficiency may not be the only variable that affected the development of symbolic competence, as most third-year students had traveled to Russia and spent a minimum of two months living with host families. In addition, the third-year students' advanced literary and area studies may have affected their performances in this study. By far the most important variables affecting the students' acquisition of symbolic competence were the instructors' reactions to the students' performances.

Throughout the study it became evident that all humorous performances were intended first and foremost for the instructors, whether they were observing or directly engaged in the exchange. Their reactions, in turn, significantly manipulated the students' symbolic development. Thus, the third-year students' highest acquisition of symbolic competence can be attributed to particular pedagogical practices. Unlike their colleagues in lower levels, the third-year instructors usually directly engaged in role-playing with students and enhanced the students' performances by teaching them new social roles and stances with the accompanying linguistic means to index these social meanings. Studies in pragmatics support such explicit instruction that connects form with its social context and speakers' intentions (Bardovi-Harlig, 2001; Bardovi-Harlig & Hartford, 1996).

The divergent practices among the instructors were due to their beliefs about what constituted legitimate teaching goals: The first- and second-year instructors believed that they were responsible for imparting grammatical structures and textbook vocabulary to the students, and they cautiously guarded classroom time so that it was not wasted on "jokes." The third-year instructors, on the other hand, did not believe in the artificial division of classroom time into valuable (curriculum-driven) and non-valuable (spontaneous) interactions. They treated all classroom activity as meaningful. And of course the instructors' own symbolic competence and ability to mediate between the first and second languages and American and Russian cultures proved indispensable. This paper argues that FL instructors should use every opportunity to bring culture into the classroom, treating every moment, including playful exchanges, as opportunities for cultural and symbolic development.

This study reveals several directions for future research. It will be worthwhile to examine the effect of the learning context – foreign language versus second language – on students' symbolic development. It also raised the question whether students' extensive literary or area studies affect their symbolic development (cf. recommendations to bring literature to the FL classroom in Kramsch, 2006, 2011; Warford & White, 2012). A more ambitious project may investigate the combined effects of classroom language use and students' and instructors' subject positions and identities on symbolic development. Finally, longitudinal studies may shed new light on how students acquire second symbolic competence and what motivates their development, including various environmental factors such as textbook representations, instructor identity and behavior, personal interest, and socialization practices outside the classroom.

## Notes

1   Taught in English, phonetics classes were excluded from the study.
2   This type of joke is known as "Russian reversals." While often credited to a Soviet-born American comedian Yakov Smirnoff (Pokhis), these jokes can be considered a form of modern folklore.
3   Due to the fact that that up to the 18th century the written word in Russia was "carefully scrutinized and censored by church," it was "implicitly recognized as sacred" and directly referring to the ultimate truth. "[T]he writer in general and the poet in particular

became a secular saint" (Bethea, 1998, p. 167). These cultural sensibilities to some extent continue to the present day.

4   A post-field interview confirmed that the students referred to the film, not to the namesake book.

5   The instructor erroneously equates the American warning "do not play in the street"with its direct Russian translation *nel'zia igrat' na ulitse*, oblivious to the fact that the correct equivalent is *nel'zia igrat' na proezzhei chasti* 'playing in the traffic area is not allowed' (a typical parental warning in Russia).

## References

ACTFL. (2012). *ACTFL proficiency guidelines*. Retrieved from http://www.actfl.org/sites/default/files/pdfs/public/ACTFLProficiencyGuidelines2012_FINAL.pdf

Attardo, S. (1994). *Linguistic theories of humor* (Vol. 1). Berlin: Walter de Gruyter.

Austin, J. L. (1962). *How to do things with words*. New York, NY: Oxford University Press.

Back, M. (2013). "La Orquesta": Symbolic performance in a multilingual community of practice. *Modern Language Journal, 97*, 383–396.

Bardovi-Harlig, K., (2001). Evaluating the empirical evidence: Grounds for instruction in pragmatics? In K. R. Rose & G. Kasper (Eds.), *Pragmatics in language teaching* (pp. 13–32). Cambridge: Cambridge University Press.

Bardovi-Harlig, K., & Hartford, B. S. (1996). Input in an institutional setting. *Studies in Second Language Acquisition, 18*, 171–188.

Bauman, R. (1987). The role of performance in the ethnography of speaking. *Working Papers and Proceedings of the Centre for Psychosocial Studies, 11*, 3–12.

Bell, N. D. (2009). Learning about and through humor in the second language classroom. *Language Teaching Research, 13*, 241–258.

Belz, J. (2002). Second language play as a representation of the multicompetent self in foreign language study. *Journal of Language, Identity, and Education, 1*, 13–39.

Belz, J., & Reinhardt, J. (2004). Aspects of advanced foreign language proficiency: Internet-mediated German language play. *International Journal of Applied Linguistics, 14*, 324–362.

Bethea, D. M. (1998). Literature. In N. Rzhevsky (Ed.), *The Cambridge companion to modern Russian culture* (pp. 161–205). Cambridge: Cambridge University Press.

Blackledge, A., & Creese, A. (2009). Meaning-making as dialogic process: Official and carnival lives in the language classroom. *Journal of Language, Identity, and Education, 8*, 236–253.

Broner, M. A., & Tarone, E. E. (2001). Is it fun? Language play in a fifth-grade Spanish immersion classroom. *Modern Language Journal, 85*, 363–379.

Bucholtz, M., & Hall, K. (2005). Identity and interaction: A sociocultural linguistic approach. *Discourse Studies, 7*, 585–614.

Bushnell, C. (2009). "Lego my keego!": An analysis of language play in a beginning Japanese as a foreign language classroom. *Applied Linguistics, 30*, 49–69.

Canagarajah, A. S. (2004). Subversive identities, pedagogical safe houses, and critical learning. In B. Norton & K. Toohey (Eds.), *Critical pedagogies and language learning* (pp. 116–137). New York, NY: Cambridge University Press.
Carter, R. (2004). *Language and creativity: The art of common talk.* London: Routledge.
Chun, E. (2009). Speaking like Asian immigrants: Intersections of accommodation and mocking at a U.S. high school. *Pragmatics, 19,* 17–38.
Cook, G. (2000). *Language play, language learning.* Oxford: Oxford University Press.
Coupland, N. (2001). Dialect stylization in radio talk. *Language in Society, 30,* 345–375.
Cutler, C. (2008). Brooklyn style: Hip-hop markers and racial affiliation among European immigrants in New York City. *International Journal of Bilingualism, 12,* 7–24.
Derrida, J. (1978). *Writing and difference.* Chicago, IL: University of Chicago Press.
Duff, P. A. (2007). Second language socialization as sociocultural theory: Insights and issues. *Language Teaching, 40,* 309–319.
Fabian, J. (1983). *Time and the other: How anthropology makes its object.* New York, NY: Columbia University Press.
Forman, R. (2011). Humorous language play in a Thai EFL classroom. *Applied Linguistics, 32,* 541–565.
Garrett, P. B., & Baquedano-López, P. (2002). Language socialization: Reproduction and continuity, transformation and change. *Annual Review of Anthropology, 31,* 339–361.
Gutierrez, K., Rymes, B., & Larson, J. (1995). Script, counterscript, and underlife in the classroom: James Brown versus Brown v. Board of Education. *Harvard Educational Review, 65,* 445–471.
Kinginger, C. (2009). *Language learning and study abroad.* New York, NY: Palgrave Macmillan.
Kramsch, C. (2006). From communicative competence to symbolic competence. *Modern Language Journal, 90,* 249–252.
Kramsch, C. (2009). *The multilingual subject.* Oxford: Oxford University Press.
Kramsch, C. (2011). The symbolic dimensions of the intercultural. *Language Teaching, 44,* 354–367.
Kramsch, C., & Sullivan, P. (1996). Appropriate pedagogy. *ELT Journal, 50,* 199–212.
Kramsch, C., & Whiteside, A. (2008). Language ecology in multilingual settings. Towards a theory of symbolic competence. *Applied Linguistics, 29,* 645–671.
Lantolf, J. (1997). The function of language play in the acquisition of L2 Spanish. In W. R. Glass & A. T. Perez-Leroux (Eds.), *Contemporary perspectives on the acquisition of Spanish* (pp. 3–24). Somerville, MA: Cascadilla Press.
Laviosa, S. (2014). *Translation and language education: Pedagogic approaches explored.* London, : Routledge.
Lytra, V. (2007). *Play frames and social identities: Contact encounters in a Greek primary school.* Amsterdam: John Benjamins.
Markee, N. (2005). A conversation analytic perspective on off-task classroom talk: Implications for second language acquisition studies. In K. Richards & P. Seedhouse (Eds.), *Applying conversation analysis* (pp. 197–213). London: Palgrave Macmillan.

MLA Ad Hoc Committee on Foreign Languages. (2007). Foreign languages and higher education: New structures for a changed world. *Profession*, 234–245.
Morgan, C., & Cain, A. (2000). *Foreign language and culture learning from a dialogic perspective* (Vol. 15). Clevedon, : Multilingual Matters.
National Standards in Foreign Language Education Project. (2006). *Standards for foreign language learning in the 21st century*. Lawrence, KS: Allen Press.
Norrick, N. R., & Klein, J. (2008). Class clowns: Talking out of turn with an orientation toward humor. *Lodz Papers in Pragmatics, 4*(1), 83–107.
Ochs, E. (1993). Constructing social identity: A language socialization perspective. *Research on Language and Social Interaction, 26*, 287–306.
Ochs, E., & Schieffelin, B. B. (2012). The theory of language socialization. In A. Duranti, E. Ochs, & B. B. Schieffelin (Eds.), *The handbook of language socialization* (pp. 1–21). Malden, MA: Wiley-Blackwell.
Polanyi, L. (1995). Language learning and living abroad. In B. F. Freed (Ed.), *Second language acquisition in a study abroad context* (pp. 271–291). Amsterdam: John Benjamins.
Pomerantz, A., & Bell, N. D. (2007). Learning to play, playing to learn: FL learners as multicompetent language users. *Applied Linguistics, 28*, 556–578.
Pomerantz, A., & Bell, N. D. (2011). Humor as safe house in the foreign language classroom. *Modern Language Journal, 95*(s1), 148–161.
Popov, V.S. (2011). Sueveriia v sovremennoi sotsial'noi srede [Superstitions in modern public sphere]. *Analitika Kul'turologii, 20*. Retrieved from http://www.analiculturolog.ru/journal/archive/item/735-superstition-in-modern-social-environment-on-the-example-of-the-internet.html
Pratt, M. L. (1991). Arts of the contact zone. *Profession, 91*, 33–40.
Rampton, B. (1998). Language crossing and the redefinition of reality. In P. Auer (Ed.), *Code-switching in conversation* (pp. 290–317). London: Routledge.
Rampton, B. (2006). *Language in late modernity*. Cambridge: Cambridge University Press.
Richards, K. (2006). "Being the teacher": Identity and classroom conversation. *Applied Linguistics, 27*, 51–77.
Said, E. W. (1979). *Orientalism*. New York, NY: Vintage Books.
Schecter, S. R., & Bayley R. (1997). Language socialization practices and cultural identity: Case studies of Mexican descent families in California and Texas. *TESOL Quarterly, 31*, 513–542.
Schieffelin, B. B., & Ochs E. (1986). *Language socialization across cultures*. Cambridge: Cambridge University Press.
Shi-xu. (1994). Ideology: Strategies of reason and functions of control in accounts of the non-Western other. *Journal of Pragmatics, 21*, 654–669.
Sullivan, P. (2000). Playfulness as mediation in communicative language teaching in a Vietnamese classroom. In J. P. Lantolf (Ed.), *Sociocultural theory and second language learning* (pp. 115–131). New York, NY: Oxford University Press.

Tarone, E. (2006). Fossilization, social context and language play. In S. Han & T. Odlin (Eds.), *Studies of fossilization in second language acquisition* (pp. 157–172). Clevedon, England: Multilingual Matters.

Tomi, L. (2001). Critical analysis of American representations of Russians. *Pragmatics, 11*, 263–284.

van Dam, J. (2002). Ritual, face, and play in a first English lesson: Bootstrapping a classroom culture. In C. Kramsch (Ed.), *Language acquisition and language socialization* (pp. 237–65). New York, NY: Continuum.

van Lier, L. (1996). *Interaction in the language curriculum: Awareness, autonomy, and authenticity*. London: Longman.

Warford, M. K., & White, W. L. (2012). Reconnecting proficiency, literacy, and culture: From theory to practice. *Foreign Language Annals, 45*, 400–414.

Warner, C. N. (2004). It's just a game, right? Types of play in foreign language CMC. *Language Learning & Technology, 8*(2), 69–87.

Wong, W. (2005). *Input enhancement: From theory and research to the classroom*. New York, NY: McGraw-Hill.

Zimmerman, D. H. (1998). Discoursal identities and social identities. In C. Antaki & S. Widdicombe (Eds.), *Identities in talk* (pp. 87–106). London: Sage.

# Appendix

**Table.** Performed personas across study groups, less than 5% frequency of occurance

| year | personas performed | frequency (percent) |
|---|---|---|
| 1st year | Baba Yaga, bear, Putin-fan, spy (2), Vasily Zaitsev | 6 (4.8%) |
| 2nd year | bear, Colonel Spalko, grandaughter, grandmother, Putin, resident in Siberia, rodeo-business man in Siberia, spy, Stalin, student-cheater (2), thief, tourist, waitress, wild | 15 (12.1%) |
| 3rd year | aristocrat, boy, bureaucrat who takes bribes, cat-lover, correspondent, employer (2), host-mother (3), abusive husband (2), job candidate (3), lover, patriot (3), poet Pier Bezukhov (3), Putin (3), reporter (2), scandalist, soldier-disillusioned, Soviet-disillusioned-dissenter (4), Soviet nemesis (2), Soviet-extremist (3), terrorist, wife-nagging, worker at a factory, young woman | 43 (34.7%) |

# Do EFL Teachers in Serbia Have What They Need to Teach L2 Pragmatics? Novice Teachers' Views of Politeness

Milica Savić
*University of Stavanger, Norway*

*The challenges of teaching L2 pragmatics are still numerous. They include various unresolved issues concerning learner goals and assessment (Kasper & Schmidt, 1996; Taguchi, 2011), a lack of suitable teaching materials (Bardovi-Harlig, 2001; McConachy & Hata, 2013; Vellenga, 2004), and student attitudes towards adopting L2 pragmatic norms (Davis, 2007; Kim, 2014; Norton, 2000; Siegal, 1996). These and the traditionally limited role of pragmatics in teacher training programs (Cohen, 2005; Eslami, 2011; Eslami-Rasekh, 2005a; Ishihara, 2007; Vásquez & Sharpless, 2009) often result in L2 teachers' limited pragmatic competence and/or metapragmatic awareness. The present study investigates novice English teachers' metapragmatic awareness as reflected in their views of politeness in general and of L2 politeness in particular. A semi-structured interview was employed to collect data from 13 novice Serbian teachers of English as a foreign language (EFL). A content analysis of the interviews reveals the novice teachers' views of the nature of politeness, especially its universal and culture-specific aspects; their varied and often value-laden views of politeness, sometimes heavily colored by their own cultural perspective; as well as considerable individual differences. The findings suggest a need for including both theoretical and pedagogically-oriented pragmatics courses in EFL teacher education in Serbia.*

## Introduction

The rapidly growing field of interlanguage pragmatics (ILP) has provided a kaleidoscopic image of pragmatic development in a variety of second and foreign language (L2) environments, including study-abroad contexts, classrooms, and virtual environments (see Taguchi, 2015), and generated a rich body of research data on L2 learners' production and interpretation of different speech acts (see Kasper & Rose, 2002). However, studies have traditionally focused on learners' attempts to master L2 pragmatics, while teacher cognition, that is, "the unobservable cognitive dimension of teaching—what teachers know, believe, and think" (Borg, 2003, p. 81), in the domain of L2 pragmatics has not been investigated sufficiently (Ishihara, 2011; Taguchi, 2011). At the same time, it is the teacher that creates a bridge between what is known about L2 pragmatic practices and how, if at all, they are addressed in the classroom (Ishihara & Cohen, 2010), especially in foreign language settings. Since teacher cognitions and practices are "mutually informing" (Borg, 2003, p. 81) and interlinked in highly complex ways (Ishihara & Cohen, 2010) and yet have only recently begun to be investigated in relation to L2 pragmatics, the present study examines novice teachers' cognitions as reflected in their views of politeness. The term *novice teachers* here refers to a group that has started teaching English before formally graduating, that is, they had taken all the courses in the BA in English Language and Literature program, but had either not yet sat all the exams or had failed and needed to re-take some of them at the time of the study. They were selected as it was believed that they could provide valuable feedback on the quality of the program and indicate possible directions for its future development.

To become a qualified EFL teacher in Serbia, one has to complete a 4-year BA and a 1-year MA program (240+60 ECTS[1]). At least 30 ECTS points are required in Pedagogy, Psychology, and TEFL Methodology, and at least 6 ECTS in teaching practice. Additionally, in order to obtain a teaching license, teachers have to pass a practical and theoretical state exam after a year of teaching. For the English majors who started their BA studies before 2005, a 4-year BA program in English Language and Literature, followed by the state exam, was sufficient to obtain formal teaching qualifications. Moreover, all licensed teachers need to complete at least 120 hours of professional development every 5 years.

The novice teachers in the present study were all part of the English BA program at a university in south Serbia. This program is not strictly a teacher training program. It provides students with comprehensive knowledge of English linguistics, Anglo-American literatures and cultures, as well as a wide array of language and communication skills. However, the vast majority of students graduating from the program become language teachers at some point in their professional lives. No official statistics are available on the percentage of English majors entering teaching. However, based on the university instructors' insight into former students' occupations, it can be inferred that over 80% become teachers, because there are few other career opportunities in economically poorly developed south Serbia, where the university is located. Therefore, the studies conducted with the EFL students in this program are considered highly relevant as an indication of the state of EFL teacher education in the region.

The current study investigates novice teachers' metapragmatic awareness by exploring their conceptualizations of politeness in general and their perceptions of L2 politeness in particular. Politeness has been conceptualized and defined in a number of different ways, ranging from early, static views of politeness as a means to reduce social friction (e.g., Brown and Levinson,, 1987; Leech, 1983) to postmodern, dynamic conceptualizations, regarding politeness as open to re-definition in any interaction, but essentially as an "intensely problematic" term to define (Mills, 2011, p. 36). Regardless of the exact definition, in both early and more recent theories and research, "politeness is regarded as one of the most important guidelines underlying human behaviour, reflected in interactants' demonstrated consideration of each other" (House, 2012, p. 285). The current study explores an aspect of *politeness1*[2], more specifically, "metapragmatic politeness1 (perceptions of politeness), that is, how people talk about politeness as a concept in everyday interaction" (Félix-Brasdefer, 2008, p. 4).

The study of politeness has been characterized by a tension between viewing politeness (or at least some of its aspects) as universal (e.g., Brown & Levinson, 1987; Leech, 1983) and as culture- and language-specific (e.g., Wierzbicka, 1985). Culture-specific aspects have been considered a major challenge in L2 pragmatics learning because of "the very close relationship of pragmatic aspects of language behaviour to deeply held values and beliefs," largely acquired subconsciously at an early age and therefore "appear[ing] to represent universal rather than culture-specific values" (Yates, 2010, pp. 300–301). In an attempt to reconcile the universal and culture-specific aspects of politeness, House (2005, p. 17) proposes a multi-level model of politeness, consisting of two universal levels (the bio-social and philosophical) and two culture-specific levels (cultural and linguistic). The culture- and language-specific levels acknowledge that "culture-specific norms of behaviours aris[e] out of a community's individuals' cultural representations" (p. 18) and that they are captured in linguistic systems. Therefore, an understanding of L2 politeness, crucial for appropriate pragmatic performance, requires familiarity with both cultural values and their linguistic manifestations in various contexts. In Yates' (2010) words, "an appreciation of broader cultural areas of language use is particularly important if learners are to understand not only *what* they might be expected to say...but also *why*" (p. 290). Bennett's (1993) developmental model of intercultural sensitivity outlines a continuum of stages, from ethnocentric to ethnorelative, leading to growing cultural awareness, necessary for understanding deeper cultural assumptions underpinning politeness norms and pragmalinguistic behavior.

Contrastive pragmatic research on Serbian and English (Blagojević & Mišić Ilić, 2013; Mišić Ilić, 2010), although admittedly rather limited, reveals differences in the preferred levels of directness with regard to hedging in written academic discourse and prohibitives. Additionally, Milosavljević (2006) demonstrates a variety of internally or externally modified imperatives for making requests in informal communication, emphasizing that a wide range of marked modifiers, aimed at signaling closeness and familiarity, and their linguistic expression clearly reveal ethical and moral values at the heart of Serbian culture. Therefore, in order to help Serbian EFL learners understand L2 politeness and pragmatic norms, teachers need to be aware of the different values to which Serbian and English-speaking cultures orient in communication. According to Kasper and Rose (2002), teachers' metapragmatic awareness is a key to effective L2 pragmatics teaching.

Metapragmatic awareness has been defined as "knowledge of the social meaning of variable second language forms and awareness of the ways in which these forms mark different aspects of social contexts" (Kinginger & Farrell, 2004, p. 20). Similarly, it has been viewed as "the acknowledgement of those contextual features that determine the extent to which a given linguistic routine may be appropriate for a particular situation" (Safont Jordá, 2003, p. 48). McConachy (2013) highlights the potential problems with "framing meta-pragmatic awareness *exclusively* in relation to knowledge of native-speaker norms" (p. 101). Such a conceptualization, he argues, "effectively obscures the role of the learners' existing cultural knowledge in the act of interpreting L2 pragmatic phenomena" (p. 101). Therefore, McConachy (2013) advocates a wider notion of metapragmatic awareness to include "an ability to reflect on the rationales for [the] interpretations of pragmatic phenomena and to bring into awareness the particular cultural frames or assumptions which are at work in the interpretive process" (p. 102). For the purposes of the present study, McConachy's broader view of metapragmatic awareness has been adopted. While both *pragmatic* and *metapragmatic* awareness have been used as terms to refer to the above concept in the literature, the term metapragmatic awareness is used here since the research focuses specifically on the ability to verbalize, discuss and reflect on pragmatic phenomena.

The present study investigates one aspect of novice teachers' metapragmatic awareness, that is, their conceptualizations of politeness. Taguchi (2011) holds that "teacher training is critical because it inevitably influences the ways in which instructional methods and materials are utilized" but at the same time emphasizes that "the knowledge and beliefs held by teachers about sociocultural aspects of language and effective techniques for teaching pragmatics have rarely been addressed (Cohen, 2008; Eslami-Rasekh, 2005)" (p. 299). This study, therefore, is an attempt to begin to fill this research gap by addressing the strengths and weaknesses of a teacher training program at a university in Serbia.

## Novice teacher cognition regarding L2 pragmatics

This section discusses the intricacies of L2 pragmatics teaching and provides a brief overview of the studies examining teacher metapragmatic awareness development during instructional pragmatics programs, before focusing on the research conducted in the Serbian context.

While the past decade has seen a growing number of publications aimed at bridging the gap between research findings in L2 pragmatics and teaching practice, including both resource books (Bardovi-Harlig & Mahan-Taylor, 2003; Houck & Tatsuki, 2011; Ishihara & Cohen, 2010; Tatsuki & Houck, 2010) and journal articles (Bou-Franch & Garcés-Conejos, 2003; Eslami-Rasekh, 2005a; Félix-Brasdefer & Cohen, 2012; Martínez-Flor & Usó-Juan, 2006), the challenges of teaching L2 pragmatics are still numerous. They include various unresolved issues concerning learner goals (Kasper & Schmidt, 1996; Taguchi, 2011), the quality of pragmatic information available in teaching materials (Bardovi-Harlig, 2001; McConachy & Hata, 2013; Vellenga, 2004), learner attitudes to adopting L2 pragmatic norms (Davis, 2007; Kim, 2014; LoCastro, 2001; Norton, 2000; Siegal, 1996), and the traditionally limited role of pragmatics in teacher training programs (Cohen, 2005; Eslami, 2011; Eslami-Rasekh, 2005a; Ishihara, 2007; Vásquez & Sharpless, 2009), often resulting in L2 teachers' limited communicative competence and/or metapragmatic awareness.

Achieving a degree of L2 pragmatic competence has long been claimed to be one of the goals of L2 learning, and various attempts have been made to refine the notion of pragmatic competence and delineate its domain (Bachman, 1990; Bachman & Palmer, 1996; Council of Europe, 2001). However, approximating the native-speaker (NS) norm has traditionally been seen as the ultimate goal against which to measure learner attainment. A goal conceptualized in such a way has repeatedly been challenged (Kasper & Schmidt, 1996), but has recently attracted severe criticism, with the advent of the poststructuralist perspective, which calls for a reconceptualization of pragmatic competence. The multitude of contexts in which English is used nowadays, together with the realization that users of English as a lingua franca continuously renegotiate and redefine pragmatic norms (House, 2010), raise numerous questions about the adequacy of NS pragmatic norms (Taguchi, 2011). Additionally, "at the intersection of multiple native and target cultures," learners need to "define for themselves...this 'third place'...that they can name their own" (Kramsch, 1993, p. 257), through an awareness of their own positioning within the complex realm of native and target pragmatic norms. Such a changing landscape creates an urgent demand for well-trained teachers capable of making informed choices and assisting learners to set goals for their own pragmatic learning.

According to Kasper and Rose (2002), when it comes to non-native speaker teachers,

> the critical qualification is that teachers themselves have been sufficiently socialized to L2 pragmatic practices, that they can comfortably draw on those practices as part of their communicative and cultural repertoire, and

that their metapragmatic awareness enables them to support students' learning of L2 pragmatics effectively. (p. 52)

While metapragmatic awareness represents a complex construct, only one of its aspects has been chosen for investigation in this research. The focus is on novice teachers' views of politeness in general, and of politeness in English in particular, for two reasons: firstly, politeness has been one of the central issues in teaching L2 pragmatics; secondly, the ability to express oneself in accordance with L2 politeness norms is one of the learning outcomes defined in the English subject curriculum in Serbia, both in primary and secondary education. For instance, after the fifth grade, learners should be able to use language appropriate to the formality of the situation, in keeping with L2 politeness norms; similarly, learners at all levels are expected to master "sociocultural interaction norms," including appropriate ways to produce various speech acts. However, regarding the exact topics to be covered in each grade, the curriculum provides an extensive list of the grammatical forms to be mastered (in terms of syntax, morphology, and lexicology), while pragmatic elements, including what is meant by "politeness norms," are omitted. In Félix-Brasdefer and Cohen's (2012) words, "a focus on grammatical forms in their role as pragmalinguistic resources...used to express pragmatic intent, such as respect or politeness, in socially appropriate situations" (p. 651) is completely missing. This lack of guidance for the teacher in the curriculum was particularly significant in deciding to focus on novice teachers' conceptualizations of politeness. Due to the lack of support in the curriculum, it is the teachers' perceptions of politeness in general and awareness of L2 politeness in particular that considerably influence whether and how various issues related to L2 politeness are covered in the classroom. The participants' actual classroom practices, however, are outside the scope of this study.

In spite of the intricacies of teaching L2 pragmatics, its place in teacher training programs is still not clearly defined. A recent study by Vásquez and Sharpless (2009), examining the role of pragmatics in 94 master's TESOL programs in the United States, revealed that these varied substantially in terms of the place of pragmatics in the curricula, the time devoted to pragmatics, the topics covered, the resources used (reflecting a more theoretical or a more applied orientation), as well as the faculty members' attitudes to and beliefs about the most appropriate ways to address pragmatics. While the considerable variability among the programs in the treatment of pragmatics lends support to the claims that pragmatics has been grossly neglected in teacher training (Cohen 2005; Eslami, 2011; Eslami-Rasekh, 2005a; Ishihara 2007; Vellenga 2011), especially the practical applications of theory (Ishihara & Cohen, 2010), Vásquez and Sharpless (2009) have also identified a growing awareness of the significance of including pragmatics in teacher education programs. Similarly, reports on the effects of recent attempts to incorporate a pragmatics component in teacher education programs, discussed below, give grounds for optimism.

A recent study by Eslami (2011) examined native and nonnative English-speaking TESOL graduate students' reflections on the content knowledge and pedagogical knowledge gained during an ESL methodology course incorporating an instructional pragmatics component. The data obtained through the students' reflective journals, online discussions, and the researcher's field notes demonstrated considerable gains in the student-teachers' pragmatic and pedagogical knowledge, and an increasing awareness of the complexities involved in understanding, mastering, and teaching L2 pragmatics.

Similarly, Vásquez and Fioramonte (2011) explored the long-term effects of a master's TESL course focusing on cross-cultural pragmatics on students' teaching practices. The course readings, topics, activities, and assignments appeared to have strongly influenced former students' language teaching. The majority of the participants, who had attended the course over five years prior to the study, reported addressing various pragmatic issues in their own classrooms within the curricular constraints. Additionally, they reported having greatly benefited from a raised awareness of pragmatic issues, both inside and outside the language classroom.

Several studies have investigated the effects of professional development programs on in-service teachers' pragmatic awareness and/or L2 pragmatics teaching skills. In an EFL setting, Ishihara (2011) examined the development of Japanese teachers' pragmatic awareness through an ethnographic case study, describing an episode leading to a teacher's increased pragmatic awareness. Ishihara (2012) investigated the value of critical narratives as a tool to dispel cultural stereotypes in L2 pragmatics teaching, demonstrating their usefulness in the process of arriving at a more comprehensive understanding of pragmatic diversity, but also presenting potential challenges to their classroom use. Yates and Wigglesworth (2005) reported significant gains in Australian ESL teachers' subject and pedagogical knowledge, and their understanding of interpersonal communication in the classroom, following a series of workshops in pragmatics. In the same vein, Vellenga (2011) found that in-service teachers' continuing professional development in the area of pragmatics yielded obvious benefits in both ESL and EFL contexts.

In contrast to the above studies, which investigated the effects of pedagogically-oriented courses and seminars in L2 pragmatics on teachers' pragmatic awareness and/or their teaching practices, the few studies examining pre-service and novice teachers' metapragmatic awareness in the Serbian context (Paunović, 2013; Savić, 2012, 2013) did not focus on the effects of pragmatically-focused courses. Rather, they explored the participants' metapragmatic awareness upon completing (part of) their coursework at the university, since a course in pragmatics was not included in the English BA curriculum at the university at the time of the studies.

In a recent study, Savić (2012) examined advanced Serbian EFL learners' metapragmatic awareness as mirrored in their metapragmatic assessment of L2 request, refusal, and apology listening texts, and the reasoning behind their choices. The findings demonstrated that few participants could identify the prosodic and syntactic features that contributed to their assessment of the contextual variables. More specifically, while a number of respondents identified various lexical features of informal language in the listening texts (e.g., contractions, fillers, phrasal verbs), far fewer could enumerate the relevant syntactic and prosodic features. Such findings clearly showed that instruction in the pragmatic functions of various syntactic structures (as pointed out by Félix-Brasdefer & Cohen, 2012) and prosodic and paralinguistic properties of speech needs to be incorporated in the participants' teacher education.

While focusing on prospective EFL teachers' understanding of various concepts related to intercultural communicative competence and a potential impact of an intercultural communicative competence course on their conceptualization of the key notions of intercultural communicative competence, Paunović (2013) briefly examined their perceptions of politeness as a form of culturally shaped behavior. She compared the responses of first- and third-year English Department students after the latter had completed the elective intercultural communicative competence course. While the former tended to disregard the interactive aspect of politeness and the fact that it is culturally shaped, the latter generally acknowledged the culturally and socially shaped nature of politeness, which suggested that "intercultural communication training makes a difference" (Paunović, 2013, p. 198), since it provides insights into broader cultural values underlying linguistic behavior.

Finally, Savić (2013) investigated senior-year English students' awareness of the sociopragmatic factors that reportedly influenced their linguistic choices and the pragmalinguistic resources they considered relevant in English. Four groups of contextual factors, pertaining to the speaker, the hearer, their relationship, and the communicative situation, were identified in the interview and verbal protocol data, largely corresponding to the range of variables dealt with in the literature. While this testified to sound sociopragmatic knowledge of the majority of the participants, a very interesting finding was a complete shift in focus once the interviewees were asked to assume the role of the teacher; namely, their focus moved to pragmalinguistic devices and the interconnectedness of language choices with contextual variables was completely disregarded. As for their pragmalinguistic knowledge, the features identified as relevant in English ranged from individual words and phrases and modal verbs to body language and prosody. Their frequency of occurrence corresponded to the way these pragmalinguistic devices are prioritized in the literature and teaching materials, and often reflected rather stereotypical views of how to express politeness in English. Finally, the interviewees found it difficult to discuss the potential influences of the different devices on the communicative effect of the message, indicating that pragmalinguistic and sociopragmatic issues need to be addressed more thoroughly.

Against this backdrop, I now report on a study of novice Serbian EFL teachers' views of politeness. The study further explores the interview data from Savić (2013, 2014), but with a different focus of analysis. The following section discusses the methodology employed in the present study.

## Method

The data presented in this paper were taken from a broader mixed-method study aiming to investigate advanced Serbian EFL learners' pragmalinguistic and sociopragmatic knowledge through their production and interpretation of three speech acts: requests, apologies, and refusals (Savić, 2014). The present study is based on the interview data from a subset of 13 participants from the earlier study.

### Participants

All the participants in the qualitative part of the original study (Savić, 2014) were senior students majoring in English at a university in Serbia, as they could offer the best insights into the outcomes of English language courses and the Methodology of TEFL instruction at the university level. At the time of the study, a two-semester Methodology of TEFL course was the only pedagogically-oriented course in the curriculum (although several new courses have since been introduced). No one course explicitly focused on L2 pragmatics, either from a theoretical or an applied perspective. Therefore, the study investigated the metapragmatic awareness developed during the participants' university education and not within a single course.

In Jones, Torres, and Arminio's (2006) words, all the senior students were considered "*information-rich* cases that hold the greatest potential for generating insight about the phenomenon of interest" (p. 66). The sampling strategy referred to as *purposeful random sampling* (Patton, 2002, p. 244) was employed to select the research participants for the original study. Only in terms of gender was the sample not chosen completely randomly. Only female students were invited to participate, as the broader study also investigated the participants' use of intonation patterns in the production of the selected speech acts and there are considerable pitch differences between males and females.

**Table 1.** Participant background

| interviewee | age | proficiency | stay-abroad | purpose |
|---|---|---|---|---|
| 1 | 24 | C1– | US, 5 months | work-and-travel program |
| 2 | 23 | C2 | US, 10 months | student exchange |
| 3 | 23 | C2– | no | |
| 4 | 23 | C2– | no | |
| 5 | 23 | C1+ | no | |
| 6 | 23 | C1– | no | |
| 7 | 23 | C1 | no | |
| 8 | 27 | C1+ | no | |
| 9 | 24 | C2– | no | |
| 10 | 24 | C2– | US, 11 months | work-and-travel program |
| 11 | 24 | C1 | US, 5 months | work-and-travel program |
| 12 | 23 | C2 | US, 4 months | work-and-travel program |
| 13 | 24 | C2– | no | |

The criterion for selecting the interviewees for the current study from the original study pool was whether they had any teaching experience outside the obligatory teaching practice. According to the background information questionnaire employed in the broader study, 13 out of 15 interviewees had already started teaching: 10 taught in private language schools and three gave private English lessons. These 13 participants fit the definition of novice teachers in the current study and, consequently, their interviews are analyzed here.

The age of the interviewees ranged from 23 to 27, their mean age being 23.7. They all belonged to the group of students referred to as *apsolventi* in the Serbian higher education system, meaning that they had taken all the courses, but had not passed all the exams yet. Their English proficiency ranged from the C1– to the C2 level of the Common European Framework of Reference for Languages (Council of Europe, 2001). Level C represents the highest of the three broad common reference levels, C1 denoting "effective operational proficiency" and C2 corresponding to "mastery" (p. 23). Level of proficiency was determined based on the interviewees' grades on the last English Language exam they had passed prior to this study. They had had four intensive 2-semester English Language courses, each targeted at a specific CEFR proficiency level.

Five interviewees had taken part in student work-and-travel programs or exchange programs (4–11 months long), while eight had never visited an English-speaking country (Table 1). This ratio of the participants with and without stay-abroad experience is not representative of the EFL student population at the university, where few students have an opportunity to visit an English-speaking country during their studies.[3]

## Data collection and analysis

The topics covered in the interviews involved the participants' perceptions of the relevant factors when communicating in the L2, the language devices that can be manipulated to modify the effect of the message in English, the advice one would give to Serbian learners traveling to Britain and the US and foreigners coming to Serbia about how to communicate appropriately, and the interviewees' views of what politeness involves and how it is manifested in the UK, the US,[4] and Serbia. The interviewees with stay-abroad experience were invited to further expand on the influence of the experience on their perceptions of pragmatic practices in the target and home communities. The interview guide is given in Figure 1. The current paper focuses on the responses reflecting the interviewees' views of politeness and their reflections on politeness in the two target cultures and in Serbia.

The interview data were collected at the American Corner and at the Faculty of Philosophy. The interviews varied in length, from 12 to 30 minutes, the average duration being 17 minutes. They were audio-recorded, transcribed (in accordance with the transcription conventions from Spencer-Oatey, 2008, p. xi, xii; see Appendix), and analyzed qualitatively for emergent themes related to politeness in general, and British, American, and Serbian politeness in particular. The interview guide constituted the framework for the analysis (Patton, 2002, p. 439–440).

---

Discussion topics:

The factors that influence the interviewees' communicative choices in L2

- The linguistic means the interviewees employ to modify the effect of their messages in L2
- The meaning of *politeness* and/or *being polite*[5]–personal definitions and reflections
- The tips about how to communicate appropriately the interviewees would give their EFL learners planning to visit the UK
- The tips about how to communicate appropriately the interviewees would give their EFL learners planning to visit the US
- The tips about how to communicate appropriately the interviewees would give a British/American foreigner visiting Serbia

Additional topics for interviewees with stay-abroad experience:

- Experiences with L2 politeness
- The influence of the stay-abroad period on the interviewees' perceptions of politeness in the target community
- The influence of the stay-abroad period on the interviewees' perceptions of politeness in Serbia

---

**Figure 1.** Interview guide

## Results and discussion

Several recurring themes emerged as the interviewees provided their own, personal definitions of politeness and compared politeness in Britain, America, and Serbia. The themes involve the nature of politeness and its universality or culture-specificity, as well as the interviewees' perceptions and interpretations of various aspects of polite behavior in the target cultures. The most prominent themes are dealt with in the sections below.

### Politeness as universal/culture-specific

The view that politeness is universal and is expressed similarly regardless of the specific culture reverberated through seven interviews. At the same time, other interviewees appeared to be sensing a tension between two opposing and/or complementary viewpoints: politeness as universal and politeness as culture-specific. The quotes below, taken from interviews with a respondent with stay-abroad experience (Interviewee 10) and a respondent without it (Interviewee 5), present the former view. In the following transcripts a dash (-) indicates a short pause, and an underscore (_) indicates a continuing tone.

Interviewee 10: […] politeness is universal, so it's the same, people are the same.

Interviewee 5: I think that's not culturally based (-) because you are polite here […] the same way you're polite in Hungary or any other place.

Along the same lines, when asked about the advice about politeness in Serbia she would give to an English-speaking foreigner, Interviewee 6, at the C1– proficiency level and with no stay-abroad experience, responded as follows:

Interviewee 6: if that person knows how to be polite, it's easy to learn some simple Serbian words_

The quotation above, as well as several other responses, seem to be based on an implicit assumption that politeness is equated with individual words and phrases, and that behaving politely in different cultures is simply a matter of acquiring L2 expressions, while an important awareness of the cultural values underlying the words, vital for a full understanding of L2 pragmatics (Yates, 2010), seems to be missing. Such views appear to be reflective of Bennett's (1993) third ethnocentric stage of the developmental model of intercultural sensitivity–*minimization*–in which the individual recognizes superficial differences between cultures but still regards all cultures as fundamentally similar, and his/her own cultural perspective is regarded as the only valid one. The centrality of Interviewee 7's own worldview was clearly expressed when she discussed the politeness tips useful to a foreigner in Serbia. This interviewee, without any stay-abroad experience, had difficulty remembering what information would be valuable because she felt that

Interviewee 7:   [...] everything is quite normal here.

This concise statement appears to reveal a lack of an important aspect of metapragmatic awareness: an ability to "bring into awareness the particular cultural frames or assumptions which are at work in the interpretive process" (McConachy, 2013, p. 102), or to perceive that the metapragmatic judgments made are actually culturally bound (McConachy 2013, p. 101). A similarly strong culturally-bound perspective can be noticed in the response to the same question provided by Interviewee 13, with a slightly higher level of proficiency than Interviewee 7, but also without any stay-abroad experience:

Interviewee 13:   Well, if you are in Serbia; there's no problem; you can swear all the time; Serbian people love it; so_ {laughs} you don't have to worry about politeness here. I'm kidding. Well, here are not (-) no (-) I guess, from my point of view (-) there are no, no, there aren't any strict rules of behavior. People, Serbs like when foreigners, their guests, are as spontaneous as possible; so I don't think that there are some strict rules for behavior and for language; so just to be as natural as possible, to laugh a lot, to talk a lot, to swear a lot_

While it is extremely difficult to interpret behavior from a neutral standpoint (Yates & Major, 2015), language teachers need to be able to reflect more critically on what is specific about their own culture, or on "cultural representations" (House, 2005) behind pragmalinguistic behavior that foreigners might need to be instructed in. Additionally, a recognition that "speakers are rooted in their culture" and that "they can resort to their individual, socioculturally generated knowledge... in which linguistic expressions are linked with extralinguistic features of the situation" (House 2005, p. 16) is a first necessary step towards understanding the challenges language learners of a particular background could face in the process of mastering L2 pragmatics. Interviewee 13 actually acknowledged that she was only expressing her own point of view, but still appeared to be unable to recognize it as one of many possible viewpoints and single out the major similarities and differences in comparison to the UK or the US.

As mentioned earlier, some interviewees appeared to be expressing two opposing standpoints even within a single turn. For instance, Interviewee 5, quoted earlier, first claimed that politeness "is not culturally-based," but then went on to argue that "there are some cultural differences that the foreigner should be aware of" and provided examples. Such responses mirror the tension between universal and culture-specific aspects of politeness in the literature (e.g., Brown & Levinson, 1987; Leech, 1983; Wierzbicka, 1985), represented in House's (2005) multilevel model.

In addition to recognizing differences regarding politeness in different countries, Interviewee 8, without stay-abroad experience, acknowledged a much more nuanced nature of politeness, that is, a variation in the understanding of politeness *within* individual cultures, reflecting discursive thinking about politeness (Mills, 2011).

> Interviewee 8: I even think politeness doesn't mean the same to me and to some other person. So what is polite for me is not polite for you or some other person. And especially between cultures. There are cultural differences and the level of politeness is more important in England, I think, than here

Two more interviewees expressed an awareness of the fact that all their statements referring to the politeness in a specific country were generalizations, but went on to say that generalizations were still useful and inevitable when discussing pragmatic topics, as acknowledged by Yates (2010, p. 290).

The responses discussed in this section demonstrate considerable variation in the novice teachers' understanding of politeness, ranging from politeness being regarded as universal, and only a matter of learning simple expressions, to politeness as a highly culture-specific concept, varying even across individuals in a single culture.

**Politeness as indirectness and/or dishonesty**

Five novice teachers expressed a rather negative view of politeness, which came across very clearly both in the content of their responses and in the prosody and body language, as noted in the field notes. For example, Interviewee 12, who was fully proficient (C2) and had spent four months in the US, felt that politeness equaled "not saying things directly if you don't think a person would like what you're saying to them or what you're asking from them." For her, politeness seemed to be a mixture of indirectness and dishonesty, that is, "trying not to state facts as they are":

> Interviewee 12: Politeness basically means euphemisms, a lot of euphemisms, and trying not to state the facts as they are. That's what politeness basically is. [...] . No; no; seriously; politeness is a lot of euphemisms. That's what I really think. It just comes down to not saying things directly if you don't think a person would like what you're saying to them or what you're asking from them. That's about it. And a lot of phrases. Phrases; phrases; phrases; like *please_* a lot of modal verbs, a LO:T of modal verbs.

This interviewee expresses a very strong opinion about both politeness in general and politeness in the English-speaking world further on in the interview. Such views appear to be strongly rooted in orientations to different values in

Serbia and the Anglo-Saxon world (although the Anglo-Saxon world is far from homogeneous), or "differences in 'cultural logic,' encoded in language" (Wierzbicka, 1985), as shown by the scarce contrastive pragmatic research involving Serbian and English (Blagojević & Mišić Ilić, 2013; Mišić Ilić, 2010) and studies of Serbian politeness (Milosavljević, 2006). As Wierzbicka (1985) argues, "different pragmatic norms reflect different hierarchies of values characteristic of different cultures" (p. 173), "much deeper than mere norms of politeness" (p. 145), which is why they can provoke strong reactions even in highly proficient learners.

In contrast to Interviewee 12, Interviewees 3 and 4 had not spent any time abroad and had a slightly lower proficiency level (C2–). The former also perceived politeness as dishonesty, while the latter expressed a view of politeness as sugarcoating, that is, putting things "in the right package":

Interviewee 3: […] so I think it's very important […] to act up a bit; it's not maybe a nice thing to say, not to be honest.

Interviewee 4: But if you know how to […] just to put it in the right package, you can achieve a lot more.

Such views confirm that "L2 pragmatic practices may provoke affective responses in L2 learners" since especially "sociopragmatics (more so than pragmalinguistics) is closely related to people's cultural and personal beliefs and values, making it more of a personal value decision whether learners wish to converge to target practices" (Kasper & Rose, 2002, pp. 275–276). While the role of learner identity in acquiring L2 pragmatic norms has now been widely acknowledged, together with the importance of teachers recognizing and respecting learners' choices about the degree to which they want to approximate target language pragmatic norms (Ishihara & Cohen, 2010), such strong views in novice teachers call for further research. Since "teachers' cognitions…emerge consistently as a powerful influence on their practices" (Borg, 2003, p. 91), the extent to which such personal views, not uncommon among Serbian EFL learners, color the treatment of L2 politeness in the classroom would certainly be worth investigating further.

While discussing her 5-month-long stay-abroad experience, Interviewee 1 addressed her perceptions of American politeness, saying that she sometimes felt that Americans "are so polite that it seems hypocritical." She also reported struggling with making inferences based on her boss's feedback and recognizing his intentions:

Interviewee 1: I would say that generally they are more polite than here; but sometimes you don't know what they're thinking; which I don't like. Sometimes they are so polite that it seems hypocritical. Sometimes when you_ for example; I had this employer; he really is a nice guy. He really is. But sometimes I couldn't make a distinction between whether

> he is giving me a remark on my job or it was just merely a warning for me, so it was kinda_ [...] So he was really a nice guy but sometimes you really cannot make that distinction between whether they're just being polite or whether they really mean that.

This response is very much in line with one of the responses from Yates and Major's (2015) study, which discusses the difficulty of comprehending and giving less direct work-related feedback and the importance of learning "how to say without saying." Whether politeness was interpreted as dishonesty and sometimes hypocrisy because of greater challenges involved in interpreting less direct modes of expression in an L2 or because of the interviewees' own cultural perspective, which values directness more (Blagojević & Mišić Ilić, 2013; Mišić Ilić, 2010), was not completely clear, even after additional clarification questions. Regardless of the exact reasons behind this rather negative view of politeness, this seems to be a relevant issue to explore further in the Serbian EFL context, especially because such views were identified in interviewees with varying proficiency levels, both with and without stay-abroad experience.

### Politeness as a matter of degree: American, British, and Serbian politeness

Although the interviewees were not asked to directly compare American, British, and Serbian politeness, all of them discussed the differences between the three at one point in the interviews. All the interviewees, regardless of their proficiency and stay-abroad experience, considered politeness a matter of degree, describing one country as "more" or "less polite" than the other two.

> Interviewee 4: Every culture has its subtleties. I mean (-) ok Serbs are not; generally speaking (-) I mean, it's a generalization; generalizations are always wrong; and exceptions confirm the rule; so it's (-) but English people are more polite. Maybe that could be prejudice or generalization (-) or I don't know; but I have this sense_ at least the persons that are on the tapes are real polite {laughs} [...] I think that British culture is founded on politeness. It also could be generalization_ prejudice or something, but that's what I think about the British. But when it comes to Americans, I think they're less polite because it's a big melting pot of cultures, so I just don't think they're that polite or_
>
> Interviewee 3: I think we [Serbs]'re actually on place number 3.

The general impression of all the interviewees was that the British were more polite than the Americans, who, in turn, were more polite than the Serbs, but few interviewees were capable of further discussing the bases for their claims. Interviewee 12 was one of the exceptions; she referred to her personal experience of communicating in the US based on the patterns taught in school through textbooks by British publishers and being perceived as overly polite by her employers:

> Interviewee 12: I adapted very easily cos (???), it's just that I felt kind of silly at first when addressing my employers; my managers (-) I would always be like *would you please be so kind as to blah blah blah* and they would be like *ok; I'll do that for you; no need to beg me* {laughs} [...] Right now if I went to England, let's say England because I guess they're more formal, their language is more formal than American English, I think I would have to be very very careful and I would be kind of tense when speaking with people over there cos I'd probably think that my language, the language I picked up in the US, would be kind of rude_

Interestingly, all the interviewees who spent some time in the US discussed the issue of textbook language, which they equated with British English, comparing it with their perceptions of language use in the US. The participants' comments reflected the perceived inadequacy of the pragmatic uses of English presented in textbooks, also found in research (Bardovi-Harlig, 2001; McConachy & Hata, 2013; Vellenga, 2004), and mirrored Bardovi-Harlig's (2001) claim that "textbooks cannot be counted on as a reliable source of pragmatic input for classroom language learners" (p. 25). While, in the past decade, there has been an increase in the variety of teaching materials, including those making use of technology and virtual learning environments as tools for pragmatic learning (see Taguchi & Sykes, 2013), the textbook still remains the major resource in EFL classrooms around the world, making the role of the teacher all the more important.

What nearly all the responses addressing politeness in the three countries seemed to have in common was discussing different degrees rather than different conceptualizations of politeness, again reflecting a confusion regarding the tension between the universal and the culture-specific. In McConachy's (2013) words, while commenting on politeness in the target cultures, the learners "mobilize[d] the cultural frames of their first language (L1), often without explicit awareness of the particular frames through which interpretations [were] being made" (p. 101). A crucial component that appeared to be missing from the responses was an attempt to discuss politeness as a reflection of cultural values, or as related to the communicative ethos, that is, "communicative values speakers may orient to in interaction" (Yates, 2010, p. 298).

However, during their 5-month stay-abroad experience, two participants actually seemed to have begun to view politeness as a defining trait of the American communicative ethos (without referring to the notion in this way). No similar view of politeness as a defining trait of British or Serbian culture, or as a feature of every culture was found in the interviews.

Interviewee 11: Politeness in the States is a way of living. It's from every single thing, moment, you do, from the moment you get into a store, from the moment you're meeting somebody, everything is a kind of polite situation. EVERYTHING I mean. So it means a lot in the States, because the moment you're not polite they will look you at you differently. No matter whether that politeness means something or not, you just need, it's the kind of culture it is.

While the effects of the interviewees' stay-abroad experience were not the focus of the present study, the interviews clearly showed that the novice teachers with some stay-abroad experience, like Interviewees 10 and 11, had reflected more deeply on pragmatic issues and were more acutely aware of the culture-specific aspects of politeness than most interviewees who had not been abroad. This could be the result of a lack of any explicit focus on L2 pragmatics in their education and the consequent necessity to rely almost exclusively on personal experience when discussing pragmatic issues. Two interviewees commented on how their stay in the US affected both their target and native language use:

Interviewee 10: It used to be very different; my English politeness used to be very artificial because it was not my innate politeness. Because I was only using my mother language, Serbian, so it used to be different. But since I've spent some time abroad_ and since I was speaking English for a couple of years here very fluently, it somehow became the same. [...] That[6] was a good thing. That was a good thing which I accepted from Americans and I brought it into my Serbian language and the way of behaving here.

In addition to raising the interviewees' awareness of their own pragmatic language use, the stay-abroad experience also made three of them reflect more on how they could use the experience in their own teaching. When asked about the advice for Serbian learners going to the US, Interviewee 11 raised a crucial point testifying to her awareness of the great variety of contexts in which learners might find themselves, the uniqueness of each of them, and the importance of observation as a learning tool:

Interviewee 11: But I would recommend listening a lot. [...] meaning to look at the way people behave, the way they talk when they go into a store or when they go into a pharmacy or wherever they go (-) wherever you are just be observant; a lot, of people; and that's actually the best way you can learn. I mean (-) I can give you some specific advice or situations, but those would be MY situations. You'll have your own; so the best thing is to observe and take the best out of those you see.

Both Interviewees 10 and 11 tackle the issue of awareness, albeit from different perspectives. What emerges from their discussions is both the need for the awareness of L1 and L2 politeness norms and for creating a "'third place'... that they can name their own" (Kramsch, 1993, p. 257), where they can feel comfortable making informed pragmatic choices.

To sum up, neither the interviewees with nor those without stay-abroad experience mentioned the interplay of the universal and the culture-specific in politeness; instead, they tended to regard different cultures as "more" or "less polite" rather than viewing them as conceptualizing politeness differently. However, the participants with at least some stay-abroad experience, like Interviewees 10, 11, and 12, appeared to have reflected more deeply on certain aspects of politeness in the target culture they had had direct experience with and demonstrated a heightened awareness of their own pragmatic language use. Unfortunately, the majority of novice EFL teachers in Serbia do not have an opportunity to visit an English-speaking country prior to starting their teaching career. Therefore, since research has shown that both pre-service and in-service teaching methodology courses can have a considerable impact on (future) teachers' metapragmatic awareness and on their ability to cope successfully with L2 pragmatics in the classroom (Eslami, 2011; Ishihara 2011; Vásquez & Fioramonte, 2011; Yates & Wigglesworth, 2005), creating opportunities for Serbian EFL teachers to learn about, discuss, and reflect on pragmatic issues could be a promising direction for developing teacher training courses.

## Conclusion

The present study explored the views of 13 novice Serbian EFL teachers related to the nature of politeness and perceptions of politeness in the UK, the US, and Serbia. Despite the small number of participants, it was an attempt to investigate teachers since the focus in L2 pragmatics research has so far been primarily on learners.

The major tension identified in the interviews was between the universal and the culture-specific and their interplay in the enactment and interpretation of (L2) politeness. The interviewees expressed surprisingly varied views, ranging from politeness being regarded as a display of respect to it being viewed as sugarcoating and dishonesty. Their perceptions were often heavily colored by their own cultural perspective, and rarely revealed reflection on intra-cultural variation. Additionally, few novice teachers regarded politeness as a reflection of deeper cultural values and culture-specific orientations to communication.

The following quotation best sums up several participants' feelings about the topics raised in the interviews and stresses the necessity for providing an arena for discussing pragmatic issues in teacher education:

Interviewee 6: This is the first time that I'm talking to somebody about politeness, about the difference in being polite in Serbia, Britain and America, and I didn't know where I stand with it [...] It's a bit strange to talk about these things for the first time. It's just, they're such obvious things, and so normal, and so academic, and yet I have never had the opportunity to talk about them.

As part of curricular reforms, a theoretical course in pragmatics has been established at the MA level at the English Department at the university where this study was conducted, but no pedagogically-oriented pragmatics courses have yet been introduced. An interesting future research area would therefore be to examine the effects of the new course on teachers' understanding of the complex interplay between the universal and the culture-specific in politeness, and on their own positioning in relation to L1 and L2 pragmatics. Since "the uniqueness of pragmatics," reflected in the role of learners' cultural values and attitudes in acquiring it, has been stressed repeatedly (Taguchi, 2011, p. 303), an insight into whether and how the cognition in the sphere of L2 pragmatics changes is certainly worth investigating. Another promising research avenue would be to explore the influence of the course on teaching practices, preferably through a larger-scale quantitative study, which could prove useful in mapping out teachers' needs and finding ways to address them within the curriculum.

Having employed the semi-structured interview as the data collection method, the present study examined novice teachers' reported cognitions, without exploring the link between cognition and teaching practice. The next critical step is to investigate how cognitions affect classroom practices, as "ultimately…we are interested in understanding teachers' professional actions, not what or how they think in isolation of what they do" (Borg, 2003, p. 105). These issues could be explored through a combination of a range of qualitative data collection methods, including class observations, verbal protocols and teacher journals, which would certainly be a promising way forward in this area.

## Notes

1   In most European higher education institutions, 60 ECTS (European Credit Transfer and Accumulation System) study points/credits corresponds to the workload during a year of full time academic studies, one credit representing 25 to 30 hours of work for an average student (including class attendance, reading course materials, doing assignments, etc.).

2   Politeness1 refers to common perceptions and manifestations of politeness in everyday interaction, while politeness2 represents scientific conceptualizations of politeness (Félix-Brasdefer, 2008, p. 10–11).
3   The term *stay-abroad* rather than *study-abroad* is employed because four out of five interviewees were not in any way involved in university life or service learning programs during their stay in the US, but were working and traveling around the country. The term is therefore used to distinguish between a more structured and academically focused sojourn in the target community and work-and-travel programs the participants in this study were involved in. Only Interviewee 2 was involved in what would be defined as a *study-abroad* program strictly speaking.
4   The UK and the US were singled out as the two English-speaking countries Serbian EFL learners are most frequently exposed to through textbooks, the media, and/or traveling. In spite of the existence of numerous cultural differences *within* these countries, the interview questions only referred to Britain and America in order to see if the interviewees would comment on intra-cultural differences in politeness.
5   The two terms were employed because it was expected (as indeed was the case) that the interviewees would find it easier to define being polite through references to examples than politeness as an abstract concept. The two were used interchangeably to stimulate discussion and encourage deeper reflection.
6   Paying attention to "everyday politeness," in the interviewee's words.

## References

Bachman, L. F. (1990). *Fundamental considerations in language testing*. Oxford: Oxford University Press.

Bachman, L. F., & Palmer, A. S. (1996). *Language testing in practice*. Oxford: Oxford University Press.

Bardovi-Harlig, K. (2001). Evaluating the empirical evidence. Grounds for instruction in pragmatics? In K. R. Rose & G. Kasper (Eds.), *Pragmatics in language teaching* (pp. 13–32). Cambridge: Cambridge University Press.

Bardovi-Harlig, K., & Mahan-Taylor, R. (2003). *Teaching pragmatics*. Washington, DC: Office of English Programs, U.S. Department of State. Retrieved from http://www.indiana.edu/~dsls/publications/printtableofcontents.doc

Bennett, J. M. (1993). Toward ethnorelativism: A developmental model of intercultural sensitivity. In R. M. Paige (Ed.), *Education for the intercultural experience* (pp. 21–71). Yarmouth, ME: Intercultural Press.

Blagojević, S., & Mišić Ilić, B. (2013). Kontrastivno-pragmatička analiza autorovog ograđivanja u pisanom akademskom diskursu na engleskom i srpskom jeziku [A contrastive pragmatic analysis of hedging in English and Serbian written academic discourse]. In I. Živančević Sekeruš (Ed.), *Proceedings of the Sixth International Interdisciplinary Symposium "Encounter of Cultures"* (pp. 587–599). Novi Sad, Serbia: Faculty of Philosophy.

Borg, S. (2003). Teacher cognition in language teaching: A review of research on what language teachers think, know, believe, and do. *Language Teaching, 36*, 81–109.

Bou-Franch, P., & Garcés-Conejos, P. (2003). Teaching linguistic politeness: A methodological approach. *IRAL, International Review of Applied Linguistics in Language Teaching, 41*, 1–22.

Brown, P., & Levinson, S. C. (1987). *Politeness. Some universals in language usage.* Cambridge: Cambridge University Press.

Cohen, A. (2005). Strategies for learning and performing L2 speech acts. *Intercultural Pragmatics, 2*, 275–301.

Cohen, A. (2008). Teaching and assessing L2 pragmatics: What can we expect from learners? *Language Teaching, 41*, 213–235.

Council of Europe. (2001). *Common European framework of reference for languages: Learning, teaching, assessment.* Cambridge: Cambridge University Press.

Davis, J. (2007). Resistance to L2 pragmatics in the Australian ESL context. *Language Learning, 57*, 611–649.

Eslami, Z. (2011). In their own voices: Reflections of native and nonnative English speaking TESOL graduate students on on-line pragmatic instruction to EFL learners. *TESL-EJ, 15*(2). Retrieved from http://www.tesl-ej.org/wordpress/issues/volume15/ej58/ej58a5/

Eslami-Rasekh, Z. (2005). Raising the pragmatic awareness of language learners. *ELT Journal, 59*, 199–208.

Félix-Brasdefer, J. C. (2008). *Politeness in Mexico and the United States. A contrastive study of the realization and perception of refusals.* Amsterdam: John Benjamins.

Félix-Brasdefer, J. C., & Cohen, A. D. (2012). Teaching pragmatics in the foreign language classroom: Grammar as a communicative resource. *Hispania, 95*, 650–669.

Houck, N., & Tatsuki, D. (Eds.). (2011). *Pragmatics: Teaching natural conversation.* Alexandria, VA: TESOL.

House, J. (2005). Politeness in Germany: Politeness in Germany? In L. Hickey & M. Stewart (Eds.), *Politeness in Europe* (pp. 13–28). Clevedon, England: Multilingual Matters.

House, J. (2010). The pragmatics of English as a lingua franca. In A. Trosborg (Ed.), *Pragmatics across languages and cultures* (pp. 363–387). Berlin: De Gruyter Mouton.

House, J. (2012). (Im)politeness in cross-cultural encounters. *Language and Intercultural Communication, 12*, 284–301.

Ishihara, N. (2007). Web-based curriculum for pragmatics instruction in Japanese as a foreign language: An explicit awareness-raising approach. *Language Awareness, 16*, 21–40.

Ishihara, N. (2011). Co-constructing pragmatic awareness: Instructional pragmatics in EFL teacher development in Japan. *TESL-EJ, 15*(2). Retrieved from http://www.tesl-ej.org/wordpress/issues/volume15/ej58/ej58a2/

Ishihara, N. (2012). Critical narratives for teaching pragmatics: Application to teacher education. *The European Journal of Applied Linguistics and TEFL, 2*, 5–17.

Ishihara, N., & Cohen, A. (2010). *Teaching and learning pragmatics: Where language and culture meet.* Harlow, England: Longman Applied Linguistics/Pearson Education.

Jones, S. R., Torres, V., & Arminio, J. (2006). *Negotiating the complexities of qualitative research in higher education. Fundamental elements and issues.* New York, NY: Routledge, Taylor & Francis Group.

Kasper, G., & Rose, K. R. (2002). *Pragmatic development in a second language.* Oxford: Blackwell.

Kasper, G., & Schmidt, R. (1996). Developmental issues in interlanguage pragmatics. *Studies in Second Language Acquisition, 18*, 149–169.

Kim, H. Y. (2014). Learner investment, identity, and resistance to second language pragmatic norms. *System, 45*, 92–102.

Kinginger, C., & Farrell, K. (2004). Assessing development of metapragmatic awareness in study abroad. *The Interdisciplinary Journal of Study Abroad, 10*(2), 19–42. Retrieved from http://www.frontiersjournal.com/issues/vol10/vol10-02_KingingerFarrell.pdf

Kramsch, C. (1993). *Context and culture in language teaching.* Oxford: Oxford University Press.

Leech, G. (1983). *Principles of pragmatics.* London: Longman.

LoCastro, V. (2001). Individual differences in second language acquisition: Attitudes, learner subjectivity, and L2 pragmatic norms. *System, 29*, 69–89.

Martínez-Flor, A., & Usó-Juan, E. (2006). A comprehensive pedagogical framework to develop pragmatics in the foreign language classroom: The 6Rs approach. *Applied Language Learning, 16*(2), 39–64.

McConachy, T. (2013). Exploring the meta-pragmatic realm in English language teaching. *Language Awareness, 22*, 100–110.

McConachy, T., & Hata, K. (2013). Addressing textbook representations of pragmatics and culture. *ELT Journal, 67*, 294–301.

Mills, S. (2011). Discursive approaches to politeness and impoliteness. In Linguistic Politeness Research Group (Eds.), *Discursive approaches to politeness* (pp. 19–56). Berlin: de Gruyter Mouton.

Milosavljević, B. (2006). Iskazivanje molbe u neformalnoj komunikaciji [Making requests in informal communication]. *Slavistika, 10*, 160–168.

Mišić Ilić, B. (2010). Jezički i kulturni aspekti govornog čina zabranjivanja iz ugla kontrastivne pragmatike [Linguistic and cultural aspects of the prohibitive speech act—A contrastive pragmatic approach]. In Lj. Subotić & I. Živančević Sekeruš (Eds.), *Proceedings of the Fifth International Interdisciplinary Symposium "Encounter of Cultures"* (pp. 463–470). Novi Sad, Serbia: Faculty of Philosophy.

Norton, B. (2013). *Identity and Language Learning (2nd ed.): Extending the Conversation.* Harlow: Longman.

Patton, M. Q. (2002). *Qualitative research and evaluation methods* (3rd ed.). Thousand Oaks, CA: Sage Publications.

Paunović, T. (2013). *The tangled web: Intercultural communicative competence in EFL.* Niš, Serbia: Faculty of Philosophy, University of Niš.

Safont Jordá, M. P. (2003). Metapragmatic awareness and pragmatic production of third language learners of English: A focus on request acts realizations. *International Journal of Bilingualism, 7*, 43–68.

Savić, M. (2012). "Who could they be talking to?" Advanced Serbian EFL learners' metapragmatic awareness. In B. Mišić Ilić & V. Lopičić (Eds.), *Jezik, književnost, komunikacija* [Language, literature, communication] (pp. 485–498). Niš, Serbia: Faculty of Philosophy, University of Niš.

Savić, M. (2013). "Ready for professional challenges?" Senior-year English Department students' sociopragmatic and pragmalinguistic knowledge. *Teme, 2*, 683–700. Retrieved from http://teme.junis.ni.ac.rs/teme2-2013/teme%202-2013-11.pdf

Savić, M. (2014). *Politeness through the prism of requests, apologies and refusals. A case of advanced Serbian EFL learners*. Newcastle upon Tyne: Cambridge Scholars.

Siegal, M. (1996). The role of learner subjectivity in second language sociolinguistic competency: Western women learning Japanese. *Applied Linguistics, 17*, 356–382.

Spencer-Oatey, H. (Ed.). (2008). *Culturally speaking: Culture, communication and politeness theory* (2nd ed.). New York, NY: Continuum.

Taguchi, N. (2011). Teaching pragmatics: Trends and issues. *Annual Review of Applied Linguistics, 31*, 289–310.

Taguchi, N. (2015). "Contextually" speaking: A survey of pragmatic learning abroad, in class and online. *System, 48*, 3–20.

Taguchi, N., & Sykes, J. (Eds.). (2013). *Technology in interlanguage pragmatics research and teaching*. Philadelphia, PA: John Benjamins.

Tatsuki, D., & Houck, N. (Eds.). (2010). *Pragmatics teaching: Speech acts*. Alexandria, VA: TESOL.

Vásquez, C., & Fioramonte, A. (2011). Integrating pragmatics into the MA-TESL program: Perspectives from former students. *TESL-EJ, 15*(2). Retrieved from http://tesl-ej.org/pdf/ej58/a1.pdf

Vásquez, C., & Sharpless, D. (2009). The role of pragmatics in the master's TESOL curriculum: Findings from a nationwide survey. *TESOL Quarterly, 43*, 5–28.

Vellenga, H. (2004). Learning pragmatics from ESL & EFL textbooks: How likely? *TESL-EJ, 8*(2). Retrieved from http://tesl-ej.org/ej30/a3.html

Vellenga, H. (2011). Teaching L2 pragmatics: Opportunities for continuing professional development. *TESL-EJ, 15*(2). Retrieved from http://www.tesl-ej.org/wordpress/issues/volume15/ej58/ej58a3/

Wierzbicka, A. (1985). Different cultures, different languages, different speech acts. *Journal of Pragmatics, 9*(2–3), 145–178.

Yates, L. (2010). Pragmatic challenges for second language learners. In A. Trosborg (Ed.), *Pragmatics across languages and cultures* (pp. 287–308). Berlin: De Gruyter Mouton.

Yates, L., & Major, G. (2015). "Quick-chatting," "smart dogs," and how to "say without saying": Small talk and pragmatic learning in the community. *System, 48*, 141–152.

Yates, L., & Wigglesworth, G. (2005). Researching the effectiveness of professional development in pragmatics. In N. Bartels (Ed.), *Researching applied linguistics in language teacher education* (pp. 261–280). New York, NY: Springer.

# Appendix

Table. Transcription conventions, adapted from Spencer-Oatey 2008: xi-xii (based on Selting et al. 1998)

| meaning | symbol | example |
|---|---|---|
| The words themselves<br>• Unintelligible text<br>• Guess at unclear text | <br>(???)<br>(word?) | <br>I don't feel like (???) and all that stuff.<br>And I'll (completely?) understand if... |
| Pauses<br>• Brief pause<br>• Pause of indicated length | <br>(-)<br>(5 sec) | <br><br>but if you (-) Ok, there was a situation once |
| Prominence<br>• (Very) lengthened segment<br>• Emphasized syllable/word | <br>wo:rd<br>WORD | <br>a lo:t of modal verbs<br>It would also depend on MY mood |
| Intonation<br>• Strongly rising tone<br>• Slightly rising tone<br>• Slightly falling tone<br>• Final tone<br>• Continuing tone | <br>word?<br>word,<br>word;<br>word.<br>word_ | <br>The language itself?<br>It's a big part of it, of course<br>I totally forgot about that; maybe we can...<br>People can be sensitive about it.<br>In the sense that_ |
| Words spoken differently from surrounding text, indicating direct speech | *word* | so I was like, *Oh, well, it's ok, I know you won't be mad at me* |
| Relevant additional information | {comment} | It doesn't mean that I'm not polite in general {laughs} |
| Text missing | [...] | they're my friends [...] and I don't even think about it |

# Noticing of Pragmatic Features During Spoken Interaction

Tetyana Sydorenko
Gwen Heller Tuason
Portland State University, USA

*Research suggests that learners' noticing of the differences between their second language (L2) knowledge and the target language can have a facilitative effect on L2 acquisition; however, little is known about learners' noticing of specific pragmatic features. The question that has not been previously addressed and which we investigated is what and how much learners can notice and learn regarding pragmatics when repeating a task with several different native speakers (NSs). The data from five ESL learners who practiced a request role-play with NSs three times were examined quantitatively and qualitatively. Noticing was measured both by learners' uptake and their verbal reports via note-taking, interviews, stimulated recalls, and reflections. Learners predominantly noticed and incorporated into subsequent production pragmatic strategies rather than forms. Some sociopragmatic learning was also evident. However, individual variation was observed, with factors identified being knowledge of linguistic expressions, ability to memorize, awareness of differences between L1 and L2 cultures, learners' goals, proficiency level, and degree of access to NSs. Our findings suggest that while prior instruction on pragmatics may increase the benefits of NS-learner interaction, it is not a required prerequisite for learners' noticing and use of some NS input.*

## Introduction

According to Schmidt's (2001) noticing hypothesis, attention plays an important role in second language (L2) learning. The premise of this hypothesis is that the stimuli that are noticed become intake, which in turn becomes available for further processing and learning. Schmidt's hypothesis has been widely studied, with L2 research indicating that noticing can have a facilitative effect on L2 acquisition (e.g., Godfroid, Boers, & Housen, 2013; Mackey, 2006).

Studies investigating noticing in an L2 have mainly focused on grammar and vocabulary in written and oral input and output (Godfroid, Housen, & Boers, 2010; Uggen, 2012; also see Leow, 2013 for a review), identifying a variety of learner-internal and external factors that can influence noticing (Izumi, 2013) and investigating what learners decide to pay attention to during learner-initiated or spontaneous noticing (e.g., Godfroid et al., 2010; Hanaoka, 2007). However, fewer studies have examined the noticing of pragmatics. The present study adds to the limited body of research in this area by examining the aspects of pragmatics that learners can notice in the input while orally interacting with native speakers (NSs) and the factors that play a role in this process.

## Review of relevant literature

In this section, we review the literature on the noticing of L2 pragmatic features, focusing on the effects of various types of instruction. We then examine research on the effects of practice on L2 development and present a case for the potential of task rehearsal in increasing the noticing of pragmatic features. Finally, we present limited research on NS-learner interaction and its contribution to pragmatic development, and particularly to the noticing of pragmatics features; we then explain how our study fills these gaps in research.

### Noticing and L2 pragmatics

Research suggests that explicit teaching of pragmatics is more effective than implicit learning of pragmatics (e.g., Halenko & Jones, 2011; Nguyen, Pham, & Pham, 2012; Takimoto, 2009) even when implicit learning takes place in input-rich study abroad contexts (Halenko & Jones, 2011). Schmidt's noticing hypothesis is referred to as an explanation for this finding.

A few studies have investigated how instruction affects learners' noticing of pragmatic features. Takahashi (2005a) compared two tasks that varied as to the degree of input enhancement: the form-comparison condition had a higher degree of input enhancement than the form-search condition. Takahashi asserted that learners in the form-comparison condition noticed more because they compared their production to NS models. Koike and Pearson (2005) also compared the effect of various instructional treatments on learners' noticing and learning, finding that provision of instruction before practice activities led to the learners noticing strategies for making appropriate suggestions in Spanish. However, both explicit and implicit instruction were found helpful for different reasons: Explicit instruction and feedback facilitated the learners' understanding of pragmatic elements and contexts, while implicit instruction and feedback improved production. Kondo (2008) explored what learners become aware of as a result of pragmatic instruction that included metapragmatic information, NS models in a form of sample dialogs, and practice and metapragmatic discussions with peer learners, finding that learners engaged in spontaneous noticing of both semantic formulas and content. Sachtleben and Denny (2012) also investigated what learners notice in discourse samples after metapragmatic instruction, and what they subsequently decide to reflect on in their blogs. Nguyen (2013) investigated the effect of metapragmatic instruction on developing learners' ability to offer constructive criticism, and reported that all learners noticed various modifiers that were provided in instruction.

In summary, studies examining noticing in L2 pragmatics are limited to comparisons of certain instructional effects, including explicit teaching by providing metapragmatic information and raising learners' awareness, provision of explicit or implicit feedback, and use of metapragmatic discussions among learners. The following sections discuss the potential of two more environments for noticing pragmatic features: task practice and interaction with NSs.

### Effect of task practice on pragmatic development

Practice of pragmatic features is another important element in various models of pragmatics instruction (cf. Cohen 2005; Félix-Brasdefer, 2006; Martínez-Flor & Usó-Juan, 2006). Studies indicate that oral practice can help improve fluency, accuracy, and complexity of responses (e.g., Ahmadian & Tavakoli, 2011; Bygate, 2001; Bygate & Samuda, 2005; De Jong & Perfetti, 2011). However, how practice affects pragmatics has been examined only in a few studies (Li, 2013; Sydorenko, 2015; Takimoto, 2012). Both Li (2013) and Takimoto (2012) found that text-based input or output practice increased pragmatic performance. Sydorenko (2015) examined learners' noticing of NS or peer input during oral practice, and found that when practicing the exact same task (computer-simulated conversation) several times, learners noticed various pragmatic aspects of NS input and incorporated them into their subsequent performance. However, when interacting with peers, there was much less noticing and input incorporation. Since Ellis (2005) contends that task rehearsal can lower learners' cognitive load and free up attentional resources for noticing various aspects of input, it is worth devoting more attention to the potential of task rehearsal for increasing the noticing of pragmatic features.

### Effect of interaction on pragmatic development

Interaction between learners and NSs has been found beneficial for a variety of areas of an L2, both from the interaction approach perspective (see Gass & Mackey, 2006) and from the perspective of socio-cultural theory (see Lantolf & Thorne, 2006). In brief, the benefits offered by interaction are negotiation of meaning and modification of output as a result, noticing the gap between the target language and learners' interlanguage, focus on form when the need for it arises during the interaction, and scaffolding provided by expert speakers and more able peers.

Unfortunately, there is little research examining the benefits of interaction for pragmatic development, and more specifically, what learners notice during such interaction. One of the recommendations is that learners interact with a variety of expert speakers of the target language to increase their pragmatic competence (e.g., Bardovi-Harlig, 1996; Kinginger & Belz, 2005) because authentic input is crucial for pragmatic development (e.g., Bardovi-Harlig, 2001). Mori (2002) and Tateyama and Kasper (2008) examined interactions with a native-speaking classroom guest, with Mori showing that students may not perceive the task in the same way as a teacher would like them to, and Tateyama and Kasper indicating that classroom guests can help facilitate pragmatic development by providing additional NS models of various registers and offering assistance to learners during their performance. Belz and Kinginger (2002) and Kinginger and Belz (2005) showed that learner-NS interactions in a different context—namely, long-term online telecollaborations—may also facilitate pragmatic development. Kinginger and Belz provide a detailed account of one learner's moment-by-moment pragmatic development, and show how a complex interplay of interlocutors' feedback, prior instruction and learning, and individual cognition shape the learning of address terms in German. Learner–learner interactions (e.g., Mori, 2004) have also been found effective in increasing pragmatic competence due to the assistance learners can provide to each other. Finally, van Compernolle and Williams (2012) demonstrate how one task, an instructional conversation between a teacher and a whole class of students, can help in promoting learners' pragmatic development as they jointly construct and reconstruct their understanding of pragmatic concepts. The studies by Kinginger and Belz and van Compernolle and Williams to some degree examine what learners notice during interaction, but clearly, more studies, and in particular microgenetic studies looking at moment-by-moment progression and noticing, are needed to help uncover the mechanisms of how learners' interactions with various speakers may benefit pragmatic development.

## Rationale and research questions

Given that both task practice and interaction with NSs may offer benefits for pragmatic development, and in particular may enable learners to notice relevant pragmatic features in the input, we investigated both of these aspects in order to fill the gaps in research. Specifically, we examined what and how much learners can notice and learn when repeating a task with several different NSs. This approximates real life encounters as learners may find themselves in the same situation with various NSs; for example, they may ask different people for letters of recommendation.

Although explicit instruction in pragmatics appears to be more beneficial than learner exposure to input and practice alone, as in study-abroad contexts, pragmatic instruction is often not provided due to the lack of time and resources in second or foreign language courses, and lack of teacher training (Sachtleben & Denny, 2012). To achieve real-world plausibility, like Bardovi-Harlig and Griffin (2005), we did not provide any pragmatic instruction in our study. Instead, following Cohen's (2005) suggestion that students take a proactive approach to their learning of pragmatics, we asked participants to engage in intentional noticing during their interaction with NSs. While Skehan (1998) argues that instructions to pay attention facilitate noticing, Schmidt (1993) contends that it may or may not do so depending on the task set up, and no empirical studies have examined this question.

We asked two research questions:

1. When instructed to pay attention to input while interacting with NSs, what pragmatic features do learners notice and incorporate into their subsequent production?
2. What factors influence learners' noticing and incorporation of pragmatic features?

## Method

We employed a multiple-case study design, in which we analyzed the data from five learners in depth. We used a variety of data collection methods (oral production of open role-plays, as well as learners' notes on their noticing, their reflections, semi-structured interviews, and stimulated recall protocols) to triangulate our measures of noticing and to gain an in-depth understanding of factors that can either contribute to or discourage noticing.

### Context and participants

Students in a Graduate Oral Communication for Non-Native Speakers course, taught by the second author, participated in the study. This course focused on academic small group discussions, panel discussions, presentations, networking, and navigating university culture. A variety of sources of data were needed to help interpret the findings, and thus, while the whole class (10 students) participated in the study, only the data from five non-native speakers (NNSs) who participated in all data collection procedures, including semi-structured interviews and stimulated recall protocols, were analyzed. There were one female and four male participants between the ages of 23 and 34 from different countries (Table 1). These five NNSs interacted with nine NSs of English, some graduate and some undergraduate students, enrolled in a course on pragmatics (taught by the first author).

### Materials and instruments

While the Graduate Oral Communication curriculum includes some pragmatic instruction, such as practice with formulaic phrases, hedging, eye-contact, and backchanneling in academic discourse, no focused pragmatic instruction was provided specifically for this study.

### Role-play scenarios

NNSs acted out role-plays with NSs. We included one non-academic scenario (asking a friend to help with moving to a new place) and one related to university culture (apologizing to a classmate for missing a group meeting) in order to simulate NNSs' exposure to NSs in varied contexts. We included request and apology speech acts because they are the most researched (Feak, Reinhart, & Rohlck, 2009; Hudson, Detmer, & Brown, 1995). (The request scenario preceded the apology scenario). However, we only analyzed the request scenario (provided in Figure 1) because the apology scenario turned out to be too difficult to remember even for NSs. To remind participants that the focus of the activity was pragmatically appropriate communication, "be polite" was stated in the role-play scenario.

---

**Friend A**

You need to move to another place this weekend, but all the friends you have asked for help are not available. This is the only friend you haven't asked yet. But you also know that this friend will have some family visiting this weekend, so he/she might not be available either. You don't think you can move alone because you have a lot of things, and you don't drive. You know that this friend has a truck. Ask your friend for help. Remember that it is really important for you to get some help. Be polite.

**Friend B**

Your friend is asking you for help to move to another place this weekend. However, your family will be visiting you. Try to help your friend, but also remember that it is not easy for you to help due to your family's visit. In the end, whether you will or will not help your friend will depend on how the whole role-play goes. Be polite.

---

**Figure 1.** Role-play scenario.

### Noticing activities

After completing the role-play as a carousel task (described below), NNSs took notes on the expressions and strategies they noticed in the NS input. Meanwhile, NSs took notes on NNSs' language use. Then within small groups of six (three NSs and three NNSs), participants briefly discussed what they noticed and/or learned (following Bardovi-Harlig & Griffin, 2005). Next, as a homework assignment, NNSs listened to the audio of their interactions with NSs and wrote reflections on learning from this activity, including any specific expressions or strategies (following Sachtleben & Denny, 2012). These noticing activities were included to help glean learners' noticing of pragmatic features that they may not necessarily use in production in demanding tasks under pressure (House, 1996).

### *Semi-structured interviews and stimulated recall protocols*

The first author conducted semi-structured interviews and stimulated recall protocols with NNSs. Participants were first asked a general question of what they learned from the activity. Then they were asked what specifically they noticed in NS production. A stimulated recall protocol followed (see Gass & Mackey, 2000). The researcher played excerpts of the role-play audio-recordings where noticing seemed to have happened or where there were opportunities for noticing that the participants did not seem to act on. Participants were encouraged to stop the audio on their own and comment on these excerpts; additionally, the researcher periodically paused the audio and asked learners if they had any comments. As per standard stimulated recall protocol (Gass & Mackey, 2000), participants were asked to reflect on what they thought at the time of the interaction, not at the time of the stimulated recall, to ensure that participants reported on the initial noticing during the role-play rather than on what they may have additionally noticed during the stimulated recall. Then the semi-structured interview continued with questions about the resources participants used to learn about American culture and appropriate communication, the differences between L1 and L2 cultures, and participants' perceptions of the usefulness of the task.

### **Procedure**

The study took place during a two-hour class session. After the consent process, all participants completed a demographic questionnaire. Then both authors explained the goals of the activity: to use the opportunity to practice talking with NSs, as well as to observe how they politely ask for something and apologize in specific situations. Since the study focused on learner-initiated noticing, the instructions were phrased in general terms; namely, NNSs were asked to "pay attention to specific words, phrases, behaviors, and statements" used by native-speaking students that they would want to use later in a similar situation. Participants were given a handout with the role-play scenarios and task instructions. Participants were asked to complete the role-play as a carousel task (see Lynch & Maclean, 2000). They were placed in groups of six, consisting of three NNSs and three NSs. NS-NNS pairs completed a role-play once, with NNSs making the request first to serve as a pre-test of their pragmatic ability. Then the dyads switched roles and performed the same role-play. Next, different NS-NNS pairs were formed twice within the small group of six. The new dyads performed the same role-play again, also switching roles. Thus, each participant performed each of the two roles in the scenario three times, with three different partners. After completing each carousel task, participants engaged in noticing activities. Finally, within two days of the NNS-NS interactions, NNSs participated in semi-structured interviews and stimulated recall protocols.[1]

## Analysis

### Aspects of pragmatic knowledge

Pragmalinguistics subsumes the knowledge of conventional linguistic means through which actions can be accomplished. These can include strategies and linguistic forms for realizing speech acts (Leech, 1983; Thomas, 1983; van Compernolle, 2014). Sociopragmatics, on the other hand, "involves an understanding of the conventions of 'proper' or 'appropriate' social behavior, including what to say to whom and when," and it mediates the use of linguistic means (van Compernolle, 2014, p. 3). Pragmalinguistics can be further divided into strategies for realizing pragmatics and form, what Clark (1979) called convention of means and convention of form, respectively. For example, saying "I need help only for a couple hours" is a strategy, specifically, an imposition minimizer. On the other hand, a conventional expression, such as "Would you mind...?" is an example of form. We examined strategies and forms separately because we noticed that learners made changes in them to different degrees. In our analysis of strategies, we referred to the coding scheme for a request speech act by Blum-Kulka, House, and Kasper (1989). Evidence of learners' broader understanding of when to use certain strategies or forms was regarded as sociopragmatic development.[2]

### Measures of noticing

Noticing is difficult to operationalize and measure (e.g., Godfroid, Boers, & Housen, 2013). To date, some studies have employed online measures of noticing during task performance, such as think-aloud protocols (see Bowles, 2010, for a review) and written tasks, like note-taking (Hanaoka, 2007) and underlining (Izumi & Bigelow, 2000). Other studies have resorted to the use of offline measures of noticing after task performance, notably stimulated recall protocols (Mackey, 2006) and learners' uptake of the elements they noticed (Sheen, 2004), or both (Bao, Egi, & Han, 2011). In order to study the approximation of noticing during learner-native speaker interactions in natural environments (i.e., learners would not be naturally taking notes or engaging in thinking aloud during such interactions), we used only offline measures of noticing.

First, we examined learners' uptake, which we operationalized as any changes in pragmatic features between each learner's first and subsequent iterations of the role-play. To count as uptake, these features had to be initially used by NS interlocutors. Learners could acquire such features from all three NSs, but our analysis only allowed us to examine what they learned from the first two because the data collection stopped right after the third NS made a request. The number of strategies and forms used by NSs is a sum of strategies (and their verbatim statements) made by the first and the second NSs that were different from the initial statements of a given participant. The specific forms of the strategies were used to produce this count. For example, the query preparatory strategies "I was just wondering maybe if you had any time this weekend maybe you could find some time to help me out" and "Is that possible?" produced by one NS were counted as two strategies and two forms. Every time a participant subsequently used the same strategy, it was added to the count of strategies incorporated by the participant; if a participant used the same form as the NS to express this strategy, it was added to the count of forms incorporated by the participant.

To triangulate our measure of noticing, we also looked for evidence of noticing in learners' notes, reflections, stimulated recalls, and interviews.

### Quantitative and qualitative analysis

Quantitative analysis of the number of strategies and forms noticed by each learner as evidenced in their uptake was used to answer research question 1. We employed descriptive rather than inferential statistics due to the small sample size.

Qualitative analysis was used to triangulate the assessment of noticing (research question 1) and to examine individual differences regarding factors influencing noticing (research question 2). When analyzing learners' notes, reflections, stimulated recalls, and interviews we looked for overall themes. Our approach was similar to that of Kinginger and Belz (2005), who examined learners' noticing as evidenced by changes in their interactions with NSs and supplemented that with learners' reports on what influenced their noticing and pragmatic development.

## Results

To answer our first research question, we provide the summary of results for all learners, followed by a detailed account of what each learner noticed. In answering our second research question of the factors that may affect noticing, we present the results theme-by-theme.

### Research question 1: *When instructed to pay attention to input while interacting with NSs, what pragmatic features do learners notice and incorporate into their subsequent production?*

In terms of pragmalinguistics, overall the five learners noticed and incorporated more strategies (23 out of 66) than forms (3 out of 66; Table 1).

**Table 1.** Participant characteristics, number of strategies and forms noticed, and factors reported

| participant[a] | native country | proficiency[b] | experience with U.S. culture | # NS strategies/forms | # learner strategies | #learner forms | change in directness |
|---|---|---|---|---|---|---|---|
| Abdul male age 23 | Saudi Arabia | high fluency and comprehensibility, medium listening skills | little experience with Americans due to lack of access to them | 15 | 5 | 0 | somewhat indirect → indirect |
| Ali male age 34 | Iraq | high fluency, comprehensibility, and listening skills | actively sought out opportunities to interact with Americans and learn from them | 12 | 4 | 1 | direct → indirect |
| Ji-hoon male age 29 | Korea | low fluency, high listening skills, high vocabulary | little experience with U.S. culture; he was not comfortable interacting with NNS because he thought they were too direct | 15 | 7 | 1 | very indirect → indirect |
| Shota male age 25 | Japan | medium fluency, comprehensibility, and listening skills | not reported | 14 | 5 | 0 | none observed |
| Sophia female age 25 | Brazil | very high speaking and listening skills, native-like expressions and intonation | extensive experience with Americans; U.S. friends provided feedback on pragmatic appropriateness | 10 | 3 | 1 | very indirect → somewhat direct |
| total | | | | 66 | 23 | 3 | |

[a]Pseudonyms.
[b]Based on interviewer observation and instructor assessment.

Each learner noticed and incorporated some strategies used by NSs (to varying degrees), but only three learners (Ji-hoon, Ali, and Sophia) noticed and incorporated one form each. That is, the data indicate that learners were more likely to notice and incorporate strategies than forms from NS input. In terms of sociopragmatics, the data indicate that some learners paid attention to the level of directness of requests. What each participant noticed is presented case-by-case. Table 2 provides the production data from one participant (Abdul) and the two NSs who performed the request with him. The interactions between the speakers are illustrated in subsequent examples. In the following examples, strategies in italics are those that were incorporated by the given participant from NS data; the actual statements are in italics when participants produced them verbatim or close to verbatim from NS models. Pauses and hesitations were deleted from the production data as it was difficult to ascertain whether learners paid attention to them.

Table 2. Abdul's production data with NS Input

| | |
|---|---|
| **Abdul round 1 (initial request performance)** | |
| query preparatory | May you help me? |
| overwhelming reason | You are the only one who can help me and have a truck. |
| moralizing | According to the proverb, friend in need is a friend indeed. |
| **NS1 round 1** | |
| preparator | Well check it out. |
| preparator | I have to move from my apartment this weekend. |
| overwhelming reason | I'm kind of in a bind because I have a lotta stuff and I have no way to move it. |
| explicit performative | The reason I'm asking you |
| grounder | is because I know you have a truck. |
| disarmer | I don't usually ask my friends for help with moving because it's a pain. |
| query preparatory | I was just wondering maybe if you had any time this weekend maybe you could find some time to help me out. |
| query preparatory | Is that possible? |
| imposition minimizer | I'll try to make sure that we don't take very long to do it, maybe we can get it done in an hour or two. |
| **Abdul round 2** | |
| *preparator* | I will move out next weekend |
| want statement | so I want you to help me |
| *grounder | because you have the truck. |
| *grounder* | So I have all this stuff I have to move out. |
| *query preparatory | Can you help me? [changed from "may" to "can"] |
| **NS2 round 2** | |
| imposition minimizer | I don't mean to impede on you but |
| preparator | I really need to move this weekend. |
| overwhelming reason | It's my only time to do it. |
| disarmer | I know your family's in town and you don't get to see them very often |

| | |
|---|---|
| *overwhelming reason | but I really don't know who else to ask, I've asked everybody. |

**Table 2 (continued).** Abdul's production data with NS Input

| | |
|---|---|
| query preparatory | Is there any way that you could help me move? |
| promise of reward | I'll buy you breakfast, I'll walk your dog, anything, really. |
| **Abdul round 3** | |
| preparator | I will move out this weekend. |
| disarmer | I know your family will come to you and I'm embarrassed but |
| *grounder | because you have the truck |
| *moralizer | you are my friend so friend in need is a friend indeed so [laughter] |
| want statement | I wanted your help. |
| *query preparatory | I don't know if you can or not [changed from his original "Can you…"] |
| *overwhelming reason | I ask all my friend, you're the only one I have [to ask again?]. [in response to NS question "Did you ask anybody else? I'm gonna be pretty busy."] |
| imposition minimizer | Yeah any time yeah that's ok [= anytime]. |

\* Strategies and/or forms that a participant used in the initial request.

## Abdul

Abdul incorporated 5 out of 15 strategies used by NSs. For example, in rounds 2 and 3, Abdul incorporated a preparator "I will move out this/next weekend" (following NS1's statement "I have to move from my apartment this weekend"). In round 2 he used a grounder "I have all this stuff I have to move out" (following NS1's statement "I'm kind of in a bind because I have a lotta stuff and I have no way to move it"), and in round 3 a disarmer "I know your family will come to you and I'm embarrassed but" (following NS1's statement "I don't usually ask my friends for help with moving because it's a pain" and NS2's statement "I know your family's in town and you don't get to see them very often"). Abdul also incorporated an imposition minimizer "Yeah any time yeah that's ok" (round 3). In terms of forms, Abdul did not incorporate any expressions from NSs verbatim, although in some of his strategies, such as "I have all this stuff," the language was similar to that of NS expressions. His disarmer, however, was informed by NSs' ideas, but linguistically it was not target-like. His disarmer "I know your family will come to you and I'm embarrassed but" was probably informed by NS2 statement "I know your family's in town" and NS1 statement "I don't usually ask my friends…," which indicates an understanding of imposition. Interestingly, while not using the same query preparatory expressions as NSs did, Abdul did change his original query preparatory "May you help me?" to

"Can you help me?" and finally to "I don't know if you can or not." This could be simply due to rehearsal, which has been shown to improve language learners' production (e.g., Ahmadian & Tavakoli, 2011; Bygate, 2001; Bygate & Samuda, 2005; De Jong & Perfetti, 2011; Sydorenko, 2015), or Abdul could have been paying attention to NSs' expressions of uncertainty in someone's ability, such as "I was just wondering maybe if you had any time this weekend maybe you could find some time" and "Is there any way that you could help me move?" in order to compose his own query preparatories.

Interview data indicates that Abdul was also paying attention to the sociopragmatic aspect of negotiating requests. He said that American students "try to extend the conversation long. If I said 'no,' they said 'why.' If I said 'yes,' they said 'Are you sure because your family will come.'" According to Abdul, in Saudi Arabia, such negotiation is not necessary when one is asking a favor from a true friend (Example 1).

**Example 1**

    Abdul:          No if if he is my friend, I don't have to to ask him politely, yeah. I will order him. I will ask him.
    Interviewer: So you can be very direct?
    Abdul:          Yeah, yeah, yeah, very direct.

Abdul's production data also indicates that in his subsequent performance, as opposed to the initial one, he negotiated a request using a variety of strategies from NS input, including the disarmer "I know your family will come to you and I'm embarrassed but" and an overwhelming reason "I ask all my friend. You're the only one I have to ask again." This is an example of sociopragmatic learning in that, beyond the knowledge of how requests are made politely using specific strategies and expressions, Abdul saw the broader picture: that roles and obligations between friends are different in North American culture as opposed to his own.

### Ali

Ali used 4 out of 12 strategies produced by NSs and 1 of 12 forms.

In round 2, Ali used an imposition minimizer "Indeed I arranged them in boxes so it is easy to transfer them" (following NS3 combined suggestory formula and an imposition minimizer "What if I have everything ready, like packed up in boxes"). In round 3, Ali used three additional strategies: a preparator, a new grounder, and a query preparatory (Example 2).

**Example 2**

    Ali:    Indeed I uh I was planning to move to a new apartment this weekend, so

NS9: Oh, nice
Ali: yeah=
NS9: =Did you find a nice one?
Ali: It was very great. I I like uh the place, but I uh my stuff are a little bit big so I think I will need your help with your truck. Can you help me to transferring my stuff? (Ali, round 3)

**Example 3**

Indeed uh I need your help in uh moving my stuff from my apartment. I decided to move to a new apartment so [pause] I wish if you could help me [pause] transferring my stuff. That would be great. (Ali, round 1)

Ali only incorporated one form from NS input: "Can you help me?" However, although this form was produced by NS3 in NS round 1, Ali used it in round 3 rather than immediately in round 2. It is possible that Ali knew this expression, but did not know when to use it. NS4's indirectness in NS round 2 (small talk, then a hint, and only then a query preparatory) could have helped Ali understand when to use query preparatories like "Can you help me?"

Like Abdul, Ali was also paying attention to the level of directness of requests, as evidenced by his interview and production data. He stated that Iraqi culture is more direct compared to the American culture, and his request strategies, which changed from direct to indirect throughout the task, reflected this awareness. Examples (2) and (3) show his last and first request attempts, respectively. Initially, Ali started right away with the need statement (a direct strategy), only then using the preparator "I decided to move to a new apartment" to soften the request; non-target like query preparatory "I wish if you could help me transferring my stuff" that sounded demanding followed; his request ended with "That would be great" before the interlocutor indicated whether she could or could not help, which does not make it a face-saving strategy. The last request, on the other hand, is much more indirect. First, Ali did not make it all in one turn, but started with a preparator "I was planning to move to a new apartment this weekend, so" and gave his interlocutor a chance to respond. After engaging in small talk, he continued with a need statement, but he hedged it with "I think" and "a little bit big." He then ended with a query preparatory "Can you help me to transferring my stuff?" However, apart from this expression, Ali composed his own original response: none of the NSs used "a little bit big," and none of them used the hedge "I think" in the need statement. The NSs did use a variety of strategies, however, to soften their requests: small talk, preparators, hints, and imposition minimizers. It appears that Ali noticed the general indirectness of NS requests and the types of strategies they used rather than specific language they employed. This is similar to Abdul's example of composing his own disarmer based on NS examples.

## Ji-hoon

Ji-hoon used 7 out of 15 NS strategies and 1 of 15 forms. Although he did not use a query preparatory strategy in round 1, he used one in round 2, "So could you help me?" after NS5 said "I was wondering if you could help me out." Similar to other learners, Ji-hoon frequently used the same strategies as NSs did, but he worded them differently. Another example is a strategy of offering a reward. In NS round 1, NS5 said, "Afterwards I would love to take you and your parents out to a nice restaurant to thank you for helping me." Ji-hoon subsequently said, "After that I will treat you and your family maybe to dinner." The only form that Ji-hoon incorporated was "So I need your help, really" after NS6 in NS round 2 said "I just really need some help," however, even here the incorporation was partial rather than complete as there was some variation in wording (Table 3).

Table 3. Ji-hoon's round 2 production data

| | Ji-Hoon round 2 |
|---|---|
| need statement | I actually need your help this weekend. |
| preparator | I am going to a new apartment this Saturday. |
| query preparatory | So could you help me? |
| suggesting a solution | Do you think when are you guys come back [=that you can help me then?]? |
| *overwhelming reason | I already asked all of my friends and they are all busy so you are the only person, [Responding to NS question: Do you have anyone else that can help you?] |
| imposition minimizer | if you can help me. |

* Strategies and/or forms that a participant used in the initial request.

Ji-hoon also paid attention to the level of directness of requests. In the interview, he stated that compared to Korean culture, Americans seemed to be more direct. Originally, he started his request with a hint: "I'm trying to move to a new house this Saturday but I don't have a, I need a car," and then later in the interaction he provided an overwhelming reason "You are the only one who can help me move." However, after the examples of NS requests, which included preparators, query preparatories, and promises of reward, among other strategies, Ji-hoon became somewhat more direct. For example, he used a need statement, a preparator, and a query preparatory, in that order, in round 2: "I actually need your help this weekend. I am going to a new apartment this this Saturday so could you help me?" However, Ji-hoon might have misinterpreted the directness level of the first NS: This NS used a hypothetical *I'd need you* expression only later in the interaction, and as part of an imposition minimizer "I'd only need you for a few hours," while Ji-hoon directly stated "I actually need your help" as part of a request proper. However, some of the time, Ji-hoon did pay attention to the order of strategies used by NSs. For example, in the second round, NS6 started with the sequence of preparators "I have to ask you a favor. I am moving this weekend." Ji-hoon then similarly used a sequence of two preparators "Actually, I'm about to ask your help this weekend. I'm going to move out," although his first preparator is rather non-target-like.

### Shota

Shota incorporated 5 out of 14 strategies from NS input, but no forms. He did not use any strategies from NS5 in his second round, possibly because he was guided by this NS and did not have a chance to produce relevant strategies on his own, as seen in Example (4), an excerpt of Shota's exchange with NS5 in round 2. NS5 asked "Am I the last one you can ask?" thus not giving Shota a chance to produce an overwhelming reason like "You are the last person I can ask."

**Example 4**

NS5: How long do you think it will take?
Shota: Yeah I think it might be half a day [pause] yeah [pause] you don't have time?
NS5: Am I uh am I the last one you can ask?
Shota: Uh huh.

All of the five strategies that Shota incorporated from NS input surfaced in round 3: Some of these strategies were used in the first round by NS7, and some in the second round by NS5 (Table 4).

**Table 4.** Shota's round 3 production data

| | Shota round 3 |
|---|---|
| *query preparatory | Could you help me this weekend? |
| grounder | I'm gonna move to new apartment. [possibly tried to use this as a preparator used by NS2] |
| *need statement | So, to move my stuff so I need your truck. |
| imposition minimizer | but I need a cu-couple time [=a couple hours, changed from "half a day"] |
| overwhelming reason | No, my friend doesn't have only small car. [in response to NS question "Well do you have anybody else who can help you?"] |
| grounder | I have so many stuff [possibly tried to use this as a preparator used by NS2]. |
| suggestory formula | What about after you went you went to zoo? |

* Strategies and/or forms that a participant used in the initial request

Like other participants, Shota also noticed the general content and the types of strategies NSs used, and adapted those models in his subsequent responses. In NS round 1, NS7 used a suggestory formula "How about this?"

followed by a query preparatory "Can you at least help me for just like the first half of the morning?" Shota used his own version of a suggestory formula in round 3 "What about after you went to zoo?" Additionally, like Ji-hoon, Shota did not use the same order of the strategies that NSs used, which resulted in more direct requests compared to those of NSs. For example, while Shota started with a query preparatory "Could you help me..." in all three versions of his role-play, NS7 started with a disarmer in the first NS round, and NS5 began with a series of preparators in the second. Since Shota did not make any modifications to the beginning of his request, it may be that he did not pay attention to how NSs began their requests, possibly because he learned that "Could you help me..." is a polite expression to use for making requests. Shota's interview data suggests this may be the case. When asked what he learned from the activity, Shota said, "American students use like words like modals, *you could...* or *you might.* It sounds yeah polite." Then when asked how he asked for help, in real life, before participating in our study, Shota replied "Um, just, can you help me?" It appears that Shota paid more attention to how to negotiate requests as opposed to how to make one initially, as evident by his use of grounders, overwhelming reasons, imposition minimizers, and suggestory formula in subsequent performance. This is also supported by the interview, in which Shota mentioned that in his home country, Japan, people would normally help in such a situation, meaning that an extended negotiation of a request would likely not take place. Unlike the other three participants, Shota did not seem to pay attention to the directness level of requests; there was no change in the directness level in his production, and this aspect was not mentioned when Shota was asked to compare his home culture to the American culture.

### Sophia

Sophia used 3 out of 10 NS strategies and one form. However, this minimal incorporation of strategies and forms from NS input seems to be due to Sophia's already high level of pragmatic knowledge rather than her lack of noticing. She started her first request with two preparators, then an overwhelming reason, followed by an imposition minimizer, and only then used a query preparatory "Do you think that you can help me?," as shown in Table 5.

This is similar to the NSs in our sample who often began indirectly with small talk, preparators, disarmers, hints, overwhelming reasons, and grounders before they used a query preparatory strategy. The strategies that Sophia incorporated seem to suggest that she was not learning what types of strategies are appropriate in a given situation but that she was rather incorporating NS ideas to enrich the content of her request. She already used several imposition minimizers in round 1, such as "It's up to you." In round 3, she added one more imposition minimizer, "I will pack everything," that was similar in content to that used by NS7 in the second NS round: "I can have it all ready."

The form that Sophia tried to incorporate from NS6 input was "I kind of have a favor," which she rephrased as "I need a favor of you" in round 2 and "I need to ask you a favor" in round 3. Regarding the level of directness, Sophia was aware of the fact that in Brazilian culture, people tend to be more direct than Americans, and she stated in the interview that she is more direct compared to Americans. Given her production data, she was likely focusing on other aspects of NS models as she was already performing on par with NSs regarding her level of directness. During the interview, we specifically mentioned to Sophia that pragmatically she was performing at a high level, and thus we were wondering if there was anything else she could learn from these activities. She replied that she was noticing intonation and gestures.

**Table 5.** Sophia's round 1 production data

| | Sophia round 1 |
|---:|---|
| preparator | What do you wanna do this weekend, well, I mean what are you do? |
| preparator | I need to move this weekend. I need someone just to drive my furniture to there. |
| overwhelming reason | I have no one who going to help me. |
| imposition minimizer | It will like take like 30 minutes or less than that. |
| query preparatory | Do you think that you can help me? |
| imposition minimizer | It's up to you. I just need to move on the weekend. Like, the time that you can, I will be there. |
| imposition minimizer | I guess it's 15 minutes from where I am living now to where I will live. |

### Research question 2: *What factors influence learners' noticing and incorporation of pragmatic features?*

Several factors were identified. First, we found that learners' prior knowledge of the forms facilitated their noticing of them. For example, after a NS said "Well I kind of have a favor," Sophia said, "I need a favor of you" in her next round. In the interview, Sophia said she used the "favor" expression she already knew and which she had just heard because it was easier than trying to come up with her own. On the other hand, Shota did not comment on the NS expression "I need a huge favor this weekend" when presented with an audio of it. When asked if he knew what it meant, Shota said he had never heard it before. What Shota did notice in NS input were modals—possibly because he used them regularly in his own requests, as he mentioned in the interview.

We found that noticing an expression or a word one already knew did not guarantee it would be used appropriately within a larger context. For example, Sophia's initial request began indirectly with a preparator "What do you wanna do this weekend well I mean what are you do?" When a NS made a request, it also started with the preparator "What are you doing this weekend?" followed by the preparator "Well I kind of have a favor." When Sophia made her request the second time, she reversed the order of these strategies: "I need a favor of you? Like actually I want to know what you are doing this weekend." Sophia may have reversed the order of the strategies because she tried not to forget to incorporate the "favor" expression she had just heard. However, not only did she reverse the order of the strategies, which made her second request more direct than the first, but she also neglected to soften the "favor" expression with the hedge *kind of* used by the NS. This finding is discussed further in the next section.

Individual differences, such as the ability to memorize, appears to be another factor of what learners notice or focus on. From an interview with Ali, we learned that although he tried to pay attention to specific expressions and managed to write down a few of them, namely "I wonder" and "I need your help," he had difficulty remembering and recording what he had just noticed. Ali initially placed a lot of emphasis on trying to notice and subsequently use target-like expressions because, as he stated, he realized that direct translation from L1 to L2 often does not work, and therefore building a repertoire of native-like expressions is important for increasing one's L2 proficiency. Perhaps because Ali was not able to remember many of the expressions he had noticed, he decided to pay attention to strategies instead. In the interview, he said, "But the MOST important thing that I learned is ... how to deal with embarrassing situations with POLITE requests, POLITELY, not to hurt the other person," referring to the fact that he was observing how to make the whole interaction polite as opposed to attending to the specific expressions used by NSs. As described earlier, Ali in fact began using more indirect strategies in subsequent production. Like Ali, Abdul also mentioned during the interview that he could not remember and write down many of the expressions he noticed during the interaction with NSs.

Awareness of differences in the level of directness between L1 and L2 cultures also surfaced as a factor of what learners notice. Abdul, Ali, and Ji-hoon discussed the differences between their L1 and L2 cultures during the interview, and they all changed their strategies to more closely fit the level of directness of American culture. Abdul and Ali became more indirect, while Ji-hoon became more direct, which is reflective of the respective differences between their home cultures and the American culture. Sophia was already indirect initially, but she stated in the interview that she was consciously trying to be indirect based on her awareness of the differences between the Brazilian and the American cultures. Shota was the only participant who did not change his production in terms of directness level, and he was not able to articulate this issue in the interview.

Proficiency level may also affect what learners pay attention to. In our data, Sophia already used appropriate strategies and expressions in her initial request, including bi-clausal expressions like "Do you think that you can help me?" which are rarely used even by advanced learners (Taguchi, 2012; Takahashi, 2005b).

She also reported paying attention to intonation and gestures. Since none of the other learners mentioned these aspects, and since Sophia displayed the highest level of pragmatic competence, it may be that only highly proficient learners are able to attend to these features.

Based on prior research (Bardovi-Harlig & Bastos, 2011; Halenko & Jones, 2011; Sachtleben & Denny, 2012), we hypothesized that learners' access to NSs would also influence noticing and subsequent production. However, at least in our small-scale study, there did not seem to be a direct link. For example, Abdul and Ali incorporated one third of NS strategies each (5 out of 15 and 4 out of 12, respectively), yet while Ali reported seeking out and having interactions with a variety of NSs and deliberately paying attention to expressions they use, Abdul said he did not have many chances to interact with Americans. Ji-hoon incorporated almost half the NS strategies (7 of 15), and yet he reported having little experience with U.S. culture and avoided talking to NSs due to his low speaking and listening skills. The different degrees of access to NSs did not seem to directly influence the number of strategies these learners noticed and incorporated. All three of these participants also made their requests more appropriate in terms of their directness level. We elaborate on the effect of NS access in the discussion section.

Finally, what learners perceive to be the goals of a particular task may influence how they approach it and what they pay attention to. We found that all participants had highly positive attitudes towards the activity, but they made only general comments about its usefulness. Participants stated that they found speaking practice with NSs beneficial, but none of them said that such practice is helpful because they can learn more specific expressions and ideas from NSs. Only Sophia made a specific comment regarding pragmatics, saying that this activity gave her more confidence and showed her that she *can* make a request successfully. We think that our participants' perception of general usefulness of speaking practice is due to the fact that students in this course tend to have a strong desire for interaction with NSs; they seem to value any activity that involves interaction with NSs (as reported by several instructors of this course). This may be the reason that most students did not perceive the goals of the activity in the same way that was presented to them by the researchers: to get ideas from NSs on appropriate communication in a particular situation.

## Discussion

### Research question 1: *When instructed to pay attention to input while interacting with NSs, what pragmatic features do learners notice and incorporate into their subsequent production?*

We found that learners primarily noticed and incorporated strategies rather than forms from NS input, and some learners also noticed the difference and made changes to the level of directness of their request. Our finding that learners incorporated more strategies than forms from input is supported by previous research indicating that learners naturally focus on content rather than form when the task requires processing or conveying meaning (Lyster, 2007; VanPatten, 2004). Similarly, in Bardovi-Harlig and Hartford's (1993) longitudinal study, NNS graduate students changed their strategies during advising sessions before they changed their form, which was the last to change. This happened even after learners rehearsed the task (Németh & Kormos, 2001).

It is not surprising that in the activity that focused on communicating meaning, learners' attention was primarily directed toward content rather than form. Several participants in fact stated that they were engulfed by the task and forgot the instructions to pay attention to NS language. High task involvement may lower learners' ability to pay attention to form (Ranta & Lyster, 2007), but it appears that attention to strategies is still possible under such conditions. Also, Kinginger and Belz (2005) hypothesized that learner noticing of NS input in their study was facilitated by the modality of text-based online exchanges. Other studies on computer-mediated communication have also found that textual modality facilitated noticing of forms (Goertler, 2009). Our study suggests that rehearsal of a task in oral modality can likewise facilitate noticing, albeit mostly of strategies.

Sociopragmatically, several learners noticed and changed the level of directness of their requests. This was often as a result of participants' reordering of strategies used. For example, Ali and Abdul changed from using query preparatories initially to later in their requests, and placing such strategies as preparators and disarmers earlier in their requests, consistent with prior research indicating that the level of directness between L1 and L2 cultures can be noticed (e.g., Barron, 2003). Shota, on the other hand, who did not change his production in terms of the directness level, used the same query preparatory in all three rounds.

**Research question 2:** *What factors influence learners' noticing and incorporation of pragmatic features?*

In line with previous findings (Skehan, 1998; Takahashi, 2005a), we found that prior knowledge of specific expressions helps with their noticing. We also observed that while learners may notice the expressions they already know, they may not be able to use them appropriately within a larger context. Although prior knowledge may facilitate noticing of context (Hanaoka, 2007; Izumi, 2013), it does not guarantee it as measured by production. In our specific example, Sophia reported knowing the expression, and yet she did not seem to notice the surrounding context. Kinginger and Belz (2005) also reported a similar case of one participant who did not use the appropriate forms under time pressure even when having explicit knowledge of them. That is, in performance under time pressure, competence does not always translate into equivalent performance.

Individual differences were another factor in what learners focused on, and this is in line with Takahashi's (2005a) observation. *Individual differences* is, of course, a rather broad term; in our study it manifested itself as inability to remember the expressions that were noticed. Other individual difference factors, such as learners' analytic ability (Takahashi, 2005b) may also be at play, although they were not observed given our small sample size and the self-report design. We were especially intrigued by Ali's data. He reported trying to be attentive to conventional expressions, yet he could not remember many of them. This contradicts Takahashi (2005b) who found that intrinsic motivation was the most important factor in noticing target expression. From Ali's self-report, it appears that he was highly intrinsically motivated to communicate with native speakers in a target-like manner. One explanation of such different findings may be different designs of our study and that of Takahashi (2005b): Our design was more naturalistic, involving the production of open-ended role-plays and self-initiated noticing, while in Takashashi, transcripts were provided, and each target expression was followed by a rating scale, making the target expressions more salient for learners. This disparity in findings indicates that more research is needed, both quantitative and qualitative, to gain a better understanding of individual factors that affect noticing. Other individual difference factors that surfaced in our study and that can be further investigated are awareness of differences between L1 and L2 cultures and personal goals when engaging in a task.

We suspect that proficiency level is also an important factor in what learners can notice. Hanaoka (2007) found that more proficient learners were able to notice more differences between their own writing and that of NSs. On the other hand, for pragmatic noticing specifically, Takahashi (2005b) found that motivation, but not proficiency, affected learners' level of noticing of targeted pragmalinguistic features, and Matsumura (2003) indicated that proficiency only indirectly affected pragmatic competence via exposure. However, Bialystok (1993) proposed that learners of higher proficiency can pay attention to target pragmatic features faster and more accurately. House (1996) supports Bialystok's model. Bardovi-Harlig and Bastos (2011) also found that proficiency was a factor in the production of conventional expressions. Thus, it seems that proficiency can, but does not always, influence noticing. In our study, only the most proficient learner (Sophia) reported paying attention to intonation and gestures. While this may be purely accidental, it is worth investigating further whether learners attend to intonation and gestures at a later stage of their proficiency.

Access to NSs is another factor that we investigated as it has been shown to help improve pragmatic competence broadly (e.g., Halenko & Jones, 2011), recognition and production of conventional expressions (Bardovi-Harlig & Bastos, 2011), and amount of noticing of pragmatic features (Sachtleben & Denny, 2012). However, a direct link between access to NSs and amount of noticing was not apparent in our study as the number of strategies and forms noticed by Abdul, Ali, and Ji-hoon did not correlate with the degree of NS access they reported. Additional factors may have shaped different performances of these learners: aptitude and language learning history (Schmidt, 2010), ability to perform under time pressure (Kinginger & Belz, 2005), and other individual differences, such as ability to memorize, which were discussed earlier.

It may also be the quality of interaction with NSs—not the amount—that affects what learners notice and subsequently use. In our data, both Sophia and Ali reported having frequent interactions with NSs; however, Sophia displayed a much higher level of pragmatic competence than Ali did. This difference may be due to the fact that Sophia reported receiving direct feedback from NSs, in seemingly a safe joking manner, regarding her high level of directness as compared to that of Americans: "Um like my friends [Americans] make fun of us [Brazilians] all the time... Because we never ask like when we go in the restaurant like 'Can I have something?' or just we just say like 'I want this one and this one'[laugh]." On the other hand, Ali stated that he regularly spoke with NS acquaintances and strangers, thus having more surface-level interactions; he did not say that he received feedback from them. We thus subscribe to the view of Kinginger and Belz (2005) that language development, including pragmatics, "is shaped not only by individual characteristics but also, and crucially in our view, by the access that [interactancts are] willing and able to negotiate within a range of socio-cultural environments and particular, local practices" (p. 370). We also suggest that the depth of interactions may matter, and should be further examined.

In summary, we found that learners were able to notice and incorporate strategies rather than forms. Some learners also changed their level of directness, primarily by more closely approximating the order of strategies used by NSs. Factors that may play a role in what learners notice are prior knowledge of linguistic expressions, ability to memorize, awareness of differences between L1 and L2 cultures, learners' goals, proficiency level, and quality/depth of access to NSs.

We now turn to the limitations of our study, and in light of them, future directions. First, since our study did not include a practice-only condition, we cannot definitively say that changes in learners' performance were due to NS input rather than practice alone. We also do not know if the noticing can be generalized to any other situation that was not part of the study. Another limitation is that the number of participants was small, and thus the factors we identified as those affecting noticing cannot be conclusive. Nevertheless, these factors are supported by previous findings and can be a point of further investigation and confirmation. Our study is also limited in that we analyzed the data from only one role-play (although two role-plays were used in the study). All of these are important issues to consider when designing future studies on noticing.

For future research, we suggest that there be more discussions in the field on how to measure noticing, particularly with regard to pragmatics. Uptake is still a questionable measure because learners may not incorporate everything they noticed into their subsequent production, which follows Bardovi-Harlig's (2009) finding that recognition of conventional expressions is a necessary but not a sufficient condition for their production. While learners may notice an expression, they may decide not to use it and instead opt for another perfectly acceptable alternative (Kasper & Schmidt, 1996). In our study, Sophia did not use the expression "I was wondering if" from NS input. Given Sophia's high proficiency level, she could have noticed this expression, but possibly did not think that this phrase was any better than the one she originally used ("Do you think that you can help me?"). Even NSs have their own styles—not all of them used the expression "I was wondering if you could" in our data. Thus, while uptake is often employed as a measure of noticing, it may be less telling when pragmatics is examined. Ali's use of "Can you help me?" in the third round rather than soon after hearing this expression (as discussed above) is another example of the challenges of using uptake as a measure of noticing, especially in research designs that incorporate rehearsal. Asking Ali to explain what prompted him to use this expression would have been particularly helpful to understand his thought processing. Note-taking is also not a perfect measure of noticing—both Ali and Abdul reported not being able to fully record what they noticed due to memory issues. We thus contend that additional qualitative studies that examine a few participants in detail and use both measures of learners' moment-by-moment progress and verbal reports are needed: such methodology provides an in-depth understanding of what pragmatic features learners notice, under which conditions, and how individual differences may affect this. While challenging due to time constraints, to make the best use of verbal reports, transcripts of learners' production need to be thoroughly analyzed before learners are asked about their noticing.

## Limitations and Future Directions

We now turn to the implications of our findings. We are encouraged by our results which suggest that even without specific prior metapragmatic instruction, but with instructions to pay attention to input, one focused activity with NSs involving several repetitions may help learners notice some gaps in their pragmatic competence. This happens even when learners are mostly focused on speaking practice. We suspect that with increased frequency of exposure to such activities, students may revise their goals from general desire for speaking practice to more specific ones, and may benefit from more focused attention. It should be noted, however, that most changes in learners' production concerned strategies rather than linguistic forms, suggesting that more than repeated interaction with NSs is needed to draw learners' attention to various target-like expressions and to help them understand the contexts of their appropriate use. Prior exposure to expressions appearing in NS input, and possibly higher proficiency level, might facilitate the noticing from NS input during interactions. Feedback is also vital as learners may draw incorrect conclusions from the input they notice. In our study, Ji-hoon became more direct than NSs even though initially he used only indirect strategies. Nevertheless, since we found that interactions with NSs *can* help learners improve their pragmatic performance to some degree, we suggest that such activities are beneficial even when providing prior metapragmatic instruction and detailed feedback is not feasible. Alternatively, teachers may want to discuss with learners how to find opportunities to interact with NSs and why they should pay attention to how NSs communicate. Thus, even when there is little time in the curriculum to devote to pragmatics, teachers can equip learners with the prerequisite knowledge and awareness for learning about pragmatically appropriate communication on their own: They can draw learners' attention to a variety of speech acts (e.g., requests, compliments, refusals), how they compare to their own cultures, some expressions learners might hear when such speech acts are performed, and why such expressions are used. After that, learners may be ready to actively engage in learning from NSs, following Cohen's (2005) suggestion to focus on teaching strategies for learning pragmatics.

## Conclusion

Through a variety of data sources (moment-by-moment production data, learners' notes on their own noticing and their reflections, semi-structured interviews, and stimulated recall protocols), we were able to identify trends that are confirmed by prior research (e.g., attention to content before forms) as well as new aspects for further investigation, such as how memory, proficiency, and candid feedback from native-speaking friends may affect what pragmatic features learners notice and to what degree. Structured interviews and stimulated recall protocols were particularly insightful in uncovering new issues to study. We hope that future research focuses on individual differences regarding noticing and employs naturalistic designs in order to gain a better understanding of what learners can and cannot notice from interactions with NSs so that pedagogical interventions can be tailored accordingly.

### Notes

1   While conducting stimulated recall protocols immediately after an activity helps counter the effect of memory, it was not possible due to the participants' schedules.
2   Notwithstanding the given categorization of pragmalinguistic and sociopragmatic knowledge, we agree with Roever, Fraser, and Elder (2014) that "it will not be possibly [sic] to clearly tell sociopragmatic and pragmalinguistic influences apart due to their close links and mutual moderating effect" (p. 44).

# References

Ahmadian, M., & Tavakoli, M. (2011). The effects of guided careful online planning on complexity, accuracy and fluency in intermediate EFL learners' oral production: The case of English articles. *Language Teaching Research, 15*, 35–59.

Bao, M., Egi, T., & Han, Y. (2011). Classroom study on noticing and recast features: Capturing learner noticing with uptake and stimulated recall. *System, 39*, 215–228.

Bardovi-Harlig, K. (1996). Pragmatics and language teaching: Bringing pragmatics and pedagogy together. In L. Bouton (Ed.), *Pragmatics and language learning* (Vol. 7, pp. 21–39). Urbana: University of Illinois at Urbana-Champaign.

Bardovi-Harlig, K. (2001). Evaluating the empirical evidence: Grounds for instruction in pragmatics? In K. Rose & G. Kasper (Eds.), *Pragmatics in language teaching* (pp. 13–32). Cambridge: Cambridge University Press.

Bardovi-Harlig, K. (2009). Conventional expressions as a pragmalinguistic resource: Recognition and production of conventional expressions in L2 pragmatics. *Language Learning, 59*, 755–795.

Bardovi-Harlig, K., & Bastos, M.-T. (2011). Proficiency, length of stay, and intensity of interaction and the acquisition of conventional expressions in L2 pragmatics. *Intercultural Pragmatics, 8*, 347–384.

Bardovi-Harlig, K., & Griffin, R. (2005). L2 pragmatic awareness: Evidence from the ESL classroom. *System, 33*, 401–415.

Bardovi-Harlig, K., & Hartford, B. S. (1993). Learning the rules of academic talk: A longitudinal study of pragmatic development. *Studies in Second Language Acquisition, 15*, 279–304.

Barron, A. (2003). *Acquisition in interlanguage pragmatics: Learning how to do things with words in a study abroad context*. Amsterdam: John Benjamins.

Belz, J., & Kinginger, C. (2002). The cross-linguistic development of address form use in telecollaborative language learning: Two case studies. *Canadian Modern Language Review, 59*, 189–214.

Bialystok, E. (1993). Symbolic representation and attentional control in pragmatic competence.

In G. Kasper & S. Blum-Kulka (Eds.), *Interlanguage Pragmatics* (pp. 43–57). New York, NY: Oxford University Press.

Bowles, M. (2010). *The think-aloud controversy in second language research*. New York, NY: Routledge.

Blum-Kulka, S., House, J., & Kasper, G. (Eds.). (1989). *Cross-cultural pragmatics: Requests and apologies*. Norwood, NJ: Ablex.

Bygate, M. (2001). Effects of task repetition on the structure and control of oral language. In M. Bygate, P. Skehan, & M. Swain (Eds.), *Researching pedagogic tasks: Second language learning, teaching and testing* (pp. 23–48). Harlow, England: Pearson.

Bygate, M., & Samuda, V. (2005). Integrative planning through the use of task-repetition. In R. Ellis (Ed.), *Planning and task performance in a second language* (pp. 37–74). Amsterdam: John Benjamins.

Clark, H. H. (1979). Responding to indirect speech acts. *Cognitive Psychology, 11*, 430–477.

Cohen, A. (2005). Strategies for learning and performing L2 speech acts. *Intercultural Pragmatics, 2*, 275–301.

De Jong, N., & Perfetti, C. (2011). Fluency training in the ESL classroom: An experimental study of fluency development and proceduralization. *Language Learning, 61*, 533–568.

Ellis, R. (2005). Planning and task-based performance: Theory and research. In R. Ellis (Ed.), *Planning and task performance in a second language* (pp. 3–34). Amsterdam: John Benjamins.

Feak, C., Reinhart, S., & Rohlck, T. (2009). *Academic interactions: Communicating on campus*. Ann Arbor: University of Michigan Press.

Félix-Brasdefer, J. C. (2006). Teaching the negotiation of multi-turn speech acts: Using conversation-analytic tools to teach pragmatics in the classroom. In K. Bardovi-Harlig, J. C. Félix-Brasdefer, & A. Omar (Eds.), *Pragmatics and language learning* (Vol. 11, pp. 165–197). Honolulu: University of Hawai'i Press.

*Gass, S. M., & Mackey, A. (2000). Stimulated recall methodology in second language research.* Mahwah, NJ: Lawrence Erlbaum.

Gass, S., & Mackey, A. (2006). Input, interaction and output in SLA. In B. VanPatten & J. Williams (Eds.), *Theories in second language acquisition: An introduction* (pp. 175–199). Mahwah, NJ: Lawrence Erlbaum.

Godfroid, A., Boers, F., & Housen, A. (2013). An eye for words: Gauging the role of attention in L2 vocabulary acquisition by means of eye-tracking. *Studies in Second Language Acquisition, 35*, 483–517.

Godfroid, A., Housen, A., & Boers, F. (2010). A procedure for testing the Noticing Hypothesis in the context of vocabulary acquisition. In M. Pütz & L. Sicola (Eds.), *Inside the learner's mind: Cognitive processing and second language acquisition* (pp. 169–197). Amsterdam: John Benjamins.

Goertler, S. (2009). Using computer-mediated communication in language teaching. *Die Unterrichtspraxis/Teaching German, 42*, 74–84.

Halenko, N., & Jones, C. (2011). Teaching pragmatic awareness of spoken requests to Chinese EAP learners in the UK: Is explicit instruction effective? *System, 39*, 240–250.

Hanaoka, O. (2007). Output, noticing, and learning: An investigation into the role of spontaneous attention to form in a four-stage writing task. *Language Teaching Research, 11*, 459–479.

House, J. (1996). Developing pragmatic fluency in English as a foreign language. *Studies in Second Language Acquisition, 18*, 225–252.

Hudson, T., Detmer, E., & Brown, J. D. (1995). *Developing prototypic measures of cross-cultural pragmatics.* Honolulu: University of Hawai'i Press.
Izumi, S. (2013). Noticing and L2 development: Theoretical, empirical, and pedagogical issues. In J. M. Bergsleithner, S. N. Frota, & J. K. Yoshioka (Eds.), *Noticing and second language acquisition: Studies in honor of Richard Schmidt* (pp. 25–38). Honolulu: National Foreign Language Resource Center, University of Hawai'i.
Izumi, S., & Bigelow, M. (2000). Does output promote noticing in second language acquisition? *TESOL Quarterly, 34,* 239–278.
Kasper, G., & Schmidt, R. (1996). Developmental issues in interlanguage pragmatics. *Studies in Second Language Acquisition, 18,* 149–169.
Kinginger, C., & Belz, J. A. (2005). Socio-cultural perspectives on pragmatic development in foreign language learning: Microgenetic case studies from telecollaboration and residence abroad. *Intercultural Pragmatics, 2,* 369–421.
Koike, D., & Pearson, L. (2005). The effect of instruction and feedback in the development of pragmatic competence. *System, 33,* 481–501.
Kondo, S. (2008). Effects on pragmatic development through awareness-raising instruction: Refusals by Japanese EFL learners. In E. Alcón & A. Martínez-Flor (Eds.), *Investigating pragmatics in foreign language learning, teaching and testing* (pp. 153–177). Clevedon, England: Multilingual Matters.
Lantolf, J. P., & Thorne, S. (2006). *Sociocultural theory and the genesis of second language development.* Oxford: Oxford University Press.
Leech, G. (1983). *Principles of pragmatics.* London: Longman.
Leow, R. P. (2013). Schmidt's noticing hypothesis: More than two decades after. In J. M. Bergsleithner, S. N. Frota, & J. K. Yoshioka (Eds.), *Noticing and second language acquisition: Studies in honor of Richard Schmidt* (pp. 11–24). Honolulu: National Foreign Language Resource Center, University of Hawai'i.
Li, S. (2013). Amount of practice and pragmatic development of request-making in L2 Chinese. In N. Taguchi & J. Sykes (Eds.), *Technology in interlanguage pragmatics research and teaching* (pp. 43–69). Amsterdam: John Benjamins.
Lynch, T., & Maclean, J. (2000). Exploring the benefits of task repetition and recycling for classroom language learning. *Language Teaching Research, 4,* 221–250.
Lyster, R. (2007). *Learning and teaching languages through content: A counterbalanced approach.* Amsterdam: John Benjamins.
Mackey, A. (2006). Feedback, noticing and instructed second language learning. *Applied Linguistics, 27,* 405–430.
Martínez-Flor, A., & Usó-Juan, E. (2006). A comprehensive pedagogical framework to develop pragmatics in the foreign language classroom: The 6Rs approach. *Applied Language Learning, 16*(2), 39–64.
Matsumura, S. (2003). Modelling the relationships among interlanguage pragmatic development, L2 proficiency, and exposure to L2. *Applied Linguistics, 24,* 465–91.

Mori, J. (2002). Task design, plan, and development of talk-in-interaction: An analysis of a small group activity in a Japanese classroom. *Applied Linguistics, 23*, 323–347.

Mori, J. (2004). Negotiating sequential boundaries and learning opportunities: A case from a Japanese classroom. *The Modern Language Journal, 88*, 536–550.

Németh, N., & Kormos, J. (2001). Pragmatic aspects of task-performance: The case of argumentation. *Language Teaching Research, 5*, 213–240.

Nguyen, T. T. M. (2013). Instructional effects on the acquisition of modifiers in constructive criticisms by EFL learners. *Language Awareness, 22*, 76–94.

Nguyen, T. T. M., Pham, T. H., & Pham, M. T. (2012). The relative effects of explicit and implicit form-focused instruction on the development of L2 pragmatic competence. *Journal of Pragmatics, 44*, 416–434.

Ranta, L., & Lyster, R. (2007). A cognitive approach to improving immersion students' oral language abilities: The awareness-practice-feedback sequence. In R. DeKeyser (Ed.), *Practice in a second language: Perspectives from applied linguistics and cognitive psychology* (pp. 141–160). Cambridge: Cambridge University Press.

Roever, C., Fraser, C., & Elder, C. (2014). *Testing ESL sociopragmatics: Development and validation of a web-based test battery.* New York, NY: Peter Lang.

Sachtleben, A., & Denny, H. (2012). Making the implicit explicit: Raising pragmatic awareness in trainee interpreters using semiauthentic spontaneous discourse samples. *TESOL Journal, 3*, 126–137.

Schmidt, R. (1993). Awareness and second language acquisition. *Annual Review of Applied Linguistics, 13*, 206–226.

Schmidt, R. (2001). Attention. In P. Robinson (Ed.), *Cognition and second language instruction* (pp. 3–32). New York, NY: Cambridge University Press.

Schmidt, R. (2010). Attention, awareness, and individual differences in language learning. In W. M. Chan, S. Chi, K. N. Cin, J. Istanto, M. Nagami, J. W. Sew, T. Suthiwan, & I. Walker (Eds.), *Proceedings of CLaSIC 2010* (pp. 721–737). Singapore: National University of Singapore, Centre for Language Studies.

Sheen, Y. (2004). Corrective feedback and learner uptake in communicative classrooms across instructional settings. *Language Teaching Research, 8*, 263–300.

Skehan, P. (1998). *A cognitive approach to language learning.* Oxford: Oxford University Press.

Sydorenko, T. (2015). The use of computer-delivered structured tasks in pragmatic instruction: An exploratory study. *Intercultural Pragmatics.* 12(3), 333–362,

Taguchi, N. (2012). *Context, individual differences, and pragmatic competence.* Toronto: Multilingual Matters.

Takahashi, S. (2005a). Noticing in task performance and learning outcomes: A qualitative analysis of instructional effects in interlanguage pragmatics. *System, 33*, 437–461.

Takahashi, S. (2005b). Pragmatic awareness: Is it related to motivation and proficiency? *Applied Linguistics, 26*, 90–120.

Takimoto, M. (2009). The effects of input-based tasks on the development of learners' pragmatic proficiency. *Applied Linguistics, 30*, 1–25.

Takimoto, M. (2012). Assessing the effects of identical task repetition and task-type repetition on learners' recognition and production of second language request downgraders. *Intercultural Pragmatics, 9*, 71–96.

Tateyama, Y., & Kasper, G. (2008). Talking with a classroom guest: Opportunities for learning Japanese pragmatics. In E. Alcón & A. Martínez-Flor (Eds.), *Investigating pragmatics in foreign language learning, teaching, and testing* (pp. 45–71). Bristol: Multilingual Matters.

Thomas, J. (1983). Cross-cultural pragmatic failure. *Applied Linguistics, 4*, 91–112.

Uggen, M. S. (2012). Reinvestigating the noticing function of output. *Language learning, 62*, 506–540.

van Compernolle, R. A. (2014). *Sociocultural theory and L2 instructional pragmatics.* Bristol: Multilingual Matters.

van Compernolle, R. A., & Williams, L. (2012). Promoting sociolinguistic competence in the classroom zone of proximal development. *Language Teaching Research, 16*, 39–60.

VanPatten, B. (Ed.). (2004). *Processing instruction: Theory, research, and commentary.* New York, NY: Routledge.

# "Always remember to say *Please* and *Thank You*": Teaching Politeness with German EFL Textbooks

Holger Limberg
European University of Flensburg, Germany

This chapter approaches the complex issue of teaching linguistic and cultural aspects of politeness with textbooks in an EFL learning environment (Bou-Franch & Garcés-Conejos, 2003; LoCastro, 2012). In schools, textbooks are still by far the most frequently used medium for language teaching. They offer a variety of texts types for learners, ranging from written to spoken and visual as well as increasingly audio-visual texts. Many EFL textbooks adopt a linear progression in the teaching of grammar and vocabulary, oriented along the complexity and abstractness of linguistic forms. A pragmatic progression, on the other hand, is non-linear and more complex. It is connected to the communicative intents and illocutionary acts students learn to express in the course of their foreign language education. One particular issue of pragmatic and sociolinguistic concern is the aspect of politeness. For a generation of young people who grow up to live and work in a globalized world, learning how to be polite in English is an important competence when transacting businesses or interacting with speakers of other cultures. Since commercially available textbooks are a major teaching resource in the EFL classroom, the question arises, what do they teach learners in terms of politeness? In this paper, EFL textbooks for secondary schools from three major publishers in Germany are scrutinized to find out how they provide input for learners on the pragmatic issue of politeness. The focus is on what aspects of politeness are explicitly addressed in textbooks and what is suggested that learners do in class to develop their politeness competence. The analysis not only reveals how important politeness is as a learning objective, but also how textbooks conceptualize politeness as pragmatic discourse phenomenon.

## Introduction

Politeness is perhaps one of most fascinating and yet complex phenomena of pragmatics, considering the vast amount of scientific interest in its study and the conceptual debate over scientific versus folk views of this phenomenon (Culpeper, 2011). It is considered a universal feature of language (Brown & Levinson, 1987), but its theoretical conceptualization, interactional organization, and discursive realization varies widely across different languages and cultures. Politeness is encoded and decoded in culturally specific ways, which means that nonnative speakers have to acquire knowledge and skills in managing politeness norms of a specific target language community. In the field of inter- and cross-cultural pragmatics, politeness has been a research topic for over four decades, with researchers' interest spanning different languages and cultures, various speaker constellations, social practices, and a variety of discourse types (Brown & Levinson, 1987; Kádár & Haugh, 2013; Kasper, 1990; Lakoff, 1973; Leech, 1983; Watts, 2003). More recently, the field has also included acquisitional aspects of pragmatics (e.g., Alcón Soler, 2005; Bardovi-Harlig, 1999, 2013; Barron, 2003; Barron & Warga, 2007; Glaser, 2014; Ishihara & Cohen, 2010). This research strand deals with the question of how learners acquire L2 or FL[1] competence to handle both language- and culturally-related issues of social interaction. Related to that, the question of how teaching materials and instructions can contribute to pragmatic development has broadened the acquisitional perspective to include input provided in formal, instructional environments (e.g., Alcón Soler, 2005; Bardovi-Harlig, Mossman, & Vellenga, 2015; Crandall & Basturkmen, 2004; Takahashi, 2001; Vellenga, 2004; Williams, 1988).

Numerous observational and interventional studies give evidence to the teachability of L2 pragmatics. They have shown that classroom instruction can lead to an increase and improvement in appropriate speech act use, pragmatic routines, and also metapragmatic knowledge (Alcón Soler, 2005; Bardovi-Harlig et al., 2015; House, 1996; Kasper, 1997; see also synopsis in Bardovi-Harlig, 2015). Despite this converging empirical evidence, a single dominant methodological approach to L2 pragmatics teaching has not yet been established. Issues about inductive versus deductive approaches, explicit versus implicit and text-based versus technology-based teaching, productive-skills versus receptive-skills orientation, or the effectiveness of metapragmatic input are still subject to discussion (Cohen, 2005; Padilla Cruz, 2013; Taguchi, 2011; Usó Juan & Martínez-Flor, 2008). Some notable trends have surfaced from this discussion, indicating that explicit instruction, metapragmatic explanations, and cognitively demanding tasks seem to favor a pragmatic development (Taguchi, 2011). Nevertheless, Kasper's (2001) assumption "that it is not always obvious how principles proposed for instruction in grammar might translate to pragmatics" (p.

51) leaves many teachers in doubt about which choices to make when developing their learners' pragmatic skills.

In school, teachers often draw upon textbooks and other commercially available material to design lessons for their learners (Byrd & Schuemann, 2014). Textbooks have a prominent status in foreign language teaching because they present a systematic syllabus with ready-made texts, tasks and language support (Hutchinson & Torres, 1994). But without knowing what textbooks really offer for the teaching of politeness, it is difficult to decide if the input is appropriate for learners and if textbooks translate into practice what politeness research has empirically revealed. Hutchinson and Torres (1994) have pointed out the danger of "absolv[ing] teachers of responsibility" (p. 315) if the built-in curriculum is taken for granted and if the design, content, and authenticity of the material are not questioned. EFL teachers are responsible "to make students more aware that pragmatic functions exist in language" (Bardovi-Harlig, Hartford, Mahan-Taylor, Morgan & Reynolds, 1991, p. 5) and "to help learners become familiar with the range of pragmatic devices and practices in the target language" (Bardovi-Harlig & Mahan-Taylor, 2003, p. 5). This mammoth task presupposes that teachers have some expertise in speech act use, politeness norms, and discourse conventions of the target language culture. It also requires their willingness to adapt commercially available material and create input that is authentic, meaningful, and challenging for learners (Bardovi-Harlig et al., 2015; Ishihara & Cohen, 2010). Several researchers working in this field have responded to the dearth of pragmatic-focused material, designing tasks, and lesson plans as well as making methodological proposals to teach specific aspects of pragmatics in ESL and EFL contexts (Bardovi-Harlig & Mahan-Taylor, 2003; Glaser, 2014; Houck & Tatsuki, 2011; Ishihara & Cohen, 2010; Padilla Cruz, 2013; Tatsuki & Houck, 2010).

In line with current research on acquisitional pragmatics, I argue that teaching pragmatics is beneficial and that we need to understand how textbook materials—especially those designed for EFL classrooms—provide input for learners. Politeness is essential for learners' "interactional, communicative, day-to-day basis of social life and the conduct of social relationships" (Brown, 2011, p. 636). EFL learners who attain a high level of pragmatic proficiency need to be exposed to extensive materials inside the classroom because their out-of-class environment does not compensate for a lack thereof (Martínez-Flor & Usó Juan, 2010). The goal of this paper is to find out how textbooks for EFL learners treat politeness as a language-learning goal and how they conceptualize this phenomenon as part of learners' pragmatic competence. To this end, I'll outline what theories of politeness have contributed to our understanding of this concept and analyze how textbooks break down this knowledge into teachable chunks that can be used in the classroom. The textbooks are taken from the German market and are designed for German learners of English in secondary schools.

Before embarking on this analysis, I will first deal with the complex phenomenon of politeness, albeit in a concise fashion with a view towards the focus of this paper (Politeness as a socio-pragmatic phenomenon). A literature review at the interface of pragmatics teaching, textbook analysis, and politeness reveals issues on teaching politeness that have so far been identified (Teaching politeness), also with regard to findings from previous textbook studies on politeness (Textbooks and politeness). Then, the corpus of textbooks used in this study is introduced (Textbook data and analysis), followed by an analysis of how textbooks introduce and teach politeness for German learners of English (Politeness teaching in German EFL textbooks). A final chapter summarizes and discusses the main findings.

## Politeness as a socio-pragmatic phenomenon

Politeness is a form of interpersonal behavior that takes into account the feelings of others as to how they think they should be treated (Brown, 2011; Kádár & Haugh, 2013). Linguistic politeness refers to the verbal component of managing interpersonal relationships (Kasper, 1990). It encompasses language choices that seek to achieve a smooth interaction between speakers according to expected socio-cultural norms within a given community. Since the beginning of scientific research on politeness, several explanations have been proposed, equating politeness with conflict avoidance (Lakoff 1975; Leech, 1983) and face-threat mitigation (Brown & Levinson, 1987) or associating it with situationally appropriate language use (Meier, 1995; Thomas, 1995). Moreover, a "surplus" view has been offered which considers politeness as a matter of going beyond what is considered appropriate in a specific context (Locher & Watts, 2005; Watts, 2003). These different explanations reflect researchers' leaning towards a pragmatic versus socio-cultural view of politeness. The former view concentrates on communicative strategies to be polite whereas the latter emphasizes norms of politeness constructed by individuals and society (Culpeper, 2011).

Brown and Levinson's (1987) framework of politeness as a form of saving the interlocutor's face has been most influential in this research field. Despite severe criticism on its claims for universality, its speaker bias, and the ignorance of lay perceptions of politeness (Eelen, 2001; Watts, 2003), it remains a major source of inspiration for pragmatics research and also pragmatics teaching. It builds on the notion of *face* (Goffman, 1967), divided into *positive* (involvement) and *negative* (independence) face, both of which are satisfied by politeness strategies. For example, their framework suggests using in-group identity markers, small talk and agreements as strategies to avoid threatening the interlocutor's positive face (Brown & Levinson, 1987, p. 102); on the other hand, being conventionally indirect, minimizing the imposition, and apologizing are strategies to avoid a negative face threat (Brown & Levinson, 1987, p. 131). Politeness is viewed as a form of facework, achieved by the linguistic realization of strategies that satisfy addressees' wants. This pragmatic view of politeness offers a viable pedagogical tool for classroom instruction. Strategies can be taught as a knowledge base of politeness, both in a formal sense of having access to linguistic resources associated with politeness (e.g., hedging expressions, modality, questions) as well as in a functional sense in terms of using these resources to be polite towards others (e.g., when apologizing, requesting, complimenting).

Appropriateness is an important notion within politeness theories because it relates to culturally determined concepts and norms.[2] What is considered appropriate and/or polite is subject to negotiation, depending on the speakers, their cultural background and the time and space in which they interact (Fraser, 1990; Meier, 1997). Speech acts can be performed in different (pragmalinguistic) ways, but not all of them may be seen as equally appropriate or polite in a given context. Appropriateness and politeness are thus not just a matter of *linguistic* encoding through, for example, conventional indirectness, but also of *social* judgments made by individuals relative to a specific context. The sociopragmatic end of a pragmatic competence refers to the knowledge speakers have about making appropriate choices on the basis of the situational context (Leech, 1983; Thomas, 1983). Pragmatic choices of being polite are not made in a social vacuum, but in the context of an interaction, informed by speakers' experience and influenced by their expectations.

Thus, an understanding of politeness is adopted for teaching purposes that is socio-cognitive, bringing both linguistic strategies of individuals and social judgments of adequacy together (Bou-Franch & Garcés-Conejos, 2003; House, 2005). This view understands politeness as the linguistic encoding of social relations and as judgments speakers make. It is something that must be communicated and interpreted by speakers. In line with this situated view, linguistic tokens have no inherent politeness value and thus, cannot, per se, be ordered on a scale from more to less polite without taking the specific context into consideration. Likewise, it is problematic to have politeness taught as hard-and-fast rules, which, when followed, automatically lead to the desired appropriate behavior. The relationship between (linguistic) form and (pragmatic) function is nonlinear. For example, uttering a request in a very indirect way, using a complex syntactic structure and several lexical modifications, is not tantamount to being more polite per se. Grammar and pragmatic competence are two emergent systems in learners, which interact and support each other, but which are not in parallel and also do not develop sequentially (Bardovi-Harlig, 2013).

## Teaching politeness

Since politeness has a key function in establishing and maintaining social relationships, the importance of teaching learners how to be polite in the L2/FL is widely acknowledged (Bou-Franch & Garcés-Conejos, 2003; Edmondson & House, 1982; Ficzere, 2014; Meier, 1997).[3] According to an early study by

Lörscher and Schulze (1988), there seems to be a deficit of explicit politeness formulae in foreign language classroom discourse, which creates the necessity to impart knowledge of verbal means of realizing politeness in the foreign language and practice the appropriate use of these means in conversation.

Saville-Troike (1996, as cited in Félix-Brasdefer, 2004) explains what politeness as one aspect of pragmatic competence for L2/FL learners entails:

> In order to achieve approximate native-speaker (NS) levels of pragmatic competence, learners need to acquire the rules of politeness of the target culture and to develop interaction skills: knowing who may or may not speak in certain settings, how they should talk to people of different statuses and roles, what nonverbal behaviors are appropriate for them to use in various contexts, what routines they should use for turn taking in conversation, and how to perform and comprehend speech acts such as requesting or apologizing. (p. 588)

Acquiring "rules of politeness" presupposes a native-speaker norm, which establishes rules and conventions of acceptable (linguistic) behavior. In EFL teaching this is problematic in two ways: First, there are different English native speaker norms (Kasper, 1995); and second, many of these rules of politeness are not obvious even to native speakers (Bardovi-Harlig & Mahan-Taylor, 2003). Notwithstanding these challenges, politeness has to be introduced in the EFL classroom, as it is an integral part of everyday language use.

The difficult question of how to operationalize politeness for teaching purposes was first addressed by Edmondson and House (1982). The authors argue that making prescriptive rules concerning polite (and impolite) utterances is meaningless since norms, conventions, and expectations are inevitably subjective and therefore subject to negotiation. Instead, Edmondson and House (1982, p. 221) suggest framing politeness teaching in terms of conversational principles (Leech, 1983) as a middle ground between endless lists of polite utterances and empty paraphrases. Understood as principles against which conversational behavior can be judged, they include saying more than just the minimum, returning a favor, apologizing before offending somebody, and offering help in case of communication difficulties (Edmondson & House, 1982). In a similar vein, Schubert (2006, p. 205) suggests that politeness rules, maxims, and strategies provide useful guidelines to bring polite verbal behavior into the EFL classroom. Rather than presenting learners with meaningless lists of so-called polite phrases and forms of conduct, maxims and strategies help "to attribute communicative functions to grammatical and lexical forms, so that the interpersonal and contextual aspect is added to the referential meaning of utterances" (Schubert, 2006, p. 205; cf. Meier, 1997).

Reconciling the pragmalinguistic and sociopragmatic bases of pragmatics teaching is crucial for a successful development of learners' politeness competence. The former requires teaching linguistic resources to perform 'polite' language functions, while the latter demands assessing socio-cultural and situative contexts to implement those resources adequately (Taguchi, 2011). General methodological approaches to teaching politeness, as for example proposed in Bou-Franch & Garcés-Conejos (2003) and Schubert (2006), suggest a pragmalinguistic understanding of politeness as a resource for developing sociopragmatic competence. First, students learn how communicative functions are attributed to grammatical and lexical forms before learning how to choose appropriate politeness forms in a given situation and evaluating the contextual appropriateness of an utterance. These approaches highlight the importance of equipping students first with linguistic means of coding social relations, using traditional politeness frameworks as a point of reference. Awareness-raising tasks, that is, tasks that direct learners' attention to politeness as a teaching objective (Schmidt, 1993), can provide "tools needed to understand the linguistic encoding of social relationships, and to make informed choices in producing and interpreting meanings" (Bou-Franch & Garcés-Conejos, 2003, p. 16). They include a variety of activities in which learners are exposed to pragmalinguistic devices and social relations in different discourse genres, evaluate their appropriateness, compare similarities and differences between cultures, discuss personal views and practice interactions to learn how to communicate appropriately under a variety of contextual constraints (see also Cohen, 2005; Félix-Brasdefer, 2006; Howard, 2003).

## Textbooks and politeness

In addition to observations and interventions, some studies of pragmatic phenomena have looked specifically at textbooks and teaching materials to find out how pragmatic aspects of language are introduced to learners. Politeness is only rarely addressed as a primary teaching objective. LoCastro (1997) found that Japanese EFL textbooks are distinguished by a noticeable absence of politeness because "neither lessons on politeness nor multiple examples of politeness markers [are] embedded in the textbooks" (p. 246). Examples of situational appropriate language use can be found in some textbook passages, primarily on a lexical and formulaic level ("please," "you're welcome"). Such a concentration on the development of linguistic competence often corresponds to a neglect of communicative functions of the forms and patterns introduced.

A problem inherent in many textbooks is that language samples and dialogs have rarely been created on the basis of sound empirical evidence. Ishihara and Cohen (2010) comment that "the majority of published textbooks are written on the basis of the curriculum writers' intuitions" (p. 146). Dialogs do not represent spontaneous pragmatic language use (e.g., interactional features of talk are often omitted), the content is often less attractive for learners and some pragmatic aspects are only partially presented; in fact, some aspects are completely ignored, or simply taken for granted, perhaps due to perceived similarities in cultural values and communication styles. It seems that the existing empirical evidence on various speech acts studied so far has not found its way into textbooks, thus having little impact on foreign language teaching (Boxer & Pickering, 1995; Martínez-Flor & Usó-Juan, 2010; Ogiermann, 2013). This pedagogical flaw is not an isolated observation, but seems to be a repeated finding in studies on different ESL and EFL textbooks.

Williams (1988) was one of the first to document the disparity between textbook input and authentic use. The business English textbooks that she reviewed teach overtly polite forms for different language functions (e.g., explaining, disagreeing, interrupting), even though they were not used in real meetings. Vellenga (2004) noted a lack of metapragmatic discussions on both appropriateness and politeness for most speech acts in EFL and ESL textbooks. Even textbook manuals provide little metapragmatic information on politeness for teachers. Phillips (1993) found that "[a]lthough students are briefly exposed to strategies for initiating polite requests, the discussion appears to be inadequate and the practice insufficient to allow them to internalize and produce, themselves, the type of polite requests favored by native speakers" (p. 379). Petraki and Bayes (2013, p. 507) found a list of short dialogs in one textbook with extremely direct requests which students were asked to rewrite to make them sound more polite. As will be shown later, parallels seem to exist in German EFL textbooks.

The few studies on German EFL textbooks also indicate that pragmatics teaching is far from flawless. Ogiermann (2010), analyzing a series of six EFL textbooks from Bavaria, found implicit and explicit pragmatic input on different speech acts, but no systematic treatment and a decrease of input for more proficient learners. Limberg (in press) identified a noticeable gap in teaching apologies between the input given in the text and opportunities for output given via tasks. Politeness as a pragmatic topic is underrepresented and reduced in its complexity in ESL and EFL textbooks, either because it is limited to a lexical level (e.g., by teaching polite expressions) or it is associated with the performance of specific speech acts, most notably requests.

This paper investigates how politeness is presented in German EFL textbooks and compares the presentation to other reviews. Several textbook studies have looked at specific speech acts and how they are represented and taught, making only cursory reference to politeness (LoCastro, 1997; Petraki & Bayes, 2013). Moreover, many pragmatic studies of textbooks are based on materials from English/American publishers and are often designed for ESL classes (Bardovi-Harlig et al., 1991; Bardovi-Harlig et al., 2015; Boxer & Pickering, 1995; Vellenga, 2004). Investigating other textbook types, for example those aimed at EFL students, designed for secondary schools, or produced by non-English publishers, contributes to a broader picture of the state of instructional pragmatics.

## Textbook data and analysis

Three EFL textbook series currently used in German secondary schools (*Gymnasium*[4]) provide the data for this study. They all have a high circulation since their publishers belong to the three major publishing houses for ELT textbooks in Germany (Buchreport, 2014). Each series consists of six volumes, one per school year from grade 5 to 10 (age 10/11 to 15/16). These textbooks are designed for learners with different levels of proficiency in English. Grades 5 and 6 can be considered beginners, although students using these textbooks often have had two years of initial English instruction in primary school. Grades 7 and 8 are intermediate learners, who have been taught different language skills and vocabulary for topics relevant for their age group. Finally, grades 9 and 10 are upper-intermediate learners, some perhaps even advanced, with an elaborated lexicon and competence in different integrated language skills (i.e., vocabulary, grammar, reading, writing, listening, speaking and mediation skills are interwoven during instruction).

Table 1 provides an overview of the textbook data used for the analysis of teaching politeness.

**Table 1.** Textbook corpus

| no. | textbook series | abbr. | publisher | vols. | date of publication | no. of teaching units per volume |
|---|---|---|---|---|---|---|
| 1 | English G 21 | EG 21 | Cornelsen | 6 | 2006–2011 | 4–6 |
| 2 | Green Line | GL | Klett | 6 | 2006–2010 | 4–7 |
| 3 | Camden Town | CT | Diesterweg (Bildungshaus Schulbuchverlage) | 6 | 2004–2008 | 6 |

English G 21 is an established textbook series for secondary schools published by Cornelsen. It purports to train communicative skills and general study skills across a number of thematic units in each textbook. Green Line (Klett) and Camden Town (Diesterweg) are equal in many ways, as their primary goal is also to gradually develop EFL students' communicative competence throughout secondary school. Differences between the three textbook series exist in the choice of topics, types of tasks and exercises, number and organization of teaching units, and the general design. Before any of these textbooks can be commercially distributed, they need to be officially approved by the Ministries of Education in each federal state of Germany. Schools eventually make a choice over a particular series. More specifically the English teachers decide which series fits best to their target learner groups. This procedure gives teachers a certain influence on textbook choice, which makes a prior inspection of the material imperative. Language textbooks published abroad generally do not find their way into the German EFL classroom, unless used as additional material by teachers because they tend not to conform to the German curricula and thus do not get officially approved.

The three EFL series follow a content-based, integrated-skills syllabus, meaning that the teaching of different language skills is embedded in specific topics. Politeness is thus expected to occur not exclusively with reference to one specific language skill (e.g., speaking) or related to a specific topic (e.g., going shopping). Moreover, as a pragmatic topic it is likely to surface in different textbook volumes and language activities. Politeness can be part of the pragmatic input provided through different text types (e.g., dialogs, picture stories) and genres (e.g., discussions, speeches), and it can be an outcome of a task or exercise that textbooks offer learners when practicing different linguistic forms or language skills. The question is how (much) attention is drawn to it, so that learners working with the materials can become aware of its importance for communicative actions.

Eighteen textbooks were analyzed by reading each unit chapter page-by-page with its input texts, comments, and assignments. Since manifestations of politeness in language and culture are too complex to capture in their entirety, also considering the multitude of speech act realizations to which learners are exposed, this study focuses on textbook instances that explicitly mark politeness as a learning objective by investigating metapragmatic comments and activities. In addition to the thematic units, extra grammar, language, and study skills sections have also been searched for politeness input. They are usually located at the end of these textbooks and summarize important skills as well as provide a resource for learners working independently.

Metapragmatic comments on politeness, in which the relational dimension of talk is clearly addressed, draw learners' attention to establishing social relationships through talk and help them notice differences in language functions and use between their L1 and the FL. The key terms *polite/ness, appropriate/ness, formal/ity, indirect/ness,* and *friendly/ness* (cf. LoCastro, 1997) were used in the search for the explicit mention of politeness. The analysis also included language activities, exercises and tasks focusing on politeness in which learners receive the opportunity to practice "being polite" and learn how to express social functions of language. They are either presented as decontextualized activities that focus on polite expressions (e.g., gap-fill exercises), or as interactive, more authentic activities embedded in specific meaningful contexts (e.g., role play tasks).

## Politeness teaching in German EFL textbooks

The following table summarizes the findings of politeness teaching in German EFL textbooks. It captures instances of politeness that are clearly labeled in the text, thus making them the focus of attention for classroom instruction. This excludes any instance where the textbook does not highlight a relational aspect of talk, but where politeness is commonly expected in the specific communicative activity (e.g., asking for directions). Explicit forms of politeness teaching only occur occasionally in the textbooks (Table 2).

**Table 2.** Politeness in German EFL textbooks

| textbook | table of contents | tasks | exercises | | | | meta-pragmatic information | useful phrases |
|---|---|---|---|---|---|---|---|---|
| | | | total | matching | listing | transformation | | |
| GL 1 | 2 | 2 | 7 | 1 | 4 | 2 | 2 | 2 |
| GL 2 | 1 | 3 | 4 | 1 | 0 | 3 | 2 | 2 |
| GL 3 | 1 | 1 | 2 | 1 | 1 | 0 | 0 | 0 |
| GL 4 | 1 | 5 | 3 | 1 | 1 | 1 | 5 | 1 |
| GL 5 | 1 | 2 | 0 | 0 | 0 | 0 | 1 | 1 |
| GL 6 | 1 | 3 | 0 | 0 | 0 | 0 | 14 | 2 |
| **subtotal** | **7** | **16** | **16** | **4** | **6** | **6** | **24** | **8** |
| EG 21 A1 | 0 | 1 | 0 | 0 | 0 | 0 | 2 | 1 |
| EG 21 A2 | 0 | 0 | 1 | 0 | 0 | 1 | 1 | 2 |
| EG 21 A3 | 0 | 1 | 1 | 0 | 1 | 0 | 1 | 1 |
| EG 21 A4 | 0 | 1 | 0 | 0 | 0 | 0 | 1 | 1 |
| EG 21 A5 | 0 | 7 | 5 | 1 | 3 | 1 | 3 | 3 |
| EG 21 A6 | 0 | 1 | 0 | 0 | 0 | 0 | 1 | 2 |
| **subtotal** | **0** | **11** | **7** | **1** | **4** | **2** | **9** | **10** |
| CT 1 | 0 | 1 | 2 | 0 | 1 | 0 | 1 | 2 |
| CT 2 | 0 | 0 | 2 | 1 | 1 | 0 | 2 | 1 |
| CT 3 | 1 | 0 | 1 | 0 | 0 | 1 | 1 | 1 |
| CT 4 | 0 | 0 | 0 | 0 | 0 | 0 | 2 | 2 |
| CT 5 | 0 | 2 | 1 | 1 | 0 | 0 | 1 | 0 |
| CT 6 | 0 | 0 | 0 | 0 | 0 | 0 | 0 | 0 |
| **subtotal** | **1** | **3** | **6** | **2** | **2** | **1** | **7** | **6** |
| **total** | **8** | **30** | **29** | **7** | **12** | **9** | **40** | **24** |

note. GL is Green Line, EG 21 is English G 21, and CT is Camden Town; 1–6 indicate the volume of the textbook series. ToC stands for table of contents. The numbers in each row represent occurrences of politeness in each of the 18 textbooks in the corpus. Different sub-tasks or exercises (a, b, c) belonging to one assignment were counted as separate occurrences of politeness. *Matching, Listing,* and *Transformation* are types of exercises.

Textbooks have different means available for explicit politeness teaching. Naturally, the first place to check if politeness is a designated teaching objective of a volume is the table of contents (ToC). It lists areas of communicative competence that are emphasized in each unit. Politeness is seldom specified as pragmatic content in the EFL textbook corpus. If it does occur, politeness is stated as a general learning outcome, such as "to express oneself politely" (GL 1), "to talk politely to a waiter/waitress" (GL 2), "to express one's opinion politely" (CT 3), and "to discuss politely" (GL 5) or it is listed under the rubric lexical/phrasal input in the form of "polite responses" (GL 3) and "polite small talk" (GL 4). These ToC items translate into different kinds of activities for learners within the textbook units. Depending on the publisher and volume, German EFL textbooks contain between four and seven teaching units, each one having a specific content-oriented theme (e.g., pocket money, living together, and media).

### Exercises on politeness

The units have a range of texts and assignments on each page, which constitute the key component of textbook-based language teaching. Assignments are generally characterized in terms of their function and outcome. Here, a distinction between *tasks* and *exercises* is made, following Ellis (2003) who proposes that "'tasks' are activities that call for primarily meaning-focused language use" (p. 3) whereas "'exercises' are activities that call for primarily form-focused language use" (p. 3). According to this definition, an assignment that asks learners to fill in blank spaces with prefabricated language chunks is classified as an exercise, whereas a role play or partner discussion in which language is produced more freely is considered a task.

The overview in Table 1 reveals that politeness tasks and exercises are roughly equal in total, but that their distribution differs between the textbook volumes and publishers. Especially in textbooks for beginners and intermediate learners (volumes 1–3), there are a larger number of form-focused exercises on politeness. Three kinds of politeness exercises are typically found in these textbooks: (a) matching (e.g., phrases with speech intentions), (b) listing or sorting (e.g., polite vs. not so polite phrases)[5], and (c) transformation exercises (e.g., rephrasing utterances to make them more polite). They all indicate a form-based approach to politeness teaching, which suggests that a particular linguistic structure can be mapped to its functional meaning. Context is not relevant in these assignments, since the focus is on the linguistic structure. In GL 1 (p. 53, No. 6) learners are asked to sort a number of utterances under the label *polite* and *not so polite* as in (1).

**(1)**

Are these words polite or not so polite? Make two lists.
Hey, you've got my CD! • That girl is a pain. • Yes, thank you. • You're welcome. • You and your silly T-shirts. • That's OK. • Can I help you? • That's your problem. • Sorry I'm late.                GL 1 (p. 53, No. 6)

At this beginner level (first year of English in secondary school), learners are exposed to utterances that apparently have a particular relational meaning regardless of the context in which they occur. The outcome of this exercise is a grid with utterances that can be learned by heart and applied to other language activities. The formulas for expressing thanks, apologies, and agreement as well as for offering help and responding are coded as polite. The others are, at least according to the textbook, "not so polite." Even though routine formulas have to be introduced early in foreign language education, a classification only on the basis of linguistic forms could be misleading if no further explanation is given.

In matching exercises, students have to find the corresponding second pair part as in (2) where they select a polite answer to the utterance provided (GL 3, p. 88, No. 1).

**(2)**

Find the polite answer.
1. Excuse me.
   a) What do you want?
   b) How can I help you?
   c) Huh?
2. I'm sorry. I can't find your CD!
   a) Can't you do anything right?
   b) I'll never give you a CD again.
   c) Well – let's look for it together.
3. Thanks for all your help.
   a) What help?
   b) You're welcome.
   c) Forget it.
4. Could you help me, please?
   a) No.
   b) I only help nice people.
   c) I'd be glad to help you.                     (GL 3, p. 88, No. 1)

Compared to the completely decontextualized listing/sorting exercise in (1), this type of exercise makes at least a first step towards introducing a two-turn-conversation in which a discourse context can be imagined. It provides students with input that is conventionally associated with politeness (e.g., indirect requests, ritual apology formulas). However, a metapragmatic awareness of the form-function-context relationship cannot be achieved solely by finding linguistic counterparts. Unless the teacher asks further questions about their relationship, students are left on their own to decide which function the specific form tries to achieve in this context.

More active student cognitive engagement can be achieved with transformation exercises (3), in which students change a dialog to make it sound more polite (cf. Petraki & Bayes, 2013). Textbooks frequently provide lists of phrases as linguistic resources to help learners construct utterances or dialogs with different levels of politeness (GL 2, p. 50, No. 3).

**(3)**

> A girl is looking for a sweatshirt in "Street Style". She is not very polite. Change her sentences. What should she say? The useful phrases on p. 39 can help you.
> Assistant: Hello. Can I help you?
> Girl: Where are the sweatshirts?
> Assistant: They're over here. Are you looking for any special colour?
> Girl: Yellow. Size M.
> Assistant: I'm very sorry, but we don't have any more yellow ones in M.
> Girl: What? No yellow ones? Show me other colours.
> Assistant: How do you like this orange sweatshirt?
> Girl: The colour is horrible.
> Assistant: Would you like this blue one? It's only £20.
> Girl: I want a cheaper sweatshirt. But blue is OK.
> Assistant: This one is only £15.
> Girl: OK. Where can I pay?                     GL 2 (p. 50, No. 3)

The modification of the shopping dialog is a guided assignment, framed by the dialog structure and supported by a handful of phrases to be used when talking politely to a shop assistant. Students at this level (second year of English) have to replace particular utterances that appear direct and impolite to make them sound more polite. Examples for the polite shopping phrases are "No, thanks. I'm just looking."; "Sorry,... too big/expensive/..."; and "I'd like to try on..." Students are supposed to realize that utterances such as "Show me other colours" are too direct and explicit and that changing it, for example, to a "Do you have other colours?" is more hearer-oriented and therefore less threatening. The result is a revised shopping dialog with conventionalized phrases that are apparently expected as part of a customer's polite behavior. However, teachers cannot really be sure whether students have understood their particular choice of language. The only indicator of a metapragmatic understanding is the replacement of a 'not very polite' utterance for one is that less direct and face-threatening.

Transformation exercises are typically found in connection with requests and questions. Ordering your food at a café or restaurant by saying "We want two pizzas" is not considered so polite (GL 1, p. 84, No. 5); instead, this EFL textbook teaches "We'd like two pizzas, please." Both the modal construction *I'd like* as well as the politeness marker *please* are presented as expected features when placing food orders. The goal of teaching politeness to beginning EFL learners is attained by introducing routine phrases that are conventionally associated with softening the illocutionary force of a directive. Since German learners of English seem to prefer more direct expressions of requests (House, 2005, 2006), their attention needs to be drawn to how they phrase their requests or express their wishes. However, a linear form-function mapping can be problematic in cases where the situational circumstances require a direct utterance due to reasons of expediency or urgency. In CT 3 (p. 86, No. LG3) a number of parents' statements are presented (together with a drawing) and the instructions ask students to make them more polite using the modal constructions *should (not)/ought (not)*. One situation depicts a mother telling her child who is riding a tricycle on the street: "Don't ride in the middle of the road! It's dangerous!" The exercise suggests being polite by lowering the level of directness regardless of the circumstances. Here, politeness conflicts with issues of safety and urgency, which make a direct, explicit, and perhaps authoritative order perfectly acceptable (cf. Brown & Levinson, 1987). Instances like these mislead learners into thinking that modal auxiliaries are the essence of politeness, when in fact they are not always the norm of appropriate behavior (cf. White, 1993).

## Tasks on politeness

Tasks are central to the learning of a foreign language (Ellis, 2003). They require learners to function primarily as language users, generating language processes that resemble those involved in real-world activities. Textbook tasks with a clear focus on politeness are rather rare. Textbooks sometimes have listening tasks in which learners listen to a spoken text played from a CD and note down what they hear. In CT 5 (p. 61, No. A4) the difference between American and German conversational behavior is discussed. The instructions first inform learners about differences in politeness between English and German given in (4).

(4)

> One reason why native speakers of English sometimes think Germans are rude, impolite or even aggressive is because many Germans have not learned to use everyday phrases and expressions which express politeness in English. Listen carefully to the dialogues on CD. Say what the situations are and note down phrases that make the dialogues sound polite.   CT 5 (p. 61, No. A4)

In addition to collecting expressions used to express politeness, students are asked to remember the situations in which they are used. The results of this listening-comprehension task are collected in class, followed by a task in which learners use these phrases to say what they would do in a given situation (e.g., reject an invitation to a party, request to check emails at someone else's house). The information about the context is limited, because learners do not know whose party or house is meant. This lack of specific contextual information prevents learners from producing speech acts in accordance with the situation.

More typical textbook tasks include role-plays and dialogs. These are interactive, conversation-like and thus more authentic forms of language use. They ask learners to employ their pragmalinguistic repertoire for a spoken activity about a specific topic. In EG 21 (A 5, p. 37) two students have to perform a telephone call, requesting information about courses at a language school in the US. One student acts as the person at the information desk and the second inquires about the courses. Prior to this, students have been taught language to ask for and give information, with special emphasis on politeness and indirectness. Metapragmatic information given as advice and highlighted with a different color on the same page reads: "When talking English to someone you don't know, you should always try to be polite. English-speakers often find Germans too direct, which makes them sound impolite" (EG 21, A 5, p. 37, No. P3f). This issue of German's level of directness is openly addressed in EFL textbooks, as a reason for pragmatic divergence in intercultural situations (cf. House, 2005, 2006). House (2006) claims "there is converging evidence that Germans prefer more direct expressions when complaining or making a request" (p. 251), a pattern that is also noticeable in other speech act utterances and conversational situations. The practice of verbal routines that English native speakers commonly have available in their pragmatic repertoire is one aspect that EFL textbooks try integrate into the teaching of politeness.

Pragmalinguistic competence receives more attention via teaching language options to perform pragmatic actions than sociopragmatic competence. Knowledge and skills to assess the contextual factors that influence language choices and to make appropriate choices given a particular goal in a particular setting is almost completely ignored. One exception found in the textbook corpus occurs in GL 6 (p. 74) on a page entitled "Avoiding social gaffes in the US."

(5)

> People you've just recently met might say, "We should go to lunch together!" This, though, is not the moment to say "OK, when?" It's just something nice to say, like "How are you?" GL 6 (p. 74)

Here, learners find a list of typical American behaviors, for first time travelers. The sociopragmatic task following the information in the box asks learners to discuss what aspects of American politeness are similar and different to their own country. Clearly, performing this kind of task in the classroom presupposes a sufficient proficiency in English if discussions are conducted in the target language (which is why the task occurs in volume 6 for upper-intermediate learners). The goal of questions like these is to raise learners' awareness. Drawing comparisons provides access to a level of awareness about how the native and target culture value rules of politeness in a similar or different way (cf. Holmes & Brown, 1987; Ishihara & Cohen, 2010). Knowledge about target culture norms when having a conversation, discussing a topic, going shopping or eating in a restaurant has to be explicitly taught, but not every EFL textbook series provides this kind of instruction.

## Metapragmatic information on politeness

The kind of information textbooks provide on the function of certain expressions that communicate politeness as well as information about the significance of politeness in certain situations or cultures is part a metapragmatic knowledge for learners (cf. Eelen, 2001; Watts, 2003). Textbook users can find this information next to an exercise or task in a unit or study skills section, most often highlighted in a framed text or with a different color. Due to space limitations, the quality and amount of metapragmatic information is restricted. Condensed to intercultural suggestions and short comments, all three German EFL textbook series remind their learners to

a) use the modal verbs *may* and *can* to ask politely for permission or to request something
b) use *please* to utter a request politely
c) use *sorry* and *excuse me* as polite forms to address or interrupt somebody

In CT 1 (first year of English) in a section called "How to talk," learners are advised "to always be friendly and polite. ...When you say *please* and *thank you*, others will understand and help you" (p. 123). The corresponding utterance given underneath this advice is "Excuse me? Can you help me, please? Thank you!" The comment prompts beginning learners to use these formulaic lexical items in order to appear friendly towards others. EFL textbooks tend to teach these comments as maxims to be followed, but do not mention consequences of inappropriate behavior.

Linguistic markers of politeness, specific modal constructions, and the use of verbal routines are features that have been closely connected to politeness in traditional pragmatics studies (e.g., Blum-Kulka, House, & Kasper, 1989; Brown & Levinson, 1987). They seem to constitute a viable way of operationalizing the concept of politeness for a textbook teaching approach. Metapragmatic suggestions like (a-c) above indicate that textbooks understand politeness as an inherent property of a particular language choice without defining explicitly what politeness is. Further comments on what is considered polite in English include

d) *Greetings* are polite (*Hello, How are you*) (EG 21 A2, p. 96; CT 3, p. 129)
e) *Question tags* are polite (*isn't it, haven't you*) (EG 21 A2, p. 86)
f) Small talk is polite (GL 4, p. 51)
g) Responses in more than one utterance are considered to be polite (EG 21 A2, p. 96)

Specific syntactic constructions can also be used to express politeness:

- h) *I'd like* is polite, *I want* is not so polite (GL 1, p. 84)
- i) With phrases like *Could you... Would you...* and *Please* you can change the register from casual to polite. (GL 4, p. 88)
- j) *Have you got* is more polite than *I need* (GL 1, p. 84)

Genre-specific comments on politeness include

- k) Writing a formal letter: Whenever you write a formal letter, the language and style should be polite and factual. (GL 6, p. 114)
- l) In a debate: Even if you strongly disagree, always express yourself politely. (GL 4, p. 108)
- m) Having a discussion: Be polite. Do not interrupt. Attack the arguments of the other side, but not the people. (GL 6, p. 123; CT 6, p. 95)
- n) Giving feedback to a presentation/a written text: Give your feedback in a polite way. First tell the presenter/writer what you think s/he did well.(CT 4, p. 133)

Culture-specific information on politeness includes

- o) You can say "Native Americans" or "Indians" to talk about the people who were living in America when the Europeans arrived, but "Native Americans" is more polite. (GL 4, p. 46)
- p) For Americans it's very important to be friendly and polite to each other in public. (GL 4, p. 51)
- q) In the US, you are often asked things that sound personal, but they are just polite. (GL 4, p. 51)
- r) The American way is to be polite: Americans are very friendly and polite—and expect the same from visitors to their country. (GL 6, p. 74)
- s) If you are staying with an exchange family in the US, your language register must be extremely polite—but friendly! (GL 6, p. 123)
- t) If you don't know which register to use (formal? informal?), it is better to be more formal, i.e., more polite. Using language that is too informal is impolite in the UK and the US. (GL 6, p. 123)

Finally, general (non-linguistic) politeness comments found in German EFL textbooks remind learners to be polite

- u) when talking English to someone you don't know (EG A5, p. 37)
- v) in public (e.g., restaurants) (GL 2, p. 41)
- w) at lunch/dinner tables (with host families) (GL 3, p. 44)
- x) when you want something from somebody (EG 21 A1, p. 130)
- y) in encounters with people from other cultures (GL 5, 86)

All of these metapragmatic comments function as advice for learners, reminding them to pay attention to specific constructions to express politeness and behaving in a polite way in foreign situations or towards English speakers. The comments are given in English and are scattered across different textbook series and volumes. In sum, they seem to capture many important aspects of politeness, but they differ in quality. Some are very general hints on how to behave in public situations or with strangers (e.g., u-y) and some points are more specific, addressing research-supported findings on politeness (e.g., a-f; Blum-Kulka, House, & Kasper, 1989; Brown & Levinson, 1987).

Despite the usefulness of drawing learners' attention towards polite language and behavior, metapragmatic comments can also be problematic if they tend to generalize politeness rules (e.g., l, t, x) or simplify them (e.g., g, l). For instance, in a heated debate with friends it can be perfectly acceptable to disagree in a way that may be seen as "not so polite" (l). Similarly, sometimes utterances only consist of one word or a simple backchanneling token that is appropriate as a response to the the prior turn (g). In other words, learners may falsely infer from these comments a politeness rule that is generally applicable. It seems that for the sake of clarity and caution, textbooks advise their learners to choose politeness as a reliable way of behaving in intercultural situations, but do not deliver necessary details to help learners understand those conventions. The effect of such information on learners' politeness is difficult to assess, but the amount of metapragmatic input is fairly low if only one textbook series is considered or even only one volume of a series is used in class for teaching.

### Lexical input on politeness

In addition to maxims and strategies, EFL textbooks provide useful phrases and expressions as language input for the politeness repertoire of students. For example, GL 6 (p. 123) provides sixth-year learners a list of polite phrases in (6).

**(6)**

    Polite phrases: please • thank you • you're welcome • not at all • please do

                                                                                                               GL 6 (p. 123)

Third-year learners of English find a framed text in CT 3 with polite phrases to conduct an interview (p. 129).

**(7)**

    Would you mind if I asked you a few questions?
    May I ask you a few questions?
    Could you please tell me...?
    I'm sorry, I didn't quite understand. Could you say that again/explain it, please?
    Thank you very much for talking to me.
    Thank you for your time.                                                 GL 6 (p. 129)

GL 1 (p. 84) presents first-year learners with useful phrases as in (8).

**(8)**

    I'd/We'd like (to)..., please
    Can you show/give me...?
    Can I..., please
    Have you got...?
    Excuse me, do you sell...?                        GL 6 (p. 84)

Sometimes textbooks offer these phrases in connection with an exercise or task that students have to do, thus placing them on the same page as linguistic scaffolding for politeness. In addition, they can be also found in specific study skills sections at the end of these textbooks, which summarize and explain a specific skill, so that learners can go back and review input and rules. A potential problem of the latter presentation is that often these sections are not integrated into classroom teaching. They serve as background information and as additional reference for students to consult when doing assignments on their own. The learning effect of this linguistic input thus depends solely on the students and their initiative to read more about polite words and expressions.

## Conclusion

Politeness in German EFL textbooks is presented as a form of behavior in interpersonal relationships that is achieved by using certain phrases and expressions conventionally expected in the target language. These expressions show concern for the addressee and make the speaker appear less obtrusive and more indirect, especially when uttering a directive speech act. Politeness reduces the force of an illocution by using, for example, modal constructions and politeness markers (e.g., "please"). This textbook approach embodies a traditional concept of politeness, following Brown and Levinson's (1987) face-saving work, which provides a rigid and operationalizable framework upon which to build students' politeness competence.

Not surprisingly, the approach to teaching politeness is primarily form-focused. Many cases in which politeness is addressed in EFL textbooks consist of language exercises in which politeness is mapped to a linguistic form. Especially at beginner levels, some of these textbooks tend to suggest outright that certain words and phrases are intrinsically polite regardless of their use in context ("please," "thank you," "sorry"). Activities that textbooks offer provide pragmalinguistic choices for students to perform a communicative function, such as requesting, discussing, or giving feedback. The types of activities range from identifying polite language (either from a given list of utterances or from an audio-recorded dialog), contrasting it with "not so polite" language, matching polite phrases with corresponding situations, and formulating as well as modifying isolated utterances in a more polite way (which are apparently too direct and impolite). Production-oriented activities, mostly in the form of role-play tasks for intermediate and advanced learners, include conducting a conversation or having a discussion in class and, in doing so, employing conventionalized formulas from the textbook that make the speaker appear more indirect and friendly. Language scaffolding, offering useful phrases to be polite, is often found underneath or next to an exercise. It serves as a word or phrase bank to help students perform the language assignment successfully.

The raw number of politeness-oriented activities and explicit references to politeness in German EFL textbooks is fairly low (cf. Table 2). Even though these numbers are more promising than what previous textbook research has found (cf. LoCastro, 1997; Vellenga, 2004), politeness is more often an *implicit* learning outcome of communicative tasks and interactive activities. That means it is not highlighted in the text or introduced as being the goal of an assignment, but the communicative activity expects a certain level of politeness according to the given situation (e.g., when asking for and giving directions). Teachers must be aware of this treatment and point out to their learners that language choices are subject to socio-cultural constraints and that politeness is not automatically communicated with specific words or phrases. Many of the exercises in textbooks provide no cues about the context of language use. The focus lies on formal aspects and learners are not asked to reflect upon language choices based on social constraints. Pragmalinguistic aspects of politeness receive more attention than sociopragmatic aspects, the latter of which is almost completely neglected in German EFL textbooks (for one exception see (5)). Awareness raising tasks, which attempt "to sensitize learners to context-based variation in language use and the variables that help determine that variation" (Rose, 1994, p. 57), are almost absent in the textbook corpus. The importance of contextual variables in discussing politeness is not adequately represented and very few opportunities are created for learners to discuss how one's choice of language both affects and is affected by the social relationship between interlocutors (cf. Vellenga, 2004; Ogiermann, 2013). Also, the impact of intonation and non-verbal conduct on politeness is completely ignored. While sociopragmatic tasks and exercises are "a far more thorny issue to deal with in the classroom" (Rose & Kasper, 2001, p. 3), this challenge should not be an excuse for a lack of treatment in textbooks.

Despite some differences in their treatment of politeness, none of the three textbook series investigated in this study offers a systematic, recurrent treatment of politeness as a pragmatic phenomenon, that is, one that gradually builds up learners' competence to communicate in context-adequate and polite ways in the course of their foreign language education in secondary school. If teachers only use one series in their classes, the explicit exposure to politeness is fairly limited. Learners' sociopragmatic skills are not sufficiently addressed. However, politeness is also not ignored (but, cf., LoCastro, 1997). It appears in different forms, spread across different volumes for beginners, intermediate and upper-intermediate/advanced learners of English. In textbooks that follow an integrated skills approach, politeness is one of many teaching objectives. But none of the textbooks analyzed here provides sufficient input and language activities to do justice to the importance of this pragmatic phenomenon. If teachers are not bound to using a specific textbook, they are free to combine and adapt input and activities for their learners (cf. Ishihara & Cohen, 2010).

Research in pragmatics teaching has repeatedly pointed out the benefits of explicit instruction with attention to both linguistic form and its relationship to contextual factors (Bardovi-Harlig et al., 2015; Rose, 2005; Takahashi, 2001). It seems that EFL textbook publishers could do more to integrate this knowledge into their material and offer more tasks and exercises that help learners express and interpret politeness as well as reflect upon the value of politeness in specific contexts. This study has made an attempt to review politeness teaching in EFL textbooks because classroom teaching is often guided by material from these books. It calls for further analyses of EFL textbooks, for different learners and classroom contexts. Additionally, research has to find out how EFL teachers actually use these textbooks in class and how they implement exercises and tasks during lessons. This study cannot make any claims about textbook usage. Nevertheless, EFL teachers have to be aware of what their textbooks offer, discuss politeness conventions with their students, and provide further activities to raise their awareness of politeness and its significance for pragmatic competence. Texts and assignments that do not address politeness adequately need to be supplemented with authentic material from TV shows (available on DVD or via internet streaming services), special websites (e.g., the Center for Advanced Research on Language Acquisition [CARLA] website hosted at the University of Minnesota) and free language corpora (e.g., The Michigan Corpus of Academic Spoken English–MICASE). Textbook writers and classroom teachers both take their responsibility to develop learners' pragmatic competence; on the one hand in designing authentic and appropriate materials and, on the other hand, in using and adapting these for communicative practices inside and outside the classroom.

## Notes

1   The term foreign language (FL) as opposed to second language (L2) is used here to refer to language teaching and learning in a (secondary) school context in which the target language English has no official internal use
2   Edmondson and House (1982) point out that "appropriateness cannot be examined without taking politeness into consideration" (p. 219, *translation mine*), so that when appropriateness is defined as a teaching objective, politeness has to be inevitably approximated.
3   Mugford (2008, this volume) argues that L2 users also have a right to be impolite and that impoliteness has to be taught in the L2 classroom because learners will be confronted with it in target-language contexts.

4   A type of secondary school that prepares students for university education.
5   Note that textbooks for beginners avoid postulating a distinction between polite and impolite, but rather paraphrase the opposite as "not so polite." The word *impolite* is introduced in a later volume (4/5).

## References

Alcón Soler, E. (2005). Does instruction work for learning pragmatics in the EFL context? *System, 33*, 417–435.
Bardovi-Harlig, K. (1999). The interlanguage of interlanguage pragmatics: A research agenda for acquisitional pragmatics. *Language Learning, 49*, 677–713.
Bardovi-Harlig, K. (2013). Developing L2 pragmatics. *Language Learning, 63*(s1), 68–86.
Bardovi-Harlig, K. (2015). Operationalizing conversation in studies of instructional effect in L2 pragmatics. *System, 48*, 21–34.
Bardovi-Harlig, K., Hartford, B. A. S., Mahan-Taylor, R., Morgan, M. J., & Reynolds, D. W. (1991). Developing pragmatic awareness: Closing the conversation. *ELT Journal, 45*, 4–15.
Bardovi-Harlig, K., & Mahan-Taylor, R. (2003). *Teaching pragmatics*. Washington, DC: United States Department of State.
Bardovi-Harlig, K., Mossman, S., & Vellenga, H. E. (2015). The effect of instruction on pragmatic routines in academic discussion. *Language Teaching Research, 19*, 324–350.
Barron, A. (2003). *Second language acquisition in a study abroad context*. Amsterdam: John Benjamins.
Barron, A., & Warga, M. (2007). Acquisitional pragmatics: Focus on foreign language learners. *Intercultural Pragmatics, 4*, 113–127.
Blum-Kulka, S., House, J., & Kasper, G. (Eds.). (1989). *Cross-cultural pragmatics: Requests and apologies*. Norwood, NJ: Ablex
Bou-Franch, P., & Garcés-Conejos, P. (2003). Teaching linguistic politeness: A methodological proposal. *International Review of Applied Linguistics, 41*, 1–22.
Boxer, D., & Pickering, L. (1995). Problems in the presentation of speech acts in ELT materials: The case of complaints. *ELT Journal, 49*, 44–58.
Brown, P. (2011). Politeness. In P. H. Hogan (Ed.), *The Cambridge encyclopedia of language sciences* (pp. 635–636). Cambridge: Cambridge University Press.
Brown, P., & Levinson, S. C. (1987). *Politeness: Some universals in language usage*. Cambridge, Cambridge University Press.
Buchreport (2014, May). Die 100 größten Verlage in Deutschland, Österreich und der Schweiz [The top 100 publishing houses in Germany, Austria and Switzerland]. Retrieved from http://www.buchreport.de/analysen/100_groesste_verlage.htm?no_cache=1
Byrd, P., & Schuemann, C. (2014). English as a second/foreign language textbooks: How to choose them—how to use them. In M. Celce-Murcia, D. M. Brinton, & M. A. Snow

(Eds.), *Teaching English as a second or foreign language* (4th ed., pp. 380–393). Boston, MA: National Geographic Learning.

Cohen, A. D. (2005). Strategies for learning and performing L2 speech acts. *Intercultural Pragmatics, 2*, 275–301. doi: 10.1515/iprg.2005.2.3.275

Crandall, E., & Basturkmen, H. (2004). Evaluating pragmatics-focused materials. *ELT Journal, 58*, 38–49.

Culpeper, J. (2011). Politeness and impoliteness. In G. Andersen & K. Aijmer (Eds.), *Pragmatics of society* (pp. 393–438). Berlin: Mouton de Gruyter.

Edelhoff, C. (Ed.) (2005). *Camden Town Gymnasium* (Vol. 1–6.).Braunschweig: Diesterweg.

Eelen, G. (2001). *A critique of politeness theories*. Manchester: St. Jerome Publishing.

Edmondson, W., & House, J. (1982). Höflichkeit als Lernziel im Englischunterricht [Politeness as a learning objective in ELT]. *Neusprachliche Mitteilungen aus Wissenschaft und Praxis, 35*, 218–227.

Ellis, R. (2003). *Task-based language learning and teaching*. Oxford: Oxford University Press.

Félix-Brasdefer, J. C. (2004). Interlanguage refusals: Linguistic politeness and length of residence in the target community. *Language Learning, 54*, 587–653.

Félix-Brasdefer, J. C. (2006). Teaching the negotiation of multi-turn speech acts: Using conversation-analytic tools to teach pragmatics in the FL classroom. In K. Bardovi-Harlig, J. C. Félix-Brasdefer, & A. S. Omar (Eds.), *Pragmatics and language learning* (Vol. 11, pp. 165–197). Honolulu: National Foreign Language Resource Center, University of Hawai'i at Mānoa.

Ficzere, E. (2014). Usefulness of teaching politeness strategies in English language classrooms. *Baltic Journal of English Language, Literature and Culture, 4*, 30–43. Retrieved from http://www.lu.lv/fileadmin/user_upload/lu_portal/apgads/PDF/BJELLC-4_2014_01.pdf

Fraser, B. (1990). Perspectives on politeness. *Journal of Pragmatics, 14*, 219–236.

Glaser, K. (2014). *Inductive or deductive?: The impact of method of instruction on the acquisition of pragmatic competence in EFL*. Newcastle upon Tyne: Cambridge Scholars Publishing.

Goffman, E. (1967). *Interaction ritual*. Chicago, IL: Aldine Publishing.

Holmes, J., & Brown, D. F. (1987). Teachers and students learning about compliments. *TESOL Quarterly, 21*, 116–139.

Houck, N. R., & Tatsuki, D. H. (Ed.) (2011). *Pragmatics: Teaching natural conversation*. Alexandria, VA: Teachers of English to Speakers of Other Languages.

House, J. (1996). Developing pragmatic fluency in English as a foreign language: Routines and metapragmatic awareness. *Studies in Second Language Acquisition, 18*, 225–252.

House, J. (2005). Politeness in Germany: Politeness in GERMANY? In L. Hickey & M. Stewart (Eds.), *Politeness in Europe* (pp. 13–28). Clevedon, England: Multilingual Matters.

House, J. (2006). Communicative styles in English and German. *European Journal of English Studies, 10,* 249–267.

Howard, A. M. (2003). Politeness is more than "please." In K. Bardovi-Harlig & R. Mahan-Taylor (Eds.). *Teaching pragmatics (chapter 2).* Washington, DC: United States Department of State. Retrieved from http://www.indiana.edu/~dsls/publications/HowardRev.pdf

Hutchinson, T., & Torres, E. (1994). The textbook as agent of change. *ELT Journal, 48,* 315–328.

Ishihara, N., & Cohen, A. D. (2010). *Teaching and learning pragmatics.* London: Longman.

Kádár, D. Z., & Haugh, M. (2013). *Understanding politeness.* Cambridge: Cambridge University Press.

Kasper, G. (1990). Linguistic politeness: Current research issues. *Journal of Pragmatics, 14,* 193–218.

Kasper, G. (1995). Wessen Pragmatik? Für eine Neubestimmung fremdsprachlicher Handlungskompetenz [Whose pragmatics? Towards a redefinition of pragmatic competence in a foreign language]. *Zeitschrift für Fremdsprachenforschung, 6,* 69–94.

Kasper, G. (1997). Can pragmatic competence be taught? *NFLRC Network* #6. Honolulu: Second Language Teaching & Curriculum Center, University of Hawai'i. Retrieved from http://nflrc.hawaii.edu/networks/NW06/default.html

Kasper, G. (2001). Classroom research on interlanguage pragmatics. In K. Rose & G. Kasper (Eds.), *Pragmatics in language teaching* (pp. 33–62). Cambridge: Cambridge University Press.

Lakoff, R. (1973). The logic of politeness; or, minding your p's and q's. In C. Corum, T. Smith-Stark, & A. Weiser (Eds.), *Papers from the ninth regional meeting of the Chicago Linguistic Society* (pp. 292–305). Chicago, IL: Chicago Linguistic Society.

Lakoff, R. (1975). *Language and woman's place.* New York, NY: Harper and Row.

Leech, G. N. (1983). *Principles of pragmatics.* London: Longman.

Limberg, H. (in press). Teaching how to apologize: EFL textbooks and pragmatic input. *Language Teaching Research.* doi: 10.1177/1362168815590695

LoCastro, V. (1997). Politeness and pragmatic competence in foreign language education. *Language Teaching Research, 1,* 239–267.

LoCastro, V. (2012). *Pragmatics for language educators: A sociolinguistic perspective.* New York: Routledge.

Locher, M. A., & Watts, R. J. (2005). Politeness theory and relational work. *Journal of Politeness Research, 1,* 9–33.

Lörscher, W., & Schulze, R. (1988). On polite speaking and foreign language classroom discourse. *IRAL, 26,* 183–199.

Martínez-Flor, A., & Usó-Juan, E. (2010). The teaching of speech acts in second and foreign language instructional contexts. In A. Trosborg (Ed.), *Pragmatics across languages and cultures* (pp. 423–442). Berlin: Mouton de Gruyter.

Meier, A. (1995). Defining politeness: Universality in appropriateness. *Language Sciences, 17*, 345–356.

Meier, A. (1997). Teaching the universals of politeness. *ELT Journal, 51*, 21–28.

Mugford, G. (2008). How rude! Teaching impoliteness in the second-language classroom. *ELT Journal, 62*, 375–384.

Ogiermann, E. (2010). Teaching politeness with Green Line New? In M. Engelhardt & W. Gehring (Eds.), *Fremdsprachendidaktik: Neue Aspekte in Forschung und Lehre* [Foreign language pedagogy: New perspectives in research and teaching] (pp. 117–134). Oldenburg, Holstein: BIS Verlag.

Ogiermann, E. (2013). On pragmatic input in Green Line New. In E. Karagiannidou, C.-O. Papadopoulou, & E. Skourtou (Eds.), Language diversity and language learning: New paths to literacy. In E. Karagiannidou, C.-O. Papadopoulou, & E. Skourtou (Eds.), *Proceedings of the 42nd linguistics colloquium in Rhodos 2007* (pp. 451–460). Frankfurt: Peter Lang.

Padilla Cruz, M. (2013). An integrative proposal to teach the pragmatics of phatic communion in ESL classes. *Intercultural Pragmatics, 10*, 131–160.

Petraki, E., & Bayes, S. (2013). Teaching oral requests: An evaluation of five English as a second language coursebooks. *Pragmatics, 23*, 499–517.

Phillips, E. M. (1993). Polite requests: Second language textbooks and learners of French. *Foreign Language Annals, 26*, 372–381.

Rose, K. R. (1994). Pragmatic consciousness-raising in an EFL context. In L. Bouton & Y. Kachru (Eds.), *Pragmatics and language learning* (Vol. 5, pp. 52–63). Urbana-Champaign: University of Illinois.

Rose, K. R. (2005). On the effects of instruction in second language pragmatics. *System, 33*, 385–399.

Rose, K. R., & Kasper, G. (2001). *Pragmatics in language teaching*. Cambridge: Cambridge University Press.

Saville-Troike, M. (1996). The ethnography of communication. In S. L. McKay & N. H. Hornberger (Eds.), *Sociolinguistics and language teaching* (pp. 351–82). Cambridge: Cambridge University Press.

Schmidt, R. (1993). Consciousness, learning and interlanguage pragmatics. In G. Kasper & S. Blum-Kulka (Eds.), *Interlanguage pragmatics* (pp. 21–42). Oxford: Oxford University Press.

Schubert, C. (2006). Politeness rules: Pragmatic approaches to intercultural competence in the EFL classroom. In W. Delanoy & L. Volkmann (Eds.), *Cultural studies in the EFL classroom* (pp. 195–209). Heidelberg: Universitätsverlag Winter.

Schwarz, H. (Ed.). (2006–2011). *English G 21. A1-A6*. Berlin: Cornelsen.

Taguchi, N. (2011). Teaching pragmatics: Trends and issues. *Annual Review of Applied Linguistics, 31*, 289–310.

Takahashi, S. (2001). The role of input enhancement in developing pragmatic competence. In K.R., Rose & G. Kasper (Eds.), *Pragmatics in language teaching* (pp. 171–199). Cambridge: Cambridge University Press.

Tatsuki, D. H., & Houck, N. R. (2010). *Pragmatics: Teaching speech acts.* Alexandria, VA: Teachers of English to Speakers of Other Languages.

Thomas, J. (1983). Cross-cultural pragmatic failure. *Applied Linguistics, 4,* 91–112.

Thomas, J. (1995). *Meaning in interaction: An introduction to pragmatics.* London: Longman.

Usó Juan, E., & Martínez Flor, A. (2008). Teaching learners to appropriately mitigate requests. *ELT Journal, 62,* 349–357.

Vellenga, H. (2004). Learning pragmatics from ESL & EFL textbooks: How likely? *TESL-EJ, 8*(2), A-3.

Watts, R. (2003). *Politeness.* Cambridge: Cambridge University Press.

Weisshaar, H. (Ed.). (2006–2010). *Green Line.* Vol 1–6. Stuttgart: Klett.

Williams, M. (1988). Language taught for meetings and language used in meetings: Is there anything in common? *Applied Linguistics, 9,* 45–58.

White, R. (1993). Saying please: Pragmalinguistic failure in English interaction. *ELT Journal, 47,* 193–202.

# A Research-based Teaching Unit for ESL/EFL Students: Responses to Gratitude

Sara Gesuato
Università di Padova, Italy

*The study explores responses to gratitude as expressed in elicited oral interaction (open role-plays) by native speakers of American English. It first gives an overview of the conventions of means and conventions of forms of the head acts and supporting moves of these reacting speech acts, and reports on their frequency of occurrence and combinatorial options across situations differing in terms of the social distance and power relationships between the interactants. It then presents a proposal for familiarizing ESL/EFL students with the speech act of responding to gratitude.*

## Introduction

Learners do not easily acquire the pragmatics (i.e., rules about the use) of the target language on their own, and pragmatic failure (i.e., failure to conform to the often unconscious, but deeply felt, communicative rules of a language or culture) may negatively reflect on the speaker/writer as a social being. Students need to realize that communicating is a form of action, informed by cultural and contextual variables, and to realize that speech acts (i.e., communicative functions) are performed differently within and across languages and cultures. Instruction may contribute to learners' awareness of rules of communication, thus increasing the accuracy of their linguistic output and improving their confidence. In particular, instruction is important when dealing with a speech act that fulfills a social function, even if realized through formulaic expressions, precisely because it answers basic interactional needs. Responding to gratitude is a case in point.

Responding to gratitude is a harmony-preserving speech act: It restores the balance of debts and credits between interlocutors, and can also work as an interaction-closing device. Due to its role as a social lubricant and conversational boundary marker, second language (L2) learners should be alerted to the variety and potential complexity of its realization, which may otherwise go unnoticed, as well as be informed of its contextual appropriateness, so as to prevent misunderstandings and discomfort in interaction. At the same time, the morpho-syntactic simplicity of the formulas encoding responses to gratitude makes these speech acts relatively accessible to students both in comprehension and in production activities, and thus an appropriate object of study. This paper presents findings from a study of the production of responses to gratitude by 12 college-age speakers of American English to provide authentic language samples for teaching (Bardovi-Harlig, Mossman, & Vellenga, 2014; Félix-Brasdefer & Cohen, 2012).

### Research on responses to gratitude

Cross-linguistic findings consistently report that speakers use one or more of three main strategies in responses to gratitude: Minimizing, or denying (the magnitude of) the object of gratitude to the favor-doer (e.g., *No problem*); Expressing a favorable disposition, that is, indicating the willingness to be at the thanker's "service" (e.g., *You're welcome*; *Je vous en prie* 'You're welcome'); and Expressing pleasure at providing the benefit (e.g., *My pleasure*; see Aijmer, 1996; Ameka, 2006; Coulmas, 1981; Edmondson & House, 1981; Farenkia, 2012; Kerbrat-Orecchioni, 1997, 2005; Ohashi, 2008a, 2008b). Studies also reveal that responses to gratitude occasionally instantiate additional strategies (see, e.g., Colston, 2002; Curikova, 2008; Jacobsson, 2002; Katz, Lenhardt, & Mitchell, 2007; Ouafeu, 2009), that they vary in their degree of elaboration (e.g., they may include multiple head acts and/or supporting moves) and lexical-morphological encoding (i.e., the same function may be worded in various ways), and that their content and formulation are not perceived as equivalent in meaning and effectiveness across contexts.

Research on responses to gratitude in English is mostly based on written data from dialog completion tasks (DCTs), with only a few studies considering spontaneous interactive data (Eisenstein & Bodman, 1993; Jung, 1994, in part; Rüegg, 2014), while Edmondson and House (1981), which analyses role-play data, only briefly touches on the topic. This study considers responses to gratitude occurring in elicited oral interaction (i.e., open mimetic role-plays; Kasper 2000: 288). After briefly reporting on the frequency of occurrence of their strategies and formulations, and their distribution across situations varying in interactants' social distance and power relationships, it presents a proposal for teaching responses to gratitude in a higher education ESL/EFL teaching context on the basis of the findings of that investigation.

## Response to gratitude data

The data considered consists of the transcripts 32 role-play interactions (about 9,000 words) collected from 12 American university students. The elicitation material included descriptions of scenarios representing two interactants in the roles of beneficiary versus benefactor—and thus likely to trigger the instantiation of thanking exchanges—and comprised distinct prompts for the two participant roles.

The scenario descriptions comprised adaptations of communicative situations found in the literature of the speech act of thanking (Eisenstein & Bodman, 1986; Held, 1996), but mostly outlined real-life events experienced by me as a participant or witness. The scenario descriptions were relevant to different role-relationships in terms of the addressees' social distance (close, –D vs. distant, +D) and degree of power (equal, =P vs. subordinate, –P vs. superior, +P), while the level of imposition (i.e., cost or magnitude of the benefit) was kept constant (i.e., high).

The dialogues, recorded in a sound-proof booth, were transcribed by a native speaker and proofread by me. Four were discarded due to lack of genuine thanking exchanges. A sample scenario description and a relevant transcript are provided below. In the transcript and later excerpts, bold indicates the expressions of gratitude and italics indicate the responses to gratitude.

### Scenario TH-O1-A5: "Maths exam" (Set A: thanking intimate and equal thankees)

> A: A friend helped you to study for a demanding maths exam. A few days ago you sat for the exam and received a good mark on it. Today you call up your friend to let her/him know.
> B: You helped a friend prepare for a demanding maths exam. He/she was supposed to take it a few days ago. Today you receive a call from him/her.

## Transcript TH-O1-A5-01 "Maths exam" (added emphasis)

A: Hey Emma, I just wanted to thank you for helping me study for that hard math test I had a couple of days ago, I got a really good grade on it so, I appreciate your help.
B: *Oh you're welcome Rosina, I was happy to know that you wanted my help and, I'm always here to help you out with that kind of stuff.*
A: So do you have anything that you want me to do as a favor in return?
B: Maybe you could help me with my English test?
A: Ok, sounds good!
B: Alright, talk to you later.
A: Bye!

Gratitude expressions, with or without the objects of gratitude specified, and directly relevant replies (i.e., text segments referring to the benefit or its circumstances and/or a positive attitude towards it)[1] were identified in sequences of turns as in the following excerpts from TH-O1-C3-01 "Babysitting."

B: Hi Mrs Shee, I see that you're back.
A: Hey, Wan. Hey **so thanks for er, babysitting my er, child.**

B: **Thank you very much, Mrs Shee.**
A: *Oh, you're welcome.*

A: Um, **thank, thank you again for...** **helping**, um, like I hope you can like, help us babysit, um, Charlotte... in the future.
B: *Of course. I really enjoy... babysit*ting *her.*

Each response to gratitude was then classified by adapting Schneider's (2005) model, in terms of strategies, that is, functions; formulation types, that is, broad lexico-semantic notions; and specific realizations, that is, surface formulations. The strategies specify the functions performed by the speaker; the formulation types encode the key term or notion relevant to a set of specific realizations, or identify its relevant semantic field; and the specific realizations are the actual instances of responses to gratitude. I applied the tripartite classification scheme to both the head acts and, where present, the supporting moves of responses to gratitude. In what follows, strategies appear in regular type, formulation types in square brackets, and specific realizations in italics.

The data exemplify five head act strategies. The first, Agreeing/Confirming, ratifies (the validity of) the previous gratitude expression by confirming the provision of the benefit and acknowledging the receipt and adequacy of thanking.

It includes the formulation type [yes] (e.g., *Yeah; Ok; Ah, Sure; Mmh mmh*). Positive evaluation expresses the thankee's view on or attitude toward the benefit. It comprises the formulation type [emotional impact]—which conveys how the thankee feels as a result of learning of the positive effect of the benefit, and involves the use of adjectives of emotional experience like *glad* and *happy* (e.g., *Glad to hear that*)—and the type [aesthetic appreciation]—characterized by the use of adjectives that rate the benefit as good (e.g., *It was nice meeting you too*). Making the other feel good shows glad acceptance of and willingness to help the interlocutor through the formulation type [welcome] (e.g., *You're welcome*). Minimizing indebtedness reassures the addressee they do not need to reciprocate a non-costly benefit. Its formulation type is [no problem] (e.g., *No worries*). Reciprocating manifests the thankee's positive reacting attitude towards the thanker, perceived as a co-benefactor. Its formulation type is [thanks] (e.g., *Thank you*).

The supporting moves also exemplify five strategies. Offer indicates the speaker's willingness to provide, or signals the accessibility of, a product/service. It includes the formulation types [I will] and [you can], which encode willingness/commitment and possibility/permission, respectively (e.g., *I'm always here to help you out...; Of course you're, you're welcome to come over [...]*). Good wish/Desire conveys the speaker's desire for something good to happen. The formulation types [may X be so] and [may X happen] refer to positive expectations about situations and events, respectively (e.g., *I hope your headache is better; I hope to see you again soon*). Concern/Interest serves to inquire about or check the suitability and likeability of the benefit. Its formulation types, [was X the case?] and [did X happen?], are relevant to positive situations and events, respectively (e.g., *I hope you, enjoyed our company and our little, cabin in the mountains*). Downplaying the benefit minimizes the perceived magnitude of the benefit. The formulation types, [good] or [obvious], serve to classify the benefit as enjoyable or as provided as a matter of course, respectively (e.g., *She's such a good kid!; that's, you know, that's...part of my job*). Background provides contextualizing information about the benefit. The formulation type [history] indicates how and under what circumstances the benefit was provided (e.g., *I didn't actually leave it there, I had er, the secretary, er, leave it [...]*); the type [previous knowledge], instead, refers to shared experiences, thus hinting at the social closeness between the interlocutors (e.g., *I knew you liked durians and starfruit*); and [preferences] encodes the speaker's general emotional motivation for acting generously (e.g., *You know, we love having you kids come through here*).

After elaborating my coding scheme, I determined the frequency of occurrence of strategies and formulation types of response-to-gratitude head acts and supporting moves in the overall corpus, mapping their distribution across the datasets, and describing their combinatorial options.

Out of 76 thanking exchanges identified, 46 (i.e., 60.2%), include responses to gratitude (i.e., on average, about 1.4 per transcript), these being fairly equally distributed across the scenario sets. Their frequency of occurrence is higher than that reported in studies based on spontaneously produced data (e.g., Aijmer, 1996; Rüegg, 2014), but lower than that reported in studies on elicited data (Schneider, 2005; Farenkia, 2012, 2013).

In the head acts, four strategies and as many formulation types (i.e., Agreeing/Confirming: [yes]; Positive evaluation, [emotional impact]; Making the other feel good, [welcome]; and Minimizing indebtedness, [no-problem]), account for the majority of the data (89.8%), and are instantiated in virtually all the datasets with comparable frequencies of occurrences (i.e., 12 to 15 tokens each): only Agreeing/Confirming is unattested in one dataset. Two general trends are identified: Positive evaluation and Making the other feel good are not favored with −P addressees, while Minimizing indebtedness and Reciprocating are not favored with =P addressees.

Only 12 responses to gratitude (i.e., 26.0%) encode supporting moves, and these occur almost exclusively after the head acts, and never alone (contra Schneider 2005; Farenkia 2012, 2013). No prominent functional-semantic pattern can be identified for them, however, given their few instantiations and the variety of strategies end encoding options realizing them, which tend to be context-specific (Schneider, 2005, p. 113).

Complex responses to gratitude are much less frequent than simple ones, being attested in 26.0% of all responses to gratitude, and in 15.7% of all thanking episodes. They include a combination of head acts (e.g., *Yeah, glad to help*; *Thank you! No problem*) or, more frequently, a combination of a head act with supporting moves (e.g., *Oh, it's no problem at all. I hope your headache is better*), findings that are in line with Schneider (2005) and Farenkia (2012, 2013). All datasets exemplify one or more supporting-move strategies and formulation types. However, none instantiates them all.

In line with previous research, this study confirms that responses to gratitude favor simple utterances, which realize one of a small set of strategies, and occur less frequently as combinations of strategies or a strategy plus support material. However, the frequency of occurrence of responses to gratitude, their distribution across situations, and the range of their attested strategies and formulations differ in part from those reported in the literature. This is ascribed to the different research parameters adopted in the various studies (i.e., data collection methods, categorizations of strategies and formulation types, and eliciting situations). These findings suggest two considerations: first, responding to gratitude is a speech act with fuzzy boundaries, which contains core members converging towards a prototypical core of actional and verbal resources, and peripheral members, characterized by less conventionalized and more context-specific content and form. Second, complementary findings originating from alternative research approaches, such as the analysis of role-play data, help gain better insights into this multi-faceted speech act.

The study illustrates how responding to gratitude is a communicative function realized through a small inventory of preferred strategies, and that most of these comprise a range of encoding options—occasionally including elaborate ones—comparable to those identified in previous research. It thus appears that, even when produced under experimental conditions, responses to gratitude tend to conform to unconscious patterns of use, which may be due to the fact that they are routinized social constructs, repetitively uttered below the level of interactants' consciousness (Rüegg, 2014, p. 18). This suggests that, since they resemble those found in spontaneous language behavior, elicited instantiations of responses to gratitude can be used as suitable models for language learners to become aware of interactional patterns.

## Relevance to language teaching and learning

The data from this study of oral production of responses to gratitude by American speakers provides a potential model for pedagogy. When compared to previous studies, it shows that responding to gratitude has a fairly typical, although not fixed, format and content, and that each of its main strategies includes a small range of lexical-semantic realizations. The limited and non-random variability in the functions and encoding options of the speech act suggest that it should be possible to devise activities for teaching it effectively. Indeed, exposure to and analysis of illustrative data can guide language learners toward understanding and use of the different structural, lexical, and semantic properties of responses to gratitude, which correlate with contextual factors. A proposal for a teaching unit on this communicative function follows.

### Teaching unit on responses to gratitude

The teaching unit presented here, which incorporates some elements of communicative exercises as described in Bardovi-Harlig (1996), provides opportunities for students to reinforce their analytical and communicative skills; more specifically, it is supposed to lead them to identify variation in the content and form of responses to thanking, to become aware of variables effecting their content and form, to learn the appropriate linguistic forms for performing responses to gratitude, and to engage in supervised interaction.

The teaching unit targets upper-intermediate adult ESL/EFL learners of English. It comprises two 90-minute lessons, excluding time for homework assignments. Each lesson is organized in phases: Warm-up, Action, Reflection, Understanding and Conclusion in the first, and Warm-up, Exploration and Production in the second. These phases are meant to help students gain insights into the workings of responses to gratitude, as it gives them the opportunity to recognize, analyze and produce contextually appropriate language. The homework assignments are meant to encourage learners to become aware of the internal elaboration and variability of responses to gratitude, to think critically about them, and to partly investigate them on their own.

The lessons can be adapted to other lengths of class meetings, as well as to students at lower level of proficiency, by skipping some of their phases and/or simplifying some of the activities, as indicated below, as well as by choosing from the teacher resources (see below) only the material deemed more suitable or interesting for one's group of learners.

Teachers should familiarize themselves with the teacher resources in advance. This way they will understand why this speech act is worth teaching, and realize that its not so obvious complexity calls for explicit instruction. Also, they will be able to select the material most appropriate to their learners—this applies in particular to the advanced reading assignments for Lesson 1, and Teacher resource 4, which contains a lot of information.

Once familiar with the lesson material, teachers are in a position to sensitize students to three crucial aspects of responses to gratitude: their importance, their conformity to rules of social conduct, and their complexity. First, responses to gratitude occur frequently—people often engage in exchanges of benefits which lead to the production of thanking exchanges—and serve a harmony-preserving function—they bring a conversational exchange to a close by ratifying, or dismissing, a previous act of thanking, and thus free the interactants from the need to indefinitely engage in reciprocal thanking (Edmondson & House 1981). Second, the strategies used in responses to gratitude conform to Leech's (1983) generosity and modesty maxims: the restoration of the balance of social debts and credits between the interactants typically involves recognizing the object of gratitude as gladly provided, minimizing the difficulties encountered in providing it, denying its existence or playing it down. Third, although produced fairly automatically, as a form of ingrained polite social behavior, these reacting speech acts vary in content, form and degree of internal elaboration, and the use and distribution of their strategies and forms correlates in a non-random fashion with changing contextual variables.

## Lesson 1: Observing the forms and functions of thanking exchanges

### *Warm-up*

The teacher explains that as speakers/writers, we may use language not only to initiate interaction, such as when requesting, offering, thanking, but also to react to someone's verbal acts, for instance by accepting, rejecting, acknowledging or ignoring what has been said. The students then read a few brief excerpts from transcripts relevant to speech situations involving thanking exchanges (see Teacher Resource 1), and are asked to make explicit what they think the participants are doing in each situation (i.e., to indicate what verbal actions are being performed) and if possible, how they know this is the case (i.e., to point out linguistic and extra-linguistic cues supporting their interpretation).

For example, in the excerpt below, learners should be able to see that Speaker A is the initiating participant who thanks Speaker B, as suggested by the use of the formula "thanks SO MUCH for watching Lily today"; they should also notice that Speaker B is the responding participant, who accepts Speaker A's expression of gratitude by replying with the formula "no worries."

```
A: Hey Amanda, thanks SO MUCH for watching Lily today.
B: Oh no worries. I love watching Lily! She's such a good
   kid.
```

With lower-proficiency students, and/or in a shorter class meeting, the teacher may want to (a) select only one dialogic excerpt and (b) make it easier for the students to identify thanking formulas and the replies to them by drawing attention to only the specific turns where the thanking exchange(s) occur(s). When the activity is completed, the teacher reviews the answers with the class (see Appendix).

**Teacher Resource 1: What are the speakers doing?**

*Instructions*
Read the following excerpts from conversations between American speakers of English. The symbol "[...]" marks omitted lines. In your own words, specify what each speaker is doing, or trying to do, by paying attention to the words they use.

I) "Flat tire": A was riding his bike, and B, a stranger, helped him change a flat tire.

```
[...]
A: I'd actually like to learn a little bit about er, how
   to, how to take care of my bike as far as maintenance
   goes a little better,
[...]
B: [Definitely a good thing], you don't want to have this
   situation happen again.
A: Yeah, hopefully not. Again, again, thank you
B: [yeah]
A: [for] stopping.
B: Glad that we were able to fix it, and have a… nice
   rest of your ride!
A: Absolutely!
[...]
```

Speaker A is _____
This is clear from _____
Speaker B is _____
This is clear from _____
[These guided observations are repeated after each excerpt.]

II) "Babysitting": B has babysat Lily, A's daughter.

A: Hey Amanda, thanks SO MUCH for watching Lily today.
B: Oh no worries. I love watching Lily! She's such a good kid.
A: Awesome, it's good to hear. Um, I'm gonna go run a few errands, and then I will pay you when I get back.
B: Ok. Sounds good! I'll just be chilling here with Lily.

III) "Friendly colleagues": B has found a gift from A on her desk. B calls A up

A: Hello?
B: Hi! I'm just um, calling to say thank you for the gift that you left on my desk yesterday.
A: Oh, thank you! Um, er you're welcome. I didn't actually leave it there, I had er, the secretary, er, leave it because you weren't in when I came by.
B: Ah, that was nice of you. Er, you'll have to let me have you over to dinner to thank you... sometime.
A: Oh, that sounds... awesome.

IV) "A cabin in the mountains": A has spent a weekend at her friend's cabin in the mountains and is taking her leave from her friend's mother.

A: It was SO nice meeting you, thank you so much for your hospitality, this trip would not have been the same without you.
B: Oh, it, no problem. I hope you, enjoyed our company and our ... little ...cabin in the mountains.
A: It was SO beautiful, we've skied and... had snowball fights and, I love the snow, it's, it's so beautiful here.
B: That's good. Not many people get the chance to come out into nature and enjoy the weather.
A: Right.
[...]
A: (*Laughs*) Alright, thank you again.
B: No problem, [bye].
A:            [bye].

Next, students individually fill in incomplete dialogic exchanges (see Teacher Resource 2) by inserting relevant responses to acts of thanking (DCTs); at the end of the matching activity, students compare their answers in small groups, and finally the teacher reviews the answers with the whole class (see Answer key for Teacher Resource 2 in Appendix). The goal is for students to realize that the same function (i.e., speech act) can be realized in different ways, and at different levels of elaboration. With lower-proficiency students, and/or in shorter class meetings, the teacher could have students work in pairs on just one dialogic exchange.

**Teacher Resource 2: How do the speakers reply to expressions of gratitude?**

*Instructions*

Match the incomplete dialogue excerpts with the relevant utterances.

I) "Back to the office": Speaker A, a CEO, is back from a trip abroad organized by Speaker B, her secretary.

A: Maddie, you were the best secretary I've had yet, the hotel was amazing, and it was in the best location ever, and the service was just unbelievable, thank you so much.
B: _____


II) "A helpful TA": A has been helped by her TA, B, revising her term paper

A: Hey!
B: Hi!
A: I just wanted to come by your office hours, and thank you for all the help you've given me on this paper.
B: Um...yeah, [a] _____. Um...
A: Yeah, but it's a really big deal, I was not gonna pass this class without your help.
B: Yeah. Well you know, the university has, you know, many resources available. [...] so you know there's...lots of those sorts of resources that you should take advantage of.
A: Yeah, sure! I'll check that out. But, er, thanks again man. You know, you, you really saved me.
B: Yeah (*both laugh*) [b] _____.
A: All right. See you at next week...office hours.

**III)** "Office hours": A, a student, has been to professor B's office hours to ask for clarifications about a topic covered in class.

A: Well, I'd really like to thank you for going over this with me, er, I was quite lost before, I, but I seem to ... have a better grasp on it now.
B: _____. Er, if, if, if you could, I, I would appreciate it if, you would come to class, 'cause, believe it or not, that's actually the place where we normally explain these things
[...]


**IV)** "Croatian holiday": A has spent a few days as a paying guest a B's place.

A: Hi! Um, I just wanted to thank you for how wonderful this trip has been.
B: Oh, [a] _____.Tell your friends.
A: Thank you. You just made me feel so welcome, and you know, I learned so much about Croatia while I was here.
B: Well I, I'm glad that you, er, liked our country.
A: Mmm hmm. You, you um, you're really a wonderful host, and, I certainly will recommend this place to my friends.
B: Oh, you're too kind.
A: (*laughs*) Thanks very much.
B: [b] _____.

*Action*
Working in pairs, students are asked to identify and label in dialogue transcripts (Teacher Resource 3), the components of thanking exchanges (i.e., the act of thanking and the response to it), to motivate their interpretations by making reference to the text and/or context, as well as voice their doubts, and the reasons for them. The aim of this phase is for the teacher to see what learners can see in the texts submitted to them prior to any instruction, and capitalize on it as a source of positive reinforcement of their analytical skills. Toward the end of this phase, the instructor reviews the answers (see Answer key to Teacher resource 3 in Appendix) and synthesizes the information from the small groups for the benefit of the class, stressing the relevance and motivation of the observations students have come up with. With lower-proficiency students, and/or in shorter class meetings, the analysis of just one dialogue transcript could suffice.

## Teacher Resource 3: Where do the speakers express gratitude? Where do they respond to gratitude?

### Instructions

Read the following excerpts and label the components of the thanking exchanges.

I) "Birthday party"

B: Hi Charlotte, happy birthday!
A: Oh, thank you, thank you for the present!
B: Oh, you're welcome! I spent a long time searching for it, so I hope that you really like it.
A: Oh really? I appreciate your effort and time.
B: Yeah.
A: Oh, can I open it?
B: Yeah, sure, go ahead!
A: Wow, it's a tablet!
B: Yeah!
A: Thank you!
B: Mmm hmm.
A: Wow, it's really nice. I like the color!
B: You do?
A: Yeah!
B: That's great, cause I thought that would be really useful for you in school as well.
A: Mmm hmm, so, can I try it?
B: Yeah, go ahead!
A: Ok. Wow, it's really nice! I like it!
B: Oh, that's great.
A: It's really comfortable to use too.
B: That's great, that's, that's really awesome.


II) "PowerPoint"

A: Hey Matt, do you have a spare half an hour or so?
B: Yeah! What for?
A: I'm not very tech-savvy and I need to make a power-point for a seminar I am taking part in. Do you think you could give me some pointers?
B: Yeah, not a problem! It's really easy. I will help you with it tomorrow, and we'll figure it out!
A: That sounds good. Thank you.
B: No problem.

## III) "Ready-made dinner"

B: Hey, how was your day of studying?
A: It was alright. I didn't quite accomplish as much as was intended.
B: Yeah.
A: As usual. What exactly are you doing home from work so early for?
B: Oh! I came home early to make you a little bit of food because I knew that you have a big test tomorrow. I thought you might enjoy a nice meal and wouldn't have to spend time making it.
A: Thank you! That's actually extremely nice, what are you making?
B: Some wonderful mashed potatoes.
A: I do love mashed potatoes.
B: A bit of onions and mushrooms on top.
A: Yummy.
B: Nice. Good steak, to build some protein.
A: Well, thank you! I mean, studying the brain and such, I can tell you that those are all great brain foods, I'm excited for the steak.
B: Yeah
[...]


## IV) "Flat tire"

A: Oh my God, what's that noise? Flat tire, seriously? Oh, here comes someone.
B: Hey, do you need some help?
A: Please. I don't know how to change a tire.
B: Ok. I got this. Do you have a spare tire with you?
A: There should be one in the back, yeah.
B: And do you have a jack?
A: Yes.
B: All right. We got this.
A: Oh my God, thank you so much.
B: No problem.

## V) "Dinner party"

A: Well, thank you, Emma, for having us over, I had a great time meeting all your lovely friends.
B: Oh, we all enjoyed your company and I hope to see you again soon.
A: Likewise. Alright, so what was the recipe for that delicious lemon cake you made?
B: Well, let me write it down for you.
A: Right, thank you. I shall try it at home.
B: You're welcome.
A: Alright, see you later!
B: Bye!

## VI) "Financial report"

A: Wow, Emma, thank you for preparing that report for me, I really appreciate it!
B: Oh it's no problem at all, I hope your headache is better!
A: It's just this crazy weather we're having, my head is super sensitive.
B: Yeah. It's allergy season.
A: Yeah. So should we take the bus or get a cab?
B: I'd prefer a cab.
A: Alright, well, thank you again for the report.
B: No problem!
A: Alright, let's go.
B: See you tomorrow

### Reflection

Students are invited to actively think about the social role and import of thanking exchanges, and to become aware of communicative-interpersonal issues not previously considered. Individually, they address specific questions on the function, form, and variability of thanking exchanges (see Teacher Resource 4): Half a class will focus their attention on acts of thanking, and the rest on responses to gratitude. Given the high number of questions included for consideration, teachers should select the ones that they think would be most doable by and interesting to their students. With lower-proficiency students and/or in shorter class meetings, only Questions 1–4 about acts of thanking, and 9–10, 16, and 18 about responses to gratitude could be considered.

**Teacher Resource 4: When and why do people thank each other? When and why do they respond to gratitude?**

*Instructions*

In your group, answer the following questions by using the excerpts you have already read and your knowledge of languages that you speak.

*On thanking*
1. When do we thank someone? Give a few examples.
2. Why do we do it? That is, for what reason or to what end?
3. Give a few examples of thanking formulas.
4. Is it possible to thank someone non-verbally? If so, how?
5. Give a short definition of thanking.
6. a) How can we express extra politeness, sincerity and/or esteem (i.e., deference towards a superior interlocutor) when expressing thanking? b) When do we do it?
7. Can you think of a reason why a beneficiary/thanker may feel embarrassed about their relationship with the benefactor/thankee?
8. In your language, a) What do people thank one another for (i.e., what are possible objects of gratitude)? b) How often do they thank one another? Fairly often or only on special occasions? c) What do people say when they express gratitude? Give a few examples and translate them. d) Are expressions of gratitude short and routinized or original and elaborate?

*On responding to gratitude*
9. When do we respond to someone's thanks, if at all? Consider the following situations. Would a response to gratitude be appropriate at all times? Why or why not?

After being thanked for...
- doing a favor (e.g., holding the door for someone when they are carrying heavy bags)
- giving someone a present (e.g., on their birthday)
- volunteering to do something for them (e.g., picking them up at the airport)
- meeting their requests (e.g., picking them up at the airport)
- saying something nice to them (e.g., a good wish, a compliment, a sincere health inquiry)

10. How do we reply, if at all, to someone's thanks? List a few formulas. If you think that some are similar in content, form or function, list them together and indicate what they share.
11. Is it possible to respond to thanks non verbally? If so, how?
12. What do you think the function(s) of responding to gratitude is/are? That is, what is responding to gratitude about and for?
13. Give a definition of the act of responding to gratitude.

14. Give a definition of a sequence of an act of thanking plus a response to gratitude.
15. How can we express extra politeness, sincerity and esteem (i.e., deference towards a superior interlocutor) when responding to gratitude?
16. What additional formulas can be used to stress the sincerity of one's response to gratitude? When are they more likely to be employed?
17. Can you think of a reason/circumstance why a benefactor/thankee may feel embarrassed about their relationship with the beneficiary/thanker?
18. In your language, a) How often do people verbally respond to thanking? Fairly often or only on special occasions? b) When would it be inappropriate, if ever, to respond to thanks? And to fail to respond? c) What do people say when they respond to thanking? Give a few examples and translate them. d) Are responses to gratitude short and routinized or original and elaborate?

Students can be asked to recall their experiences as benefactors/thankees and beneficiaries/thankers in their native and second/foreign languages. By reasoning in very practical terms about the function, contextual appropriateness, and possible formulation of expressing gratitude and responding to it, they begin to make explicit their metapragmatic knowledge and build confidence about what they already know about thanking exchanges.

Understanding: Students are divided into groups of four—including two members who have worked on acts of thanking, and two on responses to gratitude—and invited to share their thoughts on thanking exchanges. They are asked to synthesize, make explicit, and account for their reasoning, but also to be open to alternative or additional interpretations coming from their classmates. With lower-proficiency students and/or in shorter class meetings, this phase could be skipped.

*Conclusion*
As a wrap-up, the instructor provides model answers to the questions in the questionnaire (see Answer key to Teacher Resource 4 in Appendix), and points out the main issues addressed. In particular, the teacher can help the students reflect on, and find ways of expressing, the social role and importance of thanking exchanges (especially through questions 1, 2, 5, 9, 12, 13) as a joint verbal attempt to restore interactional equilibrium after an exchange of benefits, which makes both parties feel reciprocally satisfied about their interaction.

### Homework

The teacher divides the students into groups of three and asks each member to do a search on the Internet on one of the following: social advice columns on how and when to thank and to respond to gratitude in English, and how and when to thank and respond to gratitude in their native language. With lower-proficiency classes, the teacher may want to assign each Internet task to pairs of students. Finally, as an alternative, with expert learners like teachers in training, the teacher may assign three distinct reading assignments on responses to gratitude to the three members of each group: Schneider (2005), Farenkia (2012), or Rüegg (2014).

## Lesson 2: Analyzing and producing responses to gratitude

### Warm-up

In small groups, students report and comment on what they have learned from their searches on the Internet or reading assignments. Given their distinct search goals or readings, their discussion is a meaningful, motivated exchange of information and observations, each student learning something from the others. The teacher encourages each group to identify the factors that may affect the choice of strategies and formulations in responses to gratitude, and to notice similarities and differences between rules of proper conduct between English and the other language(s) considered, or, in the case of trainee teachers, to notice similarities and differences in the methods and findings across the studies. Then, on the basis of the learners' observations and comments, the teacher points out the degree of functional and formal variability within responses to gratitude.

### Exploration

In pairs, students engage in a small-scale research activity, collecting samples of native speakers' spontaneously produced acts of thanking and responses to gratitude from the Spoken and/or Fiction component(s) of an on-line corpus (e.g., COCA, *The Corpus of Contemporary American English,* Davies, 2008) or a platform that grants a free trial period in consulting corpora (e.g., SketchEngine, Kilgarriff et al., 2014). Each pair is assigned a slightly different search task, that is, the retrieval of concordances of different pairs of thanking expressions and responses to gratitude (e.g., *Thank you* and *You're welcome,* or *Thanks* and *No worries,* or *I appreciate it* and *My pleasure*). They are invited to identify and label the core expressions of thanking and responding to gratitude, and their supporting material, if any. (Also, if the information is easily retrievable, they can record, for each concordance, relevant contextual variables such as the interactants' gender, role, age, and relative status.) Finally, they are asked to observe whether the data examined corresponds, in part or completely, to what they have learned from their assigned readings, and/or if new strategies or formulations are attested. With lower proficiency students, the task could be limited to the retrieval of concordances of one thanking expression, and the identification of the relevant responses to gratitude, the goal being to establish the most frequent types of responses to gratitude, and to notice their degree of similarity with previously encountered responses to gratitude.

If the corpus task is not feasible, teachers could carry out the searches in advance and prepare lists of concordances to distribute in class as handouts, where students can look for core expressions of gratitude and of responses to gratitude, and their support material, if present. The following examples are easily accessible on COCA (http://corpus.byu.edu/coca/).

Thanking exchanges from COCA include those in (5a–c).

**5a) (Fiction, 1994, Movie Dumb and Dumber)**

```
Mary:  I've got to tell you, today was really just what I
       needed. Thanks a lot, Harry.
Harry: My pleasure, Mary.
```

**5b) (Fiction, 2012, Southern Review)**

```
A: Thanks for telling me.
B: You're welcome.
```

**5c) (Fiction, 1990, Pillar of Light)**

```
Nathan: Thank you for your help with the candy. The kids
        will be grateful.
Lydia:  You're welcome. Good-bye, Nathan. Tell your
        mother happy birthday from me, will you?
Nathan: I will, thank you.
```

### *Production*

The students by this time have had a satisfactory introduction to how to use the vocabulary and expressions typical of thanking exchanges. In a mingling activity, they practice thanking and responding to gratitude. Students are given new situations (see, e.g., the scenario descriptions above and Teacher Resource 5) so that they may practice developing their own role-plays on the basis of the knowledge acquired up to this point. For the mechanics of the interaction, students form two concentric circles, facing a partner. The students in the outside circle make some plausible request of their partners (e.g., as friends, course mates). The students in the inside circle grant the requests. Together they (develop and) conclude the interaction-transaction with thanking formulas and relevant responses, and leave-taking formulas. The circles then move over by one person so that the students may change partners and repeat the exercise. When they have completed the circle, the students switch roles and go around again. An alternative way of motivating the mingling activity involves having the students in the outside circle make a plausible offer to their partners—as friends, course mates, or neighbors—and those in the inner circle accepting it. In this case too, the (development and) conclusion of the interaction-transaction should lead to the expression of thanks and responses to gratitude. An alternative way of organizing the mingling activity involves having students form two lines, each facing a partner. When a conversational exchange is concluded, the person standing at the end of one line leaves his/her spot and moves to the beginning of the line, and each person in that line slides over one spot, so that each student finds a new partner and repeats the process. By engaging in communication with different partners, students can have sufficient practice.

## Teacher Resource 5: Role play prompts

### Requesting scenarios

1 "Garage clean-out": You have moved into an apartment where a friend of yours used to live. You find a few of his/her furniture items in the garage. You want to make room for your own things.
   You: I'm going to be doing a garage clean out this weekend. Could you come and pick up your old stuff?
2. "Ride to the airport": A family member was supposed to give you a ride to the airport tomorrow, but something has come up and they no longer can. You ask a close friend if they can help you out.
   You: Look, I know it's kind of short notice, but would you be able to give me a ride to the airport tomorrow morning? My brother was supposed to drive me there, but his boss absolutely wants him to take part in a meeting, and so I can no longer count on him.
3. "House chores": You share an apartment with another student. Today it is your turn to tidy it up, but you are busy studying for an exam, so you would really need your apartment mate to do this for you this time.
   You: Pat, I know it's my turn to tidy up this place, but I am behind with my studying and I have an exam in a couple of days. So, how about YOU do it this time, and then I'll do it twice in a row? Would that be ok? It'd really help.

4. "Lecture notes": You are a university student. You and a friend are taking the same courses. He/She borrowed your notes a long time ago. You need them back for the final exam.
    You: Remember the notes from our Geography class I gave you a month or so ago? Have you made copies of them yet? I would need them for the final.
5. "Pizza parlor": You work in a pizza parlor. You are not feeling well. You ask your boss if you can leave early, even if the place is busy.
    You: Sorry, Matt, but I have a terrible toothache. I've taken a pill, but it's not helping. Can I leave early today? I'll make it up next week.

***Offering scenarios***
1. "Job interview": A close friend informs you she/he has a job interview the following day. You offer her/him to babysit her/his child.
    You: Have you already taken care of Jimmy for tomorrow? I could easily babysit him.
2. "No cash": A colleague at work realizes he/she has no cash on him/her, and needs to make a small purchase on his/her way home.
    You: Don't worry. I can lend you a few notes until tomorrow.
3. "Bus stop": Your neighbor is waiting for the bus at the bus stop as you drive by. You pull over.
    You: Wanna a ride into town?
4. "Down with the flu": A friend tells you he/she is in bed with the flu. You offer your help.
    You: Anything I can do for you, like getting you some food or something?
5. "Grocery shopping": Outside the supermarket, a man/woman accidentally drops a shopping bag full of groceries.
    You: Here, let me help you pick them up.

As an alternative to the mingling activity, students may first be presented with model dialogues for listening and role-playing (see dialogue transcripts in Teacher Resource 3, which the teacher can read aloud to the class). At first they read dialogues silently, then out loud, paying special attention to rhythm and intonation so as to render the expressiveness of the words. In the end, inspired by the model dialogues, the students develop their own interactions according to their preferences, styles, and personalities. If time allows, students are asked to think of other possible situations for their further role-play practice.

***Conclusion***
If time permits, in pairs, students write down an imaginary thanking interaction (one student writes the beneficiary/thanker's prompt, the other the benefactor/thankee's reply), and comment on how the interlocutor's prompts makes them feel, stating if it sounds appropriate and effective.

This phase may be omitted with lower-proficiency students and/or in shorter class meetings.

Optional follow-up written homework: Students may be asked to conduct a small research project, namely watching a film or a couple of sit-com episodes, and to note thanking exchanges occurring in them, reporting them in the observation sheet provided below (Teacher Resource 6). As an alternative homework assignment, in an ESL context, learners may be asked to take note of the thanking exchanges they happen to overhear naturally occurring—or sincerely thank native speakers and jot down their responses immediately after each conversation—and then to describe the structure, content/function and formulation of the thanking exchanges collected. This encourages learners to observe and analyze native speakers' thanking behavior. (If learners observe speakers of their own gender, age and student status, this provides them with language models they feel comfortable with, and encourages them to use thanks and responses to gratitude in their own conversations.) After the data is collected, findings from learner-collected data may be shared in class at the next class meeting, thus further increasing input to learners.

**Teacher Resource 6: Observations**

*Instructions*

For the next few days, pay attention to any thanks you express, receive, or overhear and write them down together with relevant responses, if any. Observe carefully the circumstances in which these thanking exchanges were given and received in terms of role, gender, status, and other factors. Fill out the following form and then decide whether or not the interaction was appropriate. An example is provided in Figure 1.

| Sample Interaction | | | | | | | |
|---|---|---|---|---|---|---|---|
| Context | Date | Place | Other | | | | |
| Interactants | Thanker | Name, if available | Gender | Status | Other | Sincerity/ Appropriateness | |
| | | *Louise* | *F* | *Student* | *Younger* | *Y* | |
| | Thankee | Name, if available | Gender | Status | Other | | |
| | | *Nancy* | *F* | *Student* | | | |
| Text | Thanker | *Thank you very much, Nancy, for sharing your lecture notes.* | | | | | |
| | Thankee | | | *Oh, you're welcome. No problem at all.* | | | |
| | Thanker | *Yeah, they were really helpful.* | | | | | |
| | Thankee | | | *I'm glad to hear that* | | | |
| Interaction 1 | | | | | | | |
| Interaction 2 | | | | | | | |

**Figure 1.** Observation worksheet.

## Summary

The teaching unit presented here, which combines insights from research on the performance of responses to gratitude, is meant to raise learners' awareness of communicative practices in thanking exchanges, and has a dual focus on theoretical/metapragmatic knowledge and activation/development of communicative skills. It shows how to alert students to the actional import of communication, to offer them opportunities to practice conversational exchanges in a supervised, sheltered environment, but also to directly and autonomously explore spontaneously produced or elicited communicative behavior without having to take the teacher's word for it as to what speakers actually do. The phases in the lessons can also be adapted to other speech acts as well (see Yoshida, Kamiya, Kondo, & Tokiwa, 2000).

## Notes

1    I disregarded responses to other discourse segments occurring in the turns containing gratitude expressions, including replies to expansions (i.e., supporting moves) of the thanking head acts (e.g., *Really? I thought you wouldn't like this artist, but you know, it was on sale so I just got it.*).

## References

Aijmer, K. (1996). *Conversational routines in English: Conventions and creativity* (Studies in Language and Linguistics). New York, NY: Longman.

Ameka, F. (2006). "When I die, don't cry": The ethnopragmatics of gratitude in West African languages. In C. Goddard (Ed.), *Ethnopragmatics. Understanding discourse in cultural context* (pp. 231–266). New York, NY: Mouton de Gruyter.

Bardovi-Harlig (1996). Pragmatics and language teaching: Bringing pragmatics and pedagogy together. In L. Bouton (Ed.), *Pragmatics and language learning* (pp. 21–39). Urbana-Champaign: Division of English as an International Language Intensive English Institute, University of Illinois at Urbana-Champaign.

Bardovi-Harlig, K., Mossman, S., & Vellenga, H. E. (2014). Developing corpus-based materials to teach pragmatic routines. *TESOL Journal*.

Colston, H. L. (2002). Pragmatic justifications for nonliteral gratitude acknowledgements: "Oh sure, anytime". *Metaphor and Symbol, 17*, 2015–2226.

Coulmas, F. (1981). "Poison to your soul": Thanks and apologies contrastively viewed. In F. Coulmas (Ed.), *Conversational routine. Explorations in standardized communication situations and prepatterned speech* (pp. 69–91). The Hague: Mouton de Gruyter.

Curikova, L. (2008). Diskursivnoe sobytie vyrazženija blagodarnosti v anglijskom i russkom jazykach [Thanking as a speech event in English and Russian]. *Kalbų Studijos* [Studies about Languages], *13,* 60–70.

Davies, M. (2008). *The corpus of contemporary American English: 450 million words, 1990-present.* Available online at http://corpus.byu.edu/coca/.

Edmondson, W., & House, J. (1981). *Let's talk and talk about it. A pedagogic interactional grammar of English*. Baltimore, MD: Urban & Schwarzenberg.

Eisenstein, M., & Bodman, J. W. (1986). "I very appreciate": Expressions of gratitude by native and non-native speakers of American English. *Applied Linguistics, 7*, 167–185.

Eisenstein, M., & Bodman, J. (1993). Expressing gratitude in American English. In G. Kasper & S. Blum-Kulka (Hg.), *Interlanguage pragmatics* (pp. 64–81). New York, NY/Oxford: Oxford University Press.

Farenkia, B. M. (2012). Face-saving strategies in responding to gratitude expressions: Evidence from Canadian English. *International Journal of English Linguistics, 2*, 1–11.

Farenkia, B. M. (2013). "All Thanks Goes to the Almighty"—a variational and postcolonial pragmatic perspective on responses to thanks. *Sino-US English Teaching, 10*, 707–724.

Félix-Brasdefer, J. C., & Cohen, A. D. (2012). Teaching pragmatics in the foreign language classroom: Grammar as a communicative resource. *Hispania, 95*, 650–669.
Held, G. (1996). Two polite speech acts in contrastive view: Aspects of the realization of requesting and thanking in French and Italian. In M. Hellinger & U. Ammon (Eds.), *Contrastive sociolinguistics* (pp. 363–384). Berlin: Mouton de Gruyter.
Jacobsson, M. (2002). Thank you and thanks in Early Modern English. *ICAME Journal 26*, 63–80.
Jung, W-H. (1994, March). *Speech act of "thank you" and responses to it in American English*. Paper presented at the 16th Annual Meeting of the American Association for Applied Linguistics, Baltimore, MD. Retrieved from http://files.eric.ed.gov/fulltext/ED404879.pdf
Kasper, G. (2000). Data collection in pragmatics research. In H. Spencer-Oatey (Ed.), Culturally speaking. Culture, communication and politeness theory (pp. 279-303). London/New York, NY: Continuum.
Katz, A. N., Lenhardt, M., & Mitchell, K. (2007). On acknowledging thanks for performing a favour. *Metaphor & Symbol, 22*, 233–250.
Kerbrat-Orecchioni, C. (1997). Le traitement des acts de langage en analyse des conversations: l'exemple du remerciement [Treatment of speech acts in the analysis of conversation: The case of appreciations]. In S. Stati, E. Weigand, & E. Hauenherm (Eds.), *Dialogue birthday*. (Beiträge zur Dialogforschung) [Contributions to dialogue research]: Vol. 13, pp. 129–143). Tübingen: Niemeyer.
Kerbrat-Orecchioni, C. (2005). *Les acts de langage dans le discours. Théorie et functionnement* [Speech acts in discourse]. Paris: Armand Colin.
Kilgarriff, A., Baisa, V., Bušta, J., Jakubíček, M., Kovář, V., Michelfeit, J., Rychlý, P. & Suchomel V. (2014). The Sketch Engine: Ten years on. Lexicography, 1(1), 1–30. Available online at http://www.sketchengine.co.uk.
Leech, G. N. (1983). *Principles of pragmatics*. London: Longman.
Ohashi, J. (2008a). Linguistic rituals for thanking in Japanese: Balancing obligations. *Journal of Pragmatics, 40*, 2150–2174.
Ohashi, J. (2008b). Thanking episodes among young Japanese: A preliminary qualitative investigation. *Japanese Studies, 28*, 291–304.
Ouafeu, Y. T. S. (2009). Thanking responders in Cameroon English. *World Englishes, 28*, 544–551.
Rüegg, L. (2014). Thanks responses in three socio-economic settings: A variational pragmatics approach. *Journal of Pragmatics, 71*, 17–30.
Schneider, K. P. (2005). "No problem, you're welcome, anytime": Responding to thanks in Ireland, England, and the USA. In A. Barron & K. P. Schneider (Eds.), *The pragmatics of Irish English* (pp. 101–139). New York, NY: Mouton de Gruyter.
Yoshida, K., Kamiya, M., Kondo, S., & Tokiwa, R. (2000). *Heart to heart: Overcoming barriers in cross-cultural communication*. Tokyo: Macmillan Language House.

## Appendix: Answer keys

### Teacher Resource 1 answer key

I)
Speaker A is thanking Speaker B.
This is clear from "Again, again, thank you" and "for stopping."
Speaker B is accepting Speaker A's gratitude.
This is clear from "Yeah" and "Glad we were able to fix it."
II)
Speaker A is thanking Speaker B.
This is clear from "thanks SO MUCH for watching Lily today."
Speaker B is accepting Speaker A's gratitude.
This is clear from "Oh no worries. I love watching Lily! She's such a good kid."
III)
Speaker B is thanking Speaker A.
This is clear from "I'm just um, calling to say thank you for the gift that you left on my desk yesterday" and "you'll have to let me have you over to dinner to thank you".
Speaker A is accepting Speaker B's gratitude.
This is clear from "you're welcome" and "that sounds… awesome."
Speaker A is also thanking Speaker B.
This is clear from "Oh, thank you!"
IV)
Speaker A is thanking Speaker B.
This is clear from "thank you so much for your hospitality, this trip would not have been the same without you." and "thank you again."
Speaker B is accepting Speaker A's gratitude.
This is clear from "Oh, it, no problem. I hope you, enjoyed our company and our…little…cabin in the mountains" and "no problem"

### Teacher Resource 2 answer key

I)
"Oh, you're so welcome, I'm really glad to hear it. Been working hard all week, but glad to have you back!"
II)
[a] "you know, no problem, that's, you know, that's…part of my job."; [b] "You're really welcome, no problem"
III)
"No problem"
IV)
[a] "I'm, I'm glad you had a good time staying here. You know, we love having you kids come through here, you know, and see our country,

and visit around, so yeah, you're welcome back any time."; [b] "you're welcome"

**Teacher Resource 3 answer key I**

I)
- i) A: Oh, thank you, thank you for the present!
  B: Oh, you're welcome! I spent a long time searching for it, so I hope that you really like it.
- ii) A: Oh really? I appreciate your effort and time.
  B: Yeah.
- iii) A: Thank you!
  B: Mmm hmm.

II)
- A: [...] Thank you.
- B: No problem.

III)
- i) A: Thank you! That's actually extremely nice, what are you making?
  B: Some wonderful mashed potatoes.
- ii) A: Well, thank you! I mean, studying the brain and such, I can tell you that those are all great brain foods, I'm excited for the steak.
  B: Yeah

IV)
- A: Oh my God, thank you so much.
- B: No problem.

V)
- i) A: Well, thank you, Emma, for having us over, I had a great time meeting all your lovely friends.
  B: Oh, we all enjoyed your company and I hope to see you again soon.
- ii) A: Right, thank you. I shall try it at home.
  B: You're welcome.

VI)
- i) A: Wow, Emma, thank you for preparing that report for me, I really appreciate it!
  B: Oh it's no problem at all, I hope your headache is better!
- ii) A: Alright, well, thank you again for the report.
  B: No problem!

**Teacher Resource 4 answer key**

1. When they do us a favor (e.g., holding the door for us when we are carrying heavy bags).
   When they give us a present (e.g., on our birthday).

When they volunteer to do something for us (e.g., picking us up at the airport).
When they meet our requests (e.g., picking us up at the airport).
When they say something nice to us (e.g., a good wish, a compliment, an interested health inquiry).
2. Otherwise our benefactor does not know if we have received what they have sent us.
Otherwise our benefactor does not know if we like what we have received from them.
To do something nice for our benefactor in return for their favor.
To make our benefactor feel good about their kind gesture.
To make sure the interaction unfolds smoothly at the interpersonal level.
To gradually and gently end an interaction.
We were taught, as children, that it is polite to do so.
3. Thank you; Thank you so much; Thanks; Thanks a lot; I appreciate that; You're a lifesaver; What would I do without you?; That's very kind of you; I owe you.
4. Yes, for example with a smile, nod, bow or hug.
5. Thanking is manifesting gratitude in words, a way of reciprocating benefits received, which cancels the beneficiary/thanker's social indebtedness to the benefactor/thankee; this is a conventional, ritual way of restoring the balance of moral debts and credits between the interlocutors; it is a symbolic form of remuneration, as if the benefit received were a gift, whether this is really the case or not.
6a). By repeating the expression of gratitude and/or by expressing it emphatically.
By accompanying the expression of gratitude with support material (e.g., reference to positive effects derived from the benefit, negative effects avoided, obstacles overcome, goals achieved, relevance and usefulness of the benefit, offer of reciprocation, paying a compliment).
6b). When the benefit exchanged is valuable and/or when it was solicited rather than spontaneously offered.
7. While they may enjoy the benefit received, acknowledging the benefit by expressing gratitude may highlight their indebtedness to the benefactor.
8. Answers may vary.
9. We tend to respond to thanks, unless the benefit received is only verbal, that is, something that did not involve a big investment of time, money or resources for the benefactor (i.e., something that they can hardly claim credit for).
10. Don't mention it; Don't worry about it; No problem; No biggie; No bother; No trouble; No worries; Not at all; It's all right; Oh, it's nothing;

It's ok; Never mind; Forget it; It didn't take me long actually. (These expressions minimize the cost or effort involved in providing the benefit. They are focused on the object of gratitude, and address the issue of the beneficiary/thanker's indebtedness.)

My pleasure; It's a pleasure; The pleasure is all mine; I enjoyed doing it actually; I'm glad I could help; Awesome; Great. (These expressions serve to claim a complementary benefit to the benefactor/thankee. They are thus focused on the thankee, who presents his/her positive experience of the object of gratitude.)

Thank you; Thank YOU. (Such expressions similarly imply the existence of an additional, complementary benefit provided by the beneficiary/thanker to the benefactor/thankee. These too, therefore, are focused on the benefactor/thankee, who presents the exchange he/she took part in as mutually beneficial.)

You're welcome; You are quite/entirely welcome; Anytime; Anything for a friend; Whatever you need; Whenever you like; I'm always here when you need me. (These expressions are invitations to engage in similar exchanges in the future. They suggest that the benefactor/thankee likes the beneficiary/thanker.) They are thus focused on the thanker.)

Yes; Yeah; Mmh mmh; Sure; Ok; You got it. (These expressions acknowledge the exchange of benefit and the expression of gratitude. They are thus focused on the transaction.)

11. Yes, with a smile, nod or shrug of the shoulders.
12. To signal that thanking was recognized as such, and perceived as welcome and accepted.

    To settle the transaction, marking the exchange of benefits as satisfactory to both parties involved.

    To express modesty, that is, that the benefit provided was not so precious/costly to the benefactor.

    To reassure the beneficiary/thanker that they are no longer indebted to the benefactor/thankee (and so that they do not need to be concerned about, or bother expressing, gratitude, let alone feel like they have to pay back in kind) because the benefit was nothing special.

    To mark the end of the interaction.
13. It is the verbal ratification of the appropriateness and adequacy of thanking, which denies or reduces the weight of the beneficiary's obligation to pay back what they have received. It thus restores social harmony by balancing out reciprocal debts and credits (i.e., it minimizes the benefactor/thankee's credits).

    It is the verbal response to an act of thanking, this being relevant to some good or service that benefits the beneficiary/thanker.

14. It is an interactional exchange comprising two dialogic units, uttered by the beneficiary/thanker and the benefactor/thankee, which describes and concludes the interaction as satisfactory to both parties.
15. By producing less literal and more elaborate responses, for example by expressing that one would be willing to grant all similar favors in the future or by combining two or more responses together.
16. Complimenting the addressee (e.g., You deserve it); stressing the low cost of the benefit (e.g., Believe me, I have plenty—you can have it); stressing the enjoyability of the benefit (e.g., I had fun too while making it); positively commenting on the transaction (e.g., I'm glad it's the right size); expressing a good wish or desire (e.g., I hope it fits); volunteering to do more of the same (e.g., Do call me again if and when you need me).

    When the benefit exchanged is valuable and/or the expression of gratitude is elaborate and emphatic.
17. When the addressee is socially superior or distant.
18. Answers may vary.

# Brief Summaries and Reports

# How Formulaic is Pragmatics?

Kathleen Bardovi-Harlig
Indiana University, USA

*With the growing interest in formulaic language in pragmatics, it is important to understand how formulaic language—here defined as conventional use—fits into the larger set of pragmalinguistic resources. This essay attempts an answer by addressing the question "How formulaic is pragmatics?" not only to characterize pragmatics, but also to situate formulaic language in the larger context of applications that derive from research into pragmatics and language learning, namely, instruction, materials development, and assessment. This essay begins by reviewing ways in which the frequency or recurrence of formulaic language has been assessed, particularly in pragmatics. It then attempts to situate formulaic language in the larger context of pragmatics as only one type of a range of pragmalinguistic resources, and finally discusses the challenges to learners that the formulaic (or not so formulaic) nature of pragmatics presents to learners, including linguistic characteristics such as nativelike selection, distribution, transfer, and the changing nature of formulas, and learner variables such as proficiency, attitude, and exposure to the target.*

## Introduction

When we hear Nice to meet you, we know that one person is being introduced to another. Stay tuned signals an impending commercial break, and No problem may vie with You're welcome for the preferred compliment response depending on region, age of the speaker, and degree of imposition of the action for which an interlocutor is being thanked. In these situations, we know with reasonable certainty what a speaker may say, and we can describe the situation with fair accuracy given the response. These are conventional expressions, and just one of the linguistic resources that are available to speakers to carry out the social business of language in a succinct and interpretable way.

Conventional expressions are social conventions like shaking hands, kissing upon greeting, and bowing. They are known by many names including *formulas, (pragmatic) routines, situation-bound utterances.* I have used *conventional expressions* in my work in order to focus on their social value. Coulmas (1981) emphasizes the social aspect of pragmatic routines describing them as "tacit agreements, which the members of a community presume to be shared by every reasonable co-member. In embodying societal knowledge they are essential in the handling of day-to-day situations" (p. 4). Terkourafi (2002) sees formulas as "ready-made solutions to the complex and pertinent problem of constituting one's own and one's addressee's face while simultaneously ensuring that one's immediate goals in interaction are achieved" (p. 196) and argues that formulas may be a significant feature of polite discourse more generally. Knowledge of conventional expressions is part of pragmalinguistic competence, and knowledge of their use and the contexts in which they occur is part of sociopragmatic competence.

There are at least four uses of the term "formula" in pragmatics: (a) as the concept of a social expression used by a speech community, which is the type of formulaic language discussed in this essay; (b) as a product of the acquisition process, that is, a string that cannot be analyzed by the interlanguage grammar; (c) as a short form of *semantic formula* (sometimes also called *pragmatic strategy*) which describes a component of a speech act; and, (d) as the key to interpreting conversational implicatures (such as "Answer the question with a question whose answer is obvious" in the Pope-Q implicature, i.e., "Is the Pope Catholic?" Bouton, 1994). (See Bardovi-Harlig, 2006, 2012a for discussion.)

Research into formulaic language in pragmatics has grown in the last two decades. The earliest review, "Developmental issues in interlanguage pragmatics" (Kasper & Schmidt, 1996), focused on formulas as a product of the acquisition process (use [b] above) and referred to "chunks." They identified formulas as one potential area for investigating the acquisition of pragmatics and asked the question *Does chunk learning (formulaic speech) play a role in acquisition of L2 pragmatics?* At the time, only four studies had been conducted. In the decade that followed, substantially more work was conducted, but as I have demonstrated previously (Bardovi-Harlig, 2006), there was a terminological entanglement between formulas as conventional expressions and formulas as chunks that cannot be analyzed by the interlanguage grammar. In the decade between 1996 and 2006, an additional use of "formula" referring to recurrent expressions that are stored and retrieved whole from the mental lexicon began to appear in the pragmatics literature. In 2006 I made a two-way distinction between social formulas and acquisitional formulas (uses [a] and [b] above). At this point, I think that a three-way distinction is warranted (especially in light of research since 2006) between the social or conventional use of expressions, acquisitional formulas that appear early and cannot be parsed by the interlanguage grammar, and the psycholinguistic, referring to storage and retrieval in and from the mental lexicon of conventional expressions. Pragmatics research and more specifically, pragmatics research design, is not constructed to be able to shed light on the psycholinguistics of formulas, and most relevant here, issues of storage and retrieval. (There, of course, can be psycholinguistic research on pragmatic aspects of language; see for example, Edmonds, 2014, for a processing study.) My 2012 review of formulaic language in pragmatics for *ARAL* focused entirely on the area of social uses, and found that the area had grown substantially. The current literature still shows some entanglement of psycholinguistic claims with the social in L2 pragmatics research, I think to the detriment of both inquiries. Establishing what expressions are used conventionally by speech communities can provide targets for investigation for both acquisitional and psycholinguistic inquiry.

With the growing interest in formulaic language in pragmatics and more generally (see, e.g., the 2012 *ARAL* volume on Formulaic Language), it is also important to understand how formulaic language—here defined as conventional use—fits into the larger set of pragmalinguistic resources. This essay attempts an answer by addressing the question *How formulaic is pragmatics?* not only to characterize pragmatics, but also to situate formulaic language in the larger context of applications that derive from research into pragmatics and language learning, namely, instruction, materials development, and assessment. This essay is divided into three parts: section 2 outlines the means by which formulas are identified empirically; section 3 situates formulaic language in the larger context of pragmatics; and, section 4 discusses of what the formulaic (or not so formulaic) nature of pragmatics means for learners.

## Features of formulas: Recurrent, contextualized, and contractual

In this paper I use *formula* to refer to recurrent strings or expressions used for specific pragmatic purposes. Formulas often succinctly capture the illocutionary force of a contribution by virtue of the fact that the speech community in which they are used has tacitly agreed on their form, meaning, and use. In pragmatics, the definition of formulaic language includes three parts: the form as a recurrent sequence, its occurrence in specific social contexts, and the idea of the social contract which extends to members of a particular speech community.

### Formulas as recurrent sequences

Some studies operationalize *formula* as a specific sequence of words, some as a rule with lexical items, and some as recurrent components with particular semantic value. Formulas that were characterized as sequences of words include *you know* (House, 2009; Pilcher, 2009), *No worries,* and *How are you going?* (Davis, 2007), *Can I leave a message?* and *For here or to go?* (Roever, 2005) or in Northern English, the nonlocal *I don't know* [*I dunno*] and *I don't think* [*I doØ think*] and localized variants (*I divn't knaa* or *I divn't think*; Pilcher, 2009).

The best known study to operationalize *formula* as a rule, and one of the first studies in empirical pragmatics, was Manes and Wolfson (1981) which identified three compliment formulas expressed (in order of frequency) as

> NP {is/looks}(really) ADJ
> I (really) {like/love} NP
> PRO is (really) (a) ADJ NP

Other formulas that have been proposed look less like syntactic rules in that their open categories are unspecified for part of speech as in *not X or anything, but Y*, for disclaimers realized as *I don't want to sound like your mother or anything, but I think you should wait* and *We don't mean to cause a fuss or anything, but this isn't what we ordered* (Overstreet & Yule, 2001) and "So TIME" realized as *That's so last year* and *Email is so 5 minutes ago* (Wee & Tan, 2008).

Somewhere between fixed expressions and rules lie formulas that seem to be best described by choices of words in fixed arrangements. Culpeper (2010) identifies a number of impoliteness formulas such as personalized negative vocatives, realized as *You rotten liar you!* as [you] [rotten /dirty/fat/little/etc.] [moron/pig/bastard/loser/brat/etc.] [you]. Other studies describe formulas by their semantic value. For example, Bing and Ruhl (2008) characterized responsibility statements that appear in academic papers as "Acknowledge the convention + Content + Shortcomings + Responsibility of the author + No responsibility of others" as in *Naturally, I remain responsible for any mistakes still present* and *The views expressed are solely those of the authors*.

As this short review shows, recurrent strings are described in a variety of ways. They are also linked to specific contexts, which is discussed next.

## Occurrence in specific contexts

Context may be defined by speech acts, interactional setting, or speech event. Within speech events, Bing and Ruhl (2008) examined responsibility statements that appear in academic papers. Bardovi-Harlig, Mossman, and Vellenga (2014/2015, 2015) identified pragmatic routines used to indicate agreement, disagreement, and clarification in academic discussion. Culpeper (2005) found that certain expressions, such as *waste of rations*, were limited to military jokes. Culpeper (2010) studied the context of impoliteness, which included reality TV shows and university library desks (as sites of graffiti) in order to investigate impoliteness formulas.

Moving from more general contexts to more specific, formulas have been investigated within specific speech acts, such as compliments, as noted earlier, by Manes and Wolfson (1981). Hasler-Barker (2014) compared the production of compliments in Spanish and English and found Spanish compliments to be less formulaic, using at least seven strategies (Félix-Brasdefer & Hasler-Barker, 2014) where English speakers use three formulas. The favorite compliment strategy seems to be Qué ADJ/ADV NP/ ("What ADJ/ADV NP!"), which may be considered to a formula candidate with more research.

Contexts also include specific speech event contexts described by scenarios in controlled tasks such as oral and written discourse completion tasks (DCTs; Bardovi-Harlig, 2009; Kecskes, 2000, 2003; Taguchi, Li, & Xiao, 2013) and multiple choice questionnaires (Roever, 2005, 2006). Some of the contexts are very specific and are more fine-grained than the speech act level. For example, we discovered that some thanking scenarios elicit very specific responses that are distinguished from other thanking scenarios. *Thanks for (your help/your time)* was reliably used in the closing to office hours whereas *Thanks so much* was used in the granting of a make-up test. Still other thanking contexts saw the use of unrelated expressions: *That'd be great*, was used in response to an offer of assistance from a roommate. In contrast, the scenario offering a ride to a person walking in the rain was a less certain thanking context because of a reluctance to accept a ride even from a friend.

The final step in establishing that a string of words is a pragmatic formula is establishing how widely it is used.

## A social contract shared by members of a particular speech community

The description of pragmatic formulas as "tacit agreements" and as "societal knowledge" shared by "every reasonable co-member" of a community (Coulmas, 1981) that show "community-wide use" (Myles, Hooper, & Mitchell, 1998, p. 325) establishes the final piece of the formula identification: Formulas must be used widely within a community. This embodies both a notion of frequency and a notion of distribution among speakers. (Formulas used frequently but idiosyncratically and formulas used only occasionally but by different speakers would both seem to fail this test.) Defining a community then becomes crucial. In my work, I first defined community very narrowly, restricted to our local university setting where the first set of conventional expressions was identified for the purposes of understanding how learners in that specific community came to acquire conventional expressions in use there. It is reasonable to note that university communities, although geographically situated, also draw speakers from other areas. Later, for the purposes of developing instructional materials for English for Academic Purpose (EAP) for a unit on expressions used during group work (Bardovi-Harlig, Mossman, & Vellenga, 2015a,b), we defined our speech community as speakers of academic English at a geographically proximate peer institution represented by the Michigan Corpus of Academic Spoken English (MICASE; Simpson, Briggs, Ovens, & Swales, 2002). In illustrating principles for developing instructional materials for teaching pragmatic routines, we further expanded our speech communities to include (in additional to academic speech communities), American English as represented by television shows and informal conversations (Bardovi-Harlig & Mossman, in press).

Methodologically, for research purposes we are probably wiser to assume that use of expressions is limited rather than to assume they are universal. In our geographic area of south-central Indiana, we seem to be on the dialect line between "I don't mind" and "I don't care to" used when a speaker is willing to comply with a request. In our faculty we have speakers who compare unlike items as "apples and oranges" or "chalk and cheese." Such differences should teach us that identifying conventional expressions is an empirical question. Speech communities are undoubtedly different sizes, and what they share as conventional will differ.

As in the case of describing formulas and defining the contexts in which they occur, the means of establishing the frequency of an expression or its use within a community differs across studies. There are some studies that seem to simply assert that certain sequences are formulas or they may be vague about the means used for identification; such studies are not considered further here. In contrast, when empirically oriented studies assert formula status, they cite their sources. For example, when Culpeper (2005) made the claim that certain strings are formulas, he backed up the claim with a search: "I searched various corpora and the web (via WebCorp at http://www.webcorp.org.uk/) to establish the fact that these all occur with a certain regularity in the language. However, some expressions are restricted to particular registers. 'Waste of rations,' for example, seems to be largely restricted to army jokes." (Culpeper, 2005, fn 8, p. 70). As noted, searches may reveal restrictions as well as regularities.

Biber, Conrad, and Cortes (2004) defined frequency for a multi-word unit as 40 occurrences per one million words for corpus studies; an earlier paper (Biber, Johansson, Leech, Conrad, & Finegan, 1999) had suggested a lower rate of 10 occurrences per one million words. Although multi-word units lack the social attributes of conventional expressions (being primarily recurrent sequences), and the usage is not limited to specific contexts as in Culpeper (2005), Biber's work with colleagues establishes an alternative way to empirically define frequency for research on pragmatic routines and expressions. Bardovi-Harlig, Mossman, and Vellenga (2015a,b) used corpus frequency counts to determine which expressions found in ESL textbooks were legitimate targets for instruction in General American English. Pragmatic routines presented as useful expressions for academic discussion by ESL textbooks were vetted by using frequency counts from the Michigan Corpus of Academic Spoken English (MICASE; Simpson et al., 2002). Expressions that occurred from 30/million words up to 135/million words were included as target pragmatic routines in a study of the effect of instruction (Bardovi-Harlig Mossman, & Vellenga, 2015b) and in materials development (Bardovi-Harlig, Mossman, & Vellenga, 2015a) and the others were discarded.

Corpus studies are still relatively rare in pragmatics because of the difficulty of identifying contexts and speakers in many corpora. Wong (2010) investigated thanking expressions used by speakers of English in Hong Kong using the Hong Kong International Corpus of English (Wong 2010). Wong reported the absence of British thanking expressions *cheers* and *ta* among the 233 thanking expressions found in the conversation of Hong Kong English speakers.

Apart from frequency in a general corpus or even a relatively specialized one like MICASE, researchers often determine how widely a formula is used in a speech act or specific scenarios in which a single speech act is expected to be dominant. This is quite different from a general frequency count. The number of occurrences cannot be calculated since the corpus is assembled to reflect pre-selected contexts. I think of these counts more as density within the sample than frequency in a general corpus. For example, Schauer and Adolphs (2006) compared the utility of a corpus search and a DCT for the purposes of materials development and found that the DCTs provided more examples of thanking expressions than the 5-million word corpus, CANCODE (Cambridge and Nottingham Corpus of Discourse in English). Controlled elicitation, including examining spontaneous conversations, may yield more densely clustered data than general corpora that were not collected for pragmatics research.

For another perspective on formulas in specific contexts, we return to the best-known formulas in pragmatics, compliments, for a look at formulas in the context of a speech act. Manes and Wolfson (1981) collected 686 examples of compliments from spontaneous conversation. They identified three main recurrent patterns in the data, the first, NP {is/looks}(really) ADJ, accounted for 53.6% of the compliments; two additional forms—I (really) {like/love} NP and PRO is (really) (a) ADJ NP—together constitute 30% of the compliments, and the three together account for 85% of the 686 compliments collected by the study. In this study Manes and Wolfson identified (a) recurrent sequences in (b) a well-defined context, and (c) established their rate of use. Moreover, the positive adjectives (represented by ADJ in the formulas) were dominated by five adjectives that occurred in 2/3 of all the compliments.

Other studies use a cut-off, below which strings of words are not considered to be conventionally employed in a pre-defined context. Bardovi-Harlig (2009, Bardovi-Harlig, Bastos, Burghart, Chappetto, Nickels, & Rose, 2010) used four steps to identify conventional expressions: 1) observation of expressions in the community, followed by 2) scenario construction capturing the contexts of the candidate expressions, 3) trial elicitation (in writing and orally) to test the scenarios, and, 4) a final revision. The scenarios were then presented to native-speaker peers (the same ages as the L2 learners), native-speaker teachers, and learners at 4 levels of proficiency. To qualify as a conventional expression, a candidate expression had to occur in 50% or more of the native-speaker responses. At greater than 50%, the formulas identified are the favorite expressions for the context.

Culpeper (2010) also employed a 50% usage criterion to identify impoliteness formulas. Culpeper combined observation in context with frequency in a corpus. He first identified contexts in which impoliteness was likely to occur: namely, television reality shows known for impolite talk, 51 graffiti dialogues collected from university library desks, and 100 diary accounts of impolite encounters. Next he identified candidate impoliteness formulas by identifying interactions in which the addressees responded in a way that indicated they understood the utterance to be impolite, including responses, retrospective comments (a feature of the TV shows in which participants are interviewed about their experiences and other participants), and non-verbal reactions. Culpeper's final step was to establish the frequency of use of the candidate impoliteness formulas in the Oxford English Corpus (OEC). For a candidate formula to be included in the final list of impolite formulas, at least 50% of the occurrences of any one variant of a formula had to involve impoliteness in more than 50% of its occurrences in the OEC. Culpeper (2010) explains,

> *Shut up* has a strong correlation with impoliteness events in the OEC data, but does not clearly exceed the 50% level (it can express, for instance, solidarity). In contrast, *shut the fuck up*, has a stronger correlation, clearly exceeding 50%. Hence, this formula type is listed. (p. 3242)

Because *shut the fuck up* was used predominately in cases involving impoliteness, it was considered to be an impolite formula whereas *shut up* was not.

Community-wide use cannot simply be asserted. The studies just reviewed show that there are multiple ways of establishing what expressions are used in a community. Measures of community-wide use interact with the type of context considered. For example, corpus measures of frequency define context broadly, such as academic discussion or impoliteness, whereas percentage of use defines context as speech acts or specific scenarios. For pragmatics research, particularly involving learners, it is crucial that a rate of use be established in well-defined contexts.

## How pervasive are formulas in pragmatics?

There is no question that speakers use formulaic language as a pragmalinguistic resource. The existence of formulaic sequences does not, however, tell us how common they are. In this section, I will try to put the use of conventional expressions into perspective vis-à-vis other pragmalinguistic resources. I will first consider conventional expressions and alternatives to them, and then consider that some speech acts seem to not be as conventional as others.

Let us start first by considering the mathematics of community-wide use. The rates of use of conventional expressions are a continuous variable that ranges hypothetically from complete agreement (100%) in contexts in which everyone says the same thing,[1] to contexts in which no one says the same thing (0%). When we consider the highest uses of conventional expressions, such as the use of *Thank you for your help/your time* by 94% of the undergraduates in the office hour setting compared to the use of *Thank you so much* by 86% of the undergraduate respondents in the make-up test scenario, we focus on the agreement; there is very little disagreement. When we move down the scale to consider the conventional expressions that are used just frequently enough to be used more frequently than any other expression or response at a 51% cut-off rate, for example, we must also consider that there is either a competing formula, or more often, non-formulaic uses; that is, for every formula that makes a 51% cut-off, 49% of the responses are different. This is amplified in those scenarios where formula use is very low. As an illustration, only 43% of the undergraduates used *No problem* in response to a request to save someone's place in line, with no other recurrent response (the Save Place scenario, Bardovi-Harlig, 2012b). That means that 57% of the responses did not employ a conventional expression. For second language acquisition studies in pragmatics that attempt to determine what constitutes a reasonable target for acquisition (e.g., Bardovi-Harlig, 2009; Edmonds, 2014) or pragmatics studies that attempt to characterize an aspect of pragmatics such as impoliteness (Culpeper, 2010), these infrequently used formulas are discarded, at least for certain contexts.

Also consider that formulas stand out against a background of non-formulas. In some cases in our data, the formula was the only response to a situation, as in *Nice to meet you* or *No thanks, I'm full*, but other times there was a following elaboration. In the "Forgot book" scenario, 23 (66%) of the 35 native English-speaking undergraduate respondents said *I'm (so) sorry* and 18 of those (or 54% of the total group) used a conventional apology plus explanation *I'm (so) sorry, I forgot* (Bardovi-Harlig, 2012b). Of the speakers who used *I'm (so) sorry, I forgot*, 12 included an offer of redress, none of which was identical: *I'll bring it to your house later; how 'bout I meet you tonight and give it to you?; Is there any way we can meet later?; I'll get it to you as soon as possible*. If any pragmatic strategy in the realization of a speech act is formulaic, the other strategies are generally left to speaker creativity, and thus the conventional stands out across speakers.[2]

A second way of exploring the formulaic nature of pragmatics is by speech act. When my students and I conducted our field work that led to the identification of formulas in the speech of the Bloomington community, we observed that speech acts are not equally formulaic; that is, the candidate expressions for which we subsequently crafted scenarios for oral elicitation were not evenly distributed across speech acts (Bardovi-Harlig et al., 2010). Thanking contexts seem to be likely contexts for the use of conventional expressions (in the high

89–94% range discussed earlier, to 66% use of *That'd be great* in an offer of help, but much lower, 29%, in the offer of a ride). In contrast, the low-imposition request scenarios derived from our field notes failed to elicit recurrent expressions. In fact, of the 77 situations of mixed speech acts that we originally observed, more than half failed to elicit consistent use upon repeated testing.

Only one context yielded multiple alternative expressions that were not variations of each other or sequentially ordered. In the context of someone talking during a movie in a theater, *Be quiet, Keep it down,* and *Shut up* were used exhaustively by native speakers in the pilot (meaning that all responses contained one of those expressions). In the final elicitation, *Be quiet* continued to dominate with 60% of the responses, supplemented by *Shut up* and *Keep it down* (11% each) and *Quiet down* (9%) and one case of *sssshhhh* (which is also conventional, but not likely to be formulaic).

The difference between speech acts that are likely to be realized with formulaic language and those that are less likely to be realized with formulaic language is amplified when we consider cross-cultural comparisons of formulaic language. Cross-cultural comparisons show that it is not the speech act itself, but rather the cultural context of a speech act that determines the degree of conventionality (Barron, 2003; Traverso, 2006). For example, shop keepers and customers engaging in service encounters in shops in France and Syria differ in their use of formulaic language in the request solicitation-request-request uptake sequence and in the verbal acceptance of goods (Traverso, 2006). No doubt speech act, culture, language, and context interact with other factors such as imposition and social distance and should be investigated further.

I am not suggesting that the calculation of how formulaic pragmatics is, is entirely clear-cut. However, I am suggesting that when concentrating on formulas in pragmatics, it is important to remember that pragmatics is not entirely formulaic. Native speakers, nonnative speakers, and learners use a range of pragmalinguistic resources.

## What's the learning challenge?

Challenges to learners come from pragmalinguistics, sociopragmatics, and external factors.

### Nativelike selection

The best-known issue in the acquisition of conventional expressions was identified by Pawley and Syder (1983): The learning challenge for second language learners and native speakers alike is to master nativelike selection. Nativelike selection describes the problem of how speakers select idiomatic (i.e., conventional) expressions from among a "range of grammatically correct paraphrases, many of which are non-nativelike or highly marked usages" (p. 90). According to Pawley and Syder (1983), language learners need to learn a means of "knowing which of the well-formed sentences are nativelike—a way of distinguishing those usages that are normal or unmarked from those that are unnatural or highly marked" (p. 94).

### Distribution

How do learners learn which situations favor the use of formulas and which do not? This is part of sociopragmatics. Contexts for formula use are not universal (see the next point regarding transfer) but they may be at least partially predictable as in openings and closings. Contexts for use may also be reasonable targets for instruction. This area bears additional exploration.

### L1 influence

L1 influence can be considered from two perspectives: distribution and transfer. The first perspective on formulaic language and L1 influence is that conventional expressions often exhibit different distribution or different contexts cross-linguistically. Barron (2003) suggests that differences in formula use between languages may lead to potential difficulties in the acquisition of L2 pragmatics: Difficulties may arise in "situations requiring a pragmatic routine in one language but an ad hoc formulation in the other; [and] situations requiring a pragmatic routine in one language but no remark in the other" (p. 186). The second perspective on formulaic language and L1 influence is that conventional expressions most often do not have direct translations; this may lead learners to use an extant target language expression in contexts where native speakers do not because of its similarity to an L1 expression. This has not yet been discussed in the pragmatics literature to my knowledge, but crosslinguistic similarity in collocations has been investigated, and perhaps such studies could inform research in the use of conventional expressions.

### Formulas are not static

Formulas show variation: region and registers may influence formula use, and so might age, occupation, and gender. In our south-central Indiana community, local speakers alternate between the less regional I don't mind and the more regional (from south central Indiana going into Kentucky) I don't care to to comply with a request. My father, in his nineties, has always been fond the cat's pajamas and the cat's meow both of which refer to excellence.

A conventional expression may also drop out of a community's lexicon. A conventional expression may also drop out of or enter a community's lexicon. Can I leave a message? was one of 12 expressions that Roever (2005) used in a multiple-choice selection task. Four years later, with the rise of individual message systems such as voicemail and the decline of central phones for dorm rooms or homes, the same item in a production task did not elicit Can I leave a message from native speakers or learners (Bardovi-Harlig, 2009). New expressions like

Google it are added to a speech community's lexicon, emphasizing the social aspect of conventional expressions.

### Learners require sufficient proficiency to parse and produce conventional expressions

Learners' ability to produce targetlike formulas increases with proficiency (Bardovi-Harlig, 2009; Bardovi-Harlig & Bastos, 2011); knowledge of the meaning and use of formulas also increases with proficiency (Bardovi-Harlig, 2014). A close analysis of learner attempts at producing the conventional expressions reveal evidence of interlanguage syntactic development en route to targetlike production (Bardovi-Harlig, 2009; Bardovi-Harlig & Stringer, 2016; Bardovi-Harlig & Vellenga, 2012).

### Attitude

Attitudes may reflect participants' view of the language community that uses the formulas and their desire to be a part of it. Davis (2007) found that Korean learners of English in Australia and EFL learners in Korea reported a reluctance to learn or use Australian formulas (e.g., *for here or to take away* and *how did you go?* meaning 'how did it go'), stating a preference for North American or British English.

Speakers' attitudes toward the use of formulas may provide insight into how they are interpreted, whether learners are aware of them, and whether they are targets of second language acquisition from the learner's perspective.

### Exposure

Learning a language in a foreign environment is a well-known challenge to the development of pragmatic competence. However, a simple change from foreign to host environments is not sufficient to guarantee acquisition of conventional expressions. In addition to the other factors mentioned, learners must engage with speakers in the environment. Intensity of interaction is a better predictor of recognition and production of conventional expressions than length of stay (Bardovi-Harlig & Bastos, 2011). Instruction may boost interaction and noticing in both host and foreign contexts, but exposure to authentic language use is key.

## Concluding remarks

The study of formulas within the framework of pragmatics emphasizes the degree to which use of a formula is part of a social contract. Using formulas for pragmatic functions not only follows tacit social agreements, it signals the membership of participants in particular speech communities. Pragmatic research also reveals that not all social talk is formulaic, nor is it equally formulaic in every context across languages. Awareness of the speech community on the part of the researcher is crucial, and to go forward, careful attention to local speech norms and the data-based identification of formulas has to be part of the research paradigm.

### Notes

1  See Bardovi-Harlig (2013) on the complexity of determining what "saying the same thing" means.
2  The conventional expressions also seem to occur in the initial position in the realization of a speech act or responding turn. Amanda Edmonds (2014) and I have noticed this position in both the native speaker and learner production for French and English, respectively (p.c., with Edmonds). We have not yet tested this observation more broadly.

## References

ARAL. (2012) Special issue on Formulaic Language.
Bardovi-Harlig, K. (2006). On the role of formulas in the acquisition of L2 pragmatics. In K. Bardovi-Harlig, J. C. Félix-Brasdefer, & A. Omar (Eds.), *Pragmatics and language learning* (Vol. 11, pp. 1–28). Honolulu: University of Hawai'i, National Foreign Language Resource Center.
Bardovi-Harlig, K. (2009). Conventional expressions as a pragmalinguistic resource: Recognition and production of conventional expressions in L2 pragmatics. *Language Learning, 59*, 755–795.
Bardovi-Harlig, K. (2012a). Formulas, routines, and conventional expressions in pragmatics research. *ARAL, 32*, 206–227.
Bardovi-Harlig, K. (2012b). Pragmatic variation and conventional expressions. In J. C. Félix-Brasdefer & D. Koike (Eds.), *Pragmatic variation in first and second language contexts: Methodological issues* (pp. 141–173). Amsterdam: John Benjamins.
Bardovi-Harlig, K. (2014). Awareness of meaning of conventional expressions in second language pragmatics. *Language Awareness, 23,* 41–56.
Bardovi-Harlig, K., & Bastos, M.-T. (2011). Proficiency, length of stay, and intensity of interaction and the acquisition of conventional expressions in L2 pragmatics. *Intercultural Pragmatics 8*, 347–384.
Bardovi-Harlig, K., Bastos, M.-T., Burghardt, B., Chappetto, E., Nickels, E., & Rose, M. (2010). The use of conventional expressions and utterance length in L2 pragmatics. In G. Kasper, H. t. Nguyen, D. R. Yoshimi, & J. K. Yoshioka (Eds.), *Pragmatics and language learning* (Vol. 12, pp. 163–186). Honolulu: University of Hawai'i, National Foreign Language Resource Center.
Bardovi-Harlig, K., & Mossman, S. (in press). Corpus-based materials development for teaching and learning pragmatic routines. In B. Tomlinson (Ed.), *SLA research and materials development for language learning.* Abington, England: Taylor and Francis.
Bardovi-Harlig, K., Mossman, S., & Vellenga, H.E. (2015a). Developing corpus-based materials to teach pragmatic routines. *TESOL Journal*, 6, 499-526.

Bardovi-Harlig, K., Mossman, S., & Vellenga, H. E. (2015b). The effect of instruction on pragmatic routines in academic discussion. *Language Teaching Research, 19,* 324–350.

Bardovi-Harlig, K., & Stringer, D. (2016). Unconventional expressions: Productive syntax in the L2 acquisition of formulaic language. *Second Language Research.* DOI: 10.1177/0267658316641725

Bardovi-Harlig, K., & Vellenga, H. E. (2012). The effect of instruction on conventional expressions in L2 pragmatics. *System, 40,* 77–89.

Barron, A. (2003). *Acquisition in interlanguage pragmatics: Learning how to do things with words in a study abroad context.* Amsterdam: John Benjamins.

Biber, D., Conrad, S., & Cortes, V. (2004). If you look at…Lexical bundles in university teaching and textbooks. *Applied Linguistics, 25,* 371–405.

Biber, D., Johansson, S., Leech, G., Conrad, S., & Finegan, E. (1999). *Longman grammar of spoken and written English.* Harlow, England: Pearson Education.

Bing, J., & Ruhl, C. (2008). It's all my fault! The pragmatics of responsibility statements. *Journal of Pragmatics, 40,* 537–558.

Bouton, L. F. (1994). Can NNS skill in interpreting implicatures in American English be improved through explicit instruction? A pilot study. In L. F. Bouton & Y. Kachru (Eds.), *Pragmatics and language learning* (Vol. 5, pp. 88–109). Urbana-Champaign: Division of English as an International Language, University of Illinois.

Coulmas, F. (1981). *Conversational routine: Explorations in standardized communication situations and prepatterned speech.* The Hague: Mouton.

Culpeper, J. (2005). Impoliteness and entertainment in the television quiz show: *The Weakest Link. Journal of Politeness Research, 1,* 35–72.

Culpeper, J. (2010). Conventional impoliteness formula. *Journal of Pragmatics, 42,* 3232–3245.

Davis, J. (2007). Resistance to L2 pragmatics in the Australian ESL context. *Language Learning, 57,* 611–649.

Edmonds, A. (2014). Conventional expressions: Investigating pragmatics and processing. *Studies in Second Language Acquisition, 36,* 69–99.

Félix-Brasdefer, J. C., & Hasler-Barker, M. (2014) Complimenting in Spanish in a short-term study abroad context. *System, 48,* 75–85.

Hasler-Barker, M. (2014). *Effects of pedagogical intervention on the production of the compliment and compliment response sequence by second language learners of Spanish.* (Unpublished doctoral dissertation). Indiana University, Bloomington.

House, J. (2009). Subjectivity in English as Lingua Franca discourse: The case of you know. *Intercultural Pragmatics, 6,* 171–193.

Kasper, G., & Schmidt, R. (1996). Developmental issues in interlanguage pragmatics. *Studies in Second Language Acquisition, 18,* 149–169.

Kecskés, I. (2000). A cognitive-pragmatic approach to situation-bound utterances. *Journal of Pragmatics, 32,* 605–625.

Kecskes, I. (2003). *Situation-bound utterances in L1 and L2.* Berlin: Mouton.

Manes, J., & Wolfson, N. (1981). The compliment formula. In F. Coulmas (Ed.), *Conversational routine: Explorations in standardized communication situations and prepatterned speech* (pp. 115–132). The Hague: Mouton.

Myles, F., Hooper, J., & Mitchell, R. (1998). Rote or rule? Exploring the role of formulaic language in classroom foreign language learning. *Language Learning, 48,* 323–363.

Overstreet, M., & Yule, G. (2001). Formulaic disclaimers. *Journal of Pragmatics, 33,* 45–60.

Pawley, A., & Syder, F. H. (1983). Two puzzles for linguistic theory: Nativelike selection and nativelike fluency. In J. C. Richards & R. W. Schmidt (Eds.), *Language and communication* (pp. 191–226). London: Longman.

Pilcher, H. (2009). The functional and social reality of discourse variants in a northern English dialect: I DON'T KNOW and I DON'T THINK compared. *Intercultural Pragmatics 6,* 561–596.

Roever, C. (2005). *Testing ESL pragmatics: Development and validation of a web-based assessment battery.* Berlin: Peter Lang.

Roever, C. (2006). Validation of a web-based test of ESL pragmalinguistics. *Language Testing, 23,* 229–256.

Schauer, G. A., & Adolphs, S. (2006). Expressions of gratitude in corpus and DCT data: Vocabulary, formulaic sequences, and pedagogy. *System, 34,* 119–134.

Simpson, R. C., Briggs, S. L., Ovens, J., & Swales, J. M. (2002). *The Michigan corpus of academic spoken English.* Ann Arbor, MI: The Regents of the University of Michigan. Available at *quod.lib.umich.edu/m/micase/*

Taguchi, N., Li, S., & Xiao, F. (2013). Production of formulaic expressions in L2 Chinese: A developmental investigation in a study abroad context. *CASLAR 2013, 2,* 23–58.

Terkourafi, M. (2002). Politeness and formulaicity: Evidence from Cypriot Greek. *Journal of Greek Linguistics, 3,* 179–201.

Traverso, V. (2006). Aspects of polite behaviour in French and Syrian service encounters: A data-based comparative study. *Journal of Politeness Research: Language, Behavior, Culture, 2,* 105–122.

Wee, L., & Tan, Y. Y. (2008). That's so last year! Constructions in a socio-cultural context. *Journal of Pragmatics, 40,* 2100–2113.

Wong, M. L.-Y. (2010). Expressions of gratitude by Hong Kong speakers of English: Research from the International Corpus of English in Hong Kong (ICE-HK). *Journal of Pragmatics, 42,* 1243–1257.

# The Design and Construction of Websites to Promote L2 Pragmatics

Andrew D. Cohen
*Professor Emeritus, University of Minnesota, USA*

*After defining the term* pragmatics *and briefly describing its coverage, the chapter takes a retrospective look at the design and construction of websites at the University of Minnesota to promote the teaching and learning of second- and foreign-language pragmatics. It is noted that this work has included both the construction of a general website and of both a website for Japanese pragmatics and one for Spanish pragmatics. The chapter then indicates that due to the continued success of these websites, future plans call for the creation of a wiki, which will serve as a repository of knowledge about pragmatics within and across languages.*

## Introduction

The University of Minnesota's Center for Advanced Research on Language Acquisition (CARLA) was established in 1993 under the umbrella of the Institute of International Studies (now the Global Programs and Strategy Alliance) to house the federally-funded Title VI national Language Resource Center (LRC) grant to support a coordinated program of research, training, development, and dissemination to improve the nation's capacity for language learning and teaching. This report is about one of CARLA's efforts over the years, namely that of promoting the teaching and learning of second- and foreign-language (L2)[1] pragmatics.

A never-ending challenge to language educators in L2 instruction is that of providing learners a sense of appropriate language behavior, and especially how to deal with *pragmatics*. Pragmatics refers to the interpretation of intended meanings, which often go beyond the literal ones. Having pragmatic ability implies that as listener or reader, you are able to interpret the intended meanings of what is said or written, the assumptions, purposes or goals, and the kinds of actions that are being performed (Yule, 1996, pp. 3–4). As speaker, pragmatic ability means that you know how to say what you want to say with the proper politeness, directness, and formality (for instance, in the role of boss, telling an employee that s/he is being laid off; or in the role of teacher, telling a student that his/her work is unacceptable). You also need to know what not to say at all and what to communicate non-verbally. As writer, pragmatic ability means knowing how to write your message intelligibly, again paying attention to level of politeness, directness, formality, and appropriateness of the rhetorical structure of the message (for instance, in the role of employee, composing an e-mail message to your boss requesting a promotion and a raise, or a paid vacation from the boss; or as neighbor, writing a note complaining about late-evening TV noise), namely, the way that meaning is conveyed through oral and written language, through facial expressions, and through gestures.

A major focus of research on pragmatics over the years has been that of speech acts. *Speech acts* are the often-predictable routines that speakers and writers use to perform language functions, such as thanking, complimenting, requesting, refusing, apologizing, and complaining, at times performed in an *indirect* manner that may be difficult to interpret (see Searle, 1976, for a classification of speech acts). *Speech-act-specific strategies* are strategies that if used alone or in combination with one or more other strategies specific to that speech act, assist in the realization of the given speech act (Blum-Kulka, House, & Kasper, 1989). For example, the speech-act-specific strategies for apologizing would include an *expression of apology, acknowledgement of responsibility, an offer of repair, an explanation,* and *a promise of non-recurrence.*

A theoretical issue which has gotten significant currency with regard to pragmatics and especially with regard to speech acts is the distinction between pragmalinguistics and sociopragmatics. *Pragmalinguistics* refers to what constitutes appropriate linguistic forms for expressing the intent of the speech act, taking into account the norms of behavior that apply in the given situation. *Sociopragmatics* refers to the norms of behavior for realizing the given speech act in a given context, taking into account (a) the culture involved, (b) the relative age and gender of the interlocutors, (c) their social class and occupations, and (d) their roles and status in the interaction (Thomas, 1983). Another theoretical issue is that of sociolinguistic variation, namely that there is regional variation in pragmatic behavior, which makes an already challenging field even more so, and adds a new challenge for curriculum writers wishing to provide materials on pragmatics for the classroom.

Pragmatics has often been associated with common speech acts like requesting and apologizing, and less commonly researched ones like criticizing, insulting, and cursing, and related issues of politeness. There are, however, numerous other language areas involving pragmatics such as the use of humor and irony, dealing with sarcasm and teasing, making and understanding small talk, engaging in conversational management including backchanneling and other listener responses, interpreting deixis[2] and conversational implicature, and the uses of discourse markers (see Cohen, in press, for a review of research in these areas). Despite having spent many hours studying the grammatical forms and vocabulary items, learners may still lack pragmatic information that is crucial both for understanding and for communicating intentions.

Studies have identified speech routines in both oral and written language that tend to have a strategic role to play in speech acts, especially with regard to the more common and sometimes even perfunctory speech acts such as "thanking." With the less perfunctory ones, such as "complaining," it can be more challenging to describe the norms since sociolinguistic behavior is by its very nature variable. The same strategies may form the basic structure for the speech act in numerous languages. The use of particular strategies in a given socio-pragmatic situation (e.g., an apology after an altercation) depends on a series of factors (see Figure 1):

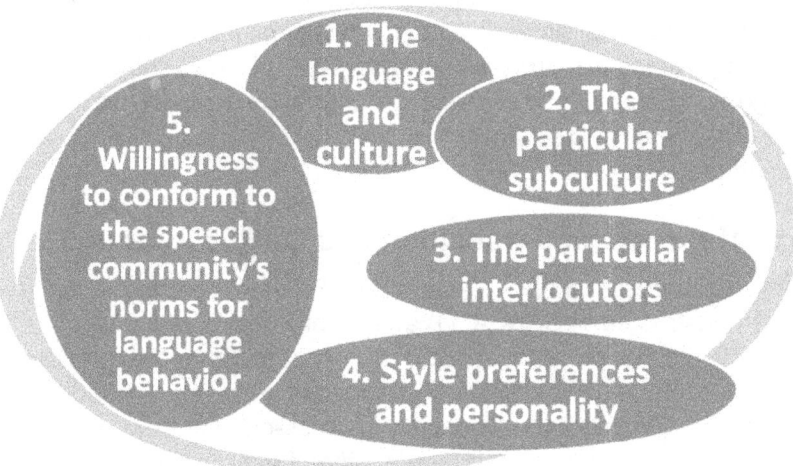

**Figure 1.** Factors determining the strategy configuration.

So, let us say we are looking at apologies in Hebrew in mainstream Israeli culture. Let us further say that the interlocutors are in the subculture of secular Israeli teenagers. The particular interlocutors are two 18-year-old males who are good friends. Let us further say, for discussion purposes, that they are both relatively outgoing and a bit pugnacious by nature. If they are native to the culture, they may be less likely to use any apology strategies at all to each other (e.g., expression of apology, acknowledgement of responsibility, or explanation) for some relatively minor infraction (like coming late to a meeting at a cafe) than would non-natives, say from the US, who have been taught to be apologetic about such matters. The Hebrew L2 speakers might offer the expression of apology ("I'm sorry to keep you waiting") and may also use another strategy like an explanation ("I waited half an hour for the bus"). The Hebrew-L1-speaking teenagers, on the other hand, may not see the need to apologize given their personalities and also given that delays are perceived by their peer group as a normal part of life.

Of course, non-native deviation from local norms may not be a result of ignorance of the appropriate behaviour, but rather an expression by the learners of their own subjectivity in the matter (see Ishihara, 2014). In other words, the non-natives may be fully aware of the normative behavior for their peer group (i.e., not to appear too apologetic), but choose to behave according to U.S., norms for such behavior. In this case, they would not be conforming to the L2 pragmatic norms out of a sense of agency – that is, a desire to be true to their own self-perceived identity.

It was out of a concern to highlight possible pragmatic differences across cultures and subcultures that efforts were made at CARLA to construct web pages[3] focused specifically on speech acts in different languages. The intention was to motivate teachers to access this material as part of their L2 instruction, as well as to serve as a resource for learners on their own to delve into the workings of speech acts across languages. This brief report takes a retrospective look at the design and construction of these web pages to promote the teaching and learning of L2 pragmatics, with a view to future efforts. The next section will describe these efforts.

## Design of pragmatics websites: The CARLA story

In this section, let us take a look at three sets of web pages appearing at a website constructed at CARLA, (1) a general website introducing pragmatics and especially speech acts in 2001, (2) a Japanese pragmatics website launched in 2003, and (3) a Spanish pragmatics website launched in 2006. All three websites benefited from research in cross-cultural pragmatics and from interventional studies investigating the effects of explicit pragmatics instruction on the development of pragmatic ability. Their goal was to employ web-based strategy instruction: to enhance learners' development and use of language learner strategies, to provide guidance in complex pragmatic language use that is difficult to "pick up," and to facilitate learning through web-based materials.

Every academic effort needs to be situated in its meaningful context. At the time that these websites were being constructed, the aim was to identify and teach both instructors and learners themselves about speech acts in a variety of languages. Describing speech acts was a keen concern then, and is still of interest to researchers and practitioners, even as the foci for pragmatics research enlarge and the means for collecting data expand. The design of pragmatics websites was viewed first and foremost as a support for busy teachers, especially non-native ones who may not be sure themselves as to the appropriate pragmatics for each and every situation. The provision of L2 pragmatics materials on a website was viewed initially as a means to mobilize L2 acquisition theories in support of classroom practice.

The perception that I had at the time, and which a small group of University of Minnesota students shared with me, was that there was a critical mass of empirical research accumulating but not much effort to get this information out into the field of language pedagogy. Hence, the design of pragmatics websites was seen as a contribution to teacher development in L2 pragmatics by providing research-based information about pragmatics. In addition, the web pages were viewed as a place that learners could go to help them in learning about appropriate choices in intercultural communication, as well as learning how to be more strategic about their learning and performance of speech acts. At the time, technology was not nearly as advanced as it is now, but still, there was a desire to incorporate technology into instructional offerings for the learning of pragmatics (see Taguchi & Sykes, 2012, for a relatively recent book on this topic).

A rationale for constructing the websites was to make it easier for teachers to include pragmatics in their instruction by supplying them empirically-based pragmatics material, providing them knowledge about pragmatics and a way to package this knowledge for students, and offering a ready means for integrating pragmatics into instruction for teachers who were already overly busy with what they were currently teaching. Along with the website development, a course for language instructors, professors, and administrators on the teaching of pragmatics was developed and started to be offered in the summer of 2006 at CARLA alongside the other summer institute offerings. Largely as an outgrowth of developing materials for that summer course, a book was written to assist teachers in L2 pragmatics instruction (Ishihara & Cohen, 2014). The material in the book was pilot-tested in those institutes over three summers (2006–2008), so that all the tasks in the book had ample field-testing. The summer institute is now offered intermittently at CARLA, and was offered in the summer of 2014.

Thanks to federal funding to the Language Resource Center at CARLA, the pragmatics website project was initiated in 2001, with the goal of providing self-access internet sites for the learning and performance of L2 pragmatics. The first effort was to construct a website for teachers, curriculum writers, and learners, entitled "Pragmatics and Speech Acts." The website provides information about six speech acts: requests, refusals, apologies, complaints, compliments, and thanking, and with examples in 10 languages (see Figure 2).The website has suggested strategies for teaching these speech acts and provides sample teaching materials, along with an annotated bibliography (updated in 2012), which includes information on other areas of pragmatics as well.

**Figure 2.** CARLA's Pragmatics and Speech Acts Web Page 4

The second project was the construction of a Japanese pragmatics website, entitled "Strategies for Learning Speech Acts in Japanese" (see Figure 3). The website has units for the learning of specific speech acts in Japanese: apologies, compliments, requests, refusals, and expressing gratitude. The initial construction and evaluation of the website was under the guidance of Gabriele Kasper (University of Hawai'i) and the curriculum adviser was Elite Olshtain (now professor emeritus from the Hebrew University of Jerusalem). Each unit was pilot-tested with learners of Japanese, revised in the Spring of 2003, and then further revised in the Fall of 2003, incorporating learners' feedback from research conducted with students using the website (Cohen & Ishihara, 2005). The units were adopted (on a trial basis) as part of the third-year Japanese course curriculum at the University of Minnesota, 2003–2004.

As part of each speech act unit, learners are to interact with audio clips of native-speaker dialogs and complete 10 exercises designed to assist them in developing appropriate strategies for learning and using each of the five speech acts in Japanese. Each speech act unit has the following components:

- comparisons of L1 and L2 norms;
- examination of contextual factors influencing each speech act (i.e., age, status, level of acquaintance, intensity of the act);
- self-evaluation of linguistic behavior;

- a focus on the speech-act-specific strategies which alone or in combination with other strategies serve to constitute the given;
- speech act, such as "an offer of repair" when apologizing;
- practice in producing output; and
- self-evaluation and feedback.

For each unit, sample interactions are based largely on empirical data from research studies. There are pragmatic awareness-raising tasks, where the norms for L2 pragmatic behavior are clearly spelled out. There are both pragmalinguistic exercises, where the focus is on language structure, with lexical and grammatical information provided (e.g., how to use the apology word *sumimasen*), and sociopragmatic exercises, where the focus is on sociocultural issues, such as what to compliment people for in Japanese. The website was intended to be used either on a stand-alone basis or as a supplement to an intermediate course in Japanese (for more on the website, see Cohen & Ishihara, 2005; Ishihara, 2007; Ishihara & Cohen, 2014).

### Exercises for Learners of Japanese

**Let's start by doing the exercises in Introduction to Speech Acts!**

In these introductory exercises, you will be asked to write down your observations in each situation. Your responses will be e-mailed to us as soon as you finish with all each question and click on 'Submit' at the end. Then, you will be able to see some comments regarding the question.

Situation 1   Situation 2   Situation 3   Situation 4

Situation 5   Situation 6   Situation 7   Situation 8

**After finishing the Introductory exercises, move on to exercises for each speech act.**

Apologies in Japanese

Compliments/Responses to Compliments in Japanese

Refusals in Japanese

Requests in Japanese

Thanks in Japanese

**In concluding all speech act strategy exercises, you are invited to view** an additional set of strategies **for learning how to perform or enhance your performance of speech acts in a second language.**

**Figure 3.** Strategies for Learning Speech Acts in Japanese[5]

Here is a comment from a student learner of Japanese after accessing the website:

> We focus on grammar the most in courses so we can produce proper sentences, but we seldom get a chance to practice the practical use of such phrases. Having a variety of situations with a detailed description of what elements are important and relevant to the speech used helps a lot. It

helps to know what to take into consideration, such as the age of the person, the situation, and the level of formality.

The third project was the construction of a Spanish pragmatics website, entitled "Dancing with Words: Strategies for Learning Pragmatics in Spanish" (see Figure 4). Its construction drew on lessons learned from the development of the Japanese website, as well as advances in web technology, and it was launched in August of 2006. The site consists of an introductory unit and eight additional units:

- compliments;
- gratitude and leave taking;
- requests;
- apologies;
- invitations;
- service encounters;
- advice, suggestions, disagreements, complaints, and reprimands; and
- considerations for pragmatic performance.

Each unit consists of unscripted video interchanges between native speakers of various regional varieties of Spanish, and activities at different levels of difficulty to cater to learners with varying pragmatic ability. All instructional material is in English with the examples, transcripts, and activities to be completed in Spanish (for more on the website, see Sykes & Cohen, 2008). The website constitutes a self-access venue for learning Spanish pragmatics with the following elements:

- empirically-based content,
- the provision of strategies-based learning and use,
- examples of acceptable pragmatic behavior,
- the pragmatics for language varieties in the Spanish-speaking world,
- encouragement of individual pragmatic development,
- a non-prescriptive approach to pragmatics, and
- accessible feedback to learners.
- Each unit has the following:
- an introduction,
- a description of the speech act (referred to as a *communicative act*),
- strategies for learning and performing the given speech act,
- identification of important social factors,
- a discussion of pragmatic variation by dialect, and
- a summary of the key points.

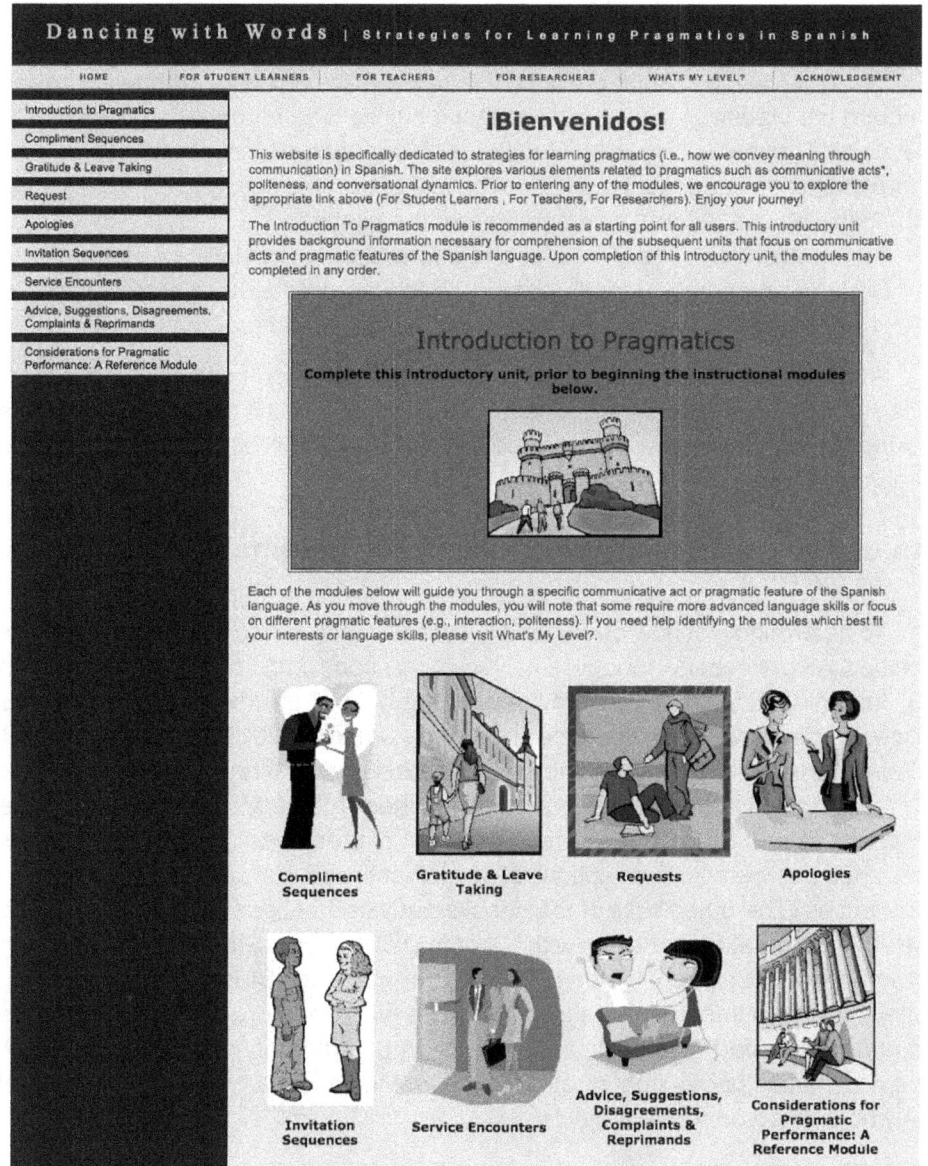

**Figure 4** Strategies for Learning Pragmatics in Spanish[6]

As indicated above, the web page included information on dialect differences in Spanish based on research available at the time (e.g., Márquez Reiter & Placencia, 2005). More research results have appeared since the construction of the website (García & Placencia, 2011; Schneider & Barron, 2008), so there is a need to update the information about Spanish dialect differences as they relate to pragmatics. Section 4, below, will deal with plans for updating the website information.

Student piloting in 2006 provided useful feedback on how to improve scrolling through the website, as well as feedback on links that were made or needed to be made. There was also useful feedback on improving the content, on providing more examples, on accent marks, on the use of terminology, and on writing style. The following is a student's comment from the piloting:

> I think overall it's really helpful and informative, especially for students who are intending to study abroad...because before you go you know it's going to be different, but you don't get the actual pragmatic stuff...

After all that work in web page construction, the good news is that this work has stood the test of time. As the next section will report, the pragmatics materials on the CARLA website continue to be popular with numerous users that visit the pragmatics web pages.

## An unobtrusive measure of use of the pragmatics web pages at CARLA

To determine just how often people were accessing the pragmatics materials on the CARLA website, Google Analytics was used,[7] with special attention given to Content Drilldown, which provides an analysis of the extent to which users access different web pages on the site. From August 29, 2013, to August 29, 2014, all the CARLA websites combined experienced a total of roughly 1,250,000 hits. Of these hits, 11% were on the pragmatics pages (133,000). The general website, "Pragmatics and Speech Acts," received 70% of these hits. The breakdown was 6% of the hits were for descriptions of speech acts and 7% were for the annotated references. The other 30% of the hits were divided between the Japanese and Spanish pragmatics websites, with "Dancing with Words: Strategies for Learning Pragmatics in Spanish" getting 23% of the hits, and "Strategies for Learning Speech Acts in Japanese" getting 7% of the hits. So, more than a dozen years after the first effort was made to construct an L2 pragmatics website at CARLA, the pragmatics pages continue to draw interest, which is gratifying for those of us who worked on these projects.

## Suggestions looking forward/The future

The question looking forward is how best to serve the international community with innovations in the design of L2 pragmatics websites. The approach that appears to be the most promising is to set up a wiki where pragmatics researchers and instructors worldwide can contribute their insights and findings to further along the action. The main strategy will be to use *crowdsourcing*, namely, soliciting contributions from a large group of people, and especially from the online community. The goal will be to make the collection of L2 pragmatics information more varied – including data from more languages, as well as more information about language variation across users and dialect variations as well. We may include simulations where learners have the opportunity to produce L2 pragmatics. The wiki will most certainly include information on additional speech acts and revised content based on the 10 or so years since the Japanese and Spanish websites were constructed.

It is the co-constructor of the Spanish pragmatics website, Julie Sykes, who had the idea of creating a wiki for which multiple people contribute in different language varieties, providing their perceptions across dialect and community (personal communication, September 2, 2014). In essence, the idea is to have a section of the current CARLA website that will function like Wikipedia or another forum with multiple contributors. This wiki will provide descriptions of a wide variety of pragmatic behaviors. People will be able, for example, to posit suggestions or questions and get input from those around the world or populate a certain area with examples from their home community. This cross-cultural effort will allow for multiple comparisons as to what is the same and what is different across cultures and subcultures.

The co-constructor of the Japanese pragmatics website, Noriko Ishihara, has as her vision for the future to see the pragmatics website include more speech acts and other areas of pragmatics. Rather than the managers of the website being responsible for reading and summarizing research papers, she sees it making more sense going forward to create a template for contributions to the wiki and to post this template to colleagues around the world (personal communication, September 8, 2014). Then the contributions will be edited (minimally) and uploaded to the wiki.[8]

CARLA's webmaster, Marlene Johnshoy, has set up a wiki for pragmatics using wikispaces.com. A graduate student monitor has been hired on an hourly basis to monitor this L2 pragmatics wiki. The grad student monitor will focus on quality control with regard to the contributions, and on categorizing and situating the offerings in the appropriate places.

The Japanese website was constructed just with audio clips, albeit of native speakers speaking in an unscripted fashion and being as natural as possible in their responses in the given speech act situations. The Spanish site has both audio and video (using a hand-held camcorder). Nowadays everyone has video capability on cell phones. Those who submit pragmatics information could easily attach video clips or include links to YouTube videos showcasing the behavior. Technology is racing ahead at such a record-breaking pace that it is difficult to foresee just what may be possible in the future for illustrating pragmatic behavior across languages and cultures.

The efforts started 12 years ago at CARLA have proven themselves to be valuable and useful. It is now time to take the next step, consistent with current technologies and interest. So, let this article serve as a call for wiki contributions.

Those interested in contributing to this instructionally-focused, L2 pragmatics wiki can write to pragmaticswiki2016@gmail.com. Those who would like to visit the wiki should go to http://wlpragmatics.pbworks.com. Here are some suggestions that may stimulate some thinking on your part and among your students and colleagues as well:

1. Video cuts from the discourse around the holiday dinner table – capturing key moments of discourse (with the permission of family members, relatives, and others). If not in English, then glosses need to be provided for those utterances.

2. A synopsis of recent pragmatics studies, with generous detail about the nature of the instruments, the efforts to validate these instruments, clever (and perhaps groundbreaking) data analysis procedures, and fascinating findings.

3. Sharing the details of research because it represents work in pragmatics which is underrepresented in the field – for instance,
   - speech acts without a solid research base like genuine criticism (e.g., for dressing sloppily, having an absurd hair style, behaving unacceptably, and the like) or efforts by nonnatives to curse that do and do not work,
   - tone of voice in English (e.g., perception or production of sarcastic or facetious utterances),
   - conversational management and mismanagement by nonnatives,
   - efforts at small talk that work or do not work, and
   - anecdotal accounts of pragmatic failure, especially cases of what have amounted to sociopragmatic goofs. Some possible examples are
     - complimenting a secretary in Israel for a job well done (not knowing that the secretary may well consider the compliment as demeaning since it implies that the other work performed is not up to par),
     - a nonnative asking an American how much s/he makes a month or how much the new house or new car cost, asking whether or not a woman is trying to have kids and how it is going (e.g., whether she is using IVF to have a baby),
     - asking certain Arab males how many children they have (since for some, divulging this information could put a curse on one or another of the children), and
     - an American telling other Chinese colleagues in Beijing about a late-night foot massage with a Chinese colleague and spouse, without realizing that the sharing this information would be deeply embarrassing to the colleague since it implied they had extra wealth do be able to afford such extravagances.

4. Getting the pragmalinguistics wrong – for instance, using "very" in an apology for inflicting bodily harm ("I'm very sorry for smashing into you") when "really"

means "regret" ("I'm really sorry about that! Are you OK?") and "very" simply is a form of etiquette ("I'm sorry to inform you that your time is up").

5. The pragmatic consequences of using certain words that have multiple meanings or connotations that can be misinterpreted in a language. For instance, *Je suis plein*, intending to indicate the woman has eaten enough can easily be misconstrued in French to mean she is pregnant, whereas *J'ai assez mangé* 'I have eaten enough' would work fine without ambiguities.

6. Posting on the wiki thorny questions dealing with topics of crucial concern to research students, where researchers with experience in those areas can jump in and provide answers (as is readily available in so many internet sites today). Here are just five sets of queries that I have culled (and edited) from emails I have received in the last few months regarding pragmatics research:
   - How do I design video clips? Or could they be downloaded from the internet? If I design the video clips, should they be silent so that the participants could produce their own response?
   - I conducted my research with nearly 150 college university students at three levels of EFL students: BA, MA, and PhD. The question is "How do I differentiate between lack of pragmatic knowledge and perceived resistance to accommodate? For example, when a student starts his letter to a faculty member with *"Hello! Are you sure you corrected my paper?"* there appears to be a lot of underlying sarcasm. How am I supposed to interpret this (i.e., as lack of pragmatic knowledge or as resistance to accommodate)?
   - I found the speech act of "genuine criticism" intriguing. I wonder what the word "genuine" means exactly and what it refers to. Is it the type of immediate criticism that interlocutors express in the very social context in which they are interacting? I wonder if you may give me some hints.
   - Does development in pragmalinguistic ability follow in an incremental way, like with the development of negation or question formation? Since there might be more than one way to perform a speech act, how do I determine which norm(s) to pay attention to? How do I determine the extent to which the alternate approaches are at similar levels of importance with respect to their impact and appropriateness?
   - I am currently hoping to do my dissertation research on interculturality and pragmatics for Hebrew as a second language, and as a base I need some study that looks at Hebrew pragmatics as a first language in Israel (for comparison purposes). There are plenty of studies from the 1980s about this, and most people who decide to mention Hebrew in their studies go back to these articles. Although these articles are vital to understanding this area, I feel that my study would not be as credible without more modern examinations of Israeli Hebrew pragmatics. Do you know if there

are more recent studies that actually collected data from native Hebrew speakers that I could use?

The above examples just serve to underscore the ubiquitous role of pragmatics in daily communication. Pragmatics makes communication in any one language a daunting task at times. How much more challenging it becomes in multilingual contexts, especially when translanguaging[9] is a factor.

## Conclusions

This article has both served as a report of the work that has been done at CARLA to design and construct web material on pragmatics. It has also served as a call for future contributions. Now that there is funding for a wiki, starting in September of 2015 efforts will be made to launch and monitor the site. Announcements will be made once the wiki is operative. It is highly likely that the field of L2 pragmatics will benefit from this development. Whether it serves to answer research questions or provides data to inform pedagogy, establishing a pragmatics wiki in the language teaching and research community can provide just the needed repository of information across languages that will furnish teachers, learners, curriculum writers, and researchers with new insights. For curriculum writers, especially, it should provide a rich source of data for enhancing their curricular materials with insights about pragmatics. Ultimately, the outcome can be beneficial to all stake-holders in the language learning effort. While pragmatic failure will continue to appear whenever languages are used, the hope is that the use of better-informed sources will contribute to diminishing the likelihood of pragmatic failure.

### Notes

1. For the purpose of expediency, the acronym L2 in this chapter represents both contexts in which the target language is a language spoken widely in the learners' community and contexts where it is not spoken widely.
2. *Deixis* refers to words and phrases that cannot be fully understood without additional contextual information. Words are deictic if their semantic meaning is fixed but their denotational meaning varies depending on time and/or place (e.g., words like *there*, *this*, and *that*).
3. *Web page* here is used to distinguish subsections of a website from the other sections. A web page may actually consist of multiple physical pages.
4. Retrieved May 15, 2015 from http://www.carla.umn.edu/speechacts/index.html
5. Retrieved May 15, 2015 from http://www.carla.umn.edu/speechacts/japanese/introtospeechacts/index.htm
6. Retrieved May 15, 2015 from http://www.carla.umn.edu/speechacts/sp_pragmatics/home.html

7   See the following link for an explanation: http://searchenginewatch.com/sew/how-to/2340779/google-analytics-content-reports-understanding-the-key-benefits#, retrieved May 15, 2015
8   Ishihara has obtained funding from the Japanese government *her university* to hire someone to monitor the wiki.
9   *Translanguaging* is "the ability of multilingual speakers to shuttle between languages, the diverse languages that form their repertoire as an integrated system" (Canagarajah, 2011, p. 401). See García and Wei (2014) for more on translanguaging

## References

Blum-Kulka, S., House, J., & Kasper, G. (1989). Investigating cross-cultural pragmatics: An introductory overview. In S. Blum-Kulka, J. House, & G. Kasper (Eds.), *Cross-cultural pragmatics: Requests and apologies* (pp. 1–34). Norwood, NJ: Ablex.

Canagarajah, S. (2011). Codemeshing in academic writing: Identifying teachable strategies of translanguaging. *The Modern Language Journal, 95*(3), 401–417.

Cohen, A. D. (in press). Teaching and learning second language pragmatics. In E. Hinkel (Ed.), *Handbook of research in second language teaching and learning* (Vol. 3). New York, NY: Routledge.

Cohen, A. D., & Ishihara, N. (2005). A web-based approach to strategic learning of speech acts. Minneapolis, MN: Center for Advanced Research on Language Acquisition (CARLA), University of Minnesota. Retrieved from http://www.carla.umn.edu/speechacts/Japanese%20Speech%20Act%20Report%20Rev.%20June05.pdf.

García, G., & Placencia, M. E. (Eds.). (2011). *Estudios de variación pragmática en español* [Studies of pragmatic variation in Spanish]. Buenos Aires: Dunken.

García, O., & Wei, L. (2014). *Translanguaging: Language, bilingualism, and education.* Basingstoke, England: Palgrave Macmillan.

Ishihara, N. (2007). Web-based curriculum for pragmatics instruction in Japanese as a foreign language: An explicit awareness-raising approach. *Language Awareness, 16*, 21–40.

Ishihara, N. (2014). Theories of language acquisition and the teaching of pragmatics. In N. Ishihara & A. D. Cohen (Eds.), *Teaching and learning pragmatics: Where language and culture meet* (pp. 99–122). Abingdon, England: Routledge.

Ishihara, N., & Cohen, A. D. (2014). *Teaching and learning pragmatics: Where language and culture meet.* Abingdon, England: Routledge.

Márquez Reiter, R., & Placencia, M. E. (2005). *Spanish pragmatics.* New York, NY: Palgrave, Macmillan.

Schneider, K., & Barron, A. (eds.) (2008). *Variational pragmatics: A focus on regional varieties in pluricentric languages.* Philadelphia, PA: John Benjamins.

Searle, J. (1976). A classification of illocutionary acts. *Language in Society, 5*(1), 1–23.

Sykes, J. M., & Cohen, A. D. (2008). L2 pragmatics: Six principles for online materials development and implementation. *Acquisition of Japanese as a Second Language,*

*11*, 81–100. Available along with other pragmatics papers at https://sites.google.com/a/umn.edu/andrewdcohen/publications/pragmatics

Taguchi, N., & Sykes, J. M. (Eds.) (2012). *Technology in interlanguage pragmatics research and teaching.* Amsterdam: John Benjamins.

Thomas, J. (1983). Cross-cultural pragmatic failure. *Applied Linguistics, 4*(2), 91–112.

Yule, G. (1996). *Pragmatics.* Oxford: Oxford University Press.

# A Corpus Linguistics Analysis of On-Line Peer Commentary

Naoko Taguchi
David Kaufer
María Pía Gómez-Laich
*Carnegie Mellon University, USA*

Helen Zhao
*The Chinese University of Hong Kong*

This report describes a preliminary attempt to apply DocuScope, a computer platform for classifying text into rhetorical categories, to the analysis of an interactive educational task. We compiled two corpora of peer comments, namely peers critiquing each other's essays in classes teaching academic and professional writing. One corpus was constructed from a graduate-level, narrative and argumentation class in a U.S. university where 12 participants shared critiques of each other's essays in a collaborative online environment. The other corpus was compiled in an undergraduate-level composition class in Hong Kong where 13 learners of L2 English commented on one another's essays online. These two corpora were automatically tagged in the DocuScope environment and statistically analyzed. Although the tasks were pragmatically similar, there were significant differences in the rhetorical features used to accomplish the task across the different classrooms. These differences are discussed and are judged to reflect differences in culture, classroom climate, and the overall purpose of the peer response activity.

## Introduction

This brief report introduces *DocuScope* (Ishizaki & Kaufer, 2011), a corpus-based tool for analyzing pragmatic language use in written texts. Previous corpus-based research on pragmatic analysis mainly falls into two categories.

One is a group of quantitative studies that examined the occurrence of pre-selected pragmalinguistic forms (e.g., discourse markers, speech act utterances). Using concordancing programs with key word search techniques, these studies presented frequency findings of target pragmalinguistic features (e.g., Carretero, Maiz-Arevalo, & Angeles Martinez, 2014; Torgersen, Cabrielatos, Hoffman, & Fox, 2011; Vaughan & Clancy, 2013). The other line of research includes qualitative studies that used human raters to identify semantic moves and pragmalinguistic forms in texts. In these studies, trained raters manually coded pragmatic features sentence-by-sentence to discern linguistic patterns of a pragmatic act (e.g., Cutting, 2001; Garcia & Drescher, 2006).

These previous approaches have several limitations. First, in quantitative studies, exclusive focus on pre-selected pragmatic forms restricts the analysis to sentence-level units (words and phrases) and does not extend to the analysis of higher-level discourse functions (e.g., constructive criticism). On the other hand, hand-coding in qualitative studies is time-consuming when analyzing a large collection of texts because several rounds of coding are necessary to establish accuracy and reliability of coding.

*DocuScope* offers solutions to these problems. This computer program provides a consistent, reliable analysis of a large compilation of natural texts. It also presents a combined analysis of lower- and higher-level units by analyzing words and phrases and their placement in larger discourse categories. In this paper, we will report on a preliminary application of the *DocuScope* technique to a pragmatic analysis. We have compiled corpora of peer comments on essays in graduate and undergraduate English writing classes. We will describe how we used *DocuScope* to analyze the corpora and the results generated by the analysis. We will conclude by discussing the potential of *DocuScope* and corpus-linguistics methods in the investigation of pragmatic behaviors.

## Target pragmatic act and purpose of the study

This study analyzes peer commenting and critiquing as the target pragmatic act. Giving peer feedback is a common social act in academic and professional writing classes. Constructive criticism has high potential to be a face-threatening act. Moderating direct face-threats, in turn, requires appropriate semantic moves, strategies, and pragmalinguistic forms (Nguyen, 2008). At the same time, people must still be effective at communicating their critiques so the critiques can be understood and acted on.

Previous studies have revealed a variety of linguistic forms used to realize the speech acts of criticism, complaint, and disagreement by native and nonnative speakers of English (e.g., Murphy & Neu, 1995; Nguyen, 2008; Salsbury & Bardovi-Harlig, 2000). Using a peer feedback task and a discourse completion task, Nguyen (2008) analyzed the linguistic characteristics of peer feedback to essays in English. Her analysis focused on the use of modifiers, defined as linguistic devices used to help reduce the offense of a criticism. External modifiers involved supportive moves to the criticism, including the use of compliments or positive remarks before or after a criticism. Internal modifiers included syntactic and lexical devices that help tone down the criticism (e.g., hedges and downtoners such as *maybe* and *possibly*, use of past tense as in *I thought you missed something*.). Results showed that native speakers of English used twice the number of modifiers that non-native speakers of English did. They also employed syntactic modifiers frequently in great variety. Complimenting was the most preferred external modifier among the native speakers. Non-native speakers, on the other hand, rarely used syntactic modifiers, and they also relied on a much narrower range of linguistic devices. Lower proficiency participants relied on a few modals and adverbs, such as *might, kind of*, and *probably/possibly/perhaps*.

Non-native speakers' restricted use of syntactic modification and their limited range of modification devices was also found in Salsbury and Bardovi-Harlig's (2000) analysis of oppositional talk (i.e., speech act of disagreement) in spontaneous conversations. Over one academic year, eight learners of English overused certain lexical devices (e.g., *maybe* and *I think*) when modifying the face-threatening speech act. They started incorporating syntactic modifications with modals (e.g., *could*) at a later period.

The goal of our *DocuScope*-based analysis is to uncover the range of linguistic features of peer critiquing and to demonstrate how these features collectively configure the discourse of critiquing. By analyzing peer commentary in two entirely different classes removed by culture and other variables, we intend to discover diverse linguistic patterns by which the act of commenting and critiquing is constructed. We thus hope to shed light on how factors such as culture, classroom environment, and curriculum can help shape what otherwise might like look like a simple and irreducible educational task.

## *DocuScope*: A corpus tool for linguistic analysis

*DocuScope* (Ishizaki & Kaufer, 2011) is a computer platform with string-matching algorithms for categorizing text and an authoring component that allows users to build their language categories for raw text. For those uninterested in building their own pattern-matching categories for language, the platform contains a built-in library of 49.1 million linguistic strings of English, which are categorized into dimensions and language action types. The actual linguistic strings are contained in language action types. Dimensions are simply groupings of related language action types into hierarchies. See the following example of the dimension *description*.

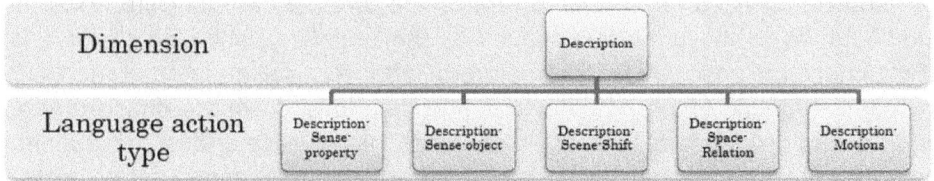

**Figure 1.** Sample dimension, and language action types

Strings of English that fall into the dimension *description* reference linguistic entities that conjure sensory (visual, auditory, tactile, olfactory, gustatory) imagery in the minds of readers. These include sense properties (e.g., *pink, velvety, grating noise*,), objects (e.g., *table, raw mushrooms, smelly towel, street lampposts*), shifts of scene (e.g., *journeyed to, departed for, trekked, left the room*), spatial relations (e.g., *sitting next to, abutting, jutting out*), and motions (e.g., *run, hop, jump, trudge, skip*).

*DocuScope* contains 198 language action types organized into 33 dimensions. The entire *DocuScope* library covers 70% of most English texts and has been used to supplement methods in discourse analysis, rhetorical criticism, and author attribution (Ishizaki & Kaufer, 2011). When texts are analyzed using the program, the *DocuScope*'s pattern matcher runs automatically and codes linguistic patterns across any corpus of interest, categorizing the texts based on the patterns found in the texts. Originally, *DocuScope* was designed as a diagnostic tool for L2 learners seeking to acquire a new genre in English (Kaufer, Geisler, Ishizaki, & Vlachos, 2005; Kaufer, Ishizaki, Collins, & Vlachos, 2004). For example, the genre of narrative texts is reliably characterized by language action types such as past tense transitive verbs, expressions of time shift (e.g., *last year*) and time duration (e.g., *for two years*). Using *DocuScope*, we can examine whether L2 narrative texts approximate the target narrative genre by incorporating these language action types.

In addition to the text tagging function, *DocuScope* provides a visualization environment that helps people visualize intended genre effects in texts. For example, people can see how similar their text is compared with the prototypical text in the given genre, and what linguistic forms and categories are present or absent compared with the prototype.

## Method and analysis

Using *DocuScope*, we analyzed two corpora of peer commentary compiled in two English writing classes during the fall semester of 2013. One class was a graduate-level narrative and argument class in a private university in the USA. A total of 21,485 words of peer comments were compiled from this class. The other class was a freshman composition class for English majors in a university in Hong Kong, which yielded a 29,900-word corpus of peer comments. Because the graduate class involved native speakers and bilinguals who were advanced writers, we refer to them as the expert group in this paper. In contrast, the undergraduate class involved freshman non-native speakers of English at the beginning of their academic study. Thus, this group is referred to as the novice group.[1] During the semester, class instructors provided no specific directions as to how to comment on peers' essays, although they pointed to several areas of focus when critiquing essays.

The expert group (graduate class in a U.S. university) had 11 students. Nine students were native speakers of English, and two were Chinese students with near-native English proficiency. The students were required to produce seven essays during the semester, each ranging 2–8 pages on a variety of genres, including self-portrait, scenic writing, and narrative history. Students uploaded 3–4 drafts for each essay, to which a peer provided comments online. The novice group (undergraduate class in a Hong Kong university) had 13 freshmen. They were all L2 writers of English, and the majority of them were L1 Cantonese. They scored 75 or above on the Michigan Test of English Language Proficiency (comparable to TOEFL iBT score of 79–80). They wrote two essays during the semester (argumentation and short story analysis; 5–6 pages each), which were commented by two peers online.

Peer comments were written and were collected from Classroom Salon, a social networking application developed at Carnegie Mellon University (http://www.classroomsalon.com/). The Classroom Salon incorporates Facebook-like features that intend to facilitate online collaborative learning (Kaufer, Gunawardena, Tan, & Cheek, 2011). The relevant aspect of Classroom Salon for this study is its ability to store, aggregate, and download into excel files on-line annotations for an individual or a whole class across the course of a semester. This makes Classroom Salon a very convenient corpus-building tool for on-line annotations. We used Classroom Salon in this way to build a corpus of all the comments made in the U.S. classroom and all the comments made in the Hong Kong classroom.

The two corpora of peer comments were analyzed on all major dimensions of the *DocuScope* built-in library. A one-way ANOVA was used to examine whether the frequency of linguistic features at the dimension-level was different between the graduate and undergraduate corpus. When there was a significant difference at a dimension level, lower-level analyses were conducted to investigate which language action types contributed to the differences. We supplemented the quantitative findings with manual analyses of extracted comments.

## Results

### Quantitative analysis

Using *DocuScope*, we found a significant difference between the two corpora of peer commentary over 13 dimensions at the alpha-level of .05. Table 1 displays those areas of differences, that is, specific dimensions or language action types where one corpus was significantly higher on frequency than the other. Below we will illustrate the notable areas of differences that are considered to typify the language of commenting in the expert and novice group.

Table 1. Areas of significant difference in linguistic features between the graduate and undergraduate students' commenting language identified by *DocuScope*

| dimension | expert group comments | novice group comments |
|---:|---|---|
| character | personal pronouns (he, she) proper nouns | |
| emotion | positive emotion | negative emotion |
| personal register | personal disclosure uncertainty self-disclosure | |
| public register | | public language public value |
| academic register | | abstract noun/adjective/adverb abstract specialized citation |
| past tense | past tense | |
| personal relations | positive relations | |
| directive | | imperative |
| narrative | biographical | |
| description | descriptive language | |
| reasoning | reason concessive | reason forward reason support reason denial |
| assertiveness | intensifier | insistence |
| interactivity | curiosity "you" subject "you" question "you" reference | "you" contingent |

The dimension *character* is active when reference is made to a person. The expert group corpus was significantly higher on this dimension than the novice group corpus, as evidenced in the students' frequent use of personal pronouns (e.g., *he* and *she*) and proper nouns (persons' names such as *Bruce* and *Mary*). The expert group corpus was also high on the dimension of *personal register*, which refers to texts containing subjective observation. As a characteristic of this dimension, the expert students' comments showed repeated use of personal disclosure language (use of disclosure verbs such as *believe* and *feel*), expressions of uncertainty (adverbs such as *perhaps* and *maybe*), and self-reference words combined with verbs indicating personal thoughts (e.g., *I think*). The expert group comments also exhibited the characteristic of personal relations, with the frequent appearance of positive relation verbs such as *love* and *admire*.

In sharp contrast, the novice group's comments were oriented toward the public and academic register. Compared with the expert group comments, their comments included more instances of public language use (reference to public authorities) and expressions of public values (e.g., words that the public in general believes or rejects, such as *justice* or *injustice*). The novice students also used language that characterizes academic register, including abstract nouns, adjectives, and adverbs (language used to describe non-concrete objects and phenomena), specialized and technical terms, and citations (e.g., *according to*). Their commenting language was also more directive and authoritative, as shown in the frequent occurrence of verb imperative forms.

Interestingly, both corpora were significantly high on the dimensions of *emotion, reasoning, assertiveness,* and *interactivity,* but the patterns of loading of linguistic features in these dimensions were markedly different. The expert group comments involved more positive emotion words, whereas the novice group used more negative emotion words. The expert students' comments included frequent use of reason-concessive language, that is, language used to acknowledge the other's point of view (e.g., *it must be acknowledged that . . .*). In addition, their comments were assertive because of their use of intensifiers (*very, really*). In contrast, the novice students' comments showed different types of reasoning expressions: language for moving a thought forward (e.g., *therefore, thus*) and language to support their point or deny others' claims. The novice students' comments were also assertive because of their use of insistence language (e.g., *you need to, you should, you must*).

Finally, on the dimension of *interactivity*, the expert students used a variety of linguistic forms that contributed to the interactive nature of their comments. Those forms included inquiry/curiosity expressions (language indicating a shared mental exploration such as *What's going on?*) and the second person pronoun *you* in different functions (as a subject and reference, and in a question). However, the novice students' comments were judged to be interactive because of the frequent occurrence of *you* in the contingent modal expressions (e.g., *you might want to*).

In summary, the *DocuScope* analysis identified a range of linguistic dimensions that were significantly different between the two corpora. These differences indicate that the common pragmatic act of critiquing others' essays was practiced differently in these two writing classes. In the undergraduate class in Hong Kong (the novice group), which consisted of L2 writers of English, peer comments were academically-oriented and sounded more public than personal, and were definitely instructive as evident in the frequent occurrence of imperatives and modals of obligation (e.g., *should* and *have to*). These characteristics seemed to reflect the nature and style of the class. It was a freshman composition class where students were explicitly taught rules and conventions of academic writing. The instructor taught these rules, and the students were expected to work with the rules. This is probably why the students' comments showed impersonal and academic characteristics. When commenting on essays, the students were acting like a teacher, passing on the rules they learned in class to their peers. They also overused *should*, *ought to*, *have to*, and *must*.

In contrast, the graduate class in a U.S. university (the expert group) was a genre-based writing class, which focused on experiential and professional writing. Unlike the class in Hong Kong, the focus of this class was to figure out the effect that the writer intended to convey on the reader and to learn how such effect could be achieved in writing. The class emphasized a holistic analysis of a text, rather than fixed rules and conventions of writing. Writing activities were more personalized than institutionalized. Students evaluated each other's writing from their own perspective, rather than imposing conventional rules and norms of writing. These characteristics of the graduate class and goals of peer feedback probably contributed to the unique linguistic features of critiquing that emerged from the corpus. The students' language was more personal, character-based, and interactive. It reflected positive emotions and personal relations, because in this class, commenting on peers' essays was a rapport-building activity in which the readers shared their personal perspectives and views with the writers, rather than teaching conventional rules of writing.

The next section presents manual analyses of select excerpts from the corpora. Manual analyses are provided to validate conclusions drawn from the quantitative analyses by presenting converging findings.

### Manual analysis

For the manual analysis, 2,000 words of comments were randomly extracted from each corpus, together yielding a total of 94 comments. Because critiquing is the major speech act in peer commentary, data were coded manually for two major criticism realization strategies: a) identifying a problematic action/choice, and b) giving a suggestion on how to change or correct the problem. In addition to these categories, following Nguyen's (2008) taxonomy, we coded the comments for the strategies used to modify a criticism (external modifiers in Nguyen), as found in the act of complimenting before criticizing (i.e., providing positive remarks for the writer either before or after a criticism to compensate for the face-threatening act). We also analyzed linguistic features involved in suggestions. We focused on the use of five features: (a) suggestions with an epistemic modal (*can, could, may, might*); (b) suggestions with a deontic modal (*have to, must, should, need to*); (c) suggestions with an imperative; (d) suggestions with an *if-clause*; and (e) suggestions using a question form. The use of assessment language (i.e., expressions of positive assessment such as *good* or *impressive* and expressions of negative assessment such as *unclear* and *inappropriate*) were also analyzed.

One striking difference between the expert and novice group was the use of criticism modifiers (i.e., compliments or the dimension of *positive relation* in *DocuScope*): The expert group provided more compliments (26%) than their novice counterparts (7%; e.g., *I love that you know this topic so well*, and *there is something I love about this line, it shows a great self-awareness, which I am personally a great fan of*). These tendencies show that the expert students used more comments to maintain positive relationships than the novices. It further suggests that insofar as experts made negative comments, they tended to mitigate the negative with positive reinforcement (compliments) more frequently than the novice students.

Another group difference was found in the suggestions. The novice group provided more suggestions (63%) than the expert group (47%). There were also qualitative differences in the manner of suggestions. The expert group used epistemic modals such as *might, could, may, might* when giving a suggestion (e.g., *a little more cohesion might help the piece as a whole*), and they also gave a suggestion by asking a question (e.g., *Maybe her heart was slowly changing and your grandma's illness made it visible. Can you interview her and ask her? Does she do email or Skype?*). Imperatives appeared less frequently in the expert group corpus. In sharp contrast, the novice students used imperatives much more frequently than the expert students, which made their suggestions strong and direct (e.g., *Use a connective to show contrast to the previous clause, cite those evidences to make your point stronger*). In addition, the use of questions was very rare in the novice group's suggestions, and they used more suggestions with the *if*-clause than the expert students. Figures 2 and 3 below illustrate these linguistic differences in the suggestion speech act.

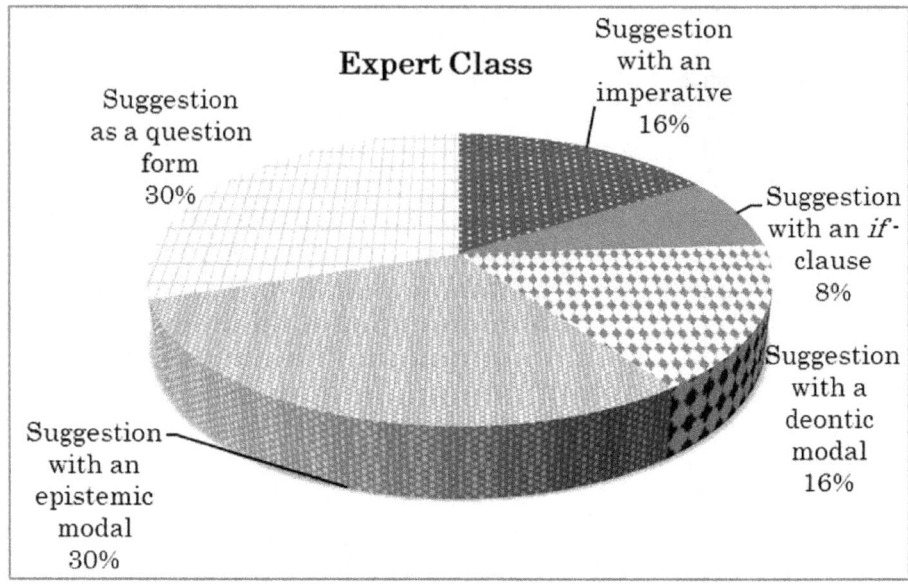

**Figure 2.** Linguistic realizations for the speech act of suggestion (expert group)

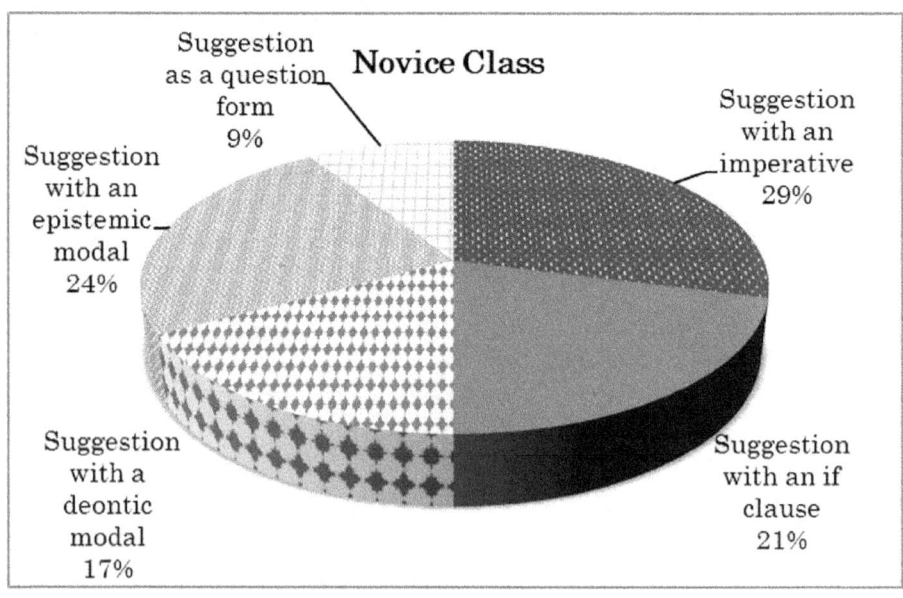

**Figure 3.** Linguistic realizations for the speech act of suggestion (novice group)

The two groups were similar in their use of suggestions with a deontic modal (e.g., *The use of past participle is inappropriate here and you have to change it to present participle*; *Honestly, your sentence structure is really messy throughout the essay. If you are using "ing" in verb, you should be parallel*). However, it is worth mentioning that the expert students usually used a hedging such as *perhaps, probably*, or *maybe* before the deontic modal (e.g., *I love that you know this topic so well, but maybe you should break this down a little more*). The use of these modifiers helped reduce the offence of the face-threatening act.

Finally, both classes exhibited great differences in their use of assessment language, with students in the expert group using more expressions of positive assessment than students in the undergraduate class (e.g., *This paragraph flows well, this description is great*; *There is something I love about this line, it shows a great self-awareness, which I am personally a great fan of*). Students in the novice group, by contrast, tended to employ more expressions of negative assessment (e.g., *Honestly, your sentence structure is really messy throughout the essay; The use of past participle is inappropriate here*; *Your writing is extremely redundant [weird];You have serious problems in your grammar because you are trying to put too much information into one sentence*).

In summary, the expert and novice groups revealed very different linguistic patterns in the speech act of giving a suggestion. The preferred strategies of the expert group involved the use of question forms and mild suggestions with epistemic modal verbs, whereas the preferred strategy of the novice group was the use of imperatives. The groups also differed in their use of positive remarks (compliments) paid to the writer either before or after a criticism to compensate for the face-threatening act: the expert students used more of them compared with the novice students. The groups also exhibited great differences in their use of assessment language, with the expert students favoring positive assessment words and the novice students favoring negative assessment words.

## Conclusion

The *DocuScope* analysis was able to capture linguistic features that differentiated the two forms of commenting language in a reliable and objective manner. The test study revealed marked differences in the nature of language of peer commenting in two different writing classes. The graduate students in a U.S. university (expert group) constructed their peer comments in a personalized, positive, and inquiring manner, as exemplified in their use of personal pronouns, positive emotion words, self-disclosing verbs, and second person pronoun *you*. In sharp contrast, the undergraduate students in a Hong Kong university (novice group) provided comments that sounded detached, objective, academic, and authoritative, as demonstrated in their use of public language, abstract expressions, imperatives, and strong suggestion formulae. The manual analysis of language data lent support to the quantitative findings gleaned from the *DocuScope* environment. The analyses agreed on the ways expert and novice students provided critiques and suggestions to their peers. For example, in the speech act of giving advice and suggestions, the novice students used deontic modals and imperatives (directives and insistence language in the *DocuScope*). The graduate students showed less use of the imperatives; instead, their suggestions were formulated more often in the form of a question (the second person pronoun *you* and inquiry language in the *DocuScope*).

The combined quantitative and manual analyses combined suggest great potential for the use of the *DocuScope* as a tool for pragmatic analysis. The computer-based method provides objective, efficient, and reliable analyses of pragmatic effects in written texts. The *DocuScope* analysis provides new insights into traditional pragmatics analyses of data that assumes one-to-one correspondence between form and force. Going beyond the sentence-level analysis, the *DocuScope* analysis enables a discourse-level, multi-dimensional analysis of a pragmatic act by revealing a constellation of linguistic forms that jointly make up the act.

This last observation leads to some final observations why *DocuScope*, as customized dictionaries, holds general promise as a tool for pragmatics research. The pragmatic force of written words in context depends on the company they keep to the left and right and on their order. Researchers can rely on the built-in dictionaries for efficient matching. But the built-in dictionaries are not likely to have anticipated all the orders and variations of pragmatic force that come with these orders. This limitation speaks to the importance of combining the default dictionaries with customized dictionaries to capture the contextual precision required for a particular data set. For example, the built-in dictionary coded *unclear* under the language action type of uncertainty (under the dimension "privy" [private state]; e.g., *I am unclear about*). But in on-line peer commentary contexts of the kind we studied, the word often appears not to express uncertainty but a negative assessment (e.g., *This is unclear to me.*). Customized dictionaries can be used to override entries in the built-in dictionary so that the actual pragmatic force of the language in the data set can be accurately captured.

More future research is necessary to explore the potential use of the *DocuScope* as an environment for corpus-based pragmatic analysis. Being exploratory in nature, the present study used ready-made corpora from already existing classes (peer comments compiled via Classroom Salon). Future research could use more principled methods in compiling a corpus of interest based on explicit research questions and use *DocuScope* as an analytical environment to answer the questions. For instance, a parallel corpus of peer comments among L2 English undergraduate students can be compiled in upper-level English classes or classes of different L1 backgrounds in order to explore different linguistic patterns in commenting, as well as the factors contributing to the differences (e.g., proficiency, level of development, L1 culture, and previous experience). In addition, since *DocuScope* is neutral to text type, it can be used to analyze spoken language. For example, we can compile a corpus of classroom language and use *DocuScope* to analyze linguistic characteristics of classroom discourse involving a range of speech acts (e.g., expressing opinions, supporting or refuting others' points of view). Such studies will help advance the use of *DocuScope* from a tool of text analysis to a means for investigating principled problems in pragmatics learning and development.

## Notes

1  We acknowledge that these two labels (expert and novice) are convenient labels. There are obviously more features that characterize the two groups. However, we decided to use these relatively simple labels because the focus of this study was not on comparing the two groups of writers: The focus was to demonstrate the use of *DocuScope* as an automated text analysis tool.

## References

Carretero, M., Maız-Arevalo, C., & Angeles Martınez, M. (2014). "Hope this helps!" An analysis of expressive speech acts in online task-oriented interaction by university students. In J. Romero-Trillo (Ed.), *Yearbook of corpus linguistics and pragmatics 2014: New empirical and theoretical paradigms* (pp. 261–289). New York, NY: Springer.

Cutting, J. (2001). The speech acts of the in-group. *Journal of Pragmatics, 33*, 1207–1233.

Garcia, P., & Drescher, N. (2006). Corpus-based analysis of pragmatic meaning. In A. M. Hornero, M. J. Luzon, & S. Murillo (Eds.), *Corpus linguistics: Applications for the study of English* (pp. 465–481). Bern, Switzerland: Peter Lang.

Garcia, P., & Drescher, N. (2006). Corpus-based analysis of pragmatic meaning. In A. M. Hornero, M. J. Luzon & S. Murillo (Eds.), Corpus linguistics: Applications for the study of English (pp.465-481). Bern, Switzerland: Peter Lang.

Ishizaki, S., & Kaufer, D. (2011). Computer-aided rhetorical analysis. In P. McCarthy & C. Boonthum-Denecke (Eds.), *Applied natural language processing and content analysis* (pp. 276–296). Hershey, PA: Information Science Reference.

Kaufer, D., Gunawardena, A., Tan, A., & Cheek, A. (2011). Bringing social media to the writingclassroom: Classroom Salon. *Journal of Business and Technical Communication, 25*, 299–321.

Kaufer, D., Geisler, C., Ishizaki, S., & Vlachos, P. (2005) Computer-support for genre analysis and discovery. In C. Yang (Ed.), *Ambient intelligence for scientific discovery* (p. 129–151). Amsterdam, The Netherlands: Springer.

Kaufer, D., Ishizaki, S., Collins, J., & Vlachos, P. (2004). Teaching language awareness in rhetorical choice using Itext and visualization in classroom genre assignments. *Journal for Business and Technical Communication, 18*, 361–402.

Murphy, B., & Neu, J. (2006). My grade's too low: The speech act set of complaining. In S. Gass & J. Neu (Eds.), *Speech acts across cultures*. New York, NY: Mouton de Gruyter.

Nguyen, T. T. M. (2008). Modifying L2 criticisms: How learners do it? *Journal of Pragmatics, 40*, 768–791.

Salsbury, T., & Bardovi-Harlig, K. (2000). Oppositional talk and the acquisition of modality in L2 English. In B. Swierzbin, F. Morris, M. E. Anderson, C. A. Klee, & E. Tarone (Eds.), *Social and cognitive factors in second language acquisition: Selected proceedings of the 1999 second language research forum* (pp. 57–76). Somerville, MA: Cascadilla Press.

Torgersen, E. N., Cabrielatos, S., Hoffman, S., & Fox, S. (2011). A corpus-based study of pragmatic markers in London English. *Corpus Linguistics and Linguistic Theory, 7*, 93–118.

Vaughan, E., & Clancy, B. (2013). Small corpora and pragmatics. In Romero-Trillo (Ed.),*Yearbook of corpus linguistics and pragmatics: New domains and methodologies* (pp. 53–73). New York, NY: Springer.

## about the contributors

**Kathleen Bardovi-Harlig**, a professor of second language studies at Indiana University, has presented at Pragmatics and Language Learning since 1987. Her work on pragmatics has appeared in *Language Learning, Studies in Second Language Acquisition, Journal of Pragmatics,* and *Intercultural Pragmatics*. She is co-editor of *Interlanguage Pragmatics: Exploring Institutional Talk* (Erlbaum) and *Pragmatics and Language Learning* (Volume 11). Her current work in L2 pragmatics focuses on the development of pragmalinguistic resources.

**J. César Félix-Brasdefer** is an associate professor at Indiana University, Bloomington. His research interests include pragmatics, discourse analysis, cross-cultural and interlanguage pragmatics, pragmatic variation, Spanish pragmatics, and (im)politeness theory. He has published numerous research articles in a variety of scholarly journals and edited volumes, including *Journal of Pragmatics, Intercultural Pragmatics, Multilingua, Language Learning, Journal of Politeness Research, System,* and *Pragmatics and Language Learning* (Volume 11). He co-edited *Pragmatic Variation in First and Second Language Contexts: Methodological Issues* (2012, John Benjamins). His most recent book is entitled *The Language of Service Encounters: A Pragmatic-Discursive Approach* (Cambridge University Press, 2015).

**Elizabeth Flores-Salgado** is currently teaching linguistics in the BA program in language teaching and master's program in TESOL in the language faculty at Benemérita Universidad Autónoma de Puebla. She published *The Pragmatics of Requests and Apologies* and several articles on pragmatics and second language acquisition. She received her doctorate in applied linguistics from

MacQuarie University in Sydney, Australia. Her current research interests include interlanguage and cross-cultural pragmatics.

**Sarah E. Blackwell** (PhD in Hispanic Linguistics, University of Pittsburgh) is an associate professor of Spanish in the Department of Romance Languages at the University of Georgia, where she teaches graduate and undergraduate courses in Hispanic linguistics and specializes in semantics, pragmatics, and discourse analysis. Her research interests include cognitive and functional linguistics, pragmatic variation, and discourse coherence in Spanish and English. She he has published articles on various topics including Spanish NP anaphora, Spanish subject pronoun use and omission, cognitive and interactional frames, and Spanish discourse connectives. She is the author of *Implicatures in Discourse: The Case of Spanish NP Anaphora* (John Benjamins, 2003) and was a special issues editor of the *Journal of Pragmatics* from 2003–2008.

**Margaret Lubbers Quesada** (PhD Linguistics, Michigan State University) is currently a professor of Spanish at the University of Georgia where she teaches a variety of graduate seminars and undergraduate courses in Spanish linguistics. Previously, she was on the faculty of the *Universidad Autónoma de Querétaro* in Mexico. Professor Quesada has investigated and published widely on the acquisition of tense, aspect and mood, subject pronouns, psychological verbs, and discourse markers in L2 Spanish from a pragmatic-discourse perspective. She is the author of the recently published (2015) volume *The L2 Acquisition of Spanish Subjects Multiple Perspectives* by Mouton de Gruyter.

**Mai Kuha** teaches linguistics at Ball State University. She investigates linguistic factors in social and environmental problems through projects in sociolinguistics and pragmatics that contribute to social justice, improve intercultural understanding, and raise awareness of environmental sustainability issues.

**Lisa M. Kuriscak** teaches Spanish at Ball State University. Her research focuses on second language acquisition of Spanish, especially as it pertains to pragmatics, study abroad effects on acquisition, the teaching of phonetics, and L2 writing.

**Elizabeth M. Riddle** teaches linguistics at Ball State University. Her main research interests are in pragmatics, including discourse-based syntax, tense, demonstratives, and speech acts. She has also worked in lexical semantics, typology, and TESOL.

**Louise Tranekjær** is an associate professor in cultural encounters and Head of the Language Profiles program at Roskilde University. She works with high school teachers on issues of intercultural competence, internationalisation, and global citizenship. She recently published a book on gatekeeping processes in work-related second language interaction and gives seminars to second language teachers of Danish, working towards developing interaction-based (CARM) teaching materials for Danish as a second language. Her general research interest is institutional interaction and the relation between membership categorization, culture and identity, currently focusing on laughables as a resource in processes of inclusion and exclusion.

**Katherine Kappa** is currently finishing her master's thesis at Roskilde University on processes of identity construction in a language learning setting aimed for asylum seekers and refugees. She has analyzed multilingual and second language interactions, and how these relate to discussions on gatekeeping, normativity, and language ideologies. Her research interest is focused on questions of identity, power and ideology as evidenced in the micro level of conversation.

**Maria Hasler-Barker** teaches courses in Spanish language, linguistics, and language teaching methodology at Sam Houston State University. Her research and publications have focused primarily on interlanguage pragmatics, instruction of pragmatics, and second language acquisition, including recent co-authored papers on the acquisition of pragmatic variables and methods of data collection in pragmatics. While continuing to research and publish on interlanguage pragmatics and instruction, she is currently working on a grant-funded interdisciplinary project investigating bilingual service encounters in public libraries.

**Gerrard Mugford** is currently teaching sociolinguistics, discourse analysis, pragmatics and lexical studies in BA and MA programmes at the Centro Universitario de Ciencias Sociales y Humanidades in la Universidad de Guadalajara, Guadalajara, Mexico. His current research interests include interpersonal second language use, politeness, impoliteness, lexical studies, and critical pedagogy. In his doctoral research, he examined foreign-language interactional language use, phatic communion and linguistic politeness among Mexican users of English as a foreign language.

**Maria Shardakova** is an assistant professor at Indiana University in Bloomington where she directs Russian Language Program. Her research focuses on interlanguage pragmatics and humor. She has published a book on interlanguage pragmatics of the apology (VDM, Germany, 2009) and a series of articles related to the acquisition of pragmatic competence in Russian by American L2 learners of Russian.

**Milica Savić** is an associate professor in the Department of Cultural Studies and Languages, University of Stavanger, Norway. She has taught courses in the methodology of TEFL, politeness in a second language, sociolinguistics, and

English phonetics and phonology, and has been actively involved in in-service teacher training in Serbia, Italy, and Norway. She has published a monograph entitled *Politeness Through the Prism of Requests, Apologies and Refusals: A Case of Advances Serbian EFL Learners,* as well as a number of research papers. Her current research interests include interlanguage pragmatics, L2 pragmatics instruction and linguistic politeness in computer-mediated communication.

**Tetyana Sydorenko** received her PhD in second language studies at Michigan State University. She is an assistant professor of applied linguistics at Portland State University. Her research interests include teaching and acquisition of second language pragmatics, computer-assisted language learning, psycholinguistic processes in second language acquisition, and assessment. Tetyana is particularly interested in studying learners' noticing of pragmatic features under various conditions, with the focus on direct implications for language teaching. She is currently investigating the use of adaptive computer-simulated conversations in the teaching of second language pragmatics

**Gwen Heller Tuason** is a senior instructor in the Intensive English Language Program at Portland State University. She received her MA TESOL degree from PSU in 2005. She is currently co-developing internet-based course materials for an intermediate-level speaking and listening course in the IELP. She has also co-designed an oral communication course for international graduate students. She enjoys collaborating with her colleague Tetyana Sydorenko in the Department of Applied Linguistics on action research in the ESL classroom.

**Holger Limberg** is currently an assistant professor of English language teaching at the European University of Flensburg, Germany. He is a former teacher of English and is currently involved in academic training for secondary school teachers of English. He received his PhD in applied linguistics from the University of Oldenburg, Germany. His current research interests include the teaching of pragmatics in instructed learning environments, pragmatic textbook analysis and the investigation of classroom discourse in primary foreign language classes.

**Sara Gesuato** is an associate professor of English at Padua University, Italy, where she teaches English language and linguistics. Her fields of activity include discourse and genre analysis, pragmatics, and corpus linguistics. She has published on the phraseology and content of academic genres, the structure and wording of expressive speech acts, and the temporal and aspectual meanings of catenative motion verbs. She has recently co-edited a volume on pragmatic issues in language teaching and learning. She earned her PhD from Padua University and the University of California at

Berkeley. Her current research interest is in pedagogical applications of speech act analysis.

**Andrew D. Cohen** was a Peace Corps Volunteer with the Aymara Indians on the High Plains of Bolivia (1965–68), taught 4 years at UCLA (ESL section, English Department), 16 years at the Hebrew University of Jerusalem (language education), and 22 years at the University of Minnesota (second language studies). He is co-editor of Language *Learning Strategies* (Cohen & Macaro, 2007, OUP), author of *Strategies in Learning and Using a Second Language* (Routledge, 2011), and co-author of *Teaching and Learning Pragmatics: Where Language and Culture Meet* (Ishihara & Cohen, Routledge, 2014), which has been translated into Japanese and Arabic. He has numerous articles and book chapters on research methods, language assessment, bilingual education, language learner strategies, and pragmatics, and is currently studying his 13th language, Mandarin.

**Naoko Taguchi** is an associate professor of Japanese and second language acquisition at Carnegie Mellon University. Her research interests include second language pragmatics, English-medium education, contexts of second language learning, and technology application to research and teaching. She serves as the co-editor of *Journal of Multilingual Pragmatics* and on the editorial/advisory board of several other journals. She has several books in production, including her co-authored monograph, *Second Language Pragmatics* (Oxford University Press).

**David Kaufer** teaches English style, grammar, and corpus rhetoric in the Department of English at Carnegie Mellon. He is a fellow of the Rhetorical Society of America and has published books and articles on written communication, genre, and technologies for text analysis and collaboration. He received his PhD from the University of Wisconsin at Madison.

**María Pía Gómez-Laich** is a third-year PhD student in second language acquisition at Carnegie Mellon University. Her research focuses on the claims of the Cognition Hypothesis and looks at the impact of manipulating task complexity on ESL students' writing performance.

**Helen Zhao** is an assistant professor in the Department of English at the Chinese University of Hong Kong. Her research interests include a usage-based approach to second language acquisition, cognitive linguistic approaches to language teaching, pedagogical grammar, computer assisted language learning, and second language writing. She is a review editor of the Asian Journal of English Language Teaching (AJELT).

# National Foreign Language Resource Center
University of Hawai'i at Mānoa

*ordering information at nflrc.hawaii.edu*

# Pragmatics & Interaction
*Gabriele Kasper, series editor*

Pragmatics & Interaction ("P&I"), a refereed series sponsored by the University of Hawai'i National Foreign Language Resource Center, publishes research on topics in pragmatics and discourse as social interaction from a wide variety of theoretical and methodological perspectives. P&I welcomes particularly studies on languages spoken in the Asia-Pacific region.

### PRAGMATICS OF VIETNAMESE AS NATIVE AND TARGET LANGUAGE
CARSTEN ROEVER & HANH THI NGUYEN (EDITORS), 2013

The volume offers a wealth of new information about the forms of several speech acts and their social distribution in Vietnamese as L1 and L2, complemented by a chapter on address forms and listener responses. As the first of its kind, the book makes a valuable contribution to the research literature on pragmatics, sociolinguistics, and language and social interaction in an under-researched and less commonly taught Asian language.

282pp., ISBN 978–0–9835816–2–8                              $30.

### L2 LEARNING AS SOCIAL PRACTICE: CONVERSATION-ANALYTIC PERSPECTIVES
GABRIELE PALLOTTI & JOHANNES WAGNER (EDITORS), 2011

This volume collects empirical studies applying Conversation Analysis to situations where second, third, and other additional languages are used. A number of different aspects are considered, including how linguistic systems develop over time through social interaction, how participants 'do' language learning and teaching in classroom and everyday settings, how they select languages and manage identities in multilingual contexts, and how the linguistic-interactional divide can be bridged with studies combining Conversation Analysis and

Functional Linguistics. This variety of issues and approaches clearly shows the fruitfulness of a socio-interactional perspective on second language learning.

380pp., ISBN 978–0–9800459–7–0 $30.

**TALK-IN-INTERACTION: MULTILINGUAL PERSPECTIVES**
HANH THI NGUYEN & GABRIELE KASPER (EDITORS), 2009

This volume offers original studies of interaction in a range of languages and language varieties, including Chinese, English, Japanese, Korean, Spanish, Swahili, Thai, and Vietnamese; monolingual and bilingual interactions; and activities designed for second or foreign language learning. Conducted from the perspectives of conversation analysis and membership categorization analysis, the chapters examine ordinary conversation and institutional activities in face-to-face, telephone, and computer-mediated environments.

420pp., ISBN 978–09800459–1–8 $30.

# Pragmatics & Language Learning
## Gabriele Kasper, series editor

Pragmatics & Language Learning ("PLL"), a refereed series sponsored by the National Foreign Language Resource Center, publishes selected papers from the International Pragmatics & Language Learning conference under the editorship of the conference hosts and the series editor. Check the NFLRC website for upcoming PLL conferences and PLL volumes.

**PRAGMATICS AND LANGUAGE LEARNING VOLUME 13**
TIM GREER, DONNA TATSUKI, & CARSTEN ROEVER (EDITORS), 2013

Pragmatics & Language Learning Volume 13 examines the organization of second language and multilingual speakers' talk and pragmatic knowledge across a range of naturalistic and experimental activities. Based on data collected among ESL and EFL learners from a variety of backgrounds, the contributions explore the nexus of pragmatic knowledge, interaction, and L2 learning outside and inside of educational settings.

292pp., ISBN 978–0–9835816–4–2 $30.

**PRAGMATICS AND LANGUAGE LEARNING VOLUME 12**
Gabriele Kasper, Hanh thi Nguyen, Dina R. Yoshimi, & Jim K. Yoshioka (Editors), 2010

This volume examines the organization of second language and multilingual speakers' talk and pragmatic knowledge across a range of naturalistic and experimental activities. Based on data collected on Danish, English, Hawai'i Creole, Indonesian, and Japanese as target languages, the contributions explore the nexus of pragmatic knowledge, interaction, and L2 learning outside and inside of educational settings.

364pp., ISBN 978–09800459–6–3                                  $30.

**PRAGMATICS AND LANGUAGE LEARNING VOLUME 11**
Kathleen Bardovi-Harlig, César Félix-Brasdefer, & Alwiya S. Omar (Editors), 2006

This volume features cutting-edge theoretical and empirical research on pragmatics and language learning among a wide variety of learners in diverse learning contexts from a variety of language backgrounds and target languages (English, German, Japanese, Kiswahili, Persian, and Spanish). This collection of papers from researchers around the world includes critical appraisals on the role of formulas in interlanguage pragmatics, and speech-act research from a conversation analytic perspective. Empirical studies examine learner data using innovative methods of analysis and investigate issues in pragmatic development and the instruction of pragmatics.

430pp., ISBN 978–0–8248–3137–0                                 $30.

# NFLRC Monographs
*Julio C Rodriguez, series editor*

Monographs of the National Foreign Language Resource Center present the findings of recent work in applied linguistics that is of relevance to language teaching and learning (with a focus on the less commonly taught languages of Asia and the Pacific) and are of particular interest to foreign language educators, applied linguists, and researchers. Prior to 2006, these monographs were published as "SLTCC Technical Reports."

### STUDENT LEARNING OUTCOMES ASSESSMENT IN COLLEGE FOREIGN LANGUAGE PROGRAMS
JOHN M. NORRIS & JOHN McE. DAVIS (EDITORS), 2015

Changes in accreditation policies and institutional practices have led to the emergence of student learning outcomes assessment as an important, increasingly common expectation in U.S. college foreign language programs. This volume investigates contemporary outcomes assessment activity, with a primary focus on useful assessment, that is, assessment that is put to use proactively by foreign language educators. Authors approach the topic from distinct perspectives, ranging from a study of national trends in outcomes assessment practices, to reflections on assessment experiences by program leaders, to case studies highlighting language educators' implementation and uses of outcomes assessment for diverse curricular and pedagogical purposes.

| | |
|---|---|
| 274pp., ISBN 978–1–943281–37–4 (paperback) | $25. |
| ISBN 978–1–943847–15–0 (eBook) | $10. |

### CULTURA-INSPIRED INTERCULTURAL EXCHANGES: FOCUS ON ASIAN AND PACIFIC LANGUAGES
DOROTHY M. CHUN (EDITOR), 2014

Although many online intercultural exchanges have been conducted based on the *Cultura* model, most to date have been between and among European languages. This volume presents several chapters with a focus on exchanges involving Asian and Pacific languages. Many of the benefits and challenges of these exchanges are similar to those reported for European languages; however, some of the difficulties reported in the Chinese and Japanese exchanges might be due to the significant linguistic differences between English and East Asian languages. This volume adds to the body of emerging studies of telecollaboration among learners of Asian and Pacific languages.

183pp., ISBN 978–0–9835816–7–3 (paperback)     $25.
ISBN 978–1–63443–578–9 (eBook)     $10.

## NOTICING AND SECOND LANGUAGE ACQUISITION: STUDIES IN HONOR OF RICHARD SCHMIDT

JOARA MARTIN BERGSLEITHNER, SYLVIA NAGEM FROTA, & JIM KEI YOSHIOKA (EDITORS), 2013

This volume celebrates the life and groundbreaking work of Richard Schmidt, the developer of the influential Noticing Hypothesis in the field of second language acquisition. The 19 chapters encompass a compelling collection of cuttingedge research studies exploring such constructs as noticing, attention, and awareness from multiple perspectives, which expand, fine tune, sometimes support, and sometimes challenge Schmidt's seminal ideas and take research on noticing in exciting new directions.

374pp., ISBN 978–0–9835816–6–6     $25.

## NEW PERSPECTIVES ON JAPANESE LANGUAGE LEARNING, LINGUISTICS, AND CULTURE

KIMI KONDO-BROWN, YOSHIKO SAITO-ABBOTT, SHINGO SATSUTANI, MICHIO TSUTSUI, & ANN WEHMEYER (EDITORS), 2013

This volume is a collection of selected refereed papers presented at the Association of Teachers of Japanese Annual Spring Conference held at the University of Hawaiʻi at Mānoa in March of 2011. It not only covers several important topics on teaching and learning spoken and written Japanese and culture in and beyond classroom settings but also includes research investigating certain linguistics items from new perspectives.

208pp., ISBN 978–0–9835816–3–5     $25.

## DEVELOPING, USING, AND ANALYZING RUBRICS IN LANGUAGE ASSESSMENT WITH CASE STUDIES IN ASIAN AND PACIFIC LANGUAGES

JAMES DEAN BROWN (EDITOR), 2012

Rubrics are essential tools for all language teachers in this age of communicative and task-based teaching and assessment—tools that allow us to efficiently communicate to our students what we are looking for in the productive language abilities of speaking and writing and then effectively assess those abilities when the time comes for grading students, giving them feedback, placing them into new courses, and so forth. This book provides a wide array of ideas, suggestions, and examples (mostly from Māori, Hawaiian, and Japanese language assessment projects) to help language educators effectively develop, use, revise, analyze, and report on rubric-based assessments.

212pp., ISBN 978-0-9835816-1-1 $25.

## RESEARCH AMONG LEARNERS OF CHINESE AS A FOREIGN LANGUAGE
MICHAEL E. EVERSON & HELEN H. SHEN (EDITORS), 2010

Cutting-edge in its approach and international in its authorship, this fourth monograph in a series sponsored by the Chinese Language Teachers Association features eight research studies that explore a variety of themes, topics, and perspectives important to a variety of stakeholders in the Chinese language learning community. Employing a wide range of research methodologies, the volume provides data from actual Chinese language learners and will be of value to both theoreticians and practitioners alike. *[in English & Chinese]*

180pp., ISBN 978-0-9800459-4-9 $20.

## MANCHU: A TEXTBOOK FOR READING DOCUMENTS (SECOND EDITION)
GERTRAUDE ROTH LI, 2010

This book offers students a tool to gain a basic grounding in the Manchu language. The reading selections provided in this volume represent various types of documents, ranging from examples of the very earliest Manchu writing (17th century) to samples of contemporary Sibe (Xibo), a language that may be considered a modern version of Manchu. Since Manchu courses are only rarely taught at universities anywhere, this second edition includes audio recordings to assist students with the pronunciation of the texts.

418pp., ISBN 978-0-9800459-5-6 $36.

## TOWARD USEFUL PROGRAM EVALUATION IN COLLEGE FOREIGN LANGUAGE EDUCATION
JOHN M. NORRIS, JOHN MCE. DAVIS, CASTLE SINICROPE, & YUKIKO WATANABE (EDITORS), 2009

This volume reports on innovative, useful evaluation work conducted within U.S. college foreign language programs. An introductory chapter scopes out the territory, reporting key findings from research into the concerns, impetuses, and uses for evaluation that FL educators identify. Seven chapters then highlight examples of evaluations conducted in diverse language programs and institutional contexts. Each case is reported by program-internal educators, who walk readers through critical steps, from identifying evaluation uses, users, and questions, to designing methods, interpreting findings, and taking actions. A concluding chapter reflects on the emerging roles for FL program evaluation and articulates an agenda for integrating evaluation into language education practice.

240pp., ISBN 978-0-9800459-3-2 $30.

## SECOND LANGUAGE TEACHING AND LEARNING IN THE NET GENERATION
RAQUEL OXFORD & JEFFREY OXFORD (EDITORS), 2009

Today's young people—the Net Generation—have grown up with technology all around them. However, teachers cannot assume that students' familiarity with technology in general transfers successfully to pedagogical settings. This volume examines various technologies and offers concrete advice on how each can be successfully implemented in the second language curriculum.

240pp., ISBN 978-0-9800459-2-5 $30.

## CASE STUDIES IN FOREIGN LANGUAGE PLACEMENT: PRACTICES AND POSSIBILITIES
THOM HUDSON & MARTYN CLARK (EDITORS), 2008

Although most language programs make placement decisions on the basis of placement tests, there is surprisingly little published about different contexts and systems of placement testing. The present volume contains case studies of placement programs in foreign language programs at the tertiary level across the United States. The different programs span the spectrum from large programs servicing hundreds of students annually to small language programs with very few students. The contributions to this volume address such issues as how the size of the program, presence or absence of heritage learners, and population changes affect language placement decisions.

201pp., ISBN 0-9800459-0-8 $20.

## CHINESE AS A HERITAGE LANGUAGE: FOSTERING ROOTED WORLD CITIZENRY
AGNES WEIYUN HE & YUN XIAO (EDITORS), 2008

Thirty-two scholars examine the sociocultural, cognitive-linguistic, and educational-institutional trajectories along which Chinese as a Heritage Language may be acquired, maintained, and developed. They draw upon developmental psychology, functional linguistics, linguistic and cultural anthropology, discourse analysis, orthography analysis, reading research, second language acquisition, and bilingualism. This volume aims to lay a foundation for theories, models, and master scripts to be discussed, debated, and developed, and to stimulate research and enhance teaching both within and beyond Chinese language education.

280pp., ISBN 978-0-8248-3286-5 $20.

## PERSPECTIVES ON TEACHING CONNECTED SPEECH TO SECOND LANGUAGE SPEAKERS
James Dean Brown & Kimi Kondo-Brown (Editors), 2006

This book is a collection of fourteen articles on connected speech of interest to teachers, researchers, and materials developers in both ESL/EFL (ten chapters focus on connected speech in English) and Japanese (four chapters focus on Japanese connected speech). The fourteen chapters are divided up into five sections:

- What do we know so far about teaching connected speech?
- Does connected speech instruction work?
- How should connected speech be taught in English?
- How should connected speech be taught in Japanese?
- How should connected speech be tested?

290pp., ISBN 978-0-8248-3136-3 $20.

## CORPUS LINGUISTICS FOR KOREAN LANGUAGE LEARNING AND TEACHING
Robert Bley-Vroman & Hyunsook Ko (Editors), 2006

Dramatic advances in personal-computer technology have given language teachers access to vast quantities of machine-readable text, which can be analyzed with a view toward improving the basis of language instruction. Corpus linguistics provides analytic techniques and practical tools for studying language in use. This volume provides both an introductory framework for the use of corpus linguistics for language teaching and examples of its application for Korean teaching and learning. The collected papers cover topics in Korean syntax, lexicon, and discourse, and second language acquisition research, always with a focus on application in the classroom. An overview of Korean corpus linguistics tools and available Korean corpora are also included.

265pp., ISBN 0-8248-3062-8 $25.

## NEW TECHNOLOGIES AND LANGUAGE LEARNING: CASES IN THE LESS COMMONLY TAUGHT LANGUAGES
Carol Anne Spreen (Editor), 2002

In recent years, the National Security Education Program (NSEP) has supported an increasing number of programs for teaching languages using different technological media. This compilation of case study initiatives funded through the NSEP Institutional Grants Program presents a range of technology-based options for language programming that will help universities make more informed decisions about teaching less commonly taught languages. The eight chapters describe how different types of technologies are used to support language programs (i.e., web, ITV, and audio- or video-based materials), discuss identifiable trends in e-language learning, and explore how technology addresses issues of equity, diversity, and opportunity. This book offers many lessons learned and decisions made as technology changes and learning needs become more complex.

188pp., ISBN 0–8248–2634–5 $25.

## AN INVESTIGATION OF SECOND LANGUAGE TASK-BASED PERFORMANCE ASSESSMENTS
JAMES DEAN BROWN, THOM HUDSON, JOHN M. NORRIS, & WILLIAM BONK, 2002

This volume describes the creation of performance assessment instruments and their validation (based on work started in a previous monograph). It begins by explaining the test and rating scale development processes and the administration of the resulting three seven-task tests to 90 university-level EFL and ESL students. The results are examined in terms of (a) the effects of test revision; (b) comparisons among the task-dependent, task-independent, and self-rating scales; and (c) reliability and validity issues.

240pp., ISBN 0–8248–2633–7 $25.

## MOTIVATION AND SECOND LANGUAGE ACQUISITION
ZOLTÁN DÖRNYEI & RICHARD SCHMIDT (EDITORS), 2001

This volume—the second in this series concerned with motivation and foreign language learning—includes papers presented in a state-of-the-art colloquium on L2 motivation at the American Association for Applied Linguistics (Vancouver, 2000) and a number of specially commissioned studies. The 20 chapters, written by some of the best known researchers in the field, cover a wide range of theoretical and research methodological issues, and also offer empirical results (both qualitative and quantitative) concerning the learning of many different languages (Arabic, Chinese, English, Filipino, French, German, Hindi, Italian, Japanese, Russian, and Spanish) in a broad range of learning contexts (Bahrain, Brazil, Canada, Egypt, Finland, Hungary, Ireland, Israel, Japan, Spain, and the US.).

520pp., ISBN 0–8248–2458–X $30.

## A FOCUS ON LANGUAGE TEST DEVELOPMENT: EXPANDING THE LANGUAGE PROFICIENCY CONSTRUCT ACROSS A VARIETY OF TESTS
THOM HUDSON & JAMES DEAN BROWN (EDITORS), 2001

This volume presents eight research studies that introduce a variety of novel, nontraditional forms of second and foreign language assessment. To the extent possible, the studies also show the entire test development process, warts and all. These language testing projects not only demonstrate many of the types of problems that test developers run into in the real world but also afford the reader unique insights into the language test development process.

230pp., ISBN 0–8248–2351–6 $20.

## STUDIES ON KOREAN IN COMMUNITY SCHOOLS
DONG-JAE LEE, SOOKEUN CHO, MISEON LEE, MINSUN SONG, & WILLIAM O'GRADY (EDITORS), 2000

The papers in this volume focus on language teaching and learning in Korean community schools. Drawing on innovative experimental work and research in linguistics, education, and psychology, the contributors address issues of importance to teachers, administrators, and parents. Topics covered include childhood bilingualism, Korean grammar, language acquisition, children's literature, and language teaching methodology. [in Korean]

256pp., ISBN 0–8248–2352–4 $20.

## A COMMUNICATIVE FRAMEWORK FOR INTRODUCTORY JAPANESE LANGUAGE CURRICULA
WASHINGTON STATE JAPANESE LANGUAGE CURRICULUM GUIDELINES COMMITTEE, 2000

In recent years, the number of schools offering Japanese nationwide has increased dramatically. Because of the tremendous popularity of the Japanese language and the shortage of teachers, quite a few untrained, nonnative and native teachers are in the classrooms and are expected to teach several levels of Japanese. These guidelines are intended to assist individual teachers and professional associations throughout the United States in designing Japanese language curricula. They are meant to serve as a framework from which language teaching can be expanded and are intended to allow teachers to enhance and strengthen the quality of Japanese language instruction.

168pp., ISBN 0–8248–2350–8 $20.

## FOREIGN LANGUAGE TEACHING AND MINORITY LANGUAGE EDUCATION
KATHRYN A. DAVIS (EDITOR), 1999

This volume seeks to examine the potential for building relationships among foreign language, bilingual, and ESL programs towards fostering bilingualism. Part I of the volume examines the sociopolitical contexts for language partnerships, including:

- obstacles to developing bilingualism;
- implications of acculturation, identity, and language issues for linguistic minorities; and
- the potential for developing partnerships across primary, secondary, and tertiary institutions.

Part II of the volume provides research findings on the Foreign Language Partnership Project, designed to capitalize on the resources of immigrant students to enhance foreign language learning.

152pp., ISBN 0-8248-2067-3 $20.

## DESIGNING SECOND LANGUAGE PERFORMANCE ASSESSMENTS

JOHN M. NORRIS, JAMES DEAN BROWN, THOM HUDSON, & JIM YOSHIOKA, 1998, 2000

This technical report focuses on the decision-making potential provided by second language performance assessments. The authors first situate performance assessment within a broader discussion of alternatives in language assessment and in educational assessment in general. They then discuss issues in performance assessment design, implementation, reliability, and validity. Finally, they present a prototype framework for second language performance assessment based on the integration of theoretical underpinnings and research findings from the task-based language teaching literature, the language testing literature, and the educational measurement literature. The authors outline test and item specifications, and they present numerous examples of prototypical language tasks. They also propose a research agenda focusing on the operationalization of second language performance assessments.

248pp., ISBN 0-8248-2109-2 $20.

## SECOND LANGUAGE DEVELOPMENT IN WRITING: MEASURES OF FLUENCY, ACCURACY, AND COMPLEXITY

KATE WOLFE-QUINTERO, SHUNJI INAGAKI, & HAE-YOUNG KIM, 1998, 2002

In this book, the authors analyze and compare the ways that fluency, accuracy, grammatical complexity, and lexical complexity have been measured in studies of language development in second language writing. More than 100 developmental measures are examined, with detailed comparisons of the results across the studies that have used each measure. The authors discuss the theoretical foundations for each type of developmental measure, and they consider the relationship between developmental measures and various types of proficiency measures. They also examine criteria for determining which developmental measures are the most successful and suggest which measures are the most promising for continuing work on language development.

208pp., ISBN 0-8248-2069-X $20.

## THE DEVELOPMENT OF A LEXICAL TONE PHONOLOGY IN AMERICAN ADULT LEARNERS OF STANDARD MANDARIN CHINESE
SYLVIA HENEL SUN, 1998

The study reported is based on an assessment of three decades of research on the SLA of Mandarin tone. It investigates whether differences in learners' tone perception and production are related to differences in the effects of certain linguistic, task, and learner factors. The learners of focus are American students of Mandarin in Beijing, China. Their performances on two perception and three production tasks are analyzed through a host of variables and methods of quantification.

328pp., ISBN 0–8248–2068–1                                         $20.

## NEW TRENDS AND ISSUES IN TEACHING JAPANESE LANGUAGE AND CULTURE
HARUKO M. COOK, KYOKO HIJIRIDA, & MILDRED TAHARA (EDITORS), 1997

In recent years, Japanese has become the fourth most commonly taught foreign language at the college level in the United States. As the number of students who study Japanese has increased, the teaching of Japanese as a foreign language has been established as an important academic field of study. This technical report includes nine contributions to the advancement of this field, encompassing the following five important issues:

- Literature and literature teaching
- Technology in the language classroom
- Orthography
- Testing
- Grammatical versus pragmatic approaches to language teaching

164pp., ISBN 0–8248–2067–3                                         $20.

## SIX MEASURES OF JSL PRAGMATICS
SAYOKO OKADA YAMASHITA, 1996

This book investigates differences among tests that can be used to measure the cross-cultural pragmatic ability of English-speaking learners of Japanese. Building on the work of Hudson, Detmer, and Brown (Technical Reports #2 and #7 in this series), the author modified six test types that she used to gather data from North American learners of Japanese. She found numerous problems with the multiple-choice discourse completion test but reported that the other five tests all proved highly reliable and reasonably valid. Practical issues involved in creating and using such language tests are discussed from a variety of perspectives.

213pp., ISBN 0–8248–1914–4                                         $15.

## LANGUAGE LEARNING STRATEGIES AROUND THE WORLD: CROSS-CULTURAL PERSPECTIVES
REBECCA L. OXFORD (EDITOR), 1996, 1997, 2002

Language learning strategies are the specific steps students take to improve their progress in learning a second or foreign language. Optimizing learning strategies improves language performance. This groundbreaking book presents new information about cultural influences on the use of language learning strategies. It also shows innovative ways to assess students' strategy use and remarkable techniques for helping students improve their choice of strategies, with the goal of peak language learning.

166pp., ISBN 0-8248-1910-1                                    $20.

## TELECOLLABORATION IN FOREIGN LANGUAGE LEARNING: PROCEEDINGS OF THE HAWAI'I SYMPOSIUM
MARK WARSCHAUER (EDITOR), 1996

The Symposium on Local & Global Electronic Networking in Foreign Language Learning & Research, part of the National Foreign Language Resource Center's 1995 Summer Institute on Technology & the Human Factor in Foreign Language Education, included presentations of papers and hands-on workshops conducted by Symposium participants to facilitate the sharing of resources, ideas, and information about all aspects of electronic networking for foreign language teaching and research, including electronic discussion and conferencing, international cultural exchanges, real-time communication and simulations, research and resource retrieval via the Internet, and research using networks. This collection presents a sampling of those presentations.

252pp., ISBN 0-8248-1867-9                                    $20.

## LANGUAGE LEARNING MOTIVATION: PATHWAYS TO THE NEW CENTURY
REBECCA L. OXFORD (EDITOR), 1996

This volume chronicles a revolution in our thinking about what makes students want to learn languages and what causes them to persist in that difficult and rewarding adventure. Topics in this book include the internal structures of and external connections with foreign language motivation; exploring adult language learning motivation, self-efficacy, and anxiety; comparing the motivations and learning strategies of students of Japanese and Spanish; and enhancing the theory of language learning motivation from many psychological and social perspectives.

218pp., ISBN 0-8248-1849-0                                    $20.

## LINGUISTICS & LANGUAGE TEACHING: PROCEEDINGS OF THE SIXTH JOINT LSH-HATESL CONFERENCE
Cynthia Reves, Caroline Steele, & Cathy S. P. Wong (Editors), 1996

Technical Report #10 contains 18 articles revolving around the following three topics:

- Linguistic issues—These six papers discuss various linguistic issues: ideophones, syllabic nasals, linguistic areas, computation, tonal melody classification, and wh-words.
- Sociolinguistics—Sociolinguistic phenomena in Swahili, signing, Hawaiian, and Japanese are discussed in four of the papers.
- Language teaching and learning—These eight papers cover prosodic modification, note taking, planning in oral production, oral testing, language policy, L2 essay organization, access to dative alternation rules, and child noun phrase structure development.

364pp., ISBN 0–8248–1851–2                                   $20.

## ATTENTION & AWARENESS IN FOREIGN LANGUAGE LEARNING
Richard Schmidt (Editor), 1995

Issues related to the role of attention and awareness in learning lie at the heart of many theoretical and practical controversies in the foreign language field. This collection of papers presents research into the learning of Spanish, Japanese, Finnish, Hawaiian, and English as a second language (with additional comments and examples from French, German, and miniature artificial languages) that bear on these crucial questions for foreign language pedagogy.

394pp., ISBN 0–8248–1794–X                                   $20.

## VIRTUAL CONNECTIONS: ONLINE ACTIVITIES AND PROJECTS FOR NETWORKING LANGUAGE LEARNERS
Mark Warschauer (Editor), 1995, 1996

Computer networking has created dramatic new possibilities for connecting language learners in a single classroom or across the globe. This collection of activities and projects makes use of email, the Internet, computer conferencing, and other forms of computer-mediated communication for the foreign and second language classroom at any level of instruction. Teachers from around the world submitted the activities compiled in this volume—activities that they have used successfully in their own classrooms.

417pp., ISBN 0–8248–1793–1                                   $30.

## DEVELOPING PROTOTYPIC MEASURES OF CROSS-CULTURAL PRAGMATICS
Thom Hudson, Emily Detmer, & J. D. Brown, 1995

Although the study of cross-cultural pragmatics has gained importance in applied linguistics, there are no standard forms of assessment that might make research comparable across studies and languages. The present volume describes the process through which six forms of cross-cultural assessment were developed for second language learners of English. The models may be used for second language learners of other languages. The six forms of assessment involve two forms each of indirect discourse completion tests, oral language production, and self-assessment. The procedures involve the assessment of requests, apologies, and refusals.

198pp., ISBN 0-8248-1763-X                                $15.

## THE ROLE OF PHONOLOGICAL CODING IN READING KANJI
Sachiko Matsunaga, 1995

In this technical report, the author reports the results of a study that she conducted on phonological coding in reading kanji using an eye-movement monitor, and draws some pedagogical implications. In addition, she reviews current literature on the different schools of thought regarding instruction in reading kanji and its role in the teaching of nonalphabetic written languages like Japanese.

64pp., ISBN 0-8248-1734-6                                 $10.

## PRAGMATICS OF CHINESE AS NATIVE AND TARGET LANGUAGE
Gabriele Kasper (Editor), 1995

This technical report includes six contributions to the study of the pragmatics of Mandarin Chinese:

- A report of an interview study conducted with nonnative speakers of Chinese; and
- five data-based studies on the performance of different speech acts by native speakers of Mandarin—requesting, refusing, complaining, giving bad news, disagreeing, and complimenting.

312pp., ISBN 0-8248-1733-8                                $20.

## A BIBLIOGRAPHY OF PEDAGOGY AND RESEARCH IN INTERPRETATION AND TRANSLATION
Etilvia Arjona, 1993

This technical report includes four types of bibliographic information on translation and interpretation studies:

- Research efforts across disciplinary boundaries—cognitive psychology, neurolinguistics, psycholinguistics, sociolinguistics,

computational linguistics, measurement, aptitude testing, language policy, decision-making, theses, and dissertations;
- training information covering program design, curriculum studies, instruction, and school administration;
- instructional information detailing course syllabi, methodology, models, available textbooks; and
- testing information about aptitude, selection, and diagnostic tests.

115pp., ISBN 0–8248–1572–6 $10.

## PRAGMATICS OF JAPANESE AS NATIVE AND TARGET LANGUAGE
GABRIELE KASPER (EDITOR), 1992, 1996

This technical report includes three contributions to the study of the pragmatics of Japanese:
- A bibliography on speech-act performance, discourse management, and other pragmatic and sociolinguistic features of Japanese;
- a study on introspective methods in examining Japanese learners' performance of refusals; and
- a longitudinal investigation of the acquisition of the particle *ne* by nonnative speakers of Japanese.

125pp., ISBN 0–8248–1462–2 $10.

## A FRAMEWORK FOR TESTING CROSS-CULTURAL PRAGMATICS
THOM HUDSON, EMILY DETMER, & J. D. BROWN, 1992

This technical report presents a framework for developing methods that assess cross-cultural pragmatic ability. Although the framework has been designed for Japanese and American cross-cultural contrasts, it can serve as a generic approach that can be applied to other language contrasts. The focus is on the variables of social distance, relative power, and the degree of imposition within the speech acts of requests, refusals, and apologies. Evaluation of performance is based on recognition of the speech act, amount of speech, forms or formulae used, directness, formality, and politeness.

51pp., ISBN 0–8248–1463–0 $10.

## RESEARCH METHODS IN INTERLANGUAGE PRAGMATICS
GABRIELE KASPER & MERETE DAHL, 1991

This technical report reviews the methods of data collection employed in 39 studies of interlanguage pragmatics, defined narrowly as the investigation of nonnative speakers' comprehension and production of speech acts, and the acquisition of L2-related speech-act knowledge. Data collection instruments are distinguished according to the degree to which they constrain informants' responses, and whether they tap speech-act perception/comprehension or production. A main focus of discussion is the validity of different types of data, in particular their adequacy to approximate authentic performance of linguistic action.

51pp., ISBN 0–8248–1419–3 $10.

www.ingramcontent.com/pod-product-compliance
Lightning Source LLC
Chambersburg PA
CBHW060105170426
43198CB00010B/778